Theatrical Jazz

PERFORMANCE, *ÀṢẸ*, AND
THE POWER OF THE PRESENT MOMENT

Omi Osun Joni L. Jones

 THE OHIO STATE UNIVERSITY PRESS | COLUMBUS

Library of Congress Cataloging-in-Publication Data

Jones, Omi Osun Joni L., 1955– author.

  Theatrical jazz : performance, Àse, and the power of the present moment / Omi Osun Joni L. Jones.

     pages cm — (Black performance and cultural criticism)

  Includes bibliographical references and index.

  ISBN 978-0-8142-1282-0 (cloth : alk. paper) — ISBN 978-0-8142-9387-4 (cd)

  1. Performance art. 2. African American theater. 3. Jazz—Philosophy and aesthetics. I. Title. II. Series:
Black performance and cultural criticism.

  PN1584.J66 2015

  781.65'112—dc23

                          2014047887

Cover design by Janna Thompson-Chordas

Text design by Omi Osun Joni L. Jones and Juliet Williams

Type set in Adobe Minion

Printed by Thomson-Shore, Inc.

Cover image: "Women on Horseback," by Carl E. Karni-Bain "BAI." The four quadrants of the painting offer repetition with a difference. The barely discernable galloping black horses arch their necks in the upper right sections while their hind legs glide forward, each quadrant offering its own experience. Photo by Elisa Durrette.

♾ The paper used in this publication meets the minimum requirements of the American National Standard for Information Sciences—Permanence of Paper for Printed Library Materials. ANSI Z39.48-1992.

9 8 7 6 5 4 3 2 1

CONTENTS

List of Illustrations   vii

A Note on Yoruba Orthography   x

Preface   xi

Acknowledgments   xiii

Introduction Troubling Jazz / *Abínibí* / Black Theatre for the Twenty-First Century   1

Part One   The Ensemble / *Ẹgbẹ́* / Community   23

                  The Marrow: Laurie Carlos   36

                  The Blue Note: Daniel Alexander Jones   78

                  The Roots: Sharon Bridgforth   118

Part Two   The Break / *Awo* / Process   165

Part Three   The Bridge / *Àṣẹ* / Transformation   199

Appendix I   Laurie Carlos: An Abbreviated Chronology of Work   227

Appendix II   Daniel Alexander Jones: An Abbreviated Chronology of Work   230

Appendix III   Sharon Bridgforth: An Abbreviated Chronology of Work   236

Notes   240

Glossary of Yoruba Terms   253

Bibliography   255

Index   263

ILLUSTRATIONS

Figure 1	"Oxum," by Werllayne Nunes	xvii
Figure 2	"Double Take," by Moyo Okediji	4
Figure 3	"Untitled," by unknown artist	12
Figure 4	"Shiny Black Stars," by Senalka McDonald	13
Figure 5	"Untitled," by Wura-Natasha Ogunji	15
Figure 6	"Miel de Abeja (Para Ochun)," by Yasmin Hernandez	17
Figure 7	Frontera@Hyde Park Theatre, Austin, Texas	19
Figure 8	FronteraFest poster	20
Figure 9	Helga Davis with ensemble in *blood pudding* at New York SummerStage Festival	35
Figure 10	Laurie Carlos in *Kshoy!/Decay!*	37
Figure 11	"Open the Sky," by Tonya Engel	43
Figure 12	Laurie Carlos teaching hip movement during *con flama* rehearsal	50
Figure 13	*con flama* gestures and language sheet	51
Figure 14	Laurie Carlos teaching gestures during *con flama* rehearsal	52
Figure 15	Laurie Carlos teaching ensemble movement during *con flama* rehearsal	53
Figure 16	Sonja Parks, Ana Perea, and Florinda Bryant performing ensemble movement during *con flama* production	54
Figure 17	Laurie Carlos indicating specific muscles during *con flama* rehearsal	55
Figure 18	Postcard from Djola Branner's *Mighty Real*	58

Figure 19   Lou Bellamy, Laurie Carlos, and Kathryn Coram Gagnon in
             Talking Bones   64

Figure 20   Daniel Alexander Jones gesturing in *The Book of Daniel 35:1*   79

Figure 21   Daniel Alexander Jones and Daniel Dodd Ellis in
             Blood:Shock:Boogie   80

Figure 22   Daniel Alexander Jones's notes for *Blood:Shock:Boogie*   81

Figure 23   Daniel Alexander Jones's poster for *The Owl Answers*   98

Figure 24   Daniel Alexander Jones's handmade book for *Phoenix Fabrik*   98

Figure 25   Daniel Alexander Jones's drawing for the *Phoenix Fabrik* program cover   99

Figure 26   *The Book of Daniel, Chapter 7: Immortality* poster, designed by
             Daniel Alexander Jones   99

Figure 27   Daniel Alexander Jones's artistic lineage   101

Figure 28   "Leroy and Moon," by Walter Kitundu   105

Figure 29   *Bel Canto,* set designed by Kat Conley, Actor's Express   110

Figure 30   Daniel Alexander Jones in *The Book of Daniel 35:1*   113

Figure 31   Sharon Bridgforth composing *River See*   119

Figure 32   L.A. map used in *con flama*   121

Figure 33   Sharon Bridgforth and her family   122

Figure 34   "Boom Boom Girls," by Tonya Engel   125

Figure 35   The root wy'mn Theatre Company   127

Figure 36   The root wy'mn Theatre Company flyer   128

Figure 37   *con flama,* Penumbra Theatre program cover   135

Figure 38   Florinda Bryant, Ana Perea, Zell Miller III, and Sonja Parks
             during *con flama* production   146

Figure 39   Florinda Bryant, Ana Perea, and Sonja Parks
             during *con flama* production   147

Figure 40   The ensemble during *blood pudding* production   149

Figure 41   "Yemaya," by Yasmin Hernandez   155

Figure 42   "Boddica," by Carl E. Karni-Bain "BAI"   166

Figure 43   *Alaskan Heat* rehearsal   169

Figure 44   The ensemble on the bed during *Alaskan Heat* production   171

Figure 45   The ensemble with gestures during *Alaskan Heat* production   173

Figure 46   *Heavenly Shades of Night* poster   175

Figure 47   Zell Miller III, Sarah Richardson, and Omi Osun Joni L. Jones in *Heavenly Shades of Night* production   176

Figure 48   Raul Castillo and Omi Osun Joni L. Jones in *Heavenly Shades of Night* production   177

Figure 49   Florinda Bryant and Omi Osun Joni L. Jones in *Heavenly Shades of Night* production   178

Figure 50   Laurie Carlos carrying Ana Perea during *con flama* rehearsal   181

Figure 51   Ana Perea carrying Sonja Parks during *con flama* rehearsal   181

Figure 52   *Half-Breed Southern Fried (check one)* poster   188

Figure 53   Daniel Alexander Jones's floor plan for *The Book of Daniel 35:1*   190

Figure 54   "Untitled," by Wura-Natasha Ogunji   201

Figure 55   "Self Portrait," by Minnie Marianne Miles   202

Figure 56   Program for *The Book of Daniel, Chapter 7: Immortality,* designed by Daniel Alexander Jones   204

Figure 57   Robbie McCauley in *Sugar*   213

Figure 58   Erik Ehn's *Maria Kizito,* the Soulographie Series   214

Figure 59   Program cover from Grisha Coleman's *The Desert*   217

Figure 60   Walter Kitundu's "Ocean Edge Device"   218

Figure 61   "The Three Graces," by Carl E. Karni-Bain "BAI"   220

Figure 62   The Soulographie Series reading at Daniel Alexander Jones's apartment   221

Figure 63   "Devotee," by Arleen Polite   225

A NOTE ON YORUBA ORTHOGRAPHY

FOLLOWING conventional Yoruba orthography, I have used diacritics on Yoruba words to mark Yoruba tones and to distinguish between /s/ and /sh/ throughout the book. I have also adopted the customary practice of not applying such marks to persons' names and to words such as *Yoruba* that have become recognizable by many English speakers. Words that are not in general use in Yorubaland, such as *Legba* and *Ellegua,* and words that are onomatopoetic drum sounds, such as *iragbagba,* have not been given diacritics. In quoting passages with Yoruba words, I have retained the English spellings and absence of diacritics as used by the author. These marks have been applied in consultation with Yoruba speakers and linguists, although any errors are solely my own.

PREFACE

AS I BEGAN WRITING this book—not just talking about it, or researching in preparation for it, but actually beginning to make sentences across the simulated page of the computer screen—I was told over and over again that it was urgent that I get the word out. Urgent. There was a pressing need, to chart this territory, to tell these stories. My self, my identity, was wrapped up in this telling. In the Yoruba-based practices I explore throughout this book, *Legba,* the Divine force who gives us an opportunity to be in sync with our life path or in opposition to it, let me know that I must do this writing work daily. Because of *Legba*'s particular relationship to words, to *àṣẹ* or the life force, and to communication, I knew it was a message designed to pierce my stubborn *Orí* (head as destiny) and compel me to work *now.*

What exigency could there be about a book that looks at the intersections of jazz aesthetics, theatrical performance, and Yoruba-based theology? While I may never know precisely what the *Òrìṣà* or Deities/Divinities and the ancestors deemed imperative about this work, I believe the urgency is about transformation using the tools I have been trained to employ—words and interaction, networks and communities, art and intellect that is intimately guided by the heart and spirit. This urgency is about not being distracted by an illusory reality in order to immerse myself in the *awo,* or mystery, that is the nature of art and writing. In so doing I may provide others with the desire and courage to transform personally and communally as well.

A fundamental principle of the jazz aesthetics discussed in this book is the act of opening one's intuitive powers. One learns to soar in performance when one's instincts are primed, and this priming means responding to the forces of nature, to instincts. The times demand that we envision and implement new strategies for living our lives, and this is precisely what the artists in this book are doing with their seriate, polyphonic, transtemporal work.

The urgency of the times also requires that we not fear including spirituality in our intellectual and scholarly work. Artists generally have no problem acknowledging spirit, but some writings *about* performing artists fail to include the spiritual impulses that fuel so much of the work. In this way, using the term jazz in the title of this book is very helpful in that jazz giants such as John and Alice Coltrane made it clear that they were in pursuit of spiritual transcendence. I am troubling jazz, interrogating it as a concept and asking jazz not only to reference sound, improvisation, and immediacy but also to evoke spirit. This work is more about the spiritual than it is about the material, though material life-changing events may come to pass by "working the work," the phrase that some of us use to identify the process of doggedly, enthusiastically rehearsing. Living the work helps us to touch that place of genuine freedom and bring back to earth the knowledge we have gleaned, allowing us to more fully understand and transform the material world we inhabit. We return to the earth with paths to freedom—our responsibility is to share it.

I have journeyed in Austin, Minneapolis, and New York with Laurie Carlos, Daniel Alexander Jones, and Sharon Bridgforth, serving variously as performer, dramaturg, producer, director, and witness. My multiple ongoing roles with them give me a unique vantage point for charting their work. Although my understandings and sensibilities are the principle force governing the explorations in this book, this is clearly a collaborative ethnography in which the ongoing relationships between Carlos, Jones, Bridgforth, and me have generated a host of shared codes, jointly told stories, communal revelations, and fluidly intertwined memories. Given this long-standing, intricately woven union, it is sometimes difficult to know exactly who said what and when. I have discussed the ideas of this book with each of them for many years. Their thoughts have stimulated me and folded into my own knowledge of theatrical jazz. While I am the author of this book, I do not lay claim to inventing, discovering, or solely explicating what is presented here. *Theatrical Jazz* is my composition, but we—and many others—have all made this tune together.

ACKNOWLEDGMENTS

THIS BOOK has been many years in the making. I was processing ideas and experiences about art and embodiment long before I knew that my meanderings through museums, seat dancing at concerts, prayers in groves, and performances in many forms of theatre would eventually lead to *Theatrical Jazz*. I drew upon all of those chance and intentional encounters in bringing this work together.

My parents, Dorothy Mae Brown Jones and William Edward Jones, provided me with a safe and supportive space to explore many interests. My sisters, Regina McNabb, LaVerne Love, and Willetta Wordlaw, offered academic excellence, creativity of expression, and improvisation through adversity as models for my own life. My family made Markham, Illinois, in the 1960s a good *àdúgbò* in which to grow.

When the making of this book became a conscious practice, I was able to reshape the ideas through several invaluable speaking engagements, including the Wallace A. Bacon Memorial Lecture at Northwestern University, the Africa Distinguished Lecture at the University of Texas at Austin, the Women's and Gender Studies Faculty Presentations at the University of Texas at Austin, as well as presentations at Duke University, the University of Louisiana at Monroe, DePaul University, and the Chicago History Museum. The writing of the book was also supported by summer writing retreats at Yaddo and Hedgebrook, and with research funds from the John L. Warfield Center for African and African American Studies and the African and African Diaspora Studies Department at the University of Texas at Austin. A generous subvention grant from the University of Texas Office of the Vice President for Research allowed for the lush images that are included in *Theatrical Jazz*. Without this institutional support, the book would exist only on my computer and in my spirit. I am grateful for the confidence in my work that this support reflects, and for the confidence I developed by having this support—a powerful circle, *yímiká.*

Several indigenous Yoruba speakers assisted me with the complex task of unpacking the densely layered meanings of their language and culture. Niyi Afolabi, Tola Mosadomi, Augustine Agwuele, Saheed Aderinto, Bukola Kpotie, and Abimbola Adelakun were patient with my many questions and generous with their discussions about the nuances of Yoruba language. Olayemi Akinola's understanding of beauty and design were instrumental in guiding me through the visual requirements of this book.

I appreciate the spiritual and life lessons from *Orílé Olókun Sànyà Awópéjú* of Cedar Creek, Texas, where I served as a Priest of *Òṣun* and had the privilege of expanding my humility and my experience with the Divine forces of nature. May each member of that community walk with joy on their Divine path.

3 Jazz Collective of Austin, Texas—Joao Costa Vargas, Bruce Saunders, and Kevin Witt—allowed me to join them onstage for improvisational explorations that informed my understanding of artistic invention. What an honor that was. My many conversations with Joao about jazz, Blackness, and the nature of being pushed me to deepen my thinking around the possibilities for social change that art affords us.

The Performance as Public Practice faculty in the Department of Theatre and Dance at the University of Texas at Austin offered important commentary on the Daniel Alexander Jones section of this book. Over lunch at the University of Texas Club, Charlotte Canning, Paul Bonin-Rodriguez, Rebecca Rossen, Deborah Paredez, and Robin Bernstein, who was visiting for the semester from Harvard, encouraged me to connect the theoretical threads more precisely. That advice was invaluable.

I am fortunate to work with people who seriously engaged with me about this work. Meta DuEwa Jones, Matt Richardson, Omise'eke Tinsley, Edmund T. Gordon, Toyin Falola, Moyo Okediji, Tshepo Masango Chery, Kali Gross, Lisa Thompson, Charles Anderson, Lisa L. Moore, Celeste Henery, and Samantha Pinto, who was a 2012 Postdoctoral Fellow at the Warfield Center, consistently offered rigorous feedback about my ideas. They created a nurturing environment where I could imagine that play and exploration were the norm and my trepidations about sharing this book with the world were significantly lessened. I have also been nourished by the Black Performance Theory gatherings of audacious improvisers; by Jane M. Saks and Emma Ruby-Sachs whose examples of radical artmaking, beauty, and commitment were always there just as my energy was flagging; and by Linda Czopek who could see what I could not.

A wide scholarly *egbẹ* has leant much-needed encouragement for my work in creating *Theatrical Jazz*. First and foremost, the John L. Warfield Center for African and African American Studies and the African and African Diaspora Studies Department have made it possible for me to dream in every direction. I am proud of the world we have created where the convergence of Blackness, performance, and spirit help us to discover bold life possibilities. D. Soyini Madison, Stephanie Batiste, Ramon Rivera-Servera, Thomas DeFrantz, Sandra Richards, Anita Gonzalez, Jill Dolan, Stacy Wolf, Joyce A. Joyce, Jennifer Brody, Judith Hamera, Hershini Young, Francesca Royster, and Joy James have each helped me to believe in the importance and usefulness of this book. Their years of successfully navigating the academy while producing innovative and necessary work has made it possible for me to dare to do the same.

E. Patrick Johnson has been an exceptional mentor and friend throughout my career. He has given me opportunities to boldly embrace the role of scholar, to honor my artist self, and to find solitude for writing one summer in the comfort of Chez Vincennes, the name lovingly given to the home he and his generous husband, Stephen Lewis, have created. Patrick is a bright spirit who makes everything around him shine.

A host of former graduate students have contributed their talents to this book: Angie Ahlgren was my research assistant and gathered information that helped me develop a context for the neighborhoods where Carlos, Jones, and Bridgforth lived; Jaclyn Pryor and Katelyn Wood read sections of the book and asked questions that helped to sharpen my thinking and my approach; and Jacqueline Lawton transcribed hours of interviews that were critical for the development of my ideas about the theatrical jazz *ẹgbẹ́*.

As I worked to ensure that the blend of seemingly disparate elements of the book created a coherent new logic for the reader, I sought the support of people who would be willing to closely read the text and give a detailed response to it. Abe Louise Young read early drafts that evolved into distinct structures for the sections on Carlos, Jones, and Bridgforth. Naminata Diabate read the manuscript and posed critical questions that allowed me to create theoretical consistency. Arielle Brown provided administrative assistance as I secured the many permissions that were required for the inclusion of photographs, posters, and paintings. Oladotun Ayobade tirelessly answered questions regarding Yoruba usage and diligently combed the endnotes for incomplete citations. He made possible the last feverish completion of details before submission of the book to the press. His keen intelligence and care were priceless.

Many theatres have produced the work of the artists who are mentioned in *Theatrical Jazz,* but special acknowledgment is due to Frontera@Hyde Park Theatre, Penumbra Theatre, Pillsbury House, and Intermedia Arts for supporting Black theatre and for hunting in archives to find images for this book. Priscilla Hale and Rose Pulliam, co-directors of allgo, not only produce the performance work of artists in this book, they also knew when to pull me away from the computer for a night at the movies or dinner and a bit of much needed processing. Not enough can said in gratitude to Vicky Boone, co-founder of Frontera@Hyde Park Theatre, who provided fertile soil for so many.

Theatrical Jazz is indebted to Adrienne Kennedy whose luminous work wafts through the content, structure, and spirit of this book. Her *People Who Led to My Plays,* which was recommended to me by Daniel Alexander Jones, dislodged my expectations around what constitutes a text. For her singular leadership, I have immeasurable respect and appreciation.

I have been profoundly inspired by the work of three Black women scholars as I was completing work on this book. Farah Jasmine Griffin's keynote address at Northwestern University's 2014 conference, "The Black Body as Archive: Writing

Black Dance," was an example of the clarity, passion, and politics that characterize outstanding scholarship. Isabel Wilkerson's *The Warmth of Other Suns* became a reminder of the transformative power of ethnographic documentation as she lovingly exposed the forces of oppression that mangle Black lives. Sarah Lewis's *The Rise* encouraged me to speak of the "failures" of theatrical jazz, and to complete the book regardless of how it might be received. I am grateful for these extraordinary models as my teachers in the potential for *ikǫ́ ̣sé ̣* that academic life can bring.

It is important that I thank the anonymous reviewers of my manuscript. Such fierce intelligence and ancient wisdom was woven into their recommendations for this book. I could not have asked for more insightful or respectful spirits to dive into my project. I hope I have done justice to their excellent suggestions.

The Ohio State University Press should be recognized for taking a chance on publishing this nontraditional brand of scholarship. Sandy Crooms (now at University of Pittsburgh Press) initially handled my manuscript, and instantly made me feel like my work was in good hands. I am completing this project with Lindsay Martin, Tara Cyphers, and the diligent staff at OSU Press. They have been thorough, enthusiastic, and good-humored even with the sprint we made to the finish. The visual nature of this book required more time and care than most, and the designers and copyeditors have earnestly tended to all the necessary details. My book is in very good company in the Black Performance and Cultural Criticism series.

To the many performers, designers, dramaturgs, audience/witnesses, directors, technicians, and writers with whom I shared so much work, I thank each of them for opening me to the magnificence that is art. I especially thank the three artists featured here, Laurie Carlos, Daniel Alexander Jones, and Sharon Bridgforth, for courageously revealing the intricacies of their lives and enduring countless intrusive questions in order to make this book. I have learned the ways of a jazz-infused life from their choices.

I conclude these acknowledgments by expressing my deepest gratitude for the love in my life. My daughter Leigh Gaymon-Jones is a jewel of brightness, the energy that keeps me buoyant. I am so happy to be an "other mother" to Sonja Perryman, a woman of power and grace. My life partner, Sharon Bridgforth—Sonja's mom and Leigh's Momo—shows me that Joy and Love are real, are necessary, and can be ours if we say yes.

I thank *Ọ̀sun—Ore yè yé O!*—for allowing her commitment to culture and beauty to manifest through me as *Theatrical Jazz: Performance, Àṣẹ, and the Power of the Present Moment.* Her flowing waters bring an abundance of all good things, along with the drive to give the ideas of this book to others. I am grateful to all the Divine energies that have made this so.

Figure 1. "Oxum," by Werllayne Nunes. This unique rendering of the riverine Òrìṣà Ọ̀ṣun offers a way to imagine her playful and mischievous nature. Wearing a symbol of her later adult role as water navigator, this Ọ̀ṣun as expressed in human form is accompanied by one of her totems in a magical torrent of flowers.

Troubling Jazz / *Abínibí* / Black Theatre for the Twenty-First Century

The goal is always God.
—Sekou Sundiata[1]

Not knowing the break
Needing a tribe
Wanting the river to claim me

Everything is everything.
Jazz and Yoruba spiritual traditions and theatre arouse my unspeakable curiosities,
arresting my attention—poised, ready, tantalized. The way Coltrane's "Dear Lord"
moves in me, and evokes so many things at the same time, is like prayer in the groves
with the calabash held high. When Thelonious Monk ka-plunks a note, and something
in me awakens, when my body moves around the circle with my back bent for Ọbàtálá
and I smile and want to just cut loose in my own improvised praise to the force of
justice and wisdom—it is all striking the same vibration, tweaking
the same root. When I stomp, wide-legged, flinging sweat around the performance
circle and declare, "this is where it all comes together"—I know that mama's biscuits
made to the harmonies of Brook Benton and Dinah Washington, I know that people
jumping with the spirit at Second Baptist Church in Harvey, Illinois, I know that my
coming out and coming in are the forces of the deepest power, are spirit, art, and
eros, are abínibí—natural, as it should be, is. At some point for me it all became the
same thing—that awe filled place of the most profound truth that when accessed, when
respected, would change everything. Could I go there? Would I choose truth and power
over a beautiful mask? I ask myself this every time I am in the presence of this work. It
takes me to the edge,

and I stop at the banks of the river, or get in with the fish and improvise.
I bring all of this together as I go wider and deeper.
It is all the same. It is the essence of being, the roots, the thang, the Spirit.
Theatre does not exist without it. Jazz couldn't be without it.
Magic cannot happen without the surrender to the mystery.
And this is how I begin to tell it as the same tune.

THIS OFFERING is humbly and audaciously about freedom. It looks at how artists are made, and how artists make art, how the singular voice can create spaces of freedom for the many. Jazz and *àṣẹ*—a Yoruba concept identifying the ability/authority to make things happen—work as tools for combating the destructive ethnocentric forces at play in the world. This work exists as a way to confront these forces and to prescribe varied, insurgent performance alternatives. More personally, this book is about finding my own voice/self/freedom through the jazz-inflected spirit-inspired traditions of three Black Theatre artists, and about passing my understandings on in the tradition of apprentice–elder relationships.

Theatrical Jazz: Performance, Àṣẹ, and the Power of the Present Moment is a study of theatrical jazz aesthetics[2] that gives particular attention to three innovative practitioners of the form—Laurie Carlos, Daniel Alexander Jones, and Sharon Bridgforth. These artists are featured here because of the scope and sway of their work, which moves around the United States while gathering in a host of new adherents and practitioners along the way. Through ethnographic documentation, close readings of texts and performances,[3] and critical analysis, I examine the major works of these artists and detail the intricate mechanics of this aesthetic.

The ethnographic strategies presented here are decidedly collaborative. While all ethnographies could lay some claim to a collaborative manifestation between the ethnographer and the fieldwork community members, *Theatrical Jazz* literally allows ample space for the voices of Carlos, Jones, and Bridgforth throughout the text. Lengthy passages from each of these artists creates a kind of call and response among them, and between them and me, what Robert G. O'Meally describes as "complicated exchanges between a single voice and other voices: soloist and the chorus of other players."[4] While I may be the soloist, at moments in the text, the chorus takes the lead. E. Patrick Johnson's *Sweet Tea* provides a sturdy model for these contrapuntal relationships as his interviews of sixty-three Black gay men of the south move between his questions and context-providing commentaries, and the stories the men tell.[5] *Sweet Tea* lets the reader experience each man—including Johnson—as both autonomous and linked. *Theatrical Jazz* offers a similar relationship as a collaborative ethnographic project.

"THE JAZZ AESTHETIC IS NOT ABOUT A SET OF AGREEMENTS OTHER THAN YOU AGREE TO DISAGREE AND RESPECT THAT. THE JAZZ AESTHETIC IS ALWAYS ABOUT THAT, ALWAYS, BECAUSE IT HAS TO BE. IT'S YOUR VERY PERSONAL DEEP SPIRITUAL JOURNEY THROUGH THE EXPERIENCE. ANYONE WHO'S DECIDED TO MAP THAT WHOLE THING OUT IS GOING TO RUN INTO A TRAFFIC JAM AT SOME POINT. BECAUSE YOU'RE GOING TO HAVE TO GIVE WAY FOR SOMEBODY ELSE'S RIFF OR JOURNEY INSIDE OF THE THING."*

—LAURIE CARLOS

* Interview by author, New York, July 2003.

The theory of theatrical jazz is this writing itself—the way this writing resists linearity even as it is bound to it, the way many speak here sometimes in contradiction to others and to themselves, the way the reader is invited to develop her or his own reading practice—start where you like, savor the visual, chew on the verbal, play with movement and sound throughout. And here is the traffic jam, invoking *Legba* of the choice-laden crossroads and *Ògún* of pulsing action. Rather than a singular prescription, this work offers the varied recipes practiced by seasoned artists.

The book has been constructed to encourage a specific visual literacy, one that complements the improvisatory nonlinear jazz aesthetics discussed throughout. Colors, fonts, images create their own communication system. Colored text is coded. Orange is the color for my critical personal narratives. The range of blues are for the primary artists featured in the book: blue for Carlos, violet for Jones, and turquoise for Bridgforth. Quotations from scholars, artists, and other thinkers who will be found in the bibliography are brown. The Yoruba glossary and proverbs are green. The African diasporic paintings throughout the book have the potential for opening up levels of awareness not prompted by verbal language, while also dialoging with the written text. At times the paintings have been positioned so as to encourage a conversation with the adjacent text, at other times the relationships between the paintings and the text are serendipitous, and the paintings can exist independent of the text if a reader wants to move through without reading the words at all. The artwork also serves as a reminder of the importance of the visual in theatrical jazz. The sentences of the text are often interrupted with additional text or with images, requiring the reader to develop his or her own reading strategy. Sometimes it may be difficult to maintain a left-to-right reading habit. The act of reading, then, simulates the active decision-making that audience/witnesses of theatrical jazz often employ, as well as reflecting the art of creation.

The titles that organize the book into an introduction and three parts provide another code for the reader by offering a triumvirate of meanings and themes that are featured in each section. Each title can be understood as a single idea experienced through three performance practices. For example, "Troubling Jazz / *Abínibí* / Black Theatre for the Twenty-First Century" comprises three mutually influencing terms. The first word in the title references jazz music, the middle term is a complementary Yoruba concept, and the final idea is a theatrical expression that corresponds to the jazz and Yoruba realities. In this way, the titles serve to remind the reader of three of the major strands of theatrical jazz that are pursued in the book.

For this introduction to the book, "Troubling Jazz" speaks to this entire project in which jazz is being examined on behalf of another artform. *Abínibí* translates roughly from the Yoruba to English as "the natural order of things," which becomes an approach to experiencing the union of theatre and jazz as a readily understandable relationship. This union creates an artform that is poised to provoke aesthetic and political transformation in the twenty-first century through its deep engagement with audience/witnesses, its commitment to Black joy, and its valorizing of the fertile strategy of improvisation. Each chapter's title can be similarly considered as individual meanings that, when joined, offer multiple overlapping understandings. The book, then, is an act of jazz making, an amalgam of performance artifacts and memories, of discoveries and frustrations.

Theatrical jazz is a distinctive way to make work and life; indeed, theatrical jazz acknowledges the necessary seamlessness of the two. While this aesthetic leans heavily on elements of jazz including ensemble and individual virtuosity, improvisation, polyrhythms, "the bridge," and "the break," it also references the modern dance idioms, the blues sensibilities, the performance art antecedents, and the ancestral calling that position theatrical jazz as a distinctive performance genre. The texts and productions made from this artistic sensibility are diverse, yet some features reoccur through the range of works. Most often, theatrical jazz is nonlinear and transtemporal. It offers a complex idea of Blackness that challenges monolithic definitions and predictable associations. The narratives most often explore power and identity, sex and desire, and are frequently subjective explorations of the writer's life. Love, joy, and community are commonly the exacting roads to transformation. In production, the bodies often share nonmimetic movements that are layered onto the verbal text as a counterpoint providing physical and visual stories of their own. Music references, especially blues and jazz, regularly appear in the work as sound, ideas, structure, or characters. In theatrical jazz, the audience is positioned as co-creators and witnesses who help shape the work and are reshaped by it.

Figure 2. "Double Take," by Moyo Okediji. The second look suggested by the title reveals many multifaceted spirits moving through the painting and, as Dr. Okediji pointed out to me, queer possibilities in the bright red lips and multiple perspectives of the musician. Photo by Moyo Okediji.

Theatrical Jazz uses Yoruba cosmology[6] to illuminate the spiritual impulses that undergird the work. The Yoruba sensibilities that pervade this book are derived from my experiences with Yoruba-based traditions, specifically my relationship with Òṣun—the Divinity of healing, culture, and abundant joy. While I acknowledge the Nigerian, Cuban, and U.S. underpinnings of my spiritual development, what is presented here is my own lived understanding of Yoruba cosmology forged from many sources, certainties, and hypotheses. Yoruba-based spiritual traditions, or Ìṣẹ̀ṣẹ̀ traditions, are African diasporic West African–derived practices in which ritual, everyday performance, and transformation mingle together in the name of creativity. Àṣẹ becomes the animating feature of this aesthetic. Yoruba cosmology, then, becomes a specific spiritual methodology for understanding how performance is generated and how performance generates change.

Like jazz itself, the book's structure is based on a fusion of intellectual, artistic, and sensory experiences. Collage, repetition, the juxtaposition of key artifacts, and critical personal narrative are central to the book's organization. In addition to scholarly analysis and ethnographic documentation, the book includes photographs of the artists' productions, discographies of their musical influences, the texts they deemed important to their development as artists and thinkers, and recipes for the community-sustaining meals so critical to their work. These distinctive artifacts are the connective tissue for the book, weaving through the analytical discussions of Carlos, Jones, and Bridgforth. In this way, I provide the reader with an ample, albeit partial, sense of the artists' lives, and how those lives come to embody the jazz principles of their art.

Throughout *Theatrical Jazz*, I employ "autocritography," what theatre scholar Kimberly W. Benston calls "a performative practice that dramatizes the roles of memory, reading, and translation in the construction of modern African-American subjectivity."[7] Through autocritography I intertwine my own personal exploration of this work with critical analysis, using production and rehearsal experiences as data for a discussion of the jazz aesthetic, Yoruba cosmology, and the diasporic realities of art and spirit. This investigation, then, is as much my own story as it is a discussion of the methods and strategies of Carlos, Jones, and Bridgforth. Indeed, our repeated collaborations have provided artistic and spiritual sustenance for us all.

"BETTY CARTER JUST CRACKED MY HEAD OPEN TO THE IDEA OF SOMETHING TO WHICH I WILL ALWAYS ASPIRE, WHICH IS A FEARLESS ABILITY TO IMPROVISE WITH ASTONISHING PRECISION, AND THE RECOGNITION THAT EVERYTHING IS CRUCIAL, THERE'S NOTHING ARBITRARY, . . . EVERYTHING HAS MEANING."*

—DANIEL ALEXANDER JONES

* E-mail message to author, June 27, 2008.

The theatrical jazz artists whose histories and art practices I present here mean to do nothing less than forge a space for a reimagined theatre and a more fully responsive world. Through the development of jazz aesthetics as experienced through theatre, they challenge traditional Western theatre making in general, and Black U.S. theatre aesthetics in particular. Freedom is indeed the goal, as these artists have been relegated to the relative obscurity of avant-garde or experimental status. For these artists, such status leaves them invisible in the Black Theatre world that resists the expansive Blackness and queer realities that characterize much of their work. In an avant-garde context, the Black aesthetics remain appropriated, fetishized idiosyncrasies rather than historically rooted through the resistive, feminist, antiracist paradigms they employ.

Carlos, Jones, and Bridgforth represent an alternative genealogy for Black Theatre. Black Theatre historians have charted the moves from Lloyd Richards that extended to Lorraine Hansberry, Sidney Poitier, Ossie Davis, and Ruby Dee of the 1950s and 1960s through August Wilson, Charles Dutton, S. Epatha Merkerson, Angela Bassett, and Delroy Lindo of the 1980s and 1990s. Historians have likewise been attentive to other far-reaching collaborations across time and space such as Robert Hooks's work in establishing both the Negro Ensemble Company and the DC Black Repertory Company, or Langston Hughes's formation of the Harlem Suitcase Theatre and the Skyloft Players in Chicago. Carlos, Jones, and Bridgforth have created a thick web of mutual influence that has sculpted their work and their lives. I have worked with them collectively on more than thirty projects to date. As of this writing, Carlos and Bridgforth have worked on eight projects together, Bridgforth and Jones have worked on five, and Jones and Carlos have worked on thirteen. In so doing, they have nurtured an impressive cadre of artists who are now conversant with the workings of theatrical jazz, artists who have created their own dense networks of theatrical-jazz-trained practitioners, artists who have established national and international reputations working across many media and theatrical forms. This spiraling as people crisscross each other's paths is common and necessary in theatrical jazz; this is how the work is shared and how it remains a living morphing form. These collaborations set in motion a constellation of fertile vast relationships that form the artistic genealogy presented in this book. I reference the complex artistic associations that extend from this trio of visionaries to offer their artistic migrations and apprenticeship relationships as evidence of the growing impact that Carlos, Jones, and Bridgforth have on theatrical performance.

"SEEING *FOR COLORED GIRLS* WAS MY FIRST MEMORY OF BEING IN A THEATRE AND IT CHANGED MY WHOLE LIFE. IT GAVE ME THE FREEDOM TO IMAGINE TELLING THE TRUTH, TO IMAGINE USING LANGUAGE IN A WAY THAT REALLY WORKED FOR ME. IT ALLOWED ME TO IMAGINE THAT I COULD DO ART. AND THAT MY STORY MATTERED."*
—SHARON BRIDGFORTH

* Phone interview with author, July 5, 2008.

It is useful to undertake this investigation of theatrical jazz through a close look at a specific artistic lineage. Because this work is learned through an apprentice–elder structure, looking at a particular lineage allows me to map in detail how the tradition operates and is passed on. Carlos is an Obie and Bessie Award–winning iconoclastic veteran who participated in the Black Arts Movement, premiered the role of the lady in blue in Ntozake Shange's *for colored girls who have considered suicide/when the rainbow is enuf,* moved through myasthenia gravis with dance and breath work, was an original player in the New York avant-garde performance scene of the 1970s, and has created a trail of legendary performances and loyal artistic associates. She has mentored many artists across several disciplines in her distinctive breath/movement/listening strategies, and her brilliance in writing, performing, and directing has been indispensable in shaping the work of Jones and Bridgforth. Jones is a 2006 Alpert Award winner for theatre and New Dramatists' Resident Writer who began his specific training in a theatrical jazz aesthetic with Aishah Rahman at Brown University, and honed his understanding through performance work with Carlos and Robbie McCauley. His friend and artistic ally, Sharon Bridgforth, is a Lambda Literary Award winner, New Dramatists' Resident Writer, and founder and director of The root wy'mn Theatre Company. Bridgforth credits *for colored girls* with giving her an artistic anchor, and Carlos with bringing her fully into the power of a jazz aesthetic. Examining these artists together in this book provides an opportunity to explore the distinctive features of their specific expression of a jazz aesthetic while clarifying the theatrical jazz aesthetic generally, and noting the many overlaps in artistic experiences, such as the influence Shange has had on all three. Taken together, Carlos, Jones, and Bridgforth represent an array of jazz possibilities in art and in life, thereby providing readers with a variety of approaches for a common goal: an invigorated sense of humanity through the rigors of artmaking, or as Sekou Sundiata said simply in an interview, "The goal is always God."[8]

Theatrical jazz has artistic impulses akin to Western theatrical avant-garde traditions[9]—a particular kind of resistance to existing sociopolitical structures, an interactive relationship with audience/witnesses, a reimagining of what theatre itself might be and *do* in the world. Indeed, the artists I examine here have often found homeplace more comfortably in so-called experimental or avant-garde theatre communities—a complicated position to occupy when Black artists have rarely set the terms of what constitutes avant in Western art.

HARRY ELAM: "Historically, Western avant-garde art has celebrated and appropriated the 'avant' energy of the racial other even as it excluded the work of the racial other. Thus, it has included race by excluding it."°

° "The *TDR* Black Theatre Issue: Refiguring the Avant-Garde," 44.

Theatre historian Harry Elam speaks to this dilemma as he examines how white artists and scholars hold tight to defining what the avant-garde might be, and who might participate.[10] Poet/scholar Fred Moten has discussed the complexities of a contemporary Black avant-garde art, an art that challenges the unstated presumptions of both Black art and a white-defined and white-dominated avant-garde art. He identifies "freedom drive" as the resistance to objectification and the "essence of black performance,"[11] while acknowledging that some Black critics would not embrace the resistance fostered by the avant-garde at the expense of a distinctive (and perhaps narrow) reading of Black aesthetics.[12] This conundrum is all too real for the artists discussed here, who have generally been produced by "experimental" venues such as P.S. 122 and the Soho Rep in New York, Pillsbury House in Minneapolis, Link's Hall in Chicago, and Frontera@Hyde Park Theatre in Austin, Texas. The primary artists featured here are creating—in quite different ways—a kind of populist modernism that speaks across high–low art divisions while offering new experiences of Blackness.[13]

The expression of a Black avant-garde stands in sharp contrast to traditional Black U.S. theatre, though the two have similar aims. Theatrical resistance and insurgency can manifest in distinctive, and seemingly contradictory, ways. Some traditionally structured Black Theatre grows out of an impulse to prove its worth by adopting established standards of dramatic excellence. In this way, the well-made play, the proscenium, and readily identifiable characters and locations become acts of resistance in a world that does not allow full participation of Black artists in mainstream theatrical work. The Black avant-garde, instead, dismantles and re-envisions the very notion of what theatre might be. In this way, Black Theatre benefits from both August Wilson and Sekou Sundiata, from Lorraine Hansberry and Robbie McCauley.

Traditional Black Theatre has found a way to encourage certain types of social change and transcendence through familiar characters, locations, and situations. The Black avant-garde pulls on that sense of the familiar, but finds new structures for it as it dares to give audience/witnesses the familiar, like a gospel choir with a fan-waving congregation, *and* an unexpected Blackness to grapple with, a new way to social and spiritual transcendence.

MARGO JEFFERSON: "Experimental theater, after all, is an acquired taste—like aged cheese or raw fish. It is an experience that needs some effort, some study and some time."°

° "The Avant-Garde, Rarely Love at First Sight."

In titling this book, I am troubling jazz, as in calling on jazz to once again take on the job of standing in for both a politicized Blackness and a counterhegemonic set of aesthetic principles. Here, jazz is not allowed to merely be itself—a music of complex origins and structures. As with jazz dance of the 1920s and 1930s and jazz poetry of the1950s through the 1970s,[14] theatrical jazz signals a self-naming that at once conjures a Black collectivity, and expresses Black innovation and individuality.

This book also troubles jazz by interrogating the term and its usage. Not only for the pejorative connotations that musician-scholar Fred Wei-han Ho[15] suggests, the term jazz may also work against the very freedom these artists are striving to achieve. Jazz seems to bind us to race, and thereby already to constrain the possi-

FRED WEI-HAN HO: "I do not use the term 'jazz' just as I do not use such terms as 'Negro,' 'Oriental,' or 'Hispanic.'"°

° "'Jazz,' Kreolization and Revolutionary Music for the 21st Century," 132.

bility of absolute freedom. The very free space that some of the artists in this book want to create and live in—the very space that the free jazz of Ornette Coleman seems to activate—is not at all free if it is hooked to race or any other identity feature. As a musical tradition, jazz has come to be associated with Blackness, sensuality, freedom, "primitivism," and democracy. All of these are loaded associations. While some of these ideas seem forward thinking and apt (as in some understandings of democracy, Blackness, and freedom), even these carry the potential taint of stereotype and essentialism—not even a strategic essentialism deployed for political solidarity and agency, but an essentialism that boxes the art into categories and, by extension, limits.

Indeed, some have attempted to define jazz as a polyglot form, not assigning originary status to African Americans. This may seem to be a testimonial for a simplistic interpretation of U.S. society that flies in the face of George Lewis's careful articulation of jazz as afrological,[16] but it also speaks a truth about the way jazz

WYNTON MARSALIS: "Jazz developed from a blending of European, African, Latin and Native American musical ideas . . . none are solely responsible for its inception. That distinction can be given to only one group of people—Americans. Just as America is a melting pot of diverse cultures, jazz, too, is a melting pot of diverse musical ideas passed down through generations."°

° *Making the Music: A Teacher's Guide to Jazz*, 10.

functions, if not about jazz's origins. Spirit is not bound by identity features. Jazz is complicated in that it both is Black and is materially transcendent; it allows us to know the specifics of our selves and to unhook from them at the same time. Spiritual transcendence does not require an absence of race, but instead an absence of race as restriction or prediction.

For the three artists featured in this book Blackness is a continual presence in their work, rarely revealed as theme or idea, but more materially present as character and detail. Some audience/witnesses might not recognize this brand of Blackness because it lives inside the blue note,—"Any note that is bent, scraped, smeared, and is generally a half step away from the obvious note."[17] In theatrical jazz, the blue note is the presence of Black references or experiences that are just enough off-center to make one's head cock to the side—curious, fascinated.[18] To varying degrees, Carlos, Jones, and Bridgforth bend traditional Black referents (gospel harmonies, civil rights video footage, Motown melodies, *Jet Magazine*) to create something new, thereby situating themselves at a powerful crossroads of traditional Black aesthetics, the Western avant-garde, and any other traditions that serve the particular experience they are sharing. Carlos's physical repertoire is shaped by modern dance and the force of breath, Jones's dramatic structure sometimes pays homage to modernist forms, and Bridgforth's ancestral memory draws almost equally from Native Americans and from Africans. Theirs is a Blackness that is expansive and inclusive, one that renders joy, hope, and freedom rather than exposes/invents a series of pathologies and/or subjugations in need of attention. They resist the politics of respectability that can prevent Black artists from telling the truth for fear of middle-class reprisals. Such resistance allows for a full range of Blackness in their work in which race, gender, class, sexuality, and nationality are varied, porous, and dynamic. They are well versed in Black literary and performance tropes, and critique or recuperate them by blending and bending them into new ideas of Blackness revealing the particular constructions of U.S. racialized identities. Their artistic choices reveal an understanding of the inextricability of aesthetics and politics, so that their very artmaking is the decidedly political act of imagining Blackness anew.

From 2008 to 2011,
I attended an array of what might be called "Black Theatre." The works were variously written by Black, white, and Asian-American writers—from two reimaginings of Porgy and Bess *at major U.S. theatres, to original works by up-and-coming Black writers at alternative spaces, to a student-directed production of* Difficulty of Crossing a Field *to an Asian American writer's skillful treatment of racial expectation. Some of these works rest on tried and true social stereotypes as well as established theatrical conventions. I sometimes left the theatre furious at what happened on stage that was then replicated in the racial relations among the audience/witnesses, and on other occasions I really felt lifted and moved. These experiences have me wondering what Black Theatre is today, and who cares about it. Can aesthetic excellence supersede political naivety and artistic privilege? Artistic skill is captivating and impressive. But what of Blackness? What happens to "the fact of Blackness" when the goals of the production do not include an investigation or historically responsible rendering of race? Can artists put Black stories on stage without any regard to real live Black people and our histories? Can white artists who appear to operate with such disregard begin to examine the racial privilege or economic privilege or perhaps yearning for acclaim and credibility that even makes such choices possible? Where is the space for honest discussion about the racial myopia that some playwrights exhibit, and the commercially viable hackneyed choices that others make? And is this book the space to call them out—*

a forum where they cannot speak back?
I have had so many provocative
conversations about art with my academic friends in the social sciences and
humanities who often argue that performance applauds even the most racist images
and ideas if the work is of high artistic quality. They often cite Monster's Ball *as a*
prime example. It seems a clear case—a Black woman who can't seem to make her life
work without a white man who is her husband's executioner. Black men are killed off,
Black women must rely on the power and privilege of whiteness, and white men are
saviors and sexual conquerors of Black women once again. My attempts at protest—a
complex Black female character, an exceptional performance, the possibility for hope
and love in a ravaging world—seem naïve and misguided, even to my ears. With
those friends I have the unenviable task of trying to demonstrate how the politics they
sometimes narrowly see represents only an element of the overall experience, not the
sum total of it.
Serious considerations of how race operates in a production do not detract from
the artistic power of a work—indeed, they enhance it by adding more density and
richness to the experience. It is dangerous to celebrate aesthetic achievement without
simultaneously offering rigorous political clarity. The danger rests in the relentlessness
of hegemony to cement the social ills art has the power to redirect.
Aesthetics is not a retreat from the social responsibility and political facts of artmaking.
Race, like theatre,
is a series of carefully coded constructions—and theatre can implode when it refuses
to deal with all the codes available to it. Only those with race privilege are allowed to
be cavalier about race. As long as racism, sexism, homophobia, and nationalism exist,
there is no art for art's sake. Aesthetics and politics are locked in an intricate dance
of intertwining meanings. We cannot get beyond race until we courageously walk the
blistering coals of race. Theatre artists have an opportunity
to abandon the distorted conversations that have sullied U.S. stages for centuries. It
is not enough to articulate intellectual and/or artistic positions without attending to
the decidedly real—albeit constructed—facts of race that envelope art. I have ancestors
who are depending on me to make this point comprehensible. Theatrical jazz is my
freedom place of possibility, an art that no longer needs a hush harbor because now
we are prepared to be loud.

The jazz aesthetic in theatre is the spatial, aural, linguistic embodiment of queer, the expression of a self-naming that is consciously and insurgently liminal, unfixed. In queerness, nonnormative eros is the norm—morphing, shape-shifting, being fully present inside of one's sexual—and political—desires. In examining the competing and often contradictory definitions of queer, Annamarie Jagose concludes, "By refusing to crystallize in any specific form, queer maintains a relation of resistance to whatever constitutes the normal."[19] Queerness is knowing/living the permeability of reality markers, it is embracing the varieties of eros regardless of what the specific practice might be—hetero, homo, or whatever. Queer is more about naming sites of possibility than naming a *particular* possibility. Queer foregrounds sexuality, the necessity of pleasure, and places it in the middle of the conversation, permits play and exploration to be the goal. Queer as permeable and multideterminant suggests an experiential relationship with liminality which need not be conceptualized solely as "not this and not that" but, more fruitfully, "this *and* that." Like queerness, liminality is the space of possibility in which people are not bound to the social structures, but are given freedom to conceive, to imagine, to invent, to make. Liminality is the space of improvisation—invention within a prescribed structure, the making of something that did not exist before.

While the concept of liminality has deep associations with the work of Victor Turner, this association carries tensions. Though Turner expanded on the work of Arnold van Gennep, he developed the details of his understanding of liminality through his work with the Ndembu of Zambia. Given that Turner deepened his understanding of liminality in working with an African people, it might be more sound to use ideas and concepts drawn from Black experiences to name the state commonly known as "betwixt and between." Rather than identifying such a state as liminal, it might be more culturally grounded to name the state "the break," thereby acknowledging important associations with the pause at the end of a vocal blues line and the solo improvisations in jazz. Naming this fertile space "the break" also allows for a useful inclusion of Fred Moten's conceptualization of "the break" as a site of radical possibility that Black aesthetics affords.[20] Similarly, in exploring the aesthetic force of "the break" as a manipulation of rhythm, artist/scholar Thomas DeFrantz identifies "the break" as "the crossroads of performance execution."[21] In so doing, DeFrantz establishes "the break" as a spiritual site of agency and self-determination by invoking *Legba,* the Yoruba Divinity who oversees the crossroads and offers us choices—for good, ill, or in between.

Jazz, "the break," and queer enact similar transgressive strategies, moving from mimesis (imitation that can lead to stasis and maintenance of the status quo) to poeisis (the literary imagination with emphasis on language) to kinesis (the forging, the sweating, the calloused hands that offer up the not known). Queer and jazz unabashedly revel in the will to traverse the new right now. They share a sense of time that is unfettered by State-controlled, future-oriented, progress-driven mandates. Queer time is a critical feature of jazz aesthetics; it supports both the aesthetic and the political dimensions of jazz through its nonnormative and transgressive rhythms, its simultaneous narrative strategies and its nonmimetic embodiments. Jazz encourages an experience that is beyond the expectation of linearity (fixed) and a mechanized timeliness (predictable), and moves into a now time that is relational (improvised) and body-centered (vulnerable). Band leader Christopher Calloway Brooks notes his grandfather's insistence on a very particular formation of time in talking about Cab Calloway's unique jazz stylings. According to Brooks, Cab Calloway required the bass player to "pull the whole groove forward" by playing just ahead of the beat while the drummer played right in the center, and the saxophonist played slightly behind the beat.[22] Calloway invented a new way of experiencing time that helped mark the swing in the music. Poet, playwright, and jazz theorist/critic Amiri Baraka, in a 1958 letter to poet Charles Olson, referred to time as a phenomenon of "the integrated body-mind."[23] Jazz time

Figure 3. "Untitled," by unknown artist. I purchased this painting from the African Heritage and Antique Collection near Leimert Park in Los Angeles. The owner did not know who the artist was. On the front of the painting are the letters G O S. On the back there appears to be an indecipherable signature and the phrase "For the love of the music! Nov 1998." Who created this strong jazz image full of queer possibilities? Photo by Wura-Natasha Ogunji.

is an innovation that happens deep in the body, creating a fluid, nuanced metronome of enactment. These body-valorizing principles that give primacy to the now of nonsanctioned gender habitations and sexual manifestations are the foundation for queer conceptualizations of time. Queer and jazz are active choices predicated on pleasure—both erotic desire and improvisation come from the same drive. In these ways, queer time and jazz are family. And herein lies the danger and threat. Queer places desire/process/now of all kinds above procreation/product/result. And in the present-tense reality of "the break," all things are possible. Queer allows the space for identity to tussle with itself rather than don socially prescribed performances. Queer, like jazz, crosses borders, borrows, samples so that the recognizable is seen anew, and ultimately a new something exists—this is not a binary world, but a fertile multitemporaneous one. In this world, beings dance in the intersection with the energy of all the directions coming to bear on that spot.

Queer is integral to the work of Carlos, Jones, and Bridgforth in that nonnormative sexualities and gender constructions are ever present. Carlos's characters frequently resist standard notions of the female, explicitly challenging gender norms and expectations. Jones's *The Book of Daniel* series regularly includes discussions about his distinctive racial, gendered, and sexual identities,[24] and Bridgforth is known for creating queer as the sexual/gendered backdrop against which everything takes place. For these artists then, queer is the everyday as their understanding of Blackness encompasses transgressive sexualities and gender constructions.

In the *Ifá* divination system of Yoruba-based spiritual traditions, an *òpèlè*, or divining chain, is often used for spiritual consultations. Each side of the chain has a story/vibration/lesson. These sides could be understood as a binary system, each side bringing its own history. When the two sides of the chain are revealed after a diviner's toss, they actually create something new, no longer a binary existence, but a truth that is the union of each side. This Yoruba-based divination system is not this or that, but quite powerfully this and that. Art, eros, and spirit are sourced from the same river of liminal possibilities.

Figure 4. "Shiny Black Stars," by Senalka McDonald. McDonald's images morph across ambiguous gender identifications. Photos by Senalka McDonald.

In spite of queer theory's association with what David Kessler calls a "radical liberationist agenda,"[25] queer theory has suffered from the same racial myopia that once plagued feminist theory, what E. Patrick Johnson and Mae Henderson call the "totalization and homogenization"[26] of queer theory. I follow the political move made by many Black feminist scholars who, in naming the particularities of their feminist agenda and practice, retained the potent, though "white," term feminism and refashioned the term with the insertion of Black as the critical modifier.[27] Likewise, I retain the potentially insurgent term queer, and following Johnson, Henderson, Wahneema Lubiano, and Bryant Alexander among others, I add Black as the animating force that retrieves queer from a stifling privileged whiteness. Here, I call on Fred Moten's work in exploring the possibilities that queer holds for a radical understanding of Blackness. Building on Eve Sedgwick's acknowledgment of the *gravitas* given to queer as deployed by intellectuals and artists of color, Moten argues, "I want to move in the trajectory of [Sedgwick's use of queer] in order to range as much as possible across the entirety of the experimental field of blackness that it opens."[28] Queer sensibilities broaden Black artistic and political possibilities.

CATHY COHEN: "In its current rendition, queer politics is coded with class, gender and race privilege, and may have lost its potential to be a politically expedient organizing tool for addressing the needs—and mobilizing the bodies—of people of color."°

° "Punks, Bulldaggers, and Welfare Queens: The Radical Potential of Queer Politics," 34.

Black itself is queer in that *self*-generated notions of Blackness and gender are counterhegemonic—after all, Aunt Jemima, the brut Negro, and Jezebel are not Black constructions but convenient hegemonic distortions of a Black spirit of survival. Aunt Jemima is a mangling of *Yemọnja,* the Yoruba Divinity of motherhood and the cresting of the ocean; the brut Negro spawns from the fear of Ṣàngó's maleness, Ṣàngó as the Divine force of vitality and electricity; and Jezebel is the opportunistic misunderstanding of Ọ̀ṣun's sensuality, Ọ̀ṣun as the Divinity charged with the sensory perpetuation of culture. Our very sense of what it means to fully be rests outside of racist definitions and therefore outside of the structures the mainstream has used to encapsulate us. True Black, Blue Black—as concept, not color—is queer. The confluence of racialized, gendered, and sexualized realities becomes, as E. Patrick Johnson's grandmother would say, "Quare."[29]

Johnson's notion of quare aptly situates queerness as a reality with a particular clarity when examined through a Black lens. In discussing how queer and Black speak across experiences, Johnson rescues queer theory from the domain of white theorists who seldom acknowledge how people of color operate within and outside the white theorists' intellectual frames.

By employing queer in this way, I run the risk of erasing the profound politicized embodiment of sexuality—specifically, criminalized, pathologized, and ostracized sexualities. If jazz is queer, and Black is queer, and even joined sides of a divining chain might be queer in their commitment to making a truth in the now, then how are gay, lesbian, bisexual, and transgender lives to be understood as distinctive queer realities? By utilizing the idea of queer in these ways, I intend to both amplify the transgressive nature of jazz, Yoruba-based spiritualities, and Blackness *and* encourage a deep consideration of how these realities have concealed/rejected their gay, lesbian, bisexual, and transgender histories. Rather than erase the particularities of queer sexualities, I hope to encompass and extend them.

I have always been queer.
Regardless of my sexual partners, I have always been queer—my identity living in a liminal space where many years ago some straight men said "There's something different about you," and women just wondered with eyebrows raised. I wasn't "out" overtly but the truth of my self seeped through my walk, my gaze, my talk. The price of a clandestine daily life is a cramped artistic and spiritual life; as a performer I would not cross the limen threshold into spirit magic but held tight to excellent technique and a melodious voice. Likewise, I would not use my àṣẹ to make things happen, but instead adhered to fixed and static religious doctrines. To claim my àṣẹ would mean to radically reorder the structures that have supported me. To live in the break on stage would mean living the break in life. The two are inextricably bound. In performance, one allows a kind of exposure, the deepest visibility—letting one's stuff get some air. Not having practiced this present-tense truth-telling in life, I found it difficult to access it in performance. It was the difference between work that others deemed good and work that took me closer to the Divine with no concern for human assessment.

Throughout the book, the spiritual worldview I use as an analytical methodology is Yoruba-based. I am interested in resonances, not continuities, among jazz aesthetics, these artists, and Yoruba cosmology. Yoruba becomes a way to see into and experience the works rather than a conscious artistic choice. I offer Yoruba cosmology as a strategy for bringing artistic, political, and everyday clarity to the works examined here in much the same way that concepts of sin, salvation, redemption, meditation, and sacrifice have become common analytical tools borrowed from other spiritual traditions. Elsewhere, I have looked at the work of Pepe Carrill of Cuba, Shay Youngblood of the United States, and Abdias do Nascimiento of Brazil to examine the conscious diasporic use of Yoruba-ness in their plays.[30] Here, I explore how Yoruba sensibilities move through the works as presences rather than as overt strategies.

Figure 5. "Untitled," by Wura-Natasha Ogunji. Ogunji's woman announces her politics with her hair, her clothes, and her reading material—popular novels by Nigerian authors. Her mesh bag carries Sebastian Okechukwu Mezu's novel about the Biafran war, *Behind the Rising Sun,* and Cyprian Ekwensi's popular novel of female autonomy, *Jagua Nana.* Photo by Wura-Natasha Ogunji.

At the bẹ̀mbẹ̀,[31] *the drums*
begin for Ọ̀ṣun—iragbagba / iragbagba / iragbagba—and once again the spiritual
spotlight was on me. My movements from Òṣogbo refined by Miami and tested in
Harlem are often called upon to help bring Ọ̀ṣun down. It is my job and my joy—
though anxieties impede the process. The drums beat with greater sharpness—slap!
thump thump thump!—as the drummers focus on my fading consciousness. The
bell is played directly in my ear, the singer vibrating right over my Orí, the circle of
practitioners moving back, giving me, giving Ọ̀ṣun her room.
A fan is shoved in my waving hand, I feel giddy and awkwardly seductive. Exposed,
vulnerable, ready. Almost ready. Just peeking through. The laughter comes through my
lips and the tears come to my lids at the same time: I frown and laugh, and cry and
giggle, and then I/we/she spins spins spins spins! I am present and
not, here and there, aware and numb. Ọ̀ṣun came to say hello, in the moment when
my connection to her was more important than the people present, when the Divine
was the primary energy, not accuracy or praise. Exhaustion and exhilaration. And so it
is in the sharp present tense that is Yoruba-based spiritual life.
And so it is.

Some African American jazz artists and scholars have had direct repeated connections with Yoruba religious traditions. In the 1940s, Dizzy Gillespie collaborated with famed drummer and Lukumi practitioner Luciano "Chano" Pozo, who brought the Yoruba-based *Lukumi* sensibility to his drumming, and to Gillespie's band. Years later, Gillespie opened "Swing Low Sweet Cadillac" with a Yoruba praise to The Primordial Mothers, the *Ìyámi,* and continued with a standard Yoruba invocation. The liner notes to the 1967 album refer to these praises as "wordless sounds," but even a cursory understanding of Yoruba language reveals that Gillespie absorbed more than Cuban rhythms, and infused Yoruba spiritual chants into his work. Marta Moreno Vega details the union of African American and Cuban musicians in her documentary *When the Spirits Dance Mambo.* This film illustrates how the spiritual practice was absorbed through extended musical partnerships. John Coltrane's "Ogunde" pays homage to the Yoruba *Òrìṣà* of metallurgy, and Louis Armstrong reportedly made frequent visits to Marie Laveau's home with his aunt.[32] The Yoruba and jazz connection in New Orleans[33] was ripened with Native American practices that paved the way for the Mardi Gras Indians, Second Lines, and a coded tradition of survival. Joyce Jackson and Fehintola Mosadomi look explicitly at the Yoruba-ness of Mardi Gras Indians and their kinship to *Egúngún* masquerades,[34] while filmmaker Maurice Martinez has focused his attention on how the spiritual realities of Native Americans blended with the spiritual practices of African Americans to create a sacred experience camouflaged by public carnival revelry in much the same way that Trinidadian spiritual life is concealed in an annual public carnival.[35] Trinidadian Calypso and Soca—critical components of carnival—have obvious associations to Yoruba *oríkì* or praise singing.

Figure 6. "Miel de Abeja (Para Ochun)," by Yasmin Hernandez. Hernandez's lush image of Ọ̀ṣun is private and introspective, a side of this Òrìṣà that is not often represented. Photo provided by Yasmin Hernandez. Courtesy of the John L. Warfield Center for African and African American Studies, University of Texas at Austin.

Jazz and Ìṣẹ̀ṣẹ̀ traditions sync up in specific and meaningful ways. Both Yoruba-based traditions and jazz are insurgent resistive practices. Both have been taken up by people who want to create their own rivers against the mainstream. Both have declared Blackness as resistance, both have been underground to grow, both have a unique relationship to Black people, and both have moved around the African diaspora. Both have also been maligned—Yoruba as malevolent cult practices, jazz as dangerously erotic (as in swing of the 30s) and alienatingly esoteric (as in some critiques of Free Jazz).[36] Jazz is a worldview like *Ìṣẹ̀ṣẹ̀*, and Yoruba-based spiritual traditions rely on the incorporative, improvisational multivalent realities that also constitute jazz. So they are sisters, twins perhaps.

Jazz and *Ìṣẹ̀ṣẹ̀* traditions exist as the very signs of Blackness in the collective imagination. Jazz is "cool" and therefore Black, while Yoruba is "African" and therefore Black. Both practices tantalizingly suggest that the practitioners have secrets, belong to a private powerful group, know more, see more, feel more, intuit more than nonpractitioners. The Yoruba traditions discussed in this book are specifically derived from practices primarily seasoned outside of Nigeria, while acknowledging Nigeria as the homeland for these traditions. Many chose these practices rather than inheriting them, as they sought a spiritual life that matched their political and aesthetic drives. In this way, "being Yoruba" is a source of pride, a badge of commitment as displayed through dress, *ilẹ̀kẹ̀s* (beaded necklaces), *idès* (bracelets), drum rhythms, and Yoruba-language prayers. Sadly, this is *not* the Yoruba tradition as it presently exists in much of Southwestern Nigeria, where African Traditional Religions (ATR) are on the sharp decline publicly, where practicing ATR is too "primitive," too antimodern for those striving to demonstrate their fluency with all things Western. By contrast, in the West, one's "Black quotient" rises when practicing an ATR. In addition to Yoruba and jazz standing in for Blackness itself, Yoruba and jazz are incorporative and improvisational. Both Yoruba-based spiritual practices and jazz embrace the forms they encounter through an amalgamating force. The old, then, is always new. The *Òrìṣà* or Divinities/Deities consume the new ideas and practices, weaving the new into the established understanding thereby creating a continually reinvigorated present, what Harry Garuba calls an "animist unconscious" through the process of a "re-enchantment with the world."[37] In jazz, Cab Calloway could take Yiddish sounds and instrumentation to create "Minnie the Moocher" and "St. James Infirmary," and Don Byron could infuse jazz sensibilities into Klezmer music for his recordings with the Klezmer Conservatory Band. These incorporations have a strong kinship with the improvisatory impulse. Without innovation and improvisation, ritual becomes hollow and impotent. Yoruba, like jazz, asks everyone present to fine-tune their senses, to touch other worlds, to respond to the now, to embrace rather than reject, and to support the journey through life. Jazz and the *Ìṣẹ̀ṣẹ̀* traditions examined in this book are doings. Their goal is to make something happen. They are enactments on the spot. They conjure that which did not exist before.

Yoruba and jazz also share common experiences of time and community. Time is *bíríbírí,* always changing, always circulating, not linear but cyclical and cumulative. With this sense of time, improvisation is inevitable as one lives deeply connected to the present moment through each innovation. The artist must respond to

WOLE SOYINKA: "The deistic approach of the Yoruba is to absorb every new experience, departmentalize it and carry on with life."°

° "From a Common Back Cloth: A Reassessment of the African Literary Image," 9.

MARGARET THOMPSON DREWAL: "Practitioners of Yoruba religion are aware that when ritual becomes static, when it ceases to adjust and adapt, it becomes obsolete, empty of meaning and eventually dies out."°

° *Yoruba Ritual: Performers, Play, Agency,* 8.

"Bíríbírí l'aiyé ń yí, aiyé ò tò bí òpá ibon."

"The worlds keep on changing
and they are never straight like the barrel
of a gun."

time as it evolves. The Òrìṣà have their own requirements that may not coincide with human desires. We participate in rituals until they are complete, and completion has a Divine determination. Because participants must be fully present, they cannot have an agenda beyond the work at that moment. One can *anticipate* what *might* happen, but one cannot force what will. To do so takes one out of the present and into the future.

Jazz and Yoruba require community for fulfillment. Yoruba is a communal practice where the elders serve as master teachers for priests in apprenticeship through the experience of *ìkọ́ṣé*, and where rituals gain force from the collective *àṣẹ* of community members. Likewise, jazz relies on rigorous on-the-job training and a group of like-minded souls able to meet the demands of the work. The work is a way of life. It is breathing the break, it is supporting the tribe,[38] it is knowing that each action is its own bridge.

The work of Carlos, Jones, and Bridgforth captures a prolific era in the development of theatrical jazz that took place primarily in Austin, Texas, and almost exclusively at Frontera@Hyde Park Theatre under the visionary guidance of then artistic director Vicky Boone, along with cofounders Annie Suite, Jason Phelps,

Figure 7. Frontera@Hyde Park Theatre, Austin, Texas. This small brick building on 43rd Street near Guadalupe in Austin, Texas, was the home to some of the most vibrant theatrical jazz explorations of the 1990s. The alley and the front parking space were sometimes used as additional performance sites. Photo by Bret Brookshire.

Figure 8. FronteraFest poster. This early incarnation of Daniel Alexander Jones's Jomama Jones graced the cover of the promotional materials for Frontera@Hyde Park Theatre's annual festival of innovative performance.

and later Eva Paloheimo. Their productions, workshops, parties, and spontaneous adventures were the heart of a very specific theatrical moment that inspired the evolution of distinctive voices for the many artists with whom they worked. It was a time of deep repetitive collaborations.[39]

Since that fruitful period when Austin was a nexus for theatrical jazz, the artists have of necessity become even more nomadic than they were when they discussed their lives as "itinerant preachers" with Austin arts columnist and actor Robert Faires in 1999. While Austin continues to occasionally present theatrical jazz work, such work can increasingly be found around the country.[40] In an interview with Erik Ehn, I suggested to Ehn that he had been the one to introduce the idea that the theatrical jazz artists were nomads or itinerant preachers. Bridgforth, who was also at the interview, confirmed that it had been Ehn who created this analogy. However, in examining Faires's 1999 interview published in the *Austin Chronicle,* it appears as though Faires initiated the idea when he wrote "The playwright today as itinerant preacher. Thinking about some of the playwriting talent gathered in Austin this autumn, that image rises up. Erik Ehn, Daniel Alexander Jones, Sharon Bridgforth, Ruth Margraff— these are not the monumental playwrights of yore, the Tennessee Williamses and Arthur Millers, at home on Broadway, their messages proclaimed in the grand temples of the theatre. They are playwrights who do not have a home on Broadway, who do not have a home anywhere. They have many homes, all across the country, in mostly small, mostly cash-poor theatres where they come, stay long enough to deliver their latest message, then are gone again, on the road to another community."[41] In the same conversation with Faires, Ehn picks up the idea when he argues that "Place to place, we're looking to get home. I'm trying to get home in Austin. I'm trying to get home in Minneapolis."[42] The oral recounting of who said what has now popularly assigned this image of artist-as-country-preacher to Ehn.

Artists, like other great innovators, need space to explore, to struggle, to stumble, and to try again. Institutions do not usually have the fiscal patience for such development. With the closing of Frontera@Hyde Park Theatre in 2001 when artistic director Vicky Boone moved into a career as a filmmaker, these nomadic artists lost a key visionary and venue for the germination of their distinctive approach to theatre. To some extent, the John L. Warfield Center for African and African American Studies at the University of Texas at Austin began to fill this void with the Performing Blackness Series (pBs) and the Austin Project (tAP).[43] The Warfield Center has made long-term commitments to several artists who employ a theatrical jazz aesthetic including Carlos, Jones, and Bridgforth, who have premiered works through both pBs and tAP.

Part One of *Theatrical Jazz*, "The Ensemble / Ẹgbẹ́ / Community," examines who is doing the work in theatrical jazz, and how this community sustains itself. Laurie Carlos's upbringing in the culturally eclectic East Village of New York City, Daniel Alexander Jones's childhood in the working-class and racially diverse Springfield, Massachusetts, and Sharon Bridgforth's adolescent bus rides across various Los Angeles neighborhoods established a sense of place and identity for each artist that shaped the work they would later create. The jazz aesthetic in theatre requires master teachers and willing apprentices; in this way a new cadre of practitioners is continually developed as the lineage extends and spirals back through an acknowledgment of ancestors who laid the foundation. The artistic genealogy for each artist is presented while the Yoruba concepts of ẹgbẹ́ (work kin), ìkọ́ṣẹ́ (transmission of knowledge), Òrìṣà (Divinities), and àdúgbò (neighborhood) provide the spiritual backdrop for the discussion.

Part Two, "The Break / Awo / Process," gets at how the work is done. Performance methods, directorial approaches, rehearsal process, relationship to the audience/witnesses, the spiritual release, casting choices, scripting techniques are all part of *awo*, or mystery, that gives the jazz aesthetic its force. Being utterly present is fundamental to the work, for this allows the *awo* to open, allows each experience to uncover its own particular vitality as the artists sweat to find a state akin to possession. In addition to exploring *awo*, this part also takes up the importance of *ìyíká*,[44] the protective circle, and *ìwà*, virtuosity as good character.

Theatrical Jazz: Performance, Àṣẹ, and the Power of the Present Moment ends with Part Three, "The Bridge / Àṣẹ / Transformation." Àṣẹ (the power and authority to make things happen) encourages audience/witnesses to dislodge former ideas about art and life. This active participation, or *ìkópa*, is evidence of the work's force. The goal for these artists—in varying degrees and ways—is the act of transformation in which one's artistic choices become one's lived choices. The artists seek to create work that writes their own identities into the world and thereby generates a distinctive set of possibilities for others. This closing chapter also speculates on the possibilities a jazz aesthetic holds for future artists. The very fact that many of the artists are also teachers themselves suggests that the necessary tradition of elder and apprentice will continue. Several of the artists in "The Bridge /

Àṣẹ / Transformation" are also now engaged in work that has an overt social or ecological consciousness. It stands to reason that an artform that aspires to make transformation would eventually link with the Earth. *Ẹbọ dá*—the sacrifice has been accepted—ensures that the work of Carlos, Jones, and Bridgforth will be passed on through an ever-widening artistic lineage and legacy.

Can I go? Can I travel in
and out and through? On the verge, right there, right there, almost, it's peeking
through, it's there, oh yes, almost, here, almost, here, but no. No. I stop. Almost. Almost
there. Not quite. But maybe. It's lurking there.
Waiting for me to step up, for me and it to be one.

The Ensemble / Ẹgbẹ́ / Community

This preparation [for making jazz] begins long before prospective performers seize upon music as the central focus of their lives.

—Paul Berliner[1]

Jazz is not only a music to define, it is a culture. Which is to say that not only might one study Bunk and Monk as individual musicians in a broad stream of musicians . . . One also can consider the immeasurably complex worlds through which they moved.

—Robert G. O'Meally,
Brent Hayes Edwards,
and Farah Jasmine Griffin[2]

THE JAZZ AESTHETIC in theatre relies on a particular brand of collaboration that extends beyond the rehearsals and the productions. It is a binding and intimate collaboration that blends daily caretaking with apprenticeship, which closely resembles the Yoruba concept of *ẹgbẹ́*, a group of people joined by a common goal. My experience with *Ìṣẹ̀ṣẹ̀*-based communities in the United States and my work with *Òrìṣà* communities in Nigeria have informed my understanding of *ẹgbẹ́,* in which members are expected to consistently, and, among some communities, unquestioningly, support the group's needs and traditions. The *ẹgbẹ́* is an intricate strand in the social structure; it teaches community building, responsibility, and accountability. Perhaps the greatest breach in an *ẹgbẹ́* is lack of reliability. One's actions are situated within the frame of the *ẹgbẹ́* and within the context of the larger society. *Ẹgbẹ́* is also related to the idea of tribe in the sharing of customs and the family-like closeness of its members. In an important way both the concept of *ẹgbẹ́,* which exists within specific sociopolitical structures, and the concept of tribe, which is often conceptualized as its own unit independent of city-state formations, are useful in understanding the relations that bind theatrical jazz practitioners. The jazz aesthetic can trace its lineage both within traditional theatre and through its own independent genealogy. In my usage throughout, tribe is a reclaimed term of communal pride rather than an evaluative description of a group's social development.

Through continual and varied interactions the *ẹgbẹ́* itself evolves into a process so that *ẹgbẹ́* slides from a noun to a verb—caretaking, truth telling, self-confrontation with the *ẹgbẹ́* as witness, an organic apprenticeship in which the members both model for and learn from each other. The daily interaction with the tribe serves to solidify the aesthetic—be present, tell the truth, work for peace and joy. As Wynton Marsalis puts it, "The choices you make on the bandstand are exactly like the choices you're going to make in society."[3] In a similar vein, in discussing what the performance ensemble teaches us about life, Daniel Alexander Jones suggested, "A selfish decision fails every time."[4]

The jazz aesthetic tribe is the *ẹgbẹ́*. While some U.S.-based Yoruba practitioners believe that *ẹgbẹ́* is for life, a Yoruba proverb asserts, "*Òrìṣà bí o kò bá lè gbèmí ṣe mí bí o ṣe bá mi.*" The proverb can be literally translated as "Divinity, if you don't support me, restore me to my original state," and, more precisely to the point being made here—"*Òrìṣà*, if you cannot help me, leave me the way you found me."[5] This suggests that while *ẹgbẹ́*s function at the behest of *égún* (ancestors) and *Òrìṣà* (Divine forces), one's own *Orí* (head, destiny) is also a Divinity that must be considered when choosing or being chosen by an *ẹgbẹ́* for participation. *Orí* may determine that a shift in a Divine relationship is necessary. Commitment to an *ẹgbẹ́* is serious, and undoing that commitment requires Divine support. This complex relationship between the individual, the *ẹgbẹ́*, and the Divine creates interlocking personal, communal, and spiritual responsibilities. Through this binding union, the tradition preserves and reimagines itself. Once members are bound to each other, it is no small gesture to turn away. One can participate in an *ẹgbẹ́* in support of community-building even while having conflict with individual members. If one's *Orí* counsels against *ẹgbẹ́* participation, the individual may leave but the *ẹgbẹ́* continues. In this way, the tradition will prevail in spite of individual human conflicts. Commitment and sustained connection result in more than collaboration; they generate community and collective responsibility.

WYNTON MARSALIS: "No one thinks that maybe a democratic act means that you have to surrender something that's yours and give it to someone else. That is, in essence, the proposition of jazz. You can be the greatest soloist in the world, but if you don't have anybody to play with you're just not going to sound good. It is important for the student to view herself or himself in the context of everyone else. And that requires listening."[*]

[*] *Making the Music: A Teacher's Guide to Jazz, 5.*

When the Warfield Center for African and African American Studies first presented *Sharon's love conjure/blues* in the spring of 2004 there were eight cast members with Helga Davis conducting. When the production was remounted in the fall of 2004 the cast had expanded to eleven with the inclusion of two musicians—Fred Cash Jr. on bass and Greg Rickard on piano—and teenaged Yoruba priest Olaiya, who served to crystallize Isadora Africa Jr.'s presence in the work. There was also a dramaturg who developed a lobby installation as part of the performance experience. Returning from *the spring production were Florinda Bryant, Daniel Alexander Jones, Daniel Dodd Ellis, Sean Tate, Sonja Perryman, and me. Gina Houston replaced Marlah Fulgham, and Carsey Walker's lines were redistributed throughout the company. Because most of us had worked together before, we brought a level of comfort and familiarity to the experience. This didn't mean that we always got along—in fact some of the brewing rifts among us at that time were not directly confronted*

until much later. What we brought was a knowledge of one another that generated a critical trust in our ability to carry out the work. In addition to the daily casual phone calls and meals that some of us shared, Helga also

scheduled outings that would help us experience each other in new ways. We spent one afternoon at the Pedernales River, where I talked about Ọ̀ṣun and we played in the water to her trickling laughter. On another occasion, we gathered one evening at my home for an informal meal. Most of us played, teased, and talked trash throughout that night,

but one person stood apart from the group.

I recognized the behavior because it was so similar to my own. For years, I had seen Laurie, Daniel, Sharon, Florinda, Sonn (as many of us call Sonja Perryman), and Zell Miller III as a closed group of intimate friends. The inside jokes, the shared histories, the productions together seemed to keep me on the outside of what appeared to be the "in group." At that time, I did not realize that the supposed "in group" actually bonded because of their outsider status—

outside mainstream life, outside mainstream theatre, outside the habits/values of their blood families. When invited to meals or movies, I would shyly decline, thinking that I would be an intruder in spite of the fact that I had been invited. I was closed to the challenges and uncertainties of personal interaction as well as to the demands of being present on stage. The two go hand in hand. I thought my option not to participate created a kind of safety through invisibility, when in reality the very safety I sought was akin to being in a room with no air—I was choking rather than saving myself. Art requires the courage to expose oneself, and the joyful foolishness to risk certainty. What I didn't understand then was that the jazz aesthetic is incorporative; it borrows, includes, stirs many elements into the roux. The people who develop the jazz aesthetic are—like the aesthetic itself—

an amalgam. This is not an ẹgbẹ́ of similar people. Indeed, the power of the group is directly related to the distinctiveness of each member. It is an ẹgbẹ́ based on the deep understanding that one must be present to fully live, must feel and tell the truth, must risk being accepted or included, must be absolutely one's self. And when you create such realities together, you work to protect and preserve that.

Ẹgbẹ́ helps sustain the breath of life.

So when one of the members of the newly constituted love conjure/blues company chose to stand apart during all the party activities—

in fact, once, left the house to sit alone on the concrete driveway while others ate, listened to music, and joked inside

*—I immediately recognized the simultaneous desire to be rooted inside the group and
the debilitating fear that I did not fit, that I would
not measure up. By removing oneself from the group, one shouts, "You can't rely on
me. I am not to be trusted." This is the enactment of passive/aggressive violence that
lives as a rupture inside of the group and reveals one's inability to sustain the rigors
of an ẹgbẹ́.*

The jazz aesthetic relies on everyone standing inside of her or his own power, and supporting those around them. This happens in performance and in life. The daily conversations, making of meals, planning events, gossip—all are ways to preserve the jazz aesthetic, to solidify the clan, to make the tribe fully known to each other. This everyday intimacy creates a confidence and willing risk-taking in performance.

When one lives tribally, eventually the work becomes a way of life. The rules and structures developed through the making of the work begin to supersede the norms operating outside of the group. Without really thinking about it or making it happen, one begins to move with the other tribe members in mind. The phone calls throughout the day, the e-mails containing bits of work and thoughts about all manner of things, remembering birthdays, the unplanned "roll ups" when the *ẹgbẹ́* whisks you away from your planned activities for a trip to the barbecue joint—all of this is as important as the rehearsals in the studio. One learns the ways of the artistic work in the everyday encounters with one another. These encounters teach spontaneity and flexibility, the importance of play, and significantly, the role of impulse in shaping the jazz aesthetic. When tribe members surprise you by showing up at your job and tempting you with an escape from those tensions for a moment, your decision about joining them or remaining at work has everything to do with facing that moment in performance where one can go against the expected or remain solidly predictable. Exercising this muscle in everyday life primes one for flexing that same muscle of spontaneity and freedom in performance. The continuity of the tradition is built in the everyday interactions; this makes it truly a lifestyle, not only a way of making art.

A primary virtue of an *ẹgbẹ́* is access to those who are trained in the work. Rather than beginning with the confusion and resistance that often accompanies an introduction to theatrical jazz, an *ẹgbẹ́* can begin at a deeper place. Confusion, uncertainty, and doubt may still appear, but there is significantly less resistance to the process for those who are trained, and indeed, there is an acceptance of confusion as a vital part of the internal and external work that must be done in embodying theatrical jazz. When Virginia Grise returned to Austin with a draft of *blu,* a script that was developed in the California Institute of the Arts (CalArts) writing program and that later won

VIRGINIA GRISE: "This community understands my work at a base level. They allow me to really hear my work. They understand breath, punctuation, structure in ways that traditionally trained actors don't—so we begin a conversation about the work that's not from a place of explanation or defense of the aesthetic but from a deeper understanding. This is essential to my growth and very survival as an artist."°

° E-mail message to author, January 11, 2007.

the 2010 Yale Drama Series Award, she knew she could gather a cadre of artists able to engage with her jazz-inflected work. Grise had been an ensemble member with the Austin Project (tAP) for two years when she became one of two writers accepted into the prestigious CalArts Writing for Performance Program in 2006. Through her longstanding apprenticeship with Bridgforth and her participation in tAP, where she worked with Jones, Carlos, McCauley, and me, she came to develop her artistic identity through theatrical jazz principles. When *blu* was read in Austin, Grise immediately called on tAP members Florinda Bryant, Monique Cortez, Ana-Maurine Lara, Jen Margulies, and me, who were conversant with the requirements of theatrical jazz, along with Jackie Cuevas and Wura-Natasha Ogunji, who were a part of tAP extended family.[6] Grise's experience with casting in Austin reflects the maintenance of shared codes that evolve among dispersed artistic allies as they strive to preserve and deepen their aesthetic identities across disparate geographic regions.

　　An *ẹgbẹ́* needs diversity among the members in order to be resilient and ready. The skills that may be lacking in some may be present in others. This is the kind of community strength that is most apparent in urban life where the sheer variety of people creates the potential for shared overlapping power. This is the urbanness that Aristotle imagined when he considered his own locale, a city where different people were required to interact and thereby create the possibility for understanding each other and themselves. In his analysis of democratic spaces, Richard Sennett states, "a democracy supposes people can consider views other than their own."[7] Sennett suggests that in ancient Greek societies, this consideration of "other views" happened in the marketplace, where a wide range of people conducted various forms of business, and in the theatre, where the semicircular shape of the traditional Greek theatre allowed spectators to experience one another through the performance. This direct interaction with people unlike one's self, for Sennett, was at the heart of Aristotle's democracy. Democracy, at its best, is inclusive and inherently diverse. The urban environment provides a means for deeply knowing many truths; the more such varied truths exist in an *ẹgbẹ́* the more flexible and durable the *ẹgbẹ́* can be. City dwellers have the opportunity to know worlds beyond those of their immediate family. As Sennett points out, the city's diversity is not only in the range of ideas but, more importantly, in the range of behaviors that it can accommodate. It is this urbanness that spawned musical jazz, and this fact of urban complexity that was the childhood reality for Carlos, Jones, and Bridgforth. The experiences in the cities of their youth primed them for an aesthetic life rich in the urban density of jazz.

　　In the previous section of this book, I discuss the way in which Yoruba cosmology provides a useful method for understanding theatrical jazz. Because the diversity of urban life is fundamental to the development of jazz, and given the resonances between jazz and Yoruba worldviews noted earlier, it is not surprising that sixteenth-century Yoruba people were among the first urban African societies.[8] Family compounds were built around the *Ọba*'s, or king's, palace and the market.

RICHARD SENNETT: "The essence of democracy lies in displacing conflict and difference from the realm of violence to a more peaceable, deliberative realm."°

° "The Spaces of Democracy," 12.

Specialists developed, often in relationship to the life of the Ọba—metalworkers, praise singers, beaders, tailors, musicians—thus creating a web of interlocking relationships common in city life. Jazz and Yoruba life share an urban vitality.

In a Yoruba worldview, *àdúgbò*, or neighborhood, is integral to the well-being of an individual as it serves as a vehicle for social integration. In this way, *àdúgbò* has an intimate link to both *ẹgbẹ́* as community responsibility and to *ìwà* as character. The importance of *ìwà* in Yoruba cosmology is revealed in the fact that it is an attribute that is carried with a person until the end of her or his life. Most simply, *ìwà* references character, but also includes grace, demeanor, and the very essence of a person that determines his or her inner and outer beauty. Tribal associations are with one's *ẹgbẹ́*, the people with whom one lives and works, while *àdúgbò* references more generally one's environment. Many Yoruba are more accustomed to naming the region of their birth and childhood as their identifying markers rather than finding identity under the colonially imposed title of Yoruba. Where you are from, where you were raised says much about your specific relationship to the world. In this way, one's neighborhood leaves an indelible stamp on one's personhood.

The tribalness that characterizes an *ẹgbẹ́* also relates to the apprentice–elder relationship that is used for learning the features of theatrical jazz. Within a community, the elder teaches directly and indirectly. As much learning occurs in the market when sniffing cheeses for an opening night reception as when rehearsing a script in the theatre. Learning theatrical jazz happens body to body, breath to breath; no matter how carefully I chart the work, this book cannot and should not replace the visceral knowledge exchanged between elder and apprentice. This relationship is one of the most profound correspondences between theatrical jazz and Yoruba-based spiritual practices. Although there has been a proliferation of published *Ifá* texts in the past fifteen years,[9] a priest cannot learn to divine by reading a book. Such training is *gb'ẹ̀kọ́*, receiving knowledge, or more precisely, *ikọ́ṣ'ẹ́*, learning a skill through the transmission of wisdom from a master. Divination skill—as well as beading, drumming, feeding *Òrìṣà*, reciting *itanlẹ̀*, and other talents needed in Yoruba-based spiritual life—comes from sitting alongside a master and, over much time, remapping intuition and acquiring wisdom. Similarly, theatrical jazz is internalized through the inherent embodiment of rehearsals and daily living.

Within the *ẹgbẹ́* and apprentice–elder structure, there is a complex paradox. Although *ẹgbẹ́* requires a solemn and steadfast commitment, there are times when the apprentice must break from the elder, when the *Orí* (personal destiny) of the apprentice dictates that she/he must find a path separate from that of the elder—joined to *ẹgbẹ́* yet separate from the elder at the same time.

In jazz, the legendary example of such a split occurred in 1923 when Louis Armstrong decided to leave his mentor King Oliver in order to fully explore his own distinctive sound. When Armstrong left New Orleans to join Oliver in Chicago, the two developed a tandem trumpet playing that let them share the role of lead trumpet. Armstrong felt constrained by this shared playing, and his wife, the

"YOU CAN'T WRITE THIS STUFF DOWN!"*
—LAURIE CARLOS

* Phone interview with author, June 16, 2008.

pianist Lil Hardin, suggested that Oliver did not want to be eclipsed by Armstrong's growing skill and popularity.[10] The apprentice left the master, and became a master himself.

It is a delicate thing, this apprentice–elder relationship, and the *egbẹ́* that nurtures it. The student in the tribe must be beholden to the teacher. The Yoruba priest in many Western variants of the practice must daily call the names of the spiritual elders or godparents reverently. The godparent must also be remembered in acts of faith and kindness—and these acts teach the lessons of the tradition. The apprentice is tasked with moving beyond the elder while creating an individual path that can simultaneously advance and critique the traditions that have provided a foundation. In Yoruba-based practices, the stories of such breaks are filled with trauma—ungrateful godchildren, dismissive godparents—but some of these shifts seem to be the natural order of things. Separation can happen without rupture.

The clearest example of moving away from theatrical jazz aesthetics while acknowledging and incorporating the contributions of artistic elders can be found in the work of Florinda Bryant and Zell Miller III. Both Bryant and Miller have mapped their own aesthetic terrain through close work with Carlos, Jones, and Bridgforth over many years. Although distinctive in their art practice, Bryant and Miller have morphed their jazz training into Hip Hop sensibilities. Bryant's 2002 *Sister Overpass,* in collaboration with Piper Anderson and Yalini (then Marian Thambynayagam),[11] and *Half-Breed Southern Fried (check one)* directed by Carlos, reveal her fluency with simultaneity of time, place, and action, a specific movement vocabulary, and an engaged relationship with the audience/witnesses even as *Sister Overpass* was specifically developed through the structure of the cipher and *Half-Breed* included a DJ and a B-Girl who amplified the improvisation imbedded in the verbal text. Bryant refers to the theatrical jazz principles she acquired through the Austin Project as "the science of the cipher."[12] For five years, Miller produced an annual "Hip Hop Explosion" in Austin, Texas, that featured many manifestations of Hip Hop sensibilities, from B-Boys and B-Girls on roller skates to high school spoken-word collectives to his own precisely crafted solo work. Miller's *Arrhythmia,* directed as a staged reading by Jones, dramaturged by Bridgforth, and hosted by Carlos for Penumbra Theatre's Cornerstone Reading Series, was followed by *Evidence of Silence Unbroken,* with Walter Kitundu as DJ and directed by Jones, along with the establishment of the spoken-word venue Xenogia with frequent collaborator Jeffrey Da'Shade Moonbeam. Miller's dedication to Hip Hop aesthetics can also be seen in his *Windtalkers and Mythmakers,* in which he pays homage to his dear mentor whom he affectionately calls Mama Carlos. In that production, Carlos was performed by Bryant. In a different vein, scholar/poet Lisa L. Moore's work with theatrical jazz began with her participation in the Austin Project. She adapted the principles of tAP into a distinctive pedagogical strategy that she used in graduate writing seminars. At each public sharing of her students' work, Moore acknowledges her Austin Project elders and *egbẹ́* even as she admittedly moved beyond those teachings. Although these seminars bear the truth-telling and ancestral exploration characteristic of the Austin Project, Moore infuses the work with her own exercises, assignments, and discussions, which reflect her unique artistic and scholarly impulses.

There are many roots of theatrical jazz; however, three visionary institution-builders had a specific and overlapping impact on Carlos, Jones, and Bridgforth. Ellen Stewart, Aishah Rahman, and Dianne McIntyre opened the way for the theatrical jazz lineage being charted here. Each of these artists is an institution builder whose influence extended well beyond those in their immediate reach. Ellen Stewart founded La Mama E. T. C. in 1961 as an international experimental theatre company. Unfortunately, because of the often narrow ways that Black Theatre is conceived and the separatist vision of most strands of Black nationalism, Stewart was seldom acknowledged for the role she played in encouraging innovative theatrical forms for Black artists. Her commitment to the avant-garde and to European collaborations was thought of as white and therefore not within the scope of Black aesthetics. La Mama has presented over a thousand productions, including work by Amiri Baraka and Ed Bullins. In describing her work with Black artists during the 1960s, Stewart said, "One writer, who was a La Mama Playwright, got to be 'minister of culture' for the black movement. I would see him and he wouldn't speak to me, but he'd always call me up late that night and say, 'Mama, forgive me, I couldn't speak to you in front of my friend, but you're my mama.' And he wasn't the only one. It was heavy, heavy."[13] In an interview with Stewart in 2007, I asked her about this incident and her relationship to Black Theatre generally. She affirmed this story and mentioned the many Black artists who worked for La Mama, though these stories are seldom included in historical accounts of the Black Arts Movement. Stewart was invested in making art in which Black people did not have to denigrate themselves with caricatures and stereotypes.[14] Stewart's dedication to experimental forms and to an expansive Blackness make her a foremother to Carlos, Jones, and Bridgforth. Stewart's sense of *ẹgbẹ́* was a strong foundation for her artmaking. She invested in people, not in plays. She says, "If the play's a flop, I'm not bothered because I believe in that person."[15]

Aishah Rahman's *Unfinished Woman Cries in No Man's Land While Bird Dies in Gilded Cage* was a groundbreaking work that, as Carlos put it, "broke open female character" by presenting complex Black women characters that theatre audiences had little opportunity to experience. Her texts are early examples of theatrical jazz in print and in production. She has theorized about and written in a jazz aesthetic, and may well be the first to use the term "jazz aesthetic" as it relates to theatre.[16] She asks, "I knew we African Americans were a jazz people who lived improvisatory lives in multi-realities so why couldn't The Music be adopted as a dra-

---

"LA MAMA HAS HAD A STRONG HAND IN THE ENVIRONMENT THAT IS THE AVANT GARDE OF AMERICAN THEATRE . . . IN THE 60S WHEN I MET ELLEN AT 15 SHE WAS DOING STUFF IN BARS. ELLEN WANTED A COLOR FREE SPACE TO WORK. SHE FOUND THAT SPACE ON EAST 4TH STREET WHERE ROD RODGERS AND ELEO POMARE WERE ALSO WORKING."*

—LAURIE CARLOS

* E-mail message to author, January 12, 2012.

"AISHAH RAHMAN WAS A MASTER OF CRAFT. SHE HAD INCREDIBLE RIGOR IN HER PRACTICE. THERE WASN'T A BREATH OUT OF PLACE. THE WAY I USE THE PAGE, THE WAY I THINK ABOUT SENTENCE STRUCTURE, I LEARNED THAT FROM HER FOR SURE."*

—DANIEL ALEXANDER JONES

* Phone interview with author, January 11, 2007.

matic structure? Form following content." Rahman has demonstrated what Brandi Catanese calls "a persistent devotion to the possibility of a culturally autonomous black theatre"[17] and has manifested that commitment through her plays, essays, journal editorship, memoir, and pedagogy. Her teaching at Brown University was the training ground for many in the form, including Daniel Alexander Jones, who took classes from her while he completed his M.A. in theatre history and criticism. As founder and editor of *NuMuse,* a journal of new dramatic writing and essays, she published the works of many nontraditional theatre artists affiliated with Brown including Alice Tuan, Nilo Cruz, Shay Youngblood, Daniel Alexander Jones, Michael S. Weaver, Bridget Carpenter, and Ruth Margraff.

Dianne McIntyre, founder of Sounds in Motion Dance Studio of Harlem, established a breath-inspired movement vocabulary in collaboration with jazz musicians that was passed on to several artists including Laurie Carlos, Marlies Yearby, Ntozake Shange, and Jawole Willa Jo Zollar. McIntyre wanted to develop what she called "Total Theatre,"[18] performance that drew upon music, dance, and text as necessary ingredients in expressing an idea or experience. McIntyre began working with musicians on stage while she was studying dance at The Ohio State University. She developed her specific movement idioms from the music and poetry that was moving through Harlem during the 1960s. Sounds in Motion became a salon where artists came to improvise, to make new work, and to hang out in each other's company. She has been a longtime collaborator with musician Olu Dara, and was one of five African diasporic women choreographers invited to perform in "Fly: Five First Ladies of Dance" at 651 Arts in 2009.[19] McIntyre's way with movement is the forerunner to the nonmimetic physicality that characterizes much of the theatrical jazz of Carlos, Jones, and Bridgforth.

In considering those artists who provide background and foundation to theatrical jazz, it is essential to include Ntozake Shange, who is chronologically positioned more as a peer to Carlos, Jones, and Bridgforth than as an elder. In the previous section, I gave an overview of the principal role Shange played in developing the theatrical jazz practices of the three artists featured here. Shange's aesthetics that seamlessly wove together dance, music, and narrative, that valorized a diverse Blackness and Black women's stories, as well as the popular and critical explosion of praise surrounding *for colored girls who have considered suicide/when the rainbow is enuf,* suggested that U.S. audiences and society in general might be ready to recognize alternative theatre forms and voices. In the sections that follow on each artist, I offer greater detail on how Shange and her work contributed to the aesthetics of Carlos, Jones, and Bridgforth.

In the act of *ikọ̀ṣẹ́,* the apprentice must discover how to critique or even challenge the elder. In Yoruba-based spiritual practices, this questioning can be construed as an unforgivable transgression. In theatrical jazz, it has the potential to disrupt the entire *ẹgbẹ́,* with members feeling compelled to take sides and mask their true feelings. In Yoruba theology, practitioners understand *ikọ̀ṣẹ́* within the frame of a monarchy where the *Ọba* has the undisputed authority even when under the advisement of a council of elders. Theatrical jazz straddles the lines between acknowledging elders and practicing the democratic principles of community decision-making. In both theatrical jazz and Yoruba practices, the ethics or *iwà* of the elder sets the tone for the work and for critique. When the individuals in an *ẹgbẹ́* are clear about their position within the *ẹgbẹ́*, and they have developed strong relationships with each other—not only with the elders—it is much easier for them to act as the checks and balances needed to keep the *ẹgbẹ́* functioning well. The *ẹgbẹ́* must work to ensure that the elder's wisdom is respected while not holding the elder above critique. The *iwà* of everyone involved is essential. Without the principles of good character and group accountability governing the work, elders can become unchallengeable dictators, unchecked in their personal excesses.

The theatrical jazz aesthetic *ẹgbẹ́* is migratory. These artists are dispersed around the United States, traveling from city to city presenting their work at a handful of willing venues. This is quite different than the regional theatre model established in the United States in the late 1940s. Since the development of Margo Jones's Theatre '47 and Nina Vance's The Alley Theatre, the regional theatre structure has dominated the U.S. theatrical landscape as the mark of professionalism and acceptance. Presenting work in a single venue, developing a season, nurturing subscribers, and hiring staff remain the hallmarks of success and stability that characterize even avant-garde companies such as La Mama E. T. C., Woolly Mammoth, the Rude Mechanicals, and Steppenwolf. As of this writing, the primary jazz aesthetic artists discussed in this book are situated on the fringe of traditional theatrical structures established through the advent of regional theatres.[20] An advantage to the minimal institutionalization of theatrical jazz is that the form has the potential for being a deeply transgressive medium as it challenges the structures of class, race, gender, sexuality, and nationhood that are ingrained in the very perpetuation of institutions.

"Ilé-Ifẹ́ ọ̀daiyé ibi ojúmọ́ tí ń mọ́ wa."

"Ilé-Ifẹ́ the place of creation, where the day dawns."

OLABIYI YAI: "It is important to observe that the Yoruba have always conceived of their history as diaspora. The concept and reality of diaspora are rationalized in Yorubaland as the normal or natural order of things historical."°

° "In Praise of Metonymy," 108.

The dispersed lives of the theatrical jazz *ẹgbẹ́* has a kinship with a Yoruba understanding of identity. *Ilé-Ifẹ̀* is the spiritual home for all Yoruba; it is the site of creation and dispersal. Indeed, the very name *Ilé-Ifẹ̀* implies not only origin but also "an expansive place/land/space."[21] Yoruba people, then, understand themselves to be a diasporic people. In his discussion of the centrality of spoken praise to Yoruba cultures, Olabiyi Yai notes that diasporic reach is a given in a Yoruba worldview. Diaspora exists as the hope for continuation, dispersal as the potential and desire for growth and expansion.

Diasporic realities not only create a circumstance of homelessness, they can also create new communities of comrades. Rather than an allegiance to a distant geographic home, a nostalgic past, a sorrow in the absence, these aesthetically determined diaspora dwellers create kin and home based on a set of artistic and life principles. They become their own root, intriguingly aware of ancestors but not bound by the ancestors' lands. They forge the bonds of *ẹgbẹ́*.

Ilé is home, what the theatrical jazz artists are creating with each other, a familiar place, free to experiment. But the jazz *ẹgbẹ́* resists the stationary singular home as they map out nomadic territories even with the focus on key cities—Austin, Minneapolis, New York. They find themselves homeless within the theatre world—on the fringe, fully embraced neither in avant-garde circles nor by the gatekeepers of Black Theatre, what *Washington Post* critic David Nicholson called the originators of the "image tribunals"; yet, there can be innovation in the margins. They are fashioning a new homeplace. Rather than settle for an identity of rootlessness by creating what I once called "a discourse of dislocation,"[22] these theatrical jazz artists are forging new nomadic transitory homes of artistic kin. They are moved more by a homeplace they could discover from region to region than by a homeland they left behind. In this way, home is not fashioned as an originary location, a longed-for "root," but the nomads make home as they, of necessity, gather to make art. It is essential that they come together again and again to map the contours of this form, to create a mutual embodied language, to solidify artistic identities, to hone understandings of how jazz in theatre lives. This is deeply collaborative work that builds on frequent continuous artistic transmunicipal journeys among those who are steeped in the tradition. They have made an intranational *ẹgbẹ́* of theatrical jazz artists trained in and committed to the specific rigors of the work.

In African Diasporic Studies, much attention has been given to geography, to trade routes, to the adaptations made in "new" locations, and to the forces of hegemony that strive to blunt particularities in new locations.[23] The theatrical jazz diaspora is more about doing and being than about identifying origins. In this way, Laurie Carlos, who makes no claims on African aesthetics, and Erik Ehn, a frequent collaborator with Jones and Carlos and a seasoned theatrical jazz artist of European descent, are both squarely positioned in a theatrical jazz aesthetic because their work and their lives are deeply informed by jazz aesthetic principles. Their work is grown from a diaspora, and they live the lives of diaspora dwellers making a homeplace in the *ilé* they forge with one another.

Diaspora as dispersal, and diaspora as shared rebellious identities, has a kinship to the Austin School of Activist Anthropology, which identifies diaspora as a political position for people who claim Blackness as a global identity.[24] This identification acknowledges similar and persistent oppressions across geography, class, gender, sexuality, nation, and is a call to dismantle those oppressions. For the Austin School, diaspora not only names the dispersal, it also lives as a term of collective resistance by claiming solidarity with people who live in other regions yet share similar racialized realities. Likewise, the dispersed theatrical jazz *ẹgbẹ́* recognizes its critique of society in general and of traditional theatre in particular. This work advocates for social reorganization because it insists on an honesty that cannot be supported in racist, sexist, homophobic, classist, nationalist structures. Because the jazz aesthetic is a way of daily life along with being a way to make art, these counterhegemonic aesthetic choices are also counterhegemonic social choices.

By focusing on Laurie Carlos, Daniel Alexander Jones, and Sharon Bridgforth, I am able to look at the central members of a theatrical jazz *ẹgbẹ́* as it developed in the 1990s in Austin, Texas. Their childhoods reveal the many strands that combined to create the theatrical jazz impulses that now dominate their work. The power of place, *àdúgbò,* is demonstrated in the people and sites of their youth. It sculpted their political and aesthetic lives that evolved into the theatrical jazz for which they are now known. These artists have a particular understanding of *egbẹ́* that is born of the necessity for community responsibility—a sense that was nurtured in their home landscapes. The meals they prepare, the images, the books, and the music that ground them, along with production artifacts and artistic genealogies, are keys to experiencing their particular expressions of theatrical jazz.

Figure 9. Helga Davis with ensemble in *blood pudding* at New York SummerStage Festival. In this 2010 performance, Davis (foreground) offers up sonic power while Francine Sheffield, Omi Osun Joni L. Jones, and Baraka de Soleil work a series of gestures. Photo by Sharon Bridgforth.

Laurie Carlos

B. JANUARY 25, 1949
QUEENS, NEW YORK

Anybody would find it overwhelming when you're trying to do self-examination and examination of your own body and spirit and language and staying true in the moment and creating new moments and not doing easy answers and not repeating old stuff over and over again. But of course that's the work the artist has to do, 'cause it's/that's the artists' work / that is what your work is.

You don't ask yourself to do easy things, you know.

Even though they're beautiful, some of the answers you get, some of the moments you get, some of the things you've done are beautiful. They're wonderful, they are technically fine, and brilliantly constructed, they have incredible aesthetic levels . . . that's a wonderful review, that's perfect, it's wonderful this is, is just great.

Yeah don't bring that crap to me next time,

'cause we did that, so let's go see the next thing one has to do. That's very difficult.

It's hard to do that, to not get up and just simply cliché yourself through your life as an artist. To not get up and do the shtick over and over again, because the world will tell you that the shtick is fine . . . but at the level that you make commitment to this replication over and over again of yourself as the artist you have died.

—Laurie Carlos[1]

Oya whips through and changes everything
a gale that uproots trees and human lives
subtle breezes that lick the ears with promises of something more
once she passes, nothing is the same.

Jazz Narrative   Jazz Narrative   Jazz Narrative

JAZZ NARRATIVES occur as a layering of elements. The primary layers are usually the textual, the physical, and the sonic. Because theatrical jazz sees truth-telling as foundational, the textual layer is often autobiographical explorations of family, neighborhood, era, secrets, personal history, and epiphanies. The nonlinearity of the textual layer resists the normativity of chronology, and allows for a reimagining of narrativizing that works against the deeply discursive nature of Black oppression. The physical layer may be dance in a traditional

Figure 10. Laurie Carlos in *Kshoy!/Decay!* This performance was inspired by women's relationships to land, exile, and homemaking, presented by the Ananya Dance Theatre at the Southern Theatre in Minneapolis, 2010. Photo by V. Paul Virtucio.

sense, but more often it builds on a gestural vocabulary that works as purely non-mimetic, or as synecdoche suggesting a larger experience, or as some combination of these possibilities. The abstract and metaphoric nature of nonmimetic movement pushes theatrical jazz explorations beyond the dangerous shorthand of verisimilitude that asks audience/witnesses to affirm the known rather than speculate on an array of imaginative possibilities. In the nonmimetic space, there is room for Black bodies to innovate and for audience/witnesses to experience Blackness outside of well-worn tropes. The theatrical jazz soundscape is rich in music, and can also employ breath work, aural synecdoche, and rhythmic sounds made from playing the body and using stage objects like instruments.

"I HAVE NEVER BEEN ABLE TO MOVE WITHIN THE BOUNDARIES OF EUROCENTRIC PLAY FORM . . . I HAVEN'T NAMED THE AESTHETIC: IT IS NOT ABSOLUTE . . . I HAVE NO WAY TO DEFINE IT RIGHT NOW. SO IN THAT WAY MY AESTHETIC IS WITHOUT DEFINITION, WHICH IS NOT A TERRIBLE THING. I CAN REALLY START TO LET IT DEFINE ITSELF."*

—LAURIE CARLOS

* *White Chocolate for My Father*, 5.

Carlos's jazz narrative strategies make ample use of these three planes: the textual story that is seriate, and spirals and repeats, that revisits images, characters, and ideas as if turning something over, seeking some combination of understanding and resolution; the gestural tale of nonmimetic movements that seem randomly juxtaposed against the verbal text, a hand sliding across the chest pulling the body in a new direction, a hip jutting into space while the torso remains still; and the soundscape, the bits of blues, jazz, rock and roll, children's rhymes, and Western classical music that live in her texts, the playful use of voice, the choral orchestration of performers' text, along with the audible breathing. These three modalities have their own story to tell, and move together like a free-jazz composition in which each element seems independent while being crucially interdependent.

Much like Ornette Coleman's "Lonely Woman," Carlos's pieces end even as they resist resolution. She concludes *White Chocolate for My Father*:

> LORE: Who are you?
> TONY: Do you love me?
> DEOLA: What wars do you remember?
> Lore: Yes.
> *Red light climbs out from everywhere.*
>   Yes.
> TONY: Do you love me?[2]

And *Feathers at the Flame* ends with:

> MENGA: I am returning every day.
> HALF EYE: I will be there very soon.
> POOR DOG: Expect me at dusk.
> RACHEL: I am here.
> GLENA: We are close.

SKYWALKER: Going.

MU: Where are you?

Scene: Family portraits. Home town welcome signs. Road and mileage billboards. A collage of memory rural and urban.[3]

These questions open the endings rather than close them. Carlos's verbal text encourages comprehension beyond what the words alone can bring.

Textual Strategies

Fact, fiction, myth, wish, projection, fantasy, necessity meld into a faceted set of truths that is Laurie Carlos. Her personal history, and her style of sharing it, is as dense and labyrinthine as the structure of much of her performance work. The maze of details pushes the listener to attend closely, to make individual decisions about what truth is and what really matters when stories are exchanged. Such fractured telling is an African American legacy revealing a host of celebratory storytelling practices and the deepest trauma, grief, and annihilated selfhood. Under such circumstances the details of one's life move through prisms of possibilities, where the telling itself supersedes the veracity of the tale.

"AUTOBIOGRAPHY FOR ME IS PHAN-TASMAGORICAL TO EVERYBODY ELSE."*

—LAURIE CARLOS

* Phone interview with author, July 11, 2003.

ZORA NEALE HURSTON: "Now, women forget all those things they don't want to remember, and remember everything they don't want to forget. The dream is the truth. Then they act and do things accordingly."°

° *Their Eyes Were Watching God,* 1.

TONI MORRISON: "The crucial distinction for me is not the difference between fact and fiction, but the distinction between fact and truth. Because facts can exist without human intelligence, but truth cannot."°

° "The Site of Memory," 93.

Carlos conjures a personal history of betrayal and beauty, of family intimacy and ruptures, of gentility and grotesquery, of brutality and bounty. This personal history makes its way into her texts—bits of memories, images, thoughts that she turns over and over from one writing to the next. The dexterity with which she weaves her own mythology, and her ability to help others weave theirs, is a hallmark of both her writing and her workshop facilitation.

In her autobiographical works—*The Pork Chop Wars (a story of mothers), The Cooking Show and How the Monkey Dances,* and *White Chocolate for My Father*—Carlos tells her life stories over and over, never exactly the same. *Teenytown* has a section entitled "White Chocolate" that is also found in *White Chocolate for My Father. The Cooking Show* includes "Phosphorescent," which also appears in *Nonsectarian Conversations with the Dead.*

The individual threads of the triple-strand narrative device move across texts so that when considered together, many of Carlos's works seem like movements within a single examination of a 1950s East Village childhood. In *White Chocolate* and *The Cooking Show,* the following passage appears spoken by The Monkey and Tiny, respectively:

Borinque thru azure & rain storms in ruffles, closed in fingers. An unknown listener of love and clear light playing guitar, answering questions about the origins of roaches and tears. Borinque clean washed linoleum raised against too much steam heat. High-rise 10 to 4 rooms and rice and rice and rice grateful for meat. Unable to find mangos in season or blue water. Loving everything American. Working New York brooms and Long Island gardens. Loving Ricky Nelson & Topo Gigo, Joselito on the Sullivan show.

Calling Carmen! Carmen Morales Rodriguez Ortiz Aiyala Arroacho Perez Cruz Carmen Sanchez Dominques Pinero Rivera Santiago Sonja Clara Jose Manuelo Edgar Ellia Luz Anna Borinque. Crying pleanas [*sic*] in Pentecostal basements. Just good dancers. Villains cut in brilliante. Singers leaning gorgeous in Woolworth powder. The Lord lives in us all! Borinque marching on the head of disaster. Declaring summer by congas and cheering loud for the Yankees. Parking DeSotos sideways on Columbia Street repairing nylons for the week. Borinque a world of pink rollers bringing stripes to florals orange to gold. Flirting loud on corners lined with garbage. Smelling summer in the eyes of Borinque thru azure. Eyelids lined in tragic black pencil.[4]

This is a provocative memory to mull over from 1988 (*White Chocolate*) to 1996 (*The Cooking Show*). It reveals a lush world, full of rich mundane details of people, of place, of class, of an era. In the printed texts, not one word is different across the eight years that separate the works. The memory returns. Stuck perhaps. Providing comfort or raising questions. Though the words remain the same, the truth of the memory shifts as it is positioned between conversations among apparitions and the living in *White Chocolate,* and between a recipe for chickpea salad and a loudly sung lament of dislocation in *The Cooking Show.*

She makes a return—refocusing, standing at a new angle, lilting anew—as if the revisitation is a search for some understanding or resolution. This spiraling back through moments often happens when chunks of text appear across pieces. The children's rhyme "Clap hands clap hands till daddy comes home daddy had money and mommy had none" is found in both *White Chocolate for My Father* and *The Pork Chop Wars (a story of mothers).* In *White Chocolate,* the rhyme comes after a female ancestor explains how she negotiates repeated rapes by placing a bag over her head—"He can only take me like this . . . Cant [*sic*] look at my face."[5] After the rhyme is sung by the children in the family, this elder ancestor goes on to describe the tenderness of her father. In *The Pork Chop Wars (a story of mothers),* the rhyme is inserted in the narration, creating a bridge between the description of a young wife who strained to maintain a well-kept home, and the narrating of her husband's imminent death. In both instances, the rhyme is a pivot between one tone and telling, and another. The lyrics speak of male power and female

"I WRITE IN THE TONE OF GOSSIP AND OLD METHODOLOGIES OF STORYTELLING."*
—LAURIE CARLOS

* Phone interview with author, June 2011.

impotence that is graphically referenced by the older characters. The rhyme reflects an imbalanced relationship, and disconcertingly inserts a child presence in the midst of joyless adult relationships. The effect is one of simultaneity—adults conducting their business as children conduct their own, each group marking the other. Carlos returns to details as if she is working to understand them, as if she is working through an understanding about her own life and history. Her personal storytelling style reflects the structure of her written work for performance—the story spirals back with a bit more or less detail, with a new cadence, or in another character's voice. This allows the reader or audience, and Carlos, an opportunity to feel the same image/idea/moment anew.

Characters and references also appear from one work to the next. Monkey references appear in *Teenytown, The Cooking Show, White Chocolate* and "Marion's Terrible Time of Joy." In *The Cooking Show* and "Marion's Terrible Time of Joy," The Monkey is Carlos herself. Monkey carries conflicting connotations—a child-like mischievous playfulness, an animal coerced into commercial entertainment tethered to an organ grinder's string, and a sardonic echo of racist nineteenth-century images. These contradictions are part of the very power of Carlos's verbal texts. A reader digests all of this at the same time, trying to catch up to the multiple meanings evoked. Carlos as a smart disconnected child is the protagonist of several of her autobiographical works, and with *White Chocolate,* she felt she "can now speak about other things that are not autobiographical, and that are also not in my child's voice, which I had been unable to do for a while. The language is so simple because I had to say it in the language that I knew at the time, as the child in the moment. I couldn't write it from the point of view of reflection."[6] In spite of anticipating a move from autobiography in1988, Carlos as Monkey returns in the 2003 "Marion's Terrible Time of Joy." Although "Marion" offers adult reflection, nagging vestiges of childhood may remain.

The multiterminous nature of theatrical jazz manifests in Carlos's work through the infusion of historical artifacts in current reality. There are repeated minstrel references in *Teenytown.* The opening sketch is called "Minstrel Mania," the closing stage direction indicates that "the entire cast performs 'Buck and Wing,' an original aboriginal tap dance, in silence," and throughout the first half of the performance, the performers assume traditional minstrel roles as Carlos plays the Interlocutor, Robbie McCauley plays Bones, and Jessica Hagedorn plays Jones. In *White Chocolate,* two scenes are described as "vaudevilles, improvisations told in two voices."[7] These minstrel elements are not situated in their nineteenth-century moment, but are fully integrated into the now of the work encouraging contemporary contemplation on racism, on entertainment, and on the particular surrogates Black artists often unwittingly embody when we take the stage.

While Carlos turns over a memory from one text to the next, a constant in each of these works are the adults who are consumed by sorrow and/or rage, and the children who are left to make sense of the world essentially on their own.

Lets say I want to tell you a story /
   Some gave less to a lot of them who came passing through /
   Some of us had to leave the party to raise the baby /
   Some could never go back not that way /
Lets say that as I am telling you this story I am reminded of another
story and I begin to tell that one /
   Lets say the story has a beginning /
   Lets say the second story reminds me of a third and then another /
The story crashing silver out of nostrils full of gestures / Flames of breath
churned to curl / °

° Laurie Carlos, "The Pork Chop Wars (a story of mothers)" (unpublished manuscript, draft 1, 2006), 22.

This truth telling arranges and rearranges life like a strong wind, picking up an idea here, depositing an image there, tossing a memory backwards and forwards in a whirl of historical shape-shifting. Carlos's present has porous contours, so that time and memory waft through now, creating an ever-evolving past-laden present. In *The Pork Chop Wars (a story of mothers),* the narrator tells us "Everything from back yonder time crawled and sat under the nails." Even the self-policing middle-class family of this performance novel[8] cannot rid themselves of a past they would like to erase.

Soundscape

Imagining Carlos's personal narrative style as the wind is more than a useful simile. Breath, air, and movement are key ingredients to Carlos's written work, her performance work, her directing, and her workshop facilitation. Carlos studied modern dance, and used the form's emphasis on breath to negotiate the asthma she was born with and the myasthenia gravis (MG) she acquired as an adult. Conscious controlled breathing in modern dance can intensify the contraction and release that characterize modern dance movements.[9] While MG is most often identified by the weakening of muscles that control the eye, eyelid, facial expressions, chewing, talking, and swallowing, the muscles that affect breathing are also susceptible. A myasthenia crisis can lead to paralysis of the respiratory muscles requiring ventilation assistance. In extreme cases, the fatigability of the muscles is life-threatening.

"SOUNDS IN MOTION CHANGED EVERY-THING IN TERMS OF HOW PEOPLE RELATED TO THE AVANT GARDE AND JAZZ. AUDIBLE BREATHING IS ALL ABOUT McINTYRE."*

—LAURIE CARLOS

* Phone interview with author, June 16, 2008.

A characteristic feature of Carlos's performance work and directing is the perceptible inhalation and exhalation of air, an artistic impulse she learned from

Dianne McIntyre at McIntyre's Sounds in Motion dance studio of Harlem. From McIntyre, Carlos came to understand how to take language into the body and release into breath and flight. Carlos credits McIntyre's breath work with providing her with the method for stemming the effects of MG. McIntyre was exploring improvisations between dancers and jazz musicians that sometimes included vocalized sounds and spoken narratives.[10] Her studio became a Harlem gathering place during the Black Arts Movement and beyond—Olu Dara, Sekou Sundiata, William "Butch" Morris, Craig Harris, Cecil Taylor, Thulani Davis, Ntozake Shange, Jawole Willa Jo Zollar, Marlies Yearby, and Carlos were all regulars over time.

Carlos's sounds/breaths are idiosyncratic and mostly unchoreographed, though her written texts sometimes incorporate the exact placement of the breath or explicit references to breathing. Breath, movement, and life itself intertwined as the diaphragmatic breathing encouraged her respiratory muscles to keep their rhythms full and steady. The breath informs the gesture, and the gesture carries the story. In this work, the very idea of story is often the thing being investigated.

BREATH / BREATH / TO EVERY ONE AFTER / BREATH BROKEN / CAPTURED, RELEASED STEPPING / *

* Laurie Carlos, "The Pork Chop Wars" (unpublished manuscript, 2006), 1.

In Yoruba cosmology, *Ọya,* the Divine force of nature that is dynamic air, works a duality—life-giving breath and the deadly winds of destruction. Even the Niger River with which *Ọya* is associated reflects radical change as it flows away from the sea for several miles then boomerangs near Timbuktu turning toward the sea and emptying into the Gulf of Guinea. This force sweeps into one's life and reorders everything, or sustains one's life through air itself. It is *Ọya* who claims the

Figure 11. "Open the Sky," by Tonya Engel. After Engel originally presented me with a version of the painting, she and I collaborated for weeks on how to infuse more mystery, simultaneity, and Divine energy into the work. In this final version, birds have been added as they tweet a private message and evoke the ability to move between worlds; the primary figure straddles here and there as the head seems to become one with the cosmos, and the eye takes in the unknown. The figure is both powerful and porous; distinctive and elusive. Photo by Tonya Engel.

last breath at death, and who prompts the first breath at birth. *Oya*'s unpredictability and ferocity make her a force to be respected in nature, and in the workings of one's life. As Carlos's autobiographical character Monkey notes in "Marion's Terrible Time of Joy," "The book don't tell you how strong the wind is gonna be in your life / Book don't tell you that /."[11] In the destructive mode, *Oya* is a sword-wielding warrior, ready for battle as the fierce companion to lightening, thunder, and rain.

Laurie came to my graduate course, Devising Solo Performance, during the spring of 2009. I have been in so many transformative workshops with Laurie, and seen her cut right through the very core of someone's façade. I have ducked from those sharp insightful knives of hers hoping to be spared embarrassment, and simultaneously longing to be fully exposed by her insights so that I could just get on with myself. Part of Laurie's genius is her ability to see what is needed, to ferret out artifice in order to reveal the pulsing vulnerability and power beneath. Some of my graduate students had seen her performance of "Washed" in which she offered her easy sense of command, her compelling movements in every corner of the stage, and her deliciously stimulating narrative—at once private introspection even as it was direct conversation with the audience. The students listened to her discussion of art during the talk back. They were excited by her work, and eager to talk with her after the performance. In the class period before Laurie's visit, I told the class about her work, about the jazz aesthetic, about the necessity of a rigorous self-honesty—indeed these were concepts we had been working with all semester. The class decided that it would be a great addition to our work to have her come to our class. Laurie entered the class and arranged us in her customary circle seated open-legged on the floor. After some introductions, Laurie brusquely told one student—"Just step

up! Just do the work!" and tears slowly welled in the student's eyes. We moved on, did exercises, made important self-discoveries, and then Laurie said to another student "Speak up! You always wait so that you are the last one to speak! Well now you have our attention! SPEAK!" And for the next three to four full minutes, the student tried to speak—but only a paroxysm of sobs came forward. Three minutes of watching this student agonize. And through that pain, I saw the class stand tall. When one student went to comfort the paralyzed student, and Laurie told her not to, the students' faces seemed filled with understanding rather than

horror. In the moment, it was both devastating to witness the student's tortured attempts to speak, and invigorating to feel right inside of a potential life and artistic transformation. This is what Laurie brings. This is her gift. Her extensive history of developing work with experimental sensibilities, her countless collaborations with luminaries in dance, theatre, and music, her life of doggedly pushing for honesty in performance—all of this came to bear on the moment in my classroom. Could the students see how much growth was happening as one student was forced to confront her habits and stand inside of her choices? Were they able to hold up a mirror to their own stuck spaces? I felt pretty certain that the student being addressed found no virtue at the time in Laurie's approach, but I could see more clearly than ever that sometimes a jolt is the way to bring someone into the present moment, that the classroom can be a safe space precisely because it can carry us through intense productive upheaval.

In one class session, Laurie managed to bring a profound change into the room, a change I knew was needed but one that I couldn't orchestrate. She was asking the students to examine themselves and to stand up. And though the style had mellowed over the years, the strategy remained the same, and the effect was—as before—cyclonic.

MONKEY

In the days when I'm in battle I always know I will win /

ANANYA

How / How do you know? /

MONKEY

Not how do I know / But why fight / It's always my battle with myself /

ANANYA

No / That's not what I am talking about / It's these crazy small people with their arrogance /

MONKEY

Arrogance is the best battle cry / It's what gets your feet up to dance / You should thank the little people /

ANANYA

Do you really think they deserve anything with their tiny minds? /

MONKEY

With their short visions /

ANANYA

I know you can't stand them either /

MONKEY

I can't stand anything or anybody / It all gets on my nerves /

ANANYA

So what's all this about them being helpful? /

MONKEY

I didn't say they were helpful / They sure are not the reason for my personal battles / I declare war / Supply the troupes / Bomb residential areas and sign truces / Rock in my rage I'm a good dancer / The little people really couldn't ever play the music / I got multiple rhythms with changing melody lines / And I'm addicted to the Tango°

° Laurie Carlos, "Marion's Terrible Time of Joy" (unpublished manuscript, 2007), 5.

The air travel of many of Carlos's characters reflects another union with *Oya* whose dominion is the air. A trip to Italy opens *White Chocolate*—"Opening: Everyone Knows a Dance! This is a voyage of improvisational movement and sound"—after the character Lore declares, "Someday Im gonna go all over the world. All over."[12] Tony then begins to recall her first trip to Italy with sister Tiny and friend Ida in which the Italian TWA agent printed the wrong departure time on their tickets. The girls had plans to visit Tony and Tiny's mother in Africa, but that would now have to wait. Taking full responsibility for the error, the agent promised the girls they could stay at a hotel until the next flight in three days, and all expenses would be paid by the airline. At the end of the play, we return to the three girls trying to get out of Italy when TWA refuses to pay for their three-day stay and lavish dining at the finest Italian hotel. After harrowing encounters with angry Italian TWA agents, the girls are allowed to leave the country. In the transitional site of an airport, the trip is ruined. Travel is not the freedom space the characters' fantasies imagine it to be ("I dream of Sweden and Paris in your eyes"[13]), and, importantly, the girls do not see their mother.

The mother figure is literally and figuratively distant in much of Carlos's work. In *Teenytown,* Her, who is a clear stand-in for Carlos, gives a final commentary about her mother when she says, "First she moved to Brooklyn and then to Zaire in 1971 she has not returned. She made both moves alone with her children. She has never been to Sweden."[14] Although the mother has done some traveling with her children, she and they remain alone. In *White Chocolate,* Mickey the mother says, "Tough little pudding heads. They all dance. Yes sir. All my children dance. Whirl around and sing too. These children of mine all mistakes."[15] The apparent cruelty of Mickey's comments is mitigated to some extent by knowing that she endured beatings and sexual assaults by her mother's boyfriend. Mickey tells her own absent mother: "I am sitting outside waiting my turn. Waiting. Mama, why didn't you help me? Mama, why didn't you help me? Mama, why didn't you help me?," then proceeds to sing "Dixie," a song etched in historical memory as the anthem for a racist southern United States. Mickey speaks of her abuse through this racially charged song that includes a failed romance between a deceiving man and naïve woman. In much of Carlos's work, mothers do not protect children but instead work to protect themselves from harrowing memories.

Throughout *Teenytown, Oya*'s winds of change make international travel unsettling. Laurie tells the audience,

> Paris is a stinking racist town
> Argentinians refuse to serve
> us steaks we don't even want—
> WE WANT CAFÉ! CAFÉ OLE! THAT'S
> ALL WE WANT YOU NEO-NAZI EXPATRIATES
>
> arbitrary & arrogant
> gendarmes demand

i.d.
in crowded subway stations

we whip out passports
trembling with rage.
we dream of singing
right up in their faces
but we know better.
you know the rap—

"je suis une ugly americain, bebe!"
hiss that secret litany,
protection against evil spirits:
little richard,
fats domino,
chuck berry
otis uno
otis dos
otis tres,
fontella bass.

we're international citizens,
you understand.[16]

While Carlos's characters often understand themselves to be citizens of the world, they are frequently reminded of the limitations imposed by race, gender, and nationality. Carlos's work points to the illusion of freedom for Black women regardless of their class status.

Music is vital to the soundscape in Carlos's work. It is in the language of her characters, it is indicated in the stage directions, it is on the radio, it is sung. Music becomes the reference point for her feelings, the guide in workshop exercises, and the marker for a memory. Specific songs and rhymes are essential to the way Carlos creates jazz structures. Many of the songs/rhymes speak of coded forms of oppression in the lyrics. In *White Chocolate,* that oppression is mostly gendered and/or sexualized. The power dynamics in "clap hands clap hands till daddy comes home daddy has money and mommy has none!"[17] speaks of male power and female dependence. *White Chocolate* also opens with a reference to "Little Bitty Pretty One"[18] whose lyrics disturbingly suggest pedophilia—

Oh, itty bitty pretty one
Come on and talk to me
Let me grab you lovely one
Come sit down on my knee
I could tell you a story

It happened a long time ago
Little Bitty Pretty One
I've been watchin' you grow

LAURIE'S DISCOGRAPHY OF IMPORTANT
MUSIC AS OF 2011*

JOAN ARMATRADING
JONI MITCHELL
BUFFY SAINTE-MARIE
LAURA NYRO
HARRY BELAFONTE
JOHNNY MATHIS
PRINCE
DAVE MATTHEWS
LOURDES PEREZ
GRISHA COLEMAN
HAMZA EL DIN, EVERY DAY FOR 30 YEARS

* Laurie Carlos, e-mail message to author, November 30, 2011.

—as well as a reference to the Bobettes' 1950s hit single "Mr. Lee," which also suggests a relationship between young girls and an older man.[19] Racist oppression is found in the music of *The Cooking Show* with "I'm gwine to jump down / tern round / pick a bile / o'cotton jump down, / tern round / pick a bale / a day."[20]

Fieldnotes

Rehearsal for con flama
Texas State Mental Hospital [21]
8 August 2000
6:45 pm

LAURIE: *"a lot of work initially is for us to learn each others' rhythms; everything is already in the room."*

Method—
LAURIE: *"let us hear your voices; don't go so far inside yourselves"*
—opens with short passage then has them read;
performers all unsure who starts and who continues
LAURIE: *"let's go back. Let's read it again. What do you know about it right now?'*
They read—
LAURIE: *"Did you get what you wanted? Go back and get what you want."*
Gives each performer a style; Florinda in the story; Zell is past the story; Ana telling someone else's story.
They are told they can stand. Only Florinda crouches—Zell and Ana remain seated.
LAURIE: *"Either be in it; away from it; or repeat it as gossip"*
   "Don't let it pull you into some cliché of language—'arty poo-ey'"
LAURIE: *"I want you to be able to tell me when you find the surprise"*
   "Stop! Nobody can hear anybody else. Do whatever you need to do to hear each other."
   "Everybody gets stuck in the funnel! Do what you have to to see each other."
Clear change in response to language when they looked at each other.

w/ Tommy Nakamura section
the 2 women "gossip" while Zell tells the same text as the teller of the tale.
LAURIE: *"break the language up" = don't say all the words*

Physical Idioms

In Carlos's work, the body is telling its own tale. Full of angularity and multiple simultaneous directions, her gestural vocabulary is a blend of her own movement background and her careful attention to the movements of the performers. Sometimes these movements are marked in the text, other times they evolve during rehearsal.

During rehearsals for Pork Chop Wars, *Laurie introduced a series of gestures that the eight women performers began to imitate then personalize with their own distinctive style. When Laurie did the gestures, they had a buoyancy, as if her body was floating or suspended. When we did them sitting in a semi-circle of chairs, they were individual expressions rather than a unison group commentary. I was designated to lead the gestures, and the women would echo my movements. Turn knees to the right, slide the downstage hand across chest, raise fist*
to eye level, twist the fist three times, slap thigh. Then, at one rehearsal, I missed my cue! The women were confused! Should they try to do the sequence without me? Would I suddenly remember and do the gesture at a different moment? Would this throw off the later gestures? Is this the very serendipity that makes this aesthetic fly? We fumbled forward, gestures askew. I wondered what the audience made of these movements when they saw them in performance. Do they take in the different qualities along with the similarities, and make their own meaning? Are they distracted by the movements? Do they give the gestures meaning in relationship to the verbal text? As with so much of this work, I yield to allowing my body to have a story while my words are sharing another.

The stage directions indicate that A Monkey Dance appears in *White Chocolate*—"*A trip up North. Kick up your legs and get onboard. Everyone's crossing the line. Everyone picks up a gesture,*"[22] and also in *Teenytown*—"I go camping outside on the drive looking for Canarsie. 'They got a fishin' place there.' My clothes are stuffed under the bed! I'm ready like a fleet of rubber ducks in red beak."[23] These are dances of children on a journey. In the first instance, the dance indicates the body movements the performer is to execute. In the second instance, the dance is a verbal allusion to travel as the child imagines getting away. Both, however, reference travel to somewhere presumably better than "here." Dance, for Carlos, is an expansive term suggesting travel, a transition, creating a space of pleasure, safety, and escape.

"I TELL THE STORIES IN THE MOVEMENT—THE INSIDE DANCES THAT OCCUR SPONTANEOUSLY, AS IN LIFE—THE MUSIC AND THE TEXT. IF I WRITE A LINE, IT DOESN'T NECESSARILY HAVE TO BE A LINE THAT IS SPOKEN; IT CAN BE A LINE THAT'S MOVED, A LINE FROM WHICH MUSIC IS CREATED. THE GESTURE BECOMES THE SENTENCE. SO MUCH OF WHO WE ARE AS WOMEN, AS PEOPLE, HAS TO DO WITH HOW WE GESTURE TO ONE ANOTHER ALL THE TIME, AND PARTICULARLY THROUGH EMOTIONAL MOMENTS. GESTURE BECOMES A SENTENCE OR A STATE OF FACT. IF I PUT ON A SCRIPT 'FOUR GESTURES,' THAT DOESN'T MEAN I'M NOT SAYING ANYTHING; THAT MEANS I HAVE OPENED IT UP FOR SOMETHING TO BE SAID PHYSICALLY."*
—LAURIE CARLOS

Carlos's signature breath work is linked to movement, and movement is linked to language. The

* *White Chocolate for My Father,* 5.

". . . I THINK IF WHEN YOU START TO TALK ABOUT LANGUAGE, WHEN LANGUAGE BEGINS TO HAPPEN IT AFFECTS THE BODY. IT AFFECTS MEMORY. IT AFFECTS WHAT'S IN THE BONES AND IT AFFECTS MUSIC. WHEN YOU START TO SPEAK, LANGUAGE BECOMES MUSIC . . . THERE'S REALLY NO WAY TO MOVE AWAY FROM MOVEMENT WHEN YOU ARE CREATING LANGUAGE."*

—LAURIE CARLOS

* Interview by author, New York, July 2003.

TONY AND TINY EXECUTE FIVE GESTURES THEN WALK INTO THE LIGHT AND SPEAK AT WILL.°

° *White Chocolate for My Father,* 17.

fusion of movement, breath, and language is characteristic of Carlos's performance work. A puff of air here, a hand sliding across the heart and into the sky there, spinning on the balls of her feet following a new diagonal while finding the melody inside a line of text—that is the simultaneity of expression that is quintessentially Carlos.

Fieldnotes

Rehearsal for con flama
Texas State Mental Hospital
15 August 2000

It was Florinda's birthday—
Laurie, Lourdes and Annette and Sonja
brought KFC, flowers, jelly beans.
Eating and check in

Aunt Gussie Section
Laurie gives a clap a snap and a sign to Ana and Florinda and Sonja
—she creates an auditory landscape—a soundscape
she refers to the physicality as "language"
—describes movements in detail, where the energy begins, what muscles are used
—has definite sense of how the movement looks and happens
—she dances the words "hands turning soil, toes wiggling"
—distinctly "black" gestures w/ the scooped back and rounded butt
—so she choreographs
—she hears the music of the words & she feels the movement in the words

Figure 12. Laurie Carlos teaching hip movement during *con flama* rehearsal. Carlos (foreground), Florinda Bryant (left), and Ana Perea (right). Photo by Bret Brookshire.

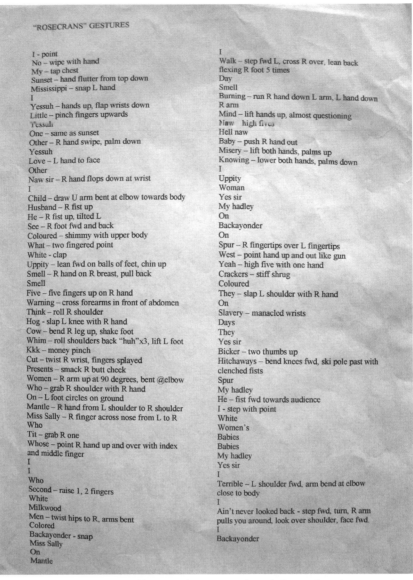

"ROSECRANS" GESTURES

I - point
No – wipe with hand
My – tap chest
Sunset – hand flutter from top down
Mississippi – snap L hand
I
Yessuh – hands up, flap wrists down
Little – pinch fingers upwards
Yessuh
One – same as sunset
Other – R hand swipe, palm down
Yessuh
Love – L hand to face
Other
Naw sir – R hand flops down at wrist
I
Child – draw U arm bent at elbow towards body
Husband – R fist up
He – R fist up, tilted L
See – R foot fwd and back
Coloured – shimmy with upper body
What – two fingered point
White - clap
Uppity – lean fwd on balls of feet, chin up
Smell – R hand on R breast, pull back
Smell
Five – five fingers up on R hand
Warning – cross forearms in front of abdomen
Think – roll R shoulder
Hog - slap L knee with R hand
Cow – bend R leg up, shake foot
Whim – roll shoulders back "huh"x3, lift L foot
Kkk – money pinch
Cut – twist R wrist, fingers splayed
Presents – smack R butt cheek
Women – R arm up at 90 degrees, bent @elbow
Who – grab R shoulder with R hand
On – L foot circles on ground
Mantle – R hand from L shoulder to R shoulder
Miss Sally – R finger across nose from L to R
Who
Tit – grab R one
Whose – point R hand up and over with index
and middle finger
I
I
Who
Second – raise 1, 2 fingers
White
Milkwood
Men – twist hips to R, arms bent
Colored
Backayonder - snap
Miss Sally
On
Mantle

I
Walk – step fwd L, cross R over, lean back
flexing R foot 5 times
Day
Smell
Burning – run R hand down L arm, L hand down
R arm
Mind – lift hands up, almost questioning
Naw   high fives
Hell naw
Baby – push R hand out
Misery – lift both hands, palms up
Knowing – lower both hands, palms down
I
Uppity
Woman
Yes sir
My hadley
On
Backayonder
On
Spur – R fingertips over L fingertips
West – point hand up and out like gun
Yeah – high five with one hand
Crackers – stiff shrug
Coloured
They – slap L shoulder with R hand
On
Slavery – manacled wrists
Days
They
Yes sir
Bicker – two thumbs up
Hitchaways – bend knees fwd, ski pole past with
clenched fists
Spur
My hadley
He – fist fwd towards audience
I - step with point
White
Women's
Babies
Babies
My hadley
Yes sir
I
Terrible – L shoulder fwd, arm bend at elbow
close to body
I
Ain't never looked back - step fwd, turn, R arm
pulls you around, look over shoulder, face fwd
I
Backayonder

Figure 13. *con flama* gestures and language sheet. During rehearsals for *con flama* in 2000, assistant stage manager Kim Burke recorded this list of gestures that Laurie Carlos generated for specific ideas in the section of text known as "Rosecrans." The gestures may suggest some quality in the words, but are not literal embodiments of the key words Carlos identified. In performance, these gestures created an ongoing flow of movement that was juxtaposed against verbal text. Photo by Ruth McFarlane.

Stage manager told performers to wear gym shoes because of the cement floor,
Laurie however is barefoot
LAURIE: *"Don't think of it as dance or you're in fucking big trouble"*
the movement is somehow mundane but gets elevated because
it is set apart in the performance
Laurie assumes women's bodies are strong
it just looks so beautiful; when it works there's a breath in it when it's beautiful

She says "go, go"—to speed them up. Like the caller in a crew squad

We worked for about 2 hours on 17 lines of text

*LAURIE: "Rehearsal is really about putting a muslin drape cloth on the body
that will later become the dress"*

Something is off
LAURIE: "everything just drops and gets very foo foo foo foo."
"It gets very ghosty because you are not breathing w/ each other."
"It's so fucking serious. I don't want it to be serious. Let's have some fun."
*"The first 12 beats are always hard for me. And they're usually at the beginning
and this time they're at the end"*

Laurie moves while Florinda says the words "voice like the wind"—p. 28
—she finds the movement in her body; she discovers as the words inform her.
LAURIE: "and then the twist, and then the twist, and then the twist"
—after she finds it in her body w/ the words, she shows it to all the others
"we're not going to illustrate the language. We're not trying to illustrate every word"

Figure 14. Laurie Carlos teaching gestures during *con flama* rehearsal. Carlos moves, and the company follows by finding their own sensibility within her choices. With Carlos as guide, the performers learn their own bodies and develop the foundation for ensemble collaborations. Left to right: Laurie Carlos, Sonja Parks, Florinda Bryant, Ana Perea. Photo by Bret Brookshire.

Rehearsal for con flama
Texas State Mental Hospital
17 August 2000

*The movement of Ana's that made everyone cry yesterday (hands around her face) is
not being used in another moment.*
The gesture is a <u>phrase</u> that Laurie returns to
She treats the script like music or dance
Performers read text, Laurie listens and <u>then</u> gives the physical idea
*By the time the performers have physicalized the piece they are clearer about the
emotions of the pieces*
When she demonstrates it doesn't have the dictatorial feeling of a line reading
LAURIE: "Does everybody know where they are right now?"
   "any moment of it that's not true, just screams"
   *"a lot of vulnerability in the stomach and the thighs that you are not working w/ yet,
    but I know that you'll get there."*

Figure 15. Laurie Carlos teaching ensemble movement during *con flama* rehearsal. Carlos suggests an image that might be useful in helping the women feel their relationships to each other. Left to right: Florinda Bryant, Laurie Carlos, Sonja Parks, Ana Perea. Photo by Bret Brookshire.

Figure 16. Sonja Parks, Ana Perea, and Florinda Bryant performing ensemble movement during *con flama* production at Frontera@ Hyde Park Theatre. The rehearsed image makes its way into the production, though Carlos's rehearsal work is not primarily about creating images that will be put on the stage. Set design by Leilah Stewart. Photo by Bret Brookshire.

Rehearsal for con flama
Texas State Mental Hospital
24 August 2000

Check in includes "how did everybody feel about the work last night?"
So much of the discussion of the play happens rather casually
Standing, going over the physical problems from the previous night.
When Ana jokingly made a leg move that was very balletic
LAURIE: "Very pretty Ana—I don't want to see it again!"

She often asks for a <u>flat</u> foot—"very colored"

Ana asks "who is it I'm kissing" and Laurie says "Ana! I don't know! We're just trying to have a party here!" and that's what they are trying to do—find the party in the spirit in the union of words/movement/body/text/experience. The spirit is the àṣẹ— They are trying to locate the àṣẹ in the work—and they do it <u>together</u>. They create it by listening and feeling each other.

Figure 17. Laurie Carlos indicating specific muscles during *con flama* rehearsal. She explains which muscles are used to achieve a particular arch and sway. From this initial precision, performers are left to make individual adjustments to the movement. Left to right: Florinda Bryant, Laurie Carlos, Ana Perea. Photo by Bret Brookshire.

DIANNE McINTYRE: "I was trying to merge the dance, the movement, and the words [in Shange's *Spell #7*]. Sometimes [Laurie Carlos and Beth Shorter] were mirroring. Sometimes the words were in Beth and the movement was in Laurie. We did it very fast. We did it very fast, but Laurie had the dance inside of her. She already had the natural wanting to do that. It was like we gave her permission to do that, she could do it from one place and show you a whole world, at the same time she and [Beth] were like one, even if they were not in the same place. She did not overshadow the dance and the dance did not overshadow her. It would not have been the same if Laurie said the poem while Beth danced.

"DIANNE WAS THE MOTHER OF DANCE FOR US ALL."*

—LAURIE CARLOS

* Phone interview with author, June 16, 2008.

This happened throughout the piece. I always loved her sense of movement connected with the word. Ntozake's writing is like that. She always loved dance and the spoken word equally, so her words are very easy to make dance. Laurie has that connection of the movement and words already in her body.

Laurie has to go to the place that is not the everyday world. It is performance possession. Such people transform us. They transcend their own bodies. Laurie brings people to new places—things they didn't know they could do."°

° Phone interview with author, June 2009.

Apprentice / Elder / Ìkọ́'sẹ
Apprentice / Elder / Ìkọ́'sẹ
Apprentice / Elder / Ìkọ́'sẹ

Carlos provides *ikọ́'sẹ́,* transformative training from a master that is required for acquiring facility with theatrical jazz. By the 1990s Carlos had worked with a wide range of artists including Samuel L. Jackson, Jawole Willa Jo Zollar, Denzel Washington, Greta Gunderson, Ntozake Shange, Suzan-Lori Parks, and Marlies Yearby; had produced work in mostly experimental venues such as BACA, Dance Theatre Workshop, Franklin Furnace, The Public Theatre, and PS 122; had premiered the role of the lady in blue on Broadway in Ntozake Shange's *for colored girls who have considered suicide/when the rainbow is enuf;* had collaborated in the formation of the avant-garde ensemble Thought Music with Robbie McCauley and Jessica Hagedorn; and had become co-director with Marlies Yearby of Movin' Spirits Dance Company and a company member of Urban Bush Women. Her distinctive gestural impulses and breath rhythms have extended into many artistic genres and traditions.

In Austin, Carlos presented Theatre Communications Group–sponsored workshops through Frontera@Hyde Park Theatre, and was a guest artist with the Austin Project from 2002 through 2009. Her facilitation is based on questions and commands that require an honesty for group cohesion and ensemble trust—"sit next to the person you feel the most kinship with in the room," and "sit next to the person you think does not want to work with you"; that require respectful and playful listening—"begin singing 'Row, Row, Row Your Boat,' and find your own instrument in the song"; that require self-clarity—"what is the most damaging mythology you create about yourself?" A master teacher's strategies are not always gentle, as the old ways of being must often be vigorously exposed and dislodged to make room for the profound spaces of art. Playwright C. Denby Swanson believes Carlos's questions that cut to the bone are designed to force a confrontation with one's self as artist.[24] Carlos often breaks open a foundation built of habit to expose the life-carrying marrow inside. These commands and questions can open participants up to themselves, and it can terrify some into isolation.

C. DENBY SWANSON: "What do you do when you are revealed? *That's* what your art is about. Don't try to hide *the thing.* That's what Laurie is interested in."°

° Interview by author, Austin, TX, July 8, 2009.

I can't quite remember the first time I worked with Laurie. It was probably in the mid-1990s in a workshop at Frontera@Hyde Park Theatre. What I do remember is that that work gave me a vitality and aliveness that was profound. I was also terrified and outraged by what seemed to be an unnecessary brusqueness. Her questions during workshops were both shocking
and simple. I knew that if I answered them honestly nothing would be the same. Laurie's way with people was spare, direct, spontaneous, interior, presentational; mine was decorous, formal, wrapped in protocols, planned, representational. Laurie

was the slashing wind, revealing truths in the wake of her stormy arrival, I was
the meandering river, laughing, comforting, caretaking; Ọya and Ọ̀ṣun in their
archetypical sisterly contrasts. After years of integrating her powerful questions into
my self-understanding, of being in productions where I felt the most vulnerable, after
countless car trips hearing her life
unfold, after picking the right asparagus and the best salmon for a communal meal,
after learning to take the opportunities her whirlwind provided, I became a more
sturdy reflection of the river, thereby able to be present and sincerely generous with
the community around me. That style of hers that is so different from my own was a
pivotal force in my naming myself an artist.

Passing on knowledge is important to Carlos, who believes it is the responsibility of the artist to train others. Through *ikọ́ṣẹ́* relationships with young artists, Bridgforth got clear about how the jazz aesthetic principles support both the apprentice and the master teacher. Being an apprentice to Carlos led to Bridgforth's role as a master teacher when she followed Carlos's directive to "just help somebody." Bridgforth's work with young artists has now become a vital feature of her own theatrical jazz practice. Without this work, the practice would fade away; the elder's very life would be singular rather than multiple.

"I DIDN'T MEET LAURIE UNTIL '98. I WAS COMPLAIN- ING. AND LAURIE SAID 'JUST HELP SOMEBODY!' SHE JUST LOOKED AT ME AND SAID, 'YOU NEED TO HELP SOMEBODY!' LUZ [GUERRA] AND I STARTED THIS GROUP IN OUR HOUSE. WE MET FOR THREE OR FOUR HOURS. LUZ AND I HAD BEEN WITH THEM CHILDREN FOR A WHOLE SUMMER—FLO[RINDA BRYANT], ZELL [MILLER III], PIPER [ANDERSON], KIM [CURETTE], AISHA [CONNER], [JEFFREY] DA'SHADE [JOHNSON]."*
—SHARON BRIDGFORTH

* Phone interview with author, July 5, 2008.

In Carlos's work, there is repeated interest in adults and their relationships with children. Some of the women elders struggle to make a good life for themselves and their children, while others succumb to the cruelties they have been dealt. In many of the works, adults do not caretake and the children are left confused, hurt, and alone. Deola, the ancestral matriarch in *White Chocolate,* chants to her children "*Oranyan ogun ma de o. Oranyan ogun ma de o.*"[25] In antiquity, this Yoruba plea for help was a special signal between Ọ̀rànmíyàn (aka Ọ̀rányàn), the son of the Yoruba progenitor *Odùduwà,* and his people. The people were only to shout this phrase when they were under attack, which would prompt Ọ̀rànmíyàn to save them. Once, some of the people shouted the phrase when there was no need. Ọ̀rànmíyàn arrived and unwittingly killed his own people. When Deola says "*Oranyan ogun ma de o,*" Lore instantly knows that they are under attack, and cannot be sure from where the threat is derived; her mother is as likely to entertain them with stories of far-off places ("I dream of Sweden and Paris in your eyes"[26]) as she is to restrain them when she goes out (". . . now I have to tie you when I leave here. Both of you. None of you will help me)."[27] Like so many of Carlos's adult–child character relationships the Yoruba phrase is paradoxical—pro- tective yet dangerous, revealing both parental care and parental carelessness. It's this very paradox that Carlos seems to explore in her work and through the many apprentice relationships she cultivates in real life. Carlos turns to an English folk song, "My Son John," in *White Chocolate* for an example of a tender parent–child relationship. Ironically, Tiny sings this song of a father lamenting the loss of his son's legs in battle, just before Tiny receives a phone call from her emotionally elusive and absent father.

Carlos has a special kinship with Sharon Bridgforth that is not characterized by the "tough love" she dispenses to many others. Bridgforth says, "Once Laurie told me I reminded her of her sister Sharon who died. And I do feel she treated me like a sister. She has protected me and been very gentle in her guidance of me."[28] Their relationship is similar to the closeness between Lore and Tony in *White Chocolate*. In the play, Lore and her sisters are left at home alone while the mother goes out. The mother has tied Tony's hands so she won't eat, and Lore knows that the consequences of untying her sister will be dire. Eventually, Lore gives in to Tony's pleas for freedom and unties her. Upon returning the mother says, "I knew you would let her go. You always choose them over me now I have to tie you when I leave here. Both of you."[29] In an interview with Sydne Mahone, Carlos explains the relationship in this way: "I had never told my sister how much I loved her but I risked everything to untie her that night . . . The risk I took was a risk my grandmother did not take for my mother while she was being raped all the time; which was also the risk my mother never took for me when she found out my stepfather had molested me. But I risked everything for my sister."[30] Carlos cares for Bridgforth as Lore cares for Tony, creating a unique *ikọ́ṣẹ́* apprentice–elder bond between these artists.

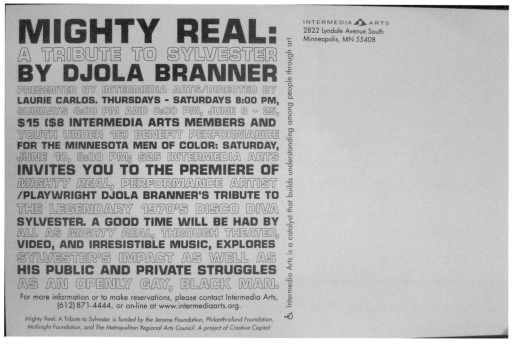

Figure 18. Postcard from Djola Branner's *Mighty Real*. In 2000 Laurie Carlos directed Branner's *Mighty Real: A Tribute to Sylvester* at Intermedia Arts in Minneapolis. For Carlos, *iko'ṣẹ́* not only is an apprentice–elder relationship but occurs among peers who learn from each other as they nurture one another's work. Photo by Ruth McFarlane.

Àdúgbò / Environment
Àdúgbò / Environment
Àdúgbò / Environment

Àdúgbò / Environment
Àdúgbò / Environment

Carlos was born in Queens, New York, in 1949, but was raised on the Lower East Side of Manhattan in the 1950s and '60s. This was the *àdúgbò*, the neighborhood, that shaped her truths about family, art, community, and politics. Raised in what she calls "a university of the street,"[31] Carlos was very aware of the vibrancy that characterized her environment and how it shaped her artmaking. At that time and in that place, an artistic and political revolution was beginning that contributed to the refashioning of the United States. The mélange of people, languages, sounds, foods, smells, clothing, music, spiritual practices, and daily habits helped establish for Carlos a specific understanding of what art and life were.

JOHN GENNARI: "The East Village proved more progressive and emerged as a center of the black avant-garde. A kind of downtown Harlem Renaissance arose on the Lower East Side, with the Umbra writer's collective, Freedomways magazine, La MaMa Experimental Theatre, and the Negro Ensemble Company foreshadowing the full flowering of the Black Arts Movement uptown in Harlem later in the decade. Black writers and artists on the Lower East Side in these years [mid-1950s to mid-1960s] included David Henderson, Ishmael Reed, A.B. Spellman, Tom Dent, Calvin Hernton, Lorenzo Thomas, Brenda Walcott, Sarah Wright, Emilio Cruz, Ted Joans, Bob Kaufman, and Bob Thomson, and such 'new thing' jazz musicians as Ornette Coleman, Don Cherry, Cecil Taylor, Albert Ayler, Archie Shepp, Marion Brown, and Sonny Murray."°

° "Baraka's Bohemian Blues," 254.

"IT ALMOST CAN'T BE ISOLATED TO A LOCATION. THERE WAS A MIND-SET THAT GENERATED A CHANGE IN FORM. A BLACK PRESENCE WAS ALWAYS THERE, BUT IT WAS WHAT WAS BOHEMIAN THAT MADE IT ALL WORK."*

—LAURIE CARLOS

* Phone interview with author, June 2009.

"It's all about environment . . . I used to go to Café Wah on McDougal. Right there, this is one of the places that Bill Cosby would work in. And Richard Pryor worked there. Dick Gregory was around all the time. He worked over at the Village Gate. And you got Miles Davis around a lot. You got Coltrane at Slugs a lot, the club on 8th Street and 3rd Avenue, the Five Spot, everybody in there. People would be playing the Five Spot 24 hours a day. It was one of those places they would go to when they left from uptown. Being at the Café Wah—and there was a place called Minneta Lane, I would just stand there and just hang out being in Paris for four or five hours in that one spot. And I would lean against a building, I would be in Paris . . . there was a theatre and a Dojo° and an art gallery. That became a hub at the time . . . for all kinds of exchanges, in '68–'69 The Stones, Jimmy Hendrix, Janis Joplin, Sly and the Family Stone hung out there at the Dojo upstairs. All

° Here Carlos is referencing the ice cream spot at 8th and St. Mark's that sold ice cream with drug-named flavors such as Panama Red and Acapulco Gold. For more information on this now gone New York favorite, see http://vanishingnewyork.blogspot.com/2010/12/ice-cream-dojo.html, and Gael Greene, "Everything You Always Wanted to Know About Ice Cream But Were Too Fat to Ask," *New York Magazine*, August 3, 1970.

these painters who hung out upstairs and downstairs. Before that, that place was a linoleum store. Upstairs was where they kept all of their stock. That's where we rehearsed *colored girls* for two weeks from noon to midnight until 6:00 in the morning . . .

I come from an experience where artists could just stand up without knowing all the answers to the questions. My experience was P.S. 122, Henry Street, Dance Theatre Workshop, New Federal, and I grew up in a jazz tradition and American folk music at Slugs—it was a big try-out place, and Café Wah was a big try-out place. Where you could go in front of an audience to discover what you could do. Coltrane, 'Jackie' McLean up at Slug's, you'd get Bob Dylan, Buffy Sainte-Marie, Odetta, all those people came through the folk tradition where you write a song the night before and you get up and say it the next day or even from the table with the coffee to the stage. That's how I understood the creation of art, what became the matter of art. The way I understand how art is created there is always that insistence in the practice.

It was musicians and traditional poets, Langston Hughes and those poets, LeRoi Jones, Loften Mitchell—lived in my projects. "Tuli" Kupferberg, Allen Ginsberg, Josh White. This way of making work translated every discipline. At the same time you are also dealing with Circle in the Square, NEC, actors and writers for the theatre . . . they came to the location and gave you permission to get the work done that wanted to get done. No matter what kind of exploration you were doing. No matter if you were Lenny Bruce or Bill Cosby or Pryor. I walked in a snow storm on my 16th birthday to see Bill Cosby—not famous, he was just very funny. The Electric Circus, where the Chambers Brothers, Sly and the Family Stone, Jimi Hendrix and Janis Joplin were. This is who is walking down the street. You had the Rolling Stones. Anybody and everybody hit this part of the world. So the 60s is when I came of age in a lot of ways."[†]

—Laurie Carlos

[†] Phone interview with author, June 16, 2008.

The gumbo of city life, so conducive to the formation of theatrical jazz, was Carlos's artistic blueprint.

Her own household provided a similarly dynamic education. Her great-grandfather was a guitar player, her grandmother a dancer on the Chitlin' Circuit, her father a drummer, her grandmother a pianist and music teacher, and her mother a dancer. Carlos's childhood living room was often filled with artists and activists testing ideas and images and sounds with one another. Carlos came to think of the world in these terms—vigorously contested and constructed, infused with art and politics as the way of daily life.[32]

This way of making work, in which the work itself is an investigation rather than a presentation of what one has already discovered, laid the foundation for the creation of the Late Nite Series—"Non-English Speaking Spoken Here"—first at Penumbra Theatre, then at Pillsbury House. Carlos hosted these events as a way to provide space for artists at every level of their development to explore in an East Village way, and in a grand gesture of institutionalized *ikǫ́ṣǫ́*. Late Nite became a training ground where artists stretched into new terrain.[33]

Blackness

Blackness

Blackness

The world of overlapping aesthetics in Carlos's home and neighborhood offered a sense of Blackness, and of the world generally, that was multiple and incorporative. While Carlos understood the legal and social limitations imposed on Black people in her world, she also felt permission to borrow from all that was around her and fold this into her own evolving aesthetic. For Carlos, Blackness exists within a wide range of social protocols, historical memories, and understood contradictions—and her written and performance work reflect this blending. Carlos describes her autobiographical performance novel *The Pork Chop Wars (a story of mothers)* as "the journey of an American family of women," and has famously called her work "American Theatre," eschewing Black Theatre or Theatrical Jazz as identifying markers. For Carlos this is not a facile declaration of apolitical art, but rather an insistence on Black being able to stand in for U.S. American.

"*WHITE CHOCOLATE* STRIVES TO CREATE A CONTEMPORARY AMERICAN AESTHETIC GROUNDED IN, AND DRAWING FROM, THE EXPERIENCE OF THE BLACK AMERICAN DIASPORA. IT SEEKS TO TELL THE STORIES OF AN AMERICAN BLACK FAMILY."*

—LAURIE CARLOS

* *White Chocolate for My Father,* 7.

Theatrical jazz brings to the stage Black people and situations not typically seen in performance. The cosmopolitan understanding of Carlos's characters often manifests in the music. At the end of *Teenytown,* Her sings "Enay ma tov u na nachiem she vech ahiem gon yah haugh," then says "Me [*sic*] casa es su casa en la dia en la noche en toda. Won't let nobody turn me around turn me around . . ."[34] as she extols the power of community and freedom across three cultural traditions. Portuguese fados, Ashkenazi Klezmer bands, Black gospels and quadrilles move through *Nonsectarian Conversations with the Dead.* In *White Chocolate,* after disdaining association with "Niggers all along the tracks," Mama sings the "Toreadors Song" from Bizet's *Carmen,* as if offering proof of her social status. Her daughter Mickey counters with the "Toreadors Song" from *Carmen Jones,* the 1954 musical film starring Dorothy Dandridge and Harry Belafonte that reimagined the Bizet opera through a contemporary Black lens. Carlos's Black folk know opera, film, as well as "ragtime and that low-count Bessie Smith."[35]

Theatrical jazz steadfastly resists stereotypes and racism, sometimes by exposing them. In early work, Carlos tackles white supremacy straight on—

This holiday where you celebrate
The freedom
Of the nation is an affront
To those who were brought involuntarily
To this place
And to all who
Were here
When you came searching
For freedom
Establishing your name
With our blood
Your freedom and the righteousness of it
Niggers of Europe
Each of you knowing the wrongfulness of slavery
For yourselves
Leaving the chains to separate us
From our Gods
No need for us
To dance at this party.[36]

Another direct confrontation with racism is found in *Teenytown* when Carlos and her Thought Music collaborators, Robbie McCauley and Jessica Hagedorn, challenge racism and sexism in the film industry ("Hollywood is too hard without a white man. The world's a bitch without a Jack not a Joe. A Joe, good or not, would never do. There is still no cure for a nigger gone bad with kisses."[37]), confront the appropriation of rhythm and blues ("who wrote the song / who gets the credit"[38]), and expose global racism ("Paris is a stinking racist town / Argentinians refuse to serve / us steaks we don't even want—"[39]). *White Chocolate for My Father* gets its name from Carlos's understanding of the decimation of Black people in the United States. The play ends with Deola, the African ancestor, warning, "When this shit gets to 1979 Im gonna board a ship the fuck out of here. Niggers will be trying to get polite with these white dogs. I remember, I shoot this shit cause I remember I still feel the pain in my head. You gonna learn how to, live with them and talk like them and see the world like them. 1979 Im not doin none of this again. Where are your gods who will cry out for?"[40] In her more recent work, the ravages of racism are woven into the everyday fabric of her characters' lives. The performance novel format of *The Pork Chop Wars (a story of mothers)* allows a fullness of detail and bifurcation of narrative perspective where the particularities of Black-

"'WHITE CHOCOLATE' WAS SOMETHING THAT WE HAD BECOME IN THIS PROCESS: WE'RE STILL HERE, BUT WE ARE UNRECOGNIZABLE TO EACH OTHER. WE DON'T KNOW WHAT TRIBES WE COME FROM, WHO THE FATHER IS, WHO THE SPIRITS ARE THAT WE'RE LOOKING AT."*

—LAURIE CARLOS

* *White Chocolate for My Father*, 3.

ness can radiate. Through first-, second-, and third-person narration, through the details of scene, summary, and description, and through an epic sweep of memory in *The Pork Chop Wars (a story of mothers),* Carlos is able to narrate/enact the richness of her character's lives in the specifics of food, music, clothing, familial relations, and class concerns; in this way, both race and racism are implicit.

On this street in Memphis slipped the best colored folks in and out of their gracious dwellings, tidy, respectable and gently used /
[. . .]
Way back imperatives of roughness were waved away with lace, with gentility / They scrubbed and washed with purpose all the time daily / Nothing from the street absorbed the rugs nothing, no dust, or muddy satin shoes / Under the glass cut lights even in French no hair on fire made entrance here /

The best pomades cooled and dressed these diverse torrents of ribboned controversy / Everyone had their own comb and brushed their secrets to be burned in the plate so the birds would not get them / Just sweet music / Only the sweetest music was ever played on her piano / No RagTime / None of that in here / Not in this house she whispered / No RagTime in here, no, no, no, no Le Jazz Hot, no / The ongoing interrogation of Boleros continued at every gathering of invited guests /

Only the best people ever associated with this family here in the new south of colored entrepreneurs / The family that had come up from Mississippi wood laid a foundation solidly into the future / First there were the general stores owned by her uncle, her father and later by her twin broths and firs cousin / The very best funeral parlors to serve any clientele in Memphis Tennessee enjoined their sterling reputation / All details were executed with distinction by a skilled and well trained staff / Nothing got past em / Taking notice of hair pins / emerald broaches / leather brad belts / stockings /
Watches / Hats important at all times no matter where you are on the ladder of life / Hats were gonna tell it all°

° Laurie Carlos, "The Pork Chop Wars" (unpublished manuscript, draft 1, 2006), 5.

Ẹgbẹ́   **Ẹgbẹ́**   **Ẹgbẹ́**   **Ẹgbẹ́**

Carlos graduated from New York High School for the Performing Arts in 1967 and began taking classes with Lloyd Richards at the Negro Ensemble Company in 1968. In the evenings, she worked with Mobilization for Youth (MFY), a city-run job corps program for teenagers (1958–70) that was part of President Johnson's War on Poverty. MFY offered actor training and filmmaking, along with training in social justice strategies. Carlos was learning new models for theatre through MFY, which was becoming an important venue for the development of new U.S. playwrights. At the NEC, she worked as an usher, and at the front of the house handing out programs. It was through the NEC that she met her fast friend Robbie McCauley, laying the foundation for a long-standing bond. They performed together in *for colored girls,* founded the revolutionary performance art company Thought Music with Jessica Hagedorn, worked together at Penumbra Theatre, and have maintained almost daily conversations for decades.

Kathi Gagnon, another of Carlos's close friends, was an artistic elder to many in the Minneapolis–St. Paul community during the 1980s and 1990s. Her influence extended to Austin when she came to St. Edward's University to perform the role of Lena Younger in *A Raisin in the Sun.* Her death from cancer left us stunned. She was Carlos's dear friend, driving Carlos on ever-eventful shopping trips, chatting like a blood sister about national politics, bickering in that well-worn way that longtime friends take comfort in, and sharing many artistic projects. They worked together on stage in Shay Youngblood's *Talking Bones* at Penumbra with Carlos in the role of Baybay and Gagnon playing Ruth. Carlos's respect for Marion Lake and

Figure 19. Lou Bellamy, Laurie Carlos, and Kathryn Coram Gagnon in *Talking Bones* at Penumbra Theatre. The 1994 Penumbra Theatre world premiere of Shay Youngblood's *Talking Bones* was directed by Robbie McCauley, with set design by Seitu Jones. Left to right: Bellamy as Mr. Fine, Carlos as Baybay, and her close friend Gagnon as Ruth. Daniel Alexander Jones played Oz in this production.

for their friendship is evidenced in the play for which Lake is named—"Marion's Terrible Time of Joy." Carlos says the stories of the play are Lake's stories. This play marks a significant departure for Carlos as she explores work outside of her child's voice and begins to imagine joy. Carlos and Lake lived in the same New York apartment building, raised their children together, and Lake created in Carlos "the ability to see the lessons in the hard times."[41]

McCauley, Gagnon, and Lake are among Carlos's most longstanding and intimate *ẹgbẹ́* members. She creates with them a stability, care, and respect that is in sharp contrast to the adult relationships found in her texts. These artistic and personal commitments are at the core of a theatrical jazz *ẹgbẹ́*.

The attention Carlos gives to food preparation reflects her distinctive brand of making *ẹgbẹ́*. Her written and performance work seems enveloped by food, and all the life-giving potential that it carries. Some of her titles—*White Chocolate for My Father; The Cooking Show and How the Monkey Dances; Persimmon Peel; If the Butter Burns, It Ain't Biscuits; The Pork Chop Wars (a story of mothers)*—reveal her penchant for the rich textures of the culinary arts. In *The Cooking Show,* while Monkey cooks for the audience, these stage directions are given: "*The recipe is a modification, an improvement, a memory without guilt. The* MONKEY *chews cilantro and hums. A way to the first memory. In the kitchen the monkey sings.*"[42] The stage directions suggest how food functions as sustenance for the body and for the spirit as Carlos likens the preparation of food to the exploration of personal history, a history that can be changed as needed without guilt. Recipes are for cooking and for ordering one's life.

In an early draft of the performance novel, *The Pork Chop Wars (a story of mothers)*, Carlos begins with

> They no longer desired to chew on sticks, crumble bones, mash leaves under tongues, fill cheeks with plum pits, and grind the rinds between to soften / They prepared for her arrival sucking back salted spit, skin off from lips, sugar culled outta gums swishing roasted parts leaking onto the throat / They were always preparing for her arrival /[43]

Later, the chorus of voices makes clear the relationship between careful cooking and the multiple life-sustaining properties of food when they say,

> So in this turn she chose to lean on disasters / while they washed potatoes to
>   boil for hours, soaked thyme in lemon juice, swallowed, laced claret in ber-
>   ries swallowed with black pepper /
> Ooooooooweee
> Make it taste like what it is /
> Some oyster, some corn cakes, stuffed fish /
> Make it taste like what it is / A thing that tastes like what's suppose to /
> That's how it has to be / They eat whatever they want to / somebody got to get
>   what they want to taste / Eat up / That's how it has got to be / Eat all you can

and leave nothing for the rest of em / Freedom does not look back for who
is eating nothing.[44]

One's freedom is bound to the very skill of the cook, for food—properly prepared
food—is required for physical and psychic survival.

In *The Cooking Show and How the Monkey Dances,* Carlos engulfs the audience in the preparation of food, by converting the space into her own kitchen
where she prepares a meal throughout the performance then offers it up to the
audience at the close of the show. I have seen two versions of this work, and while
both retain the same basic shape, the specific content of each is drawn from different moments in Carlos's family life and from current world events. As with any
good cook, she invents as she goes. The cooking itself is a communion with the
audience, a supplication, as Monkey the cook offers her lineage to the Divine for
acknowledgment:

> Donna Sears / Tedra / Ellia   Rodriquez / Cynthia   Ann   Scott / Janice
> Valentine / George   Johnson / Ellen   Woodlon / Deborah   Aikins /   Gladys
> Leon / Barbara Tepper /
>   These names are prayers /
>   Gentle ingredients / short recipes[45]

After this grace of sorts is said, the cooking begins:

> Welcome to my kitchen world where the poems start sometime and all the prob-
> lems get an airing and the possibility of dream walking with a casual visitor is
> dependent on how many of us eat garlic raw. And if you are here it's 'cause you
> want to be. Not like white boys want to just be any damn where they think it's all
> going on. But more like a true feeling for leaning long into the arms of a sister or
> a stranger who smells like wells of sadness sometime. Nothing academic to back
> up the story. Nothing to prove. No way to prove it. This is where the memory of
> smell and furious tasting goes on. Don't try to write down the recipe. Listen to
> where you are going. This is not like stealing the sheet music off the stand after
> the colored composer has finished the gig.
>   Recipe now: Chickpea salad, oh, yeah.[46]

The opening to the performance pulls spirit, politics, Black referents, history,
homeplace, and cuisine all together, thereby suggesting that each is necessary and
interdependent. Understanding the racialized history of the appropriation of Black
music is as vital as the components for a chickpea salad; what you eat predicts how
fully you can dream; the spiritual ritual of praying is sister to active listening. For
Carlos, food preparation is anything but casual, and its potency makes its way very
directly into much of her work. Food is specific, and engagement with it is intense
and visceral.

Carlos's father, Walter T. Smith, was a musician and a cook who, as she puts it, "evolved into a chef." Carlos says, "I think I cook because of him."[47] This may be true in many ways. When he left the home, the four-year-old Carlos prepared the meals for her mother and younger sister. She remembers standing on a milk crate to reach the stove so she could prepare breakfast or dinner. It is also true that her father's skill as a cook was passed along to Carlos, though she has developed her own very particular way with food. Carlos's cooking demonstrates a tender relationship between her, the ingredients, and, importantly, those who will receive the meal:

> I was a watcher . . . I learned how to cook things, not with my own point of view, with the aesthetics that the person who ran the kitchen cooked it. Tomorrow is the second anniversary of my mom's passing[48] and I'm going to make chili her way. I've always learned how to make the food how the person in the room wanted to experience the food. *I* put chorizo in chili along with ground beef. My stepmom would not do that, and my mother Mildred[49] would never cook chili. *She* would get it out of the can.

> If you made black-eyed peas for my father, they had to have smoked ham hocks. If you made meatloaf, it had to have boiled eggs on the inside. Things I wouldn't do because they are not my taste. My grandfather loved succotash, corn, tomatoes, okra. I don't eat okra. I learned to cook without tasting. I would make gefilte fish without tasting it. I would make it, and they would can it and have it all winter.[50]

Carlos's attention to the recipient of her meals is a special brand of caretaking. Her attentive watching made her a much loved cook whose many meals for a Late Nite Series reception, or an impromptu gathering of women from the Austin Project, are lessons in the precise selection of ingredients and the expert presentation of the food. Special platters and serving utensils, picked flowers standing in a vase, a garnished tray of bright vegetables, just the right table cloth. These are the details that establish food as a culturally specific ritually driven art form. Food is at once history, identity, place, community, and security.

During one of Laurie's conversations in the Performance as Public Practice graduate program in the Department of Theatre and Dance at the University of Texas, she talked about which foods can be served together, and which cannot. She spoke of rye bread and mustard, definitely not mayonnaise. The rye and the mustard work together because of the specific peoples and histories attached to each. You can't have mayo because of the egg and that wouldn't be
Kosher. She went on about which spices cannot touch which meats because of the wars people waged that were related to each condiment and each animal. Laurie told us about the trade routes that created specific relations that then led to distinctive

dishes. The history of food is shaped by human desire, travel, and commerce. To be a cook, she said without saying it, meant carrying all of that information. She spoke with such knowing, such passion. This is the way I had seen her in rehearsal, as if she was conjuring some ancient memories, as if she was steeped
in nostalgia for just the right exhalation of breath or the perfect point of a finger, as if food carried secrets that humans must master.

LAURIE'S SURVIVAL RECIPES

The most important recipe is rendering fat. We've forgotten the process. We don't eat lard and we don't know about rendering fat. That's what people used to do. Heat it until all the fat came out. And you could use it to make biscuits and everything. That's an important recipe that we have forgotten how to do.

The other is baking bones. You put them in the oven and bake them all down. So that all the marrow is cooked through, then opening up those bones, then taking the marrow. Then you crush the bones. What I don't remember is what the bones are used for after that. What I do remember is that people used them for plastering their house. Add a little liquid and you use the bones to fill up holes.

I've been thinking about these recipes.

Baking bones, rendering fat, and making fish stock. Our grandparents all had chicken stock and fish stock. Most people ate fish heads. But you took those bones and filleted something, like the whiting, you take the little parts of that and put that in the pot, then you take a sieve and mash them all the way through, what you get is bones and you get the skin. People held on to fish heads and stuff, and opened them up and put them in that stock. Fish head soup. You hear a lot about it now, but I'm not sure who does it from scratch any more. Those recipes are major to survival. People talk about the chitlins, these recipes were basic to survival and, in a lot of cases, basic to prayer. Because you would kill the animal you had ritual with. People drank the blood, made blood sausage, people kept feathers—and people are not having that relationship any more. You are not having a relationship with the action of praying, with thanking the food you are about to eat. And that gelatin stuff, the bones being mashed is part of how you created pigment. You would mix other things in with those bones, so when you got ready to do something like paint, this was part of the ingredient. All of this had to do with how people made prayer and what their relationship to God was.

I wanted to talk about good fancy food. But it just doesn't have any place right now. Part of the action of having a kitchen and household and a farm plantation was food to escape with, food to travel with, was how you gathered bones and got the marrow. Some people didn't get any meat except in the marrow of the bone. But did you know where that comes from, eating the marrow and eating the gristle? This is all very instinctual, very basic to being human. The fact that people want you to eat a piece of chicken without no skin and it's crazy. And they take the bones. They are crazy. And they wonder why people are sick all the time.

Bill Moyers* talked about people trying to keep up with the chicken on the conveyer belt. Chicken comes up and you have to cut off the breasts because that's your section. People of course lose fingers, and have problems with their wrists. Shoulders get dislodged, elbows freeze up that's because they are not doing anything that has to do with the life force of those animals. People get sick. Down in the ground sick. It violates who they are. Then we go buy 12 chicken wings. And we are complicit in this.

That's another reason why I began to think about the rendering of fat. I showed you these two places [on the tour in 2003]—a chicken market on Pitts St. and a chicken market on 13th St. And there are only two of those poultry markets all over the Lower East Side. You asked me about those knives and I start thinking about the smell, and my father had a large saw and a little saw so that you could saw the bones. When you asked me that question, all the smells came up. These smells are not very different than the smells of Jamaica Queens right now, the smells of certain parts of Brooklyn that have large populations of Blacks and Jews—and kosher, the animals have been slaughtered a certain way. You used to be able to go to these poultry markets on Saturday night mostly. They had them in Chinatown, I remember, you could buy a pound of chicken feet. After Shabbat you could buy chicken necks, you could buy backs. They would put it on the side, and nobody who was not a Jew could take those eggs and you could put it in the pot with the chicken to make the dumplings. The Chinese used to take that egg and put it in a bowl and put hot water over it. This is where you get egg drop soup. You put some noodles and you get egg drop soup. Those markets existed, and they are coming back because of the Hillel kosher connection. I mention that because the smell of where you lived was so deeply connected with how meat and poultry and fish came into your neighborhood. I told you I'm revising *The Pork Chop Wars,* but that line "They no longer sucked on bones"—that is a key to a big part of the story. In that is also, the rendering of fat is done by every single culture that eats meat. Ghee is a rendering of the fat from the butter. So there is some form of it in every single culture.

When you slaughter the animals, you've got to take that fat and put it in a pot, no water, and you've got to cook that down. What you get when you do that is you get lard, you get personal hair care products, you get body cream, you get a way to continue to cook other foods. You get something to make soap with, but I don't remember all the recipes. There is that great big pan that people put turkey in now. You put the bones in that pan or you take the bones and put them in the fire and cook them just like that in the fire and you take that marrow out and I do remember seeing the marrow up in the bone. This is a special thing. Take a thing that looks like a knife, that was a scooper about a foot long and you move all the marrow onto a surface and it gets eaten or they give you some. I do know in the Philippines they take that marrow and mix it up with rice. Those are the recipes I'm going to give you.

I think part of it too is when we're talking about the cultural things that bind us, things we all share, we never talk about this anymore. Because we are not doing it

* On the blog *Bill Moyers Journal,* there was much discussion of worker abuses in the poultry industry. Moyers documented these abuses, and supported the creation of the controversial documentary *Mississippi Chicken,* directed by John Fiege (2007).

any more. The Native Americans did this too with the bones of the bison. You used the skin, the hair, the teeth, you used the bone, you crushed the bone. You used the dung, so there's something about forgetting ourselves because we don't connect in that way anymore which brings us back to why in the hell does anybody do theatre except that we are all trying to commit to a common story in a public place and part of the issue for all of us is that there has always been only one of the stories which is why they have to tell it over and over again so they have to be sure they don't tell the truth about any of it they need to believe it as much as they need to believe it. We've gone along with it for a long time and at the same time we have to tell our stories. The reason that has been blocked so hard at the point our stories get told, their story relinquishes validity. This war in Iraq, it is harder to maintain the lie. So our story gets out anyway. Which is why we all go to the theatre. It has become our campfire again. I wish they would tell us about some chicken bones with some marrow. That's the new business we need to be in. Make some whole cakes with some cuchifrito and some beef marrow and a spoon. Cuchifrito, pork rinds—that happens because you rendered all the fat and what is left is the skin. Pigtails and all that stuff. That's why people buy the pork skin, there's something that reminds them. They know it ain't no good for them but they eat it anyway. There's nothing as good as pork rind and some coffee. Boiled coffee, pork skin and a piece of bread. That's a wonderful smell. In Texas they got the one that's hard on outside and soft on the inside, they call it crackling, and Mexicans have cuchifrito. They had a big cuchifrito place on Delancey St. They opened it in the '50s. The Jews went crazy. It was only about 3 blocks away from the poultry market. There was a big Puerto Rican migration. They opened that cuchifrito place and the people went crazy. There was a line for the pork tail, blood sausage and ox tongue and it would sit in the window. The smell would get you before you turned the corner on Clinton Street headed toward Avenue A, between Clinton and Avenue A on Delancey and that upset the Jews over there so bad, and so the Jews who lived upstairs had to move out that building. The housing then became Puerto Rican and Chinese, and lot of that had to do with the fact that that cuchifrito place opened up down there.

That's why we get up and go to different cities. There are places in the world, you can't get certain things unless you are in those cities. That's why the Europeans got up and left. They have no pepper, no cloves, no turmeric, I don't think they had cinnamon. They get up and go get something for their meat. They didn't have nothing. Everybody else had what they needed. As soon as they found out they could get up and find tomato, they got out of there. They didn't have corn or pumpkin or squash. They had to leave. They been trying to claim the silk road the spice road ever since. They didn't have palm oil, they didn't have coconut. I don't know, did they have nutmeg? I don't think so.[†]

[†] Laurie Carlos, phone interview with author, June 16, 2008.

Carlos's work is elemental. Breath and food are compulsory.

Gender Queer   Gender Queer   Gender Queer

Queer appears in Carlos's theatrical jazz through confrontations with gender expectations.

GENDER IS LOST TO GIVE WAY FOR
THE TELLING OF EACH SPIRIT STORY.*

—LAURIE CARLOS

* "Feathers at the Flame, Next Dance"
(unpublished manuscript, 5th draft, May 25,
1998), 2.

WARRIOR WOMAN LIKE I AM. WILLING
TO STAND STILL IN THE STORM ON THE
MOUNTAIN.*

—DANIEL ALEXANDER JONES, AS GLENA

* "Feathers at the Flame, Next Dance"
(unpublished manuscript, 5th draft, May 25,
1998), 17.

In *An Organdy Falsetto*, Cry—one-third of an all-girl band—says, "She was my man. My steady thought till I was eleven when some one told us kissing like that was wrong and tragic."[51] Cry tackles constraints on friendship, comfort, eros, and gender expression. In this way Carlos's work is queer in its acknowledgment of sexual *and* gender transgressions. She raises the question—"who qualifies for a kiss?"[52]

The women and men in her work are often in contentious relationships full of resentment, due, in part, to gendered prohibitions and disappointments. Hers are not tender love stories. They are pacts made for safety, power, or convenience. Men abusing women with too much or no sex, women full of disdain and sorrow.

If she wanted some part of him he would measure the time to be sure she was left dry / Too much noise for a decent woman to make with a man / There were woman who he loved to listen to when the deal was good / When he had bargained hard with whiskey and cash / Women who would hum, burn, or bark just for him as requested as bargained for / This wife of his didn't listen to his requirements / She leaked her unskilled sonatas unrestrained and this was not expected from her when they married°

° Laurie Carlos, "The Pork Chop Wars" (unpublished manuscript, 1st draft, 2006), 4.

Fine all my ladies are fine. Well packaged Good clothes. Show stoppers. All fine and eager to please. I need certain kinds of things sometime. Special things, only very special type ladies can give. And only the finest looking ladies are even considered. What it look like? That's what I want to know. Cause what it look like reflects on what I look like. Yeah damn right its vain. I like mirrors and I like ladies who like mirrors I do em in mirrors. I get into my tongue up against up against it in mirrors. I like

looking at myself. I am fine. Well packaged.
Good clothes. Show stopper. I have photos of
ladies who have been able to keep my interest
for however long they keep my interest. The
pictures with their long legs open smiling with
their less than perfect breast. And no matter
how fine they are naked they all have less
than perfect tits. That's why I will never
stop renting Vanessa del Rio. I always run
her on the VCR and make all my ladies watch.
Then come the photos I keep them so the way I
have them is different than loving
something. I got the pussy it's in my drawer
and I take it out when I want it and I don't
have to remember a thing or smell them or
hear them all fine and eager to please.°

° Laurie Carlos, "An Organdy Falsetto" (unpublished manuscript, 1985), 7.

Throughout *White Chocolate,* the girls imagine relationships laced with the heteronormative expectations they saw around them, even as those socially sanctioned relationships were rife with pain. The radio is Lore's lover, full of sad or mocking love songs—"Kisses Sweeter than Wine," "Love and Marriage," "Why Do Fools Fall in Love?," "Mama, He Treats Your Daughter Mean." The absent father of the play, who sometimes calls and delivers "chocolate kisses" to Tiny via the phone, creates a longing for male connection. Tony fantasizes, "The way I want to marry is in a big yellow dress with pretzels and my hair in bobby pins new shoes & a lot of cake & beer ahhh. My nose will point down."[53] The down-turned nose suggests a stylized image of superiority from a magazine that serves—along with the dress, the hair, and the cake—to stand in for a perfect marriage that Tony, Tiny, and Lore never saw at home with their mother Mickey.

I'm just a girl the only one
I made my mind up to have you.
Don't care what nobody say
And I ain't got no daddy
Got lipstick these eyes
Put my sneakers in the garbage
Just for you.
Don't care what nobody say.
I'm just a girl the
Only one

I made my mind up to have
You°

° Laurie Carlos, "Nonsectarian Conversations with the Dead" (unpublished manuscript, 1985),
11.

Lore's relationship fantasy does not fix on the spectacle of the wedding but reveals her childlike understandings of what marriage is:

> I told her see John O'Conner that's a boy in my class, he's in the third grade too. He asked me at the monkey bars to marry him. To be a bride with him. His father was a teacher at our school P.S. 188. And John's father and his sister were Irish. His mother was Irish too but she was dead so John and his sister came to school with their daddy. We gonna marry and have Chinese children. See he said I am pink and you are brown that makes yellow Chinese! . . . The fourth grade John went to a private Catholic school. His father said he would never come to 188 again. We laughed in celebration that day, I was happy, I was singing.
>
> There were Chinese apples. Chinese checkers. Chinese children![54]

It is telling that the journey into marriage begins at the monkey bars, evoking the mask of playfulness worn by the monkey, a common image for Carlos, coerced into entertainment. Marriage, then, is a show concealing the imbalanced power dynamics beneath. Her fantasy also pulls in all the race, class, and gender codes that serve to support the corrosiveness of patriarchy.

I'm a man. A full grown man. A natural man. When I make Love to a woman ain't that a man. M.A.N. Man. Oh child I'm a full grown hurt so good man.°

° Laurie Carlos, "An Organdy Falsetto" (unpublished manuscript, 1985), 5.

Love and Joy   Love and Joy   Love and Joy

"Marion's Terrible Time of Joy" is a significant departure for Carlos from much of her previous work. Although Carlos cites *The Pork Chop Wars (a story of mothers)* (2006) as the move away from her "little girl voice"—and by the time *The Pork Chop Wars (a story of mothers)* appears, the vexed character Monkey has gone from her work—it is earlier, in "Marion's Terrible Time of Joy" (2003) where the child's pain is not riding the top of the story. In the company of the women of "Marion's Terrible Time of Joy," Monkey/Laurie can open to an adult self-love. "Marion's Terrible Time of Joy" retains some of the autobiographical content, the attention to breath and food, and the spiraling storytelling of earlier work, but the river is now introduced as a dominant image and spiritual animator.

MONKEY

What do you dream at the river / Do the dances flow from this place? /

ANANYA

I wade and remember / The temples are behind us /

MONKEY

The regrets are all I know now / The inability to shake regret is all I know standing here at the river / I want new clothes / A disguise / a revealing look that gives comfort / New choices

ANANYA

Changing your clothes won't give you peace or bring you back time or cleanse regret / (Ananya hums)

MONKEY

I've known / I know / I have always known this / Every day for hours at a time I dig into the wounds of it / If when we hear the music we could know the emptiness of the melody at the first note / So much regret / He was dead all that time / (Oliver Lake's horn blows Ananya finds it and gestures) Which river is this?

ANANYA

My river /

MONKEY

If the sea could take me home /

ANANYA

If winds were blue in this dream /

MONKEY

If all of it would just go up /

ANANYA

If living forced some good /

MONKEY

If goodness were all there is / °

° Laurie Carlos, "Marion's Terrible Time of Joy" (unpublished manuscript, 2007), 3.

Throughout the text, as the characters ask about the river, deeper moments of personal truths are revealed. When Ananya asks Monkey "When did you find your river?," Monkey shares a story of the difficult relationship with her daughter and the bond between herself and Marion. Monkey concludes this lengthy passage with "The river over flows . . . River running fast and away to the shore." [55] This flooding strips away and replenishes. When a river exceeds the bounds of its banks, it can uproot trees, wash away homes, and reorganize the landscape, leaving layers of fertilizing silt behind. Populations along the Nile relied on annual flooding to help strengthen the soil for the next planting season.[56] The river of "Marion's Terrible Time of Joy" allows the women to pour forth the challenges they face with their children, and the river is a palliative to these struggles. After one such pouring forth, Monkey plays "Suzanne" on the jukebox—"Suzanne takes you down to the river / she has been there / she has seen things"—and the stage directions instruct, "she hums 'Suzanne' and Nina[Simone]'s version clears the night." [57] The river, the women's weeping, the subsequent path to healing, create a significant transition as Marion then begins to speak of love.

LAURIE'S LINEAGE°

Laurie . . .

works with Dianne McIntyre

originates the role of the lady in blue in Ntozake Shange's *for colored girls*

directs reading of Aishah Rahman's *Mojo and the Sayso* with Daniel Alexander Jones as Blood at Brown University

creates Thought Music with Robbie McCauley and Jessica Hagedorn

creates *Teenytown* with Robbie McCauley and Jessica Hagedorn

directs *Alaskan Heat Blue Dot* with Florinda Bryant, Zell Miller III, Emily Cicchini, Richard Smith, and Omi Osun Joni L. Jones at Hyde Park Theatre (HPT)

directs Sharon Bridgforth's *blood pudding* with Florinda Bryant, Zell Miller III, Djola Branner, Renita Martin, and Stacey Robinson for HPT

directs Djola Branner's *Mighty Real* at Pillsbury House

directs Daniel Alexander Jones's *Clayangels* with Daniel Alexander Jones and Todd Jones, Kim Koym as set designer, Grisha Coleman as composer, Omi Osun Joni L. Jones as dramaturg at New World Theatre; later Sonja Perryman as production assistant at HPT

directs Sharon Bridgforth's *con flama* with Florinda Bryant, Ana Perea, Zell Miller III, Sonja Parks, Leilah Stewart set designer, Omi Osun Joni L. Jones as dramaturg for HPT; later with Ambersunshower Smith, Djola Branner, Aimee Bryant, Mankwe Ndosi, Sonja Parks, and Seitu Jones as set designer for Penumbra

directs Renita Martin's *Five Bottles in a Six Pack* at Cherry Lane Theatre and Jumpstart Theatre with Renita, and Jane Wang on bass

writes *The Cooking Show & How the Monkey Dances*

writes *White Chocolate for My Father*

writes *An Organdy Falsetto*

writes *Persimmon Peel*

writes *Nonsectarian Conversations with the Dead*

becomes a company member of Urban Bush Women

serves as Guest Artist for the Austin Project 2002–9 (except 2008 when flooded Amtrak lines prevented her from getting to Austin)

co-directs *The Pork Chop Wars* with Deborah Artman, with Florinda Bryant, Courtney Morris, Bianca Flores, Lisa L. Moore, Renita Martin, Virginia Grise, Omi Osun Joni L. Jones, and Rene Ford, with Sharon Bridgforth as dramaturg

directs Florinda Bryant's *Half-Breed Southern Fried (check one)* with Bryant, Monique Cortez, Jaclyn Pryor, Lara Rios, Terrence Stith the DJ, and Sharon Bridgforth as dramaturg

mentors Djola Branner, Carl Hancock Rux, Grisha Coleman, Erik Ehn, Daniel Alexander Jones, Sonja Parks, Ana Perea, Cynthia Oliver, Sharon Bridgforth

° This partial listing of events, productions, and publications gives a sense of the interconnections among theatrical jazz artists. See Carlos's excerpted CV (Appendix I) for production details.

nurtures emerging artists Virginia Grise, Zell Miller III, Florinda Bryant, E. G.
Bailey, Kim Thompson, Deborah Asiimwe

directs Rebecca Rice's work

directs Luis Alfaro's *Straight as a Line* with Kathryn Coram Gagnon, Joe Wilson
Jr.

hosts the Austin Project Performance Company with Florinda Bryant, Amanda
Johnston, Kristen Gerhard, and Leigh Gaymon-Jones for Late Nite

hosts Kim Thompson and Annelize Machado for Late Nite

writes *Marion's Terrible Time of Joy*

devises *Map Lite* with Cynthia Oliver at a residency at the University of Illinois,
Urbana–Champagne

performs in Erik Ehn's *Maria Kizito*

directs Deborah Asiimwe's work at CalArts

performs *If the Butter Burns, It Ain't Biscuits* for Warfield Center / tAP

performs *Washed* for Warfield Center / tAP

directs *Venus* by Suzan-Lori Parks at Arizona State University

directs Virginia Grise's *blu* at Company of Angels in Los Angeles

Daniel Alexander Jones

B. FEBRUARY 9, 1970
SPRINGFIELD, MASSACHUSETTS

I make theatre to create a ritualized context
for the experience of radical empathy.
—Daniel Alexander Jones[1]

The power of the female is
   a force of nature embraced by those who are courageous enough to do so.
     The Ìyámi create and protect.
       They laugh loudly in the certainty of their own strength.

*I attended a double bill of performances under the title "Revolutionary Love" at Frontera@Hyde Park Theatre in 1995—*Earthbirths, Jazz, and Raven's Wings, *written and directed by Daniel Alexander Jones, and* Black Power Barbie in Hotel de Dream, *written by Shay Youngblood and directed by Daniel. These works included characters, themes, and artistic choices I had not experienced through a Black worldview. Then in 1996 I returned to Frontera to see* Blood:Shock:Boogie,*
written and performed by Daniel. When Daniel entered the space clad only in a silver lamé cloth draped sensually over his nude body, his hair a perfect 1920s coiffure with a black curl teasing around his cheek and his voice a torch singer's blend of whiskey and vibrato—all the contradictions and juxtapositions of time, place, gender, sexuality living together on that stage—I was struck. I was uneasy and mesmerized, drawn into this world of danger. No easy answers here. Instantly, order was reinvented. There was something so electric about this work. It felt like I was watching the making of the work on the spot, not the repetition of rehearsed choices. There was something in the sweat and the immediacy, in the deep responsiveness between the performers in the ensemble works, in the directness and spontaneity of the solo work, and in the attention to details and skill in everything that left me rather stunned. I sat in the anonymous position of an audience member, isolated from the people around me, and I wanted to talk back to the performance. "What did you just say?! What do you mean putting that clumsy, smelly, tenderness up there on that stage? Oh no you didn't!" As I experienced this work, I knew it was somehow wrapped up in my own freedom. Something about my own life was at stake as these courageous artists challenged me to see race and gender and sexuality with more roads than I dared believe were possible.*

Figure 20. Daniel Alexander Jones gesturing in *The Book of Daniel 35:1* at allgo. He is moving through the environmental space he created for the performance in 2005 as presented at allgo, the Texas statewide queer people of color organization based in Austin. The abstract gesture, the unique relationship with the audience, the reimagining of space are hallmarks of theatrical jazz. Photo by Bret Brookshire.

Figure 21. Daniel Alexander Jones (right) and Daniel Dodd Ellis in *Blood:Shock:Boogie* at Frontera@Hyde Park Theatre (1996). They are in the dressing room preparing for a performance. An image of Josephine Baker looks on from the mirror. Photo by Bret Brookshire.

DANIEL ALEXANDER JONES was raised in Springfield, Massachusetts, in the early 1970s. At this time Springfield still reflected the working-class Democratic bent of the parents in the neighborhood, even while much of the rest of the country was moving toward the self-centered individualism of the '80s. Springfield was home to a number of progressive thinkers who believed that courage and justice and activism were necessary ingredients for a good life. It was a place where community was manifest in the way people voted and in the way adults tended to the children, who played in the streets past sundown. Within this neighborhood, Daniel described his house as a "kind of crossroads."[2] He explains that, growing up, "Our house was the place on the street everybody came to. There were all these other houses, but in summers at seven o'clock at night, all the kids would be in our house. And I think it had to do partly with my mom being just the kind of person that let everybody come and play."[3]

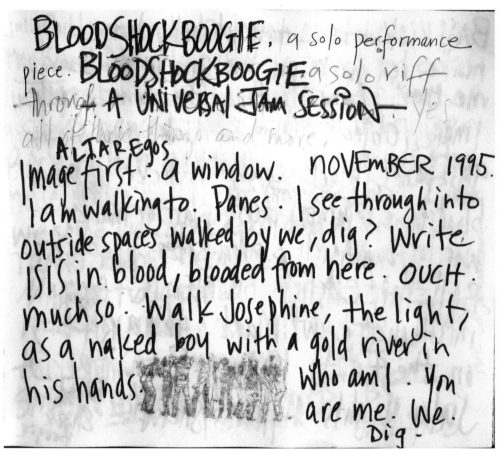

Figure 22. Daniel Alexander Jones's notes for *Blood:Shock:Boogie.* Jones often creates detailed visual conversations in conjunction with his performances. Here he provides a glimpse into the interior landscape of *Blood:Shock:Boogie,* 1996. Photo by Daniel Alexander Jones.

Jones's mother, Georgina Leslie Jones, is a white woman whose people were working-class Scottish immigrants and WASP New England farmers. As a young woman, Georgina headed the Tiny Tots preschool program at the Springfield Girl's Club, which her mother, Bernice Lucille Gould Leslie, had run for many years. Arthur Leroy Jones, a Black youth worker with the Springfield Boy's Club, was hired by Bernice to coordinate the boys' activities after the Girl's Club moved to a new location that included room for a boy's division. Arthur and Georgina had worked together at the Girl's Club for a few years before Arthur approached Bernice to ask her permission and blessing for their marriage. Bernice had long respected Arthur, and she greeted him with a New England formality and warmth that left an indelible mark on Jones. Jones writes with deep affection of his beloved Bunny, as Bernice Leslie was known, in *The Book of Daniel: jazz rite in lecture format* and in the eulogy he wrote for her in 2003—"Quietly, you encouraged me to cross the boundaries others had set . . . as you yourself had done."[4] Georgina and Arthur had two children, Daniel and Todd, who tell some of the life of their neighborhood in the jointly written *Clayangels.* Arthur's brother Gus, who appears from time to time as a figure in Jones's work, was the family activist whose ideas generated many memorable family dialogues. Mr. Uncle of *Earthbirths,* a refashioned Gus, is identified in the opening stage directions as Witness, and throughout the play tells the family history and the neighborhood horrors.

(Lights on Harper preparing pots of greens at the kitchen table. There are collards piled high, in varying states of preparation. Harper pauses from chopping and washing to serve already cooked greens to Mr. Uncle and Captain, who sit at the table. Mr. Uncle speaks in a percussive, self-assured style. He eats while he talks.)

MR. UNCLE
Most people you see with our name come out of South Carolina
Were all owned by one master
Guy was a big landlord
You know?
In that area
That area
That area's mixed up
With Indians
Who were swal . . .
Who were
What you call in a sense
Swallowed up
That meant
They married blacks
So that's what it is around that area there,
See?

Where'd you learn how to make these greens?

Like you take the Hendersons?
Hendersons
Ricky Henderson?
They're all from that same area
Y'see?
And if you lookit Henderson you see
More of the pronounced Indian
In fact, uh
Look at them sometime
You remember Ricky Henderson?
Yeah, his daughter!

Yeah . . . you know his daughter?
Look at her sometime, you'll see more
Pronounced Indian in her
See?
The African's there of course
It's pronounced
But you can see the Indian's still in there
Down there you also had a lot of
Intermarriage and half-breeding
S'you don't know who's who
SLIDE M (CAPTAIN AND LADY WEDDING)
See but, uh
What else can I tell ya?
What else you wanna know?
That I can dick my mind about
Huh?
What I know about, see?
See
That that that uh
You know about Bubba's son
young
Bubba's son
SLIDE N (WING)
SLIDE O (NOOSE)
SLIDE P (LYNCH TREE)

CAPTAIN. The one that got killed . . . ?

MR. UNCLE. The one that got killed down there
The one that got killed
Over
The tires
You know 'bout that?
Got lynched
Ask Ma about it
she's got . . .

CAPTAIN. You talkin' bout the one got killed down there . . .

MR. UNCLE. Down South . . .
Yeah
Had the
'Bout the
Tires
The guy tried to beat him
Yeah

The guys tried to beat him
Out of his money, out of his money
Out of his tires
See
Out of his car
He went and shot 'em
He went and he shot the three guys
The—the father and the two sons
'N they come and get him
And they lynched him
See he—And Ma was telling me
How she pull
Ah
Pull
Tried to pull his flesh meat out
Out of the tree
And they couldn't
There was nothing else left of him
Little sick back in those days
Hand me another piece of bread°

° Daniel Alexander Jones, "Earthbirths, Jazz, and Raven's Wings" (unpublished manuscript, 1995), 18.

Jones's Springfield was a place where Mrs. Bertoldo shared her marinara sauce with her neighbors, where boarders rented rooms in single-family homes, where Mr. Satiroupolus delivered milk and orange juice and occasionally shared a cup of coffee in Georgina's kitchen, where Rev. J. P. Morgan was pastor at Trinity Baptist Church and Rev. Ifill, then later Rev. Watts, were pastors at Arthur Jones's church home of Bethel A.M.E., where halfway houses were down the street and around the corner, where Dr. and Mrs. Mapp "were of the old school DuBoisian line,"[5] and Mr. Burr of the Iroquois Nation was like a grandfather to Jones in the care and generosity he extended to the entire Jones family.

DANIEL
Miss Vivian

TODD
Miss Lillian

**Daniel and TODD transform into
Miss Lillian and Miss Vivian. Game.**

MISS LILLIAN AND MISS VIVIAN
We like simple things

MISS LILLIAN
Preserved peaches

MISS VIVIAN
Vanilla Ice Cream

MISS LILLIAN AND MISS VIVIAN
Shortbread cookies

MISS LILLIAN
Fine entertainers. Lena Horne.

MISS VIVIAN
Lillian always has borne a strong resemblance to Lena Horne, without the flaws in Lena's figure.

MISS LILLIAN
You're too kind.

MISS VIVIAN
We're quiet people.

MISS LILLIAN
Good people.

MISS VIVIAN
We do have high expectations.

MISS LILLIAN
High standards

MISS VIVIAN
We've been on this street since nineteen forty-five. At one fifty-eight

MISS LILLIAN
And one sixty-two. Vivian's husband worked in the die-cutting factory.

MISS VIVIAN
And Lillian's husband maintained his own building.

MISS LILLIAN
We're both maiden Freedmen from North Carolina.

MISS VIVIAN
We've been on either side of one sixty long enough to see the changes.

MISS LILLIAN
It can be difficult, having standards.
Neither of them came from much.

MISS VIVIAN
Sister.

MISS LILLIAN
It has to be said to put it all in context.

MISS VIVIAN
The wife had opportunity, her father was a musician. And Scottish.

MISS LILLIAN
Her mother, the dear, embodied the social graces.

MISS VIVIAN
Old Massachusetts family. I wouldn't bear to think of what crossed her mind when that Jones boy began to come around.

MISS LILLIAN
It's not that those . . . arrangements can't work.

MISS VIVIAN
Why when we first came to the Hill there was another family like that on the next block up.

MISS LILLIAN
Not our block.

MISS VIVIAN
And they were no bother. Kept to themselves.

MISS LILLIAN
Didn't make a show of it. And their little girls were just as mannered.

MISS LILLIAN AND MISS VIVIAN
But one sixty.

MISS VIVIAN
It was like a revolving door.

MISS LILLIAN
All those different folks. All "peace and free."

MISS VIVIAN
Right next door.

MISS LILLIAN
When it comes down to it, in an arrangement like that it is always the children who suffer.

MISS VIVIAN
Children.

MISS LILLIAN
You can take the "N"-word out of the ghetto, but you can't take the ghetto out of the "N"-word.

MISS VIVIAN
It's going to show up somewhere. In the children.

MISS LILLIAN
The wife was nice enough. Although we had a word for young white ladies who fancied colored men.

MISS VIVIAN
Lillian.

MISS LILLIAN
She didn't know about that Jones family.

MISS LILLIAN AND MISS VIVIAN
We knew.

Daniel and TODD return to Pietà position.

DANIEL
Well in the first place I had asked for a brother and then around my birthday
    mom and dad
said that I was going to get one and they had found out for sure it was coming.
    So they told me and
I got ready for it and everything, cause you have to get ready.
And then
it was supposed to come but they said the um, stork was um, it was late
but I knew he just didn't want to come out yet cause I had talked to him and

so were gonna go in there and make him come out so mom and I

so we took a picture in the backyard right near the flowers. And she went in and
        . . . I went to school cause we still had five days left

because we had had all the snow days but all we had to do practically was color
        and start times tables and

Then it was flag day and Mrs. Finn had us coloring some flags

and I had already told Shannon and Porfirio that I was going to get a brother and
        Porfirio said something but he was puerto rican and me and Shannon were
        teaching him english but

he

still

didn't make sense sometimes and Shannon said was he gonna look like me

cause I was half and half

and she didn't know which half,

and you know the eyes, and I said I didn't know, and I wasn't gonna tell them
        anyway

and so the principal came in and started talking to Mrs. Finn

so I knew it was time and he came over

and told me my father was in the hall and I gave Mrs. Finn my flag and said I
        had to go

and my father said I had a baby brother and the principal shook my hand

and we went to the hospital and

went in but when we got there the lady said I couldn't go in there

cause visiting hours were over

and I didn't get to see my mom or my brother.

But they made—

my mom called and she said what should they name him

from two choices TODD or Christopher and I said easy Christopher

cause TODD sounded stupid and Christopher was his name

and anyway they named him TODD.°

° Daniel Alexander Jones, "Clayangels" (unpublished manuscript, 1997), 11–15.

Jones's neighborhood—with its variety, community responsibility, and general congeniality—laid the foundation for the specifics of his art. A jazz aesthetic develops most potently from a sense of a complex world (lots of people, lots of cultures, lots of life choices) and specifically a complex Blackness. Jones's keen writer's ear can be understood through his description of his Springfield neighborhood where multiple sonorous truths existed, even in contradiction to each other:

> . . . I grew up with all of these different sounds—double-dutch, Italian, Spanish, Caribbean music, Gospel music, two ministers on the street, the sounds of buses and cars and people yelling and people calling each other from the house, and

the summertime everybody out on the street together and the generations. So it was the idea of a melting pot, but not a melting pot, like this, this symphony of different sounds. So that was the earliest sort of sign, imprint, in addition to all the different kinds of music that everybody listened to and in our house it was folk music, Odetta, Miriam Makeba, Stevie Wonder, the Motown people, Aretha Franklin, maybe a little classical music, the radio, whatever came through on the radio . . . I just developed this love for these distinct sounds, but I loved all of them. I didn't love just any one thing. I loved the way they meshed together . . . So I think my ear was trained at an early age to accept different voices: the sounds of family members and friends of the family, different, different sounds of music, . . . and then visually, the beauty of all the people I grew up around, again, a completely diverse group of people . . . So when I later was introduced to jazz music and jazz culture it all made sense.[6]

DANIEL'S DISCOGRAPHY OF IMPORTANT MUSIC AS OF 2006*

BETTY CARTER, *THE AUDIENCE WITH BETTY CARTER*
IT QUICKENED ME. IN MANY WAYS, IT SCARED ME. I WAS DRAWN TO IT KNOWING SOME-
WHERE INSIDE ME WHEN I LISTENED TO IT, REALLY LISTENED TO IT, IT WOULD CHANGE MY
LIFE. SO I WAS TENUOUS AT FIRST. BUT HER VERSION OF *MY FAVORITE THINGS*? PLEASE.

DIANA ROSS, *DIANA*
STILL THE MOST SEDUCTIVE SURFACE I KNOW. THIS IS A TIME MACHINE TO MY YOUNG
SELF. IT IS STILL SUCH A BEAUTIFUL, MODERN COMPOSITION BY CHIC AND SUCH A BEAU-
TIFUL, MODERN PERFORMANCE BY ROSS. IT IS NOT JAZZ. BUT IT IS INDISPUTABLY *PRES-
ENCE*. IT'S A STAND IN, ON THIS LIST, AS WELL, FOR THE SWATH OF MUSIC THAT WAS THE
"SOUNDTRACK OF MY LIFE." INCLUDING STACY LATTISAW, TEENA MARIE & RICK JAMES,
EVELYN "CHAMPAGNE" KING, DONNA SUMMER, MELBA MOORE, THE JONES GIRLS, AND A
TON OF LESSER KNOWN OTHERS, ETC. I COULD SING THIS ENTIRE ALBUM, FRONT TO BACK,
WITH EVERY INSTRUMENTAL LICK, I KNOW IT SO WELL.

YOKO ONO, *IT'S ALRIGHT (I SEE RAINBOWS)*
EVERY TIME I LISTEN TO THIS, IT SOUNDS NEW. ONO TOOK US ON JOURNEYS OF THOUGHT
AND EMOTION. HER SONGS OPENED PORTALS TO SUBJECTIVE, FRAUGHT AND PASSION-
ATELY HOPEFUL UNIVERSES.

SARAH VAUGHAN, *SASSY SWINGS THE TIVOLI*
THE SHEER PLEASURE OF VAUGHAN'S VOICE, FOR HER AS THE SINGER, FOR THE BAND AS
COLLABORATORS, AND FOR US AS LISTENERS IS ALMOST OVERWHELMING.

ALICE COLTRANE, *UNIVERSAL CONSCIOUSNESS, WORLD GALAXY* AND *LORD OF LORDS*
A HOLY TRINITY.

JOHN COLTRANE, ANYTHING

BOB MARLEY, ANYTHING

* Daniel Alexander Jones, e-mail message to author, October 25, 2006.

ODETTA, ANYTHING

BJORK, *POST, HOMOGENIC,* AND *VESPERTINE*

STEVIE WONDER, *SONGS IN THE KEY OF LIFE*

JOSEPHINE BAKER, *THE FABULOUS JOSEPHINE BAKER*
FROM LATER IN HER CAREER, WHEN THE RECORDING TECHNOLOGY WAS ABLE TO CAP-
TURE THE DEPTH AND RICHNESS OF HER DISTINCTIVE VOICE. IT IS SUCH A THEATRICAL
RECORD. BAKER'S QUINTESSENTIAL SHOWMANSHIP IS ON FINE DISPLAY. IT OFTEN FEELS
LIKE A "LIVE" RECORDING.

TINA TURNER, *PRIVATE DANCER*
BREAKING OUT FROM ALL RESTRAINT. TEARING THE CAGING WALLS DOWN. OUTLAW
SELF-LOVE.

LABELLE, ANYTHING, BUT ESPECIALLY, *CHAMELEON*
I DON'T TEND TO PLAY FAVORITES, BUT LABELLE'S ALBUM, *CHAMELEON,* KEEPS SURFACING
ON MY LIST OF BELOVED RECORDINGS. THE SPECIFIC SONIC ALCHEMY OF PATTI LABELLE,
NONA HENDRYX AND SARAH DASH WAS AND IS INIMITABLE. THIS SOUNDS LIKE FREEDOM
TO ME. EMPOWERED, CONNECTED, UNABASHED, SEXUAL, SPIRITUAL, POLITICAL, UNAS-
SAILABLY EXCELLENT. IT IS ALSO A SOUND THAT FELT—FELT—LIKE MY OWN DESIRE FELT;
THE PARTICULAR LIFE-FORCE LIKE SOME PULSING STAR FROM A GALAXY FAR AWAY, ONE
WHICH MY SOUL CALLED/CALLS HOME.

Betty Carter's particular vocal stylings and her personal independence were critical in shaping Jones's understanding of the possibilities of performance. He fashions *The Book of Daniel: jazz rite in lecture format* around a jazz lesson in which Betty Carter's "My Favorite Things" becomes the text for the day. He is fond of quoting Carter as saying "It's not the melody, it's about something else—it's the song," as a way of explaining how to enter jazz. In his lecture/performance, he sketches out the key features of his brand of theatrical jazz on a flip chart, one of the few props in the performance space. Drawing from the work of Eileen Southern, Zora Neale Hurston, and his own extensive experience in the form, Jones wrote this about jazz:

"THE LIVING MATRIX OF JAZZ CREATES CONTRADICTIONS ALL AT ONE TIME. YOU CAN'T DO ONE THING AND MAKE JAZZ."*
—DANIEL ALEXANDER JONES

* E-mail message to author, March 12, 2008.

- Vocally oriented music
- Emphasizes individual
  — Performer as composer
  — Personality
  — (Hurston) Originality, Imitation
- Aural music

The lecture becomes more personal as he begins to teach about improvisation by listening to Betty Carter, and listing the salient features of her work: "Melody,

Rhythm, Syncopation, Time & Space → Call and Response, 'Employing antiphonal relationship between 2 solo instruments or between solo and ensemble.'—Southern." The flip chart then declares in bold red letters "CALL, DANIEL." The theory of call and response is demonstrated through Carter's masterful stylings, and enacted as an audience member calls Jones on his cell phone during the performance. His response to this call revolves around the question "Can you remember the sensation of birth?" Here, the lettering on the flip chart moves away from the uniform block letters on the previous pages to an eclectic array of cursive and print, capitals and lower case, huge type and tiny type, and wholly imagined fonts. This visual shift is a cue to the new terrain the performance has cracked open. It signals a disruption and entrance into deeper intimacy as Jones explores the words shame, resistance, tree, October, and joy. This seemingly random collection of words evolves into a conversation around his family. All the while, Jones as lecturer is moving animatedly around the space, calling on audience members to engage with the lecture, savoring his own words while mocking the pomposity of university professors, and eventually gazing upon a wedding photo of his mother and father projected on an upstage sheet. The flip chart asks, "What is the appropriate colour to wear to weddings?"—first in enormous red cursive letters, then on the next page in teeny black printed letters. With Jones's Black father and white mother in a wedding embrace behind him, the final page of the flip chart says in red, "Weddings. Colour?"—simultaneously invoking wedding protocols of white only for brides and racial protocols requiring monochromatic unions.

In this work, Jones reveals how the theory of jazz becomes a living practice, through the playful and dexterous improvisation of the performance itself, and through his parents' improvised road to love. In this work, he reveals how the jazz aesthetic is an art and life practice, intertwined. He would not allow me to videotape this work because he didn't want to be self-conscious about this spontaneously produced performance. This trembling aliveness is a hallmark of Jones's work.

I first worked with Daniel when he was asked to direct First Stage Productions' Shakin' the Mess Outta Misery, *by Shay Youngblood. I was excited to be a dramaturg on the production because it would give me an opportunity to work closely with Daniel. I knew that Cynthia Taylor-Edwards (now Alexander), director of First Stage Productions, was taking an artistic risk in inviting this innovative young artist to direct for her family-oriented predominantly Black theatre company. I supported Cynthia's move toward more professional and provocative*
theatre, and this gave me all the more reason to take on the role of dramaturg. The production was first performed at the Public Domain's small second-floor theatre space in downtown Austin. Until we were able to work in the theatre, we often rehearsed at Daniel's house in Hyde Park. Some of the eight cast members were regulars with First Stage. They were mostly Black women in their 50s—except for the two performers playing the bifurcated role of Daughter, one of whom was a teenager. Everyone had day jobs and/or family and school commitments that made it difficult to get to

rehearsal on time. We would arrive 5, 10, sometimes 15 minutes past the start time. And invariably, Daniel would greet us warmly and integrate each performer into the evolving rehearsal, no matter what time she arrived. One night, I was particularly late. As I pulled in front of Daniel's house, I dreaded seeing him and the women as I entered. I imaged their lips tight, their eyes averted, and Daniel brusquely reminding me of how important

time is, how everyone has to make sacrifices, and that no one should have to wait on others to arrive, that my actions were selfish and unprofessional, and that I must do better in the future. Of course, Daniel had never spoken to me in this way, but my own frustration and embarrassment prompted my imagination to create this grotesque Daniel who would punish me for my professional transgressions. As I opened the door to the house poised with an apology on my breath, I smelled greens on the stove, cornbread in the oven, and heard laughter from the two or three cast members who were present. Daniel was happily banging pots in the kitchen and the women were casually sharing stories about the best way to cook greens. I was confused. Maybe there wasn't a rehearsal that night and I wasn't even supposed to be there. Soon a few more women arrived, and well over an hour past the start time for the rehearsal everyone was present, sopping up greens

with chunks of cornbread, and rubbing our bare feet together in the ultimate sign of satisfaction and community familiarity. I relaxed into an easy evening of trash-talking and good food. Daniel understood what we would gain in trust and appreciation and camaraderie by spending an evening huddled over a hearty meal instead of crouched over the script. He didn't raise an eyebrow at the late arrivals, just handed everyone a plate and allowed any stresses from the day to dissolve. We laughed full and hard that night. And that was the energy that shaped the rest of our time together. Here was a director we could trust. He cared about us and for us. We would try

anything he tossed our way because he demonstrated just how important we were to him. The result was one of the most important productions I have experienced. The women moved each other to tears most nights of the run and moved their audiences to consistent standing ovations. There was a palpable love that surrounded this work, and I like to think that audiences sensed this even before the first words of the show began as they walked through the lobby display that I had created. Watermelons, cornmeal, and molasses on the floor for Yemọnja, who is the Divine principle of motherhood governing this play, images from Romare Bearden's river series to evoke the play's important river moments, historical information on the magic

references, the Civil Rights movement, and the role of water in African American spiritual lives—all of this to encourage the audience to open to the world they would soon enter in the theatre. Once seated in the ¾ staging with white linen draped like laundry across the entire space, with designs like veve painted on the floor, with performers whose most rigorous training came from daily living and Daniel's kindness—audiences, too, could kick off their shoes in satisfaction. Daniel told me, "what you put in rehearsal is what you get in performance," and I saw that simple dictum fully enacted. Daniel's style is not to "crack the whip" but to listen, to provide warm encouragement. And a plate of greens when needed.

DANIEL'S VEGETARIAN GREENS
THE HISTORY

Daniel says: "Greens were prepared in our house on the weekend. My father would clean out the big slate sink in our kitchen, scrubbing it down with cleanser and rinsing it well. He would have purchased the greens from a store called Blatche's Foods or he would have gotten them from the yard, depending on the time of year. Collards were not widely available, but given that a sizeable majority of the Black folks in Springfield were children of Southern migrants, there was a demand. His focus was meditative and his movements were deliberate as he washed and rinsed the greens then chopped them up. He would have cooked pigs' knuckles in the double boiler earlier that morning. The smell would funk up the whole house. I used to hate that smell, and the hot steam heat of the whole enterprise. He'd fill his double boiler, add salt, pepper and a little baking soda and then cook them up. The skkkkkettt-skkkkkkettt sound of the double boiler is one of my strongest aural childhood memories. When they were served at dinner, they were thoroughly cooked—dark dark almost brown. They were, invariably, pronounced to be 'tender.' Now, the smell of greens cooking is tinged always with a bit of nostalgia for home, for weekend days on Thompson Street.

When I stopped eating meat altogether at age 14, my decision to do so was greeted with little fanfare—and with an implicit understanding that I was welcome to eat whatever I chose from the family table, but there were not going to be any special accommodations. I was welcome, for example, to strain the meat out from my portion of spaghetti sauce. I was welcome to eat extra peas and carrots and salad. But if I wanted something else—I knew where the pots and pans were. I'd learned to cook a lot of things early in my life from my grandmother and by watching my mom and dad cook. And PBS cooking shows were a staple of my early teenage years. So, with no thought of what I couldn't do, I began making my own food. I experimented a lot—using the ingredients that were around . . . Velveeta Cheese, English muffins, Hunt's tomato paste and sauce, Mueller's vermicelli in a box, frozen corn and peas, evaporated milk, Blue Bonnet margarine, Ore-Ida frozen fries, Dreikorn's white bread . . . I made a LOT of things from these ingredients. A lot. Then, of course, I started to branch out and go shopping with one or the other parent. As I grew to be a better cook—I happily assumed some of the cooking duties in the house. Now, it's understood that when I go home to visit, I will be making the meals for everyone.

As I went off down my own path, I relished the chance to meet other people's food when I would meet them. I learned how to cook things that maybe I would have had on occasion as a young person, at a neighbor's house, etc. or in a restaurant, but learned to love as I got older—rice & beans, soups, Indian food, Vietnamese, Thai and Chinese foods, salads, alternative grains, tofu . . .

One thing I always wanted to try my hand at was collard greens. The problem was figuring out how to get all the rich flavor and salty goodness without part of a pig laying up in the pot. A lot of the people I met who were trying not to eat pork would put a smoked turkey leg up in there. But I wasn't eating that either. And I'd left the time of straining out or picking out meat well behind. I started with the great rule of cooking—learn your ingredients. I learned the cycle of the collard green—from tender young leaf to full, resilient one. I learned the different varieties, sizes, shapes. I learned the properties of the leaf as it got prepared and as it cooked. How long was too long on the flame, how long was not enough? What about adding water? What about adding spices? Should they be sliced, or chopped; should the stalk be cut out, or kept? What kind of oil to use? And on and on and on. It was a trial and error and trial and success journey. I discovered many variations on a theme. But the theme became really strong.

This recipe is the theme and there are a couple variations to play with. This is not an exact recipe. This is a point of departure. This recipe only works when you personalize it—when you make it your own. Amounts are approximate. Start with a little less than I note, then add more to fit your taste buds. Experiment with other ingredients. But pay attention to the 'rules' of the recipe. They are the result of a lot of experience."

DANIEL'S VEGETARIAN GREENS
THE RECIPE

INGREDIENTS
MAIN:

Collard Greens—Three to four large bunches.*

Garlic—One large head, separated into cloves and peeled.[†]

Peanut Butter—One heaping tablespoon.

Tomatoes—Ripe Roma, three or four, seeded and roughly chopped.[‡]

Olive Oil—Two tablespoons.[§]

Jalapeños or **Thai Chilies**—From four to six, to taste. Stem removed, but whole.[¶]

"MUST-HAVE" SPICES:

Sea Salt or Kosher Salt—One teaspoon to begin, more to taste.

Tamari—Two teaspoons to begin, more to taste.

Black Pepper—½ teaspoon to begin, more to taste.

Brown Sugar—One teaspoon.

"OPTIONAL BUT NO-JOKE" SPICES:

Ground Cumin—One teaspoon to begin, more to taste.

Ground Coriander—Two teaspoons to begin, more to taste.

---

* Use fresh Collard Greens only. Never frozen. The best is picked from your backyard. But store-bought is fine. Organic is ideal, but you do what you can.

[†] You may trim the root ends of the garlic cloves, but do not cut chop or mash them.

[‡] If you can't get your hands on good tomatoes, don't bother. You could use one or two from your garden, or some other variety—as long as they are ripe and smell like tomatoes.

[§] You may use Peanut Oil instead—but not light oil, like canola.

[¶] You may use a hotter pepper like habañero if you wish. Or you may omit them altogether, depending upon your preference.

Turmeric—¼–½ teaspoon.[**]

Spike Seasoning—1 teaspoon to start, more to taste.[††]

Chipotle Pepper Powder—This adds a wonderful smoky barbecue flavor. Go gently—½ teaspoon to start.

PREPARATION

1. After cleaning the greens well,[‡‡] get your cutting board and a sharp knife handy.
2. Place a large, heavy bottomed pot on the stove over a medium heat.
3. Begin to chop the greens. I layer several leaves, roll them into a cylinder shape, and then chop widthwise. Don't chop them too thickly, or they won't release their flavor and will take a long time getting tender. Strips about ½ wide do well. About ¼ of them should be chopped fairly finely, in chiffonade. I have found that having variation in your chopping helps to release both liquid and flavor into the overall pot. You can, of course, roughly chop all the leaves, if you'd like.
4. Here's a key. The leaves should still be wet from rinsing, not patted dry. As you chop, begin to add them to the pot. You may run your hand under the faucet and dribble a little water over them—but don't add more than a tablespoon of water to the pot. This is hugely important.
5. As you add greens, add a layer of garlic cloves and tomatoes, and one or two peppers. Add your oil.
6. Keep chopping and adding. And every once in a while, stir the greens up from the bottom of the pot with a wooden spoon. The heat should be medium to medium-high depending on your stove and the pot. The greens should not be burning or sticking, but rather should start to quickly steam. Add all your remaining garlic, tomatoes and peppers.
7. Here's the tricky part. This part gets easier to move through with practice. It is a "feel" thing. The collards will at first get very bright emerald green, then they will start to leach their liquid and steam a bit and will reduce in size and get a slightly deeper sea green. Keep "folding" them up from the bottom, gently with the wooden spoon, and letting them steam for a minute or two, then "fold" them up again. Keep the heat constant as they reduce in volume and make the pot likker.
8. After they have changed color a bit, add your peanut butter (it will be a clump at first, no worries, it will dissolve in time) and your spices. Keep stirring.
9. The greens will change color twice more as they become tender. The color you want is a deep green, almost pine green. You'll know when it happens, because all the greens in the pot will turn this color at the same time. Turn down the heat and cover. Stir them every few minutes.

[**] Turmeric can quickly overwhelm a dish. Better to start with ¼ teaspoon—a generous pinch. Adding a little bit to the greens, however, does something quite wonderful.

[††] If you use Spike, decrease the amount of both salt and tamari by half. It adds a depth of savory flavor, but will be too salty if you use it with the full amounts of the other two ingredients.

[‡‡] Even though greens today are usually well cleaned in the supermarket—you should still thoroughly clean them! If the center stems are thick/tough, you may want to cut them out—otherwise, just trim it off where it meets the leaf.

10. The time this will take varies depending upon the greens, the heat, etc. It can be anywhere from 15 minutes to 30 minutes. Keep an eye on them. And most importantly—taste them as you go. You want a green that is tender, but firm to the tooth. This is not the cook-it-til-it's-mush kind of greens. But neither should they be crunchy.[§§]

11. Tasting is also important for the balance of spices. You may need to add more salt or tamari (your choice).

12. By the way, the garlic cloves will soften, roasting in the heat. They impart a particular flavor. You can remove them before serving—often they sort of "dissolve" into the whole thing. The tomatoes should dissolve into the likker. You may remove the peppers before serving.

NOTES

1. This should become your recipe. You will increase or decrease ingredients per your taste. You may try adding some things not on this list.

2. I've experimented a lot over the years with these greens. This recipe represents the best of what I've learned. The method and the ingredients are not arbitrary. But that doesn't mean that you can't find your own way to do. Collards are resilient (in more ways than one)—so have fun!

3. I've used cayenne pepper to great effect when no fresh hot peppers are available. I like adding dried chili flakes when serving, but cooking with them seems less effective. Molasses is good instead of the brown sugar. Just a little sweetness deepens the overall flavor—trust me.

4. The peanut butter always raises eyebrows. But it (along with the whole garlic cloves) is the secret!!! Leave it out at your own risk.

5. I do not advocate the use of onion when cooking the greens. Nor do I add vinegar, as many do, to this vegetarian recipe.

6. A final note on water—the most delicious likker comes from the greens themselves. Coax it out with heat. Don't add a lot of water. Otherwise you'll end up with flavorless likker and tough greens.

SERVING SUGGESTIONS

Thinly slice a **white onion.** Place one or two slices atop individual servings of greens. Best eaten by hand with fresh, hot cornbread.
Serve with **blackeyed peas** and **white rice,** or with **field peas** and **white rice. Hot sauce** on the side.
Serve with **fried sweet plantains,** or with **plantain and red pepper fritters.**
The greens are even better the second day!

[§§] There are other recipes that are good for that, like sautéed Brazilian Collard Greens, but not this one.

While a student at Classical High School on State Street[7] in downtown Springfield (the same school both his parents attended), Jones initially planned to attend the Rhode Island School of Design upon graduation. His skill as a visual artist was encouraged by the generous direction of dedicated art teachers Sandra Camp and Dr. Elliot Dyer, both of whom pushed Jones to an advanced level of work. However, at the recommendation of the Drama Club teacher, Patricia Keenan, Jones auditioned for the drama troupe. From this moment, theatre became his primary art form, though his continued work as a painter is reflected in the visual detail of his theatre artmaking, in the many theatre posters and programs he has created,[8] and in the handmade books he created for *Phoenix Fabrik*.[9]

At the end of his first year in the Drama Club, Jones performed the lady in blue's "no more sorrys" monologue from Ntozake Shange's *for colored girls who have considered suicide/when the rainbow is enuf,* the very monologue that Carlos originated at the Henry Street Settlement and premiered on Broadway. Even before formally becoming a theatrical jazz practitioner, Jones made a profound connection with the aesthetic:

> I did the monologue and I remember the feeling of being possessed at the time . . . something transcended. I don't really remember what I did, just the feeling about what happened. And I remember afterward, the class was sort of stunned . . . and the teacher later said that it was something bigger than me . . . and I realized that it was something about entering this kind of work, this language—the music, the poetry, and the spirit of it, that was what was right. That was what I was supposed to do, and I didn't really have language for it at that time . . . it involved a transcendent artistic experience.[10]

Jones's theatrical *egbẹ́* began to evolve during his college years. As an undergraduate at Vassar College majoring in Africana Studies, Jones met his first mentor, Dr. Constance E. Berkley, whose portrait by Daniel is on loan to the John L. Warfield Center for African and African American Studies at the University of Texas. With Dr. Berkley, Jones studied Black drama, African literatures, and African Traditional Religions. Jones speaks often of the careful way Dr. Berkley would lecture from precisely penned faded notecards, her round speech and her sharp mind creating the very image of the scholar. Through her tutelage, Jones learned the importance of discipline, precision, and rigor with every aspect of his craft.

While at Vassar, Jones had to confront a world quite different than the congenial diversity of his Springfield home. He found that he had to address his discomfort with class issues as well as what he calls "institutionalized aversive racism"—the often invisible yet pervasive ways that institutions perpetuate discrimination through admissions policies, a privileged canon and curriculum, and the insidious insistence that racism does not happen at their institution.[11] Even more pressing was the conflict he experienced with both the philosophy and faculty of the Drama Department at that time. He withdrew from Vassar and enrolled at

Figure 23. Daniel Alexander Jones's poster for *The Owl Answers*. He created this poster for the Brown University George Houston Bass Kulcha Kollectiv production of Adrienne Kennedy's *The Owl Answers* directed by Rhonda Ross. This work solidified an ongoing friendship between Jones and Ross, and launched a continuing investigation for Jones into Kennedy's work. Photo by Daniel Alexander Jones.

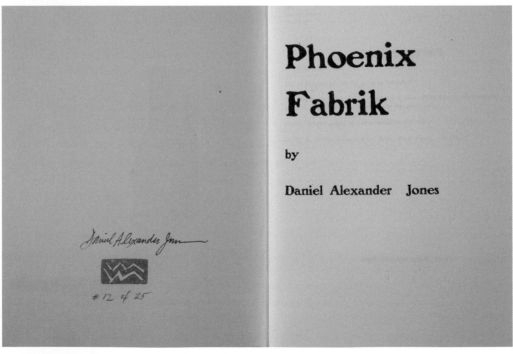

Figure 24. Daniel Alexander Jones's handmade book for *Phoenix Fabrik*. I was glad I was able to purchase one of Jones's handmade books before other audience/witnesses scooped them all up! This special book was made for the workshop production presented by allgo, the Texas statewide queer people of color organization, 2004. Photo by Elisa Durrette.

phoenix fabrik

Figure 25. Daniel Alexander Jones's drawing for the *Phoenix Fabrik* program cover. This drawing was later fashioned into the poster for the Pillsbury House Theatre production, 2006. Photo by Daniel Alexander Jones.

Figure 26. *The Book of Daniel, Chapter 7: Immortality* poster, designed by Daniel Alexander Jones. The posters and the programs are so critical in setting a tone for a production that Jones often creates his own, as with this poster for *The Book of Daniel: Immortality,* presented in the Performing Blackness Series of the John L. Warfield Center for African and African American Studies at the University of Texas at Austin, 2007. The importance of birds in the text and Jones's relationship to female energy are reflected in the bird images in the poster. Photo by Daniel Alexander Jones.

Emerson College. There he met Helen Patmon, an English professor who validated his aesthetic and political understandings, and who encouraged him to return to Vassar, where he could take full advantage of those resources while pursuing his own academic and artistic path. He did indeed return to Vassar, where he became president of the Ebony Theatre Ensemble (ETE). Through ETE he directed *Wedding Band* and performed in *Soldier's Play, Day of Absence,* and *Dutchman.* At the end of his senior year, ETE produced Jones's *Bloodletting,* a futuristic science fiction play, with an accompanying essay that served as a commentary about his experiences with "institutionalized aversive racism."

After completing his B.A. at Vassar in 1991, Jones applied to graduate programs in acting and writing, and was accepted to the Master's Program in Theatre at Brown University. The same year that Jones went to Brown, George Houston Bass, founder and artistic director of Rites and Reasons Theatre housed at Brown, passed away. Although the Black artistic community at Brown had to find new leadership, an energetic group of artists continued to create a prodigious amount of work during this period. Other students in Jones's artistic and intellectual world at Brown included Rhonda Ross,[12] Donald King (later founder and artistic director of Providence Black Repertory Theatre), Paco Gerald, and Jackie Wigfall, but it was his relationship with the writer and painter Shay Youngblood that solidified his developing aesthetic sensibilities. As Jones describes it: "[Shay] became entrée into the more sophisticated, realized and conscious application of a lot of the principles which were heretofore subliminal or intuitive . . . they hadn't really fallen into a codified language at all. That was all over when I met Shay, because all of a sudden everything that I knew in my gut was something that she did explicitly."[13] Their collaborations stretched over many years.

Jones's immersion in the nonlinear transtemporal transgeographic experience of the jazz aesthetic was stimulated by his work with Aishah Rahman. At Brown, Jones was a student in Rahman's course on the Black Arts Movement. Rahman opened up the very idea of Blackness for Jones. As he puts it, "That course was revolutionary for all of [the students]. She wouldn't let us be comfortable in our chauvinism around Blackness. I just felt free to do what I had been doing with no shame."[14] Rahman, who appears to be the first to use the term "jazz aesthetic" as it relates to theatre, describes her work in this way:

> I was trying to dramatize the unconscious or emotional levels of character. And that's why I find that I always have to make some kind of leap that might be described in some Eurocentric term like "absurdist." But I don't think of it that way. My work is in the tradition of what I call the "jazz aesthetic," which acknowledges the characters' various levels of reality. They have triple consciousness: of the unborn, the living and the dead . . . the jazz aesthetic in drama expresses multiple ideas and experiences through language, movement, visual art and spirituality simultaneously.[15]

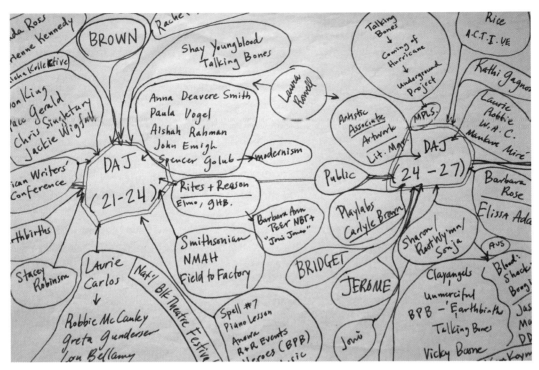

Figure 27. Daniel Alexander Jones's artistic lineage. When I asked Jones to create his artistic lineage, he presented me with a dense three-page map of his evolution as an artist. This central panel gives a sense of the many people and experiences that shaped him from twenty-one to twenty-seven years of age. Jones's thinking is informed by design concepts—font, color, and composition are key. Photo by Elisa Durrette.

Rahman's often-anthologized *The Mojo and the Sayso* clearly expresses "various levels of reality" as a Black family works through their grief when the youngest son is killed by policemen. By the end of the play, a Baptist preacher disrobes on stage as "he reveals a feathered body, a hook nose and webbed, claw feet,"[16] and the family drives through the front door in a car that the father has been repairing in the family's living room. As Rahman notes in the stage directions, "The production style should serve and illuminate the absurdity, fantasy and magic mayhem that are intrinsic in this script."[17] *The Mojo and the Sayso* created the first work experience shared by Jones and Carlos when Rahman invited Carlos to Brown as a guest director for a reading of the play at the end of Jones's second year in graduate school. Jones refers to his work with Carlos as "a soul journey" that was "life changing."[18] In Carlos's workshop at Brown and in her direction of the staged reading of *The Mojo and the Sayso,* Jones once again found himself in the presence of a master teacher who would push him into a fuller understanding of the work he is moved to create. In the reading, Jones played the role of the edgy and protective older son Blood, while fellow grad student (later, Pulitzer Prize winner) Nilo Cruz played the guilt-ridden mechanic father, provocatively named Acts.

Jones's artistic relationship with Carlos has moved between Minneapolis and Austin, across many collaborations in which they exchange roles as director, performer, writer. Carlos is one among many women with whom Jones has developed profound relationships that move him more fully into his specific expression of theatrical jazz, and extend his humanity. Kathi Gagnon, also a close friend to Carlos, was a highly acclaimed performer whom Jones describes as an "otherworldly talent." She lent her gifts to works by Jones and Bridgforth, and she worked with other members of the theatrical jazz *ẹgbẹ́* including Carlos, Djola Branner, Shay Youngblood, and Robbie McCauley. During the summer of 1994, Jones was staying with Gagnon as he worked on *Earthbirths* in her home library. Later that year, she played Ruth in Penumbra's production of *Talking Bones*, with Carlos playing Baybay, Jones playing Oz, and Lou Bellamy (then artistic director of Penumbra) as Mr. Fine, directed by Robbie McCauley, choreographed by Marlies Yearby, and with a set designed by Seitu Jones. She immediately took Jones under her wing, due in part to his close resemblance to her son Philippe, and due in large measure to the sense of artistic and personal camaraderie that they shared. Jones acknowledges her importance in his life as his "cut buddy" with "her indomitable spirit, her kindness, her take-no-mess attitude, and her consummate professionalism."[19]

Jones was also deeply bonded to the artist/activist Rebecca Rice.[20] Just as *Talking Bones* was closing, Rice came to Penumbra to star in Cheryl West's *Jar the Floor*. Rice's *Waiting in Vain* and *Everlasting Arms* (1996, directed by Carlos) had recently been produced at Penumbra, and she was part of the Minneapolis women's theatre collective At the Foot of the Mountain. Rice invited Jones to participate in The Powderhorn Project (1995), a community-based theatre initiative of interviews and community forums with local performers that evolved into a documentary theatre performance about the Powderhorn neighborhood in Minneapolis. Jones worked closely with Rice, learning the ways of community collaboration, devising, interviewing, and scavenging a set on fifty dollars. They also worked together on ACTIVE, a short-lived series of antiracist workshops sponsored by Penumbra and designed as corporate diversity trainings, as well as on the Guthrie Theatre's production of Theodore Ward's *Big White Fog* (1995) with Rice and Carlos performing, Bellamy as director, and Jones as assistant director. Along with these theatrical unions, Jones and Rice developed a powerful personal alliance that continued until her surprising death from cancer in 2002. Of his relationship with Rice, Jones says: "I credit her with unmasking a certain set of truths about myself—reminding me of my true spirit."[21]

Jones has shared a long-standing friendship and artistic partnership with Robbie McCauley, whom he first met through her performance with Carlos in *Persimmon Peel* at the National Black Theatre Festival in Winston-Salem, 1993. After finishing his summer job performing in vignettes in the "Field to Factory" exhibit at the Smithsonian Institution in Washington, DC,[22] Jones and other Smithsonian company members treated themselves to a road trip headed for the National Black Theatre Festival. In *The Book of Daniel, Chapter 7: Immortality*, Jones describes the festival in this way:

DANIEL

We pull up to the hotel and conference center where the festival is housed. I step out of the van, eyes glued to the sidewalk. I look up and who is standing there looking at me but Laurie Carlos, and she says "We've been waiting for you." She takes me by the hand, and I walk away from the Smithsonian crowd before I know it I am in a theatre, full of stars—I mean—stars

LIBRARIANS

Robbie McCauley

Rosalind Cash

Sekou Sundiata

Craig Harris

Rhodessa Jones

Carl Hancock Rux

Billie Allen

Keith Antar Mason and the Hittite Empire

TOGETHER

Ntozake Shange[23]

From this moment, he shared the festival with these Black theatre avant-garde luminaries, setting in motion a series of conversations and collaborations that continue to this day.

Following the festival, Jones returned to Springfield, not sure what he would do next. Youngblood told him that Robbie McCauley was directing *Talking Bones* at Penumbra Theatre, and she encouraged him to audition. Carlos was then an Artistic Associate at Penumbra, and she responded to Jones's inquiry about an audition with a customarily cryptic response, "We knew you would call."[24] Thus began Jones's continuing relationship with McCauley, and his multifaceted though short-lived career with Penumbra Theatre. McCauley has directed staged readings of Jones's *Bel Canto* with Oni Faida Lampley, Ebony Jo-Ann, Burl Mosley, and Lynda Gravatt for the Public Theatre and for the Sundance Playlab. She later directed a full staging of the work with Renita Martin for Theatre Offensive. Jones has directed McCauley in *Phoenix Fabrik* at the Todd Mountain Theatre Project in Roxbury, New York, and that experience deepened their already established mutual respect and trust. About her work under Jones's direction of *Phoenix Fabrik,* McCauley said it was "an exemplary jazz experience for me. His material, like Bebop, was written, and required to engage repeatable and improvisational interpretations throughout the production. We were given permission to play the play with our own instruments—which include memory . . . Daniel's work depended on trust, courage, and willingness. I heard not a wink last summer [2007] of 'I can't,' 'I won't,' or 'I don't know.' The company was mainly Black but also international. I learned from Daniel to trust and be humble to the forms of our people even more."[25]

McCauley is a key figure in Jones's artistic lineage. In the Penumbra production of *Talking Bones,* according to Jones, McCauley taught him to "play the 'now'—to hold multiple impulses in a vibrating matrix of played consciousness like a musical chord" (message to author June 11, 2008), to discard the camouflage and bring his deepest truth to each moment. Jones describes this pivotal production in this way:

> . . . Squatting at the edge of the Penumbra stage, when at the conclusion of a scene run-through she approached me and asked me, much to my surprise after I had delivered what I considered to be a fairly good performance of the sequence of events, "What are you afraid of?" "Me or Oz (my character)?" I asked back. "What are you afraid of?" she asked. I started to ruminate and list off typical character-back-story points . . . she cut me off with sound "Uh-uh-uh . . . What are you afraid of?" My face fell. My masks fell. I didn't know. And yet . . . Somewhere within me, just below my ribcage, just behind the knot in my abdomen, I felt a tickle, a small, but noticeable stirring . . . there were no words there . . . everyone was listening, waiting . . . my eyes got wet . . . I took a deep breath in . . . I . . . "There! Right now! Play the scene!" she said . . . I opened my mouth and my world changed in an instant.[26]

McCauley is an intellectual and artistic comrade who shares Jones's understanding of theatrical jazz, and enriches the many roads his work and life have explored. Of McCauley, Jones says, "Our conversation welcomes all the contradictions of what it means to be an artist and citizen. She doesn't skirt the difficulties, and she doesn't dwell in them."[27]

The presence of these exceptional women mentors in Jones's artistic and intellectual life continues a relationship with female reality that was established in childhood as he lived in a world populated and managed mostly by women. The labor and love his mother and grandmother contributed to the summer camp left an indelible understanding of power and authority. From a metaphysical standpoint, Jones believes he was called by Josephine Baker and Lena Horne to do his art. It is no surprise, then, that he would create performances in which he embodied them both. He performs as Josephine Baker in *Blood:Shock:Boogie,* and discusses her while provocatively eating and tossing bananas in *The Book of Daniel, Chapter 7: Immortality.* He created and performed the cabaret act *Cab and Lena* with his friend and collaborator Grisha Coleman. Jones's performances were more than paying homage to these legendary Black women performers, it was opening a space for Jones to fully explore the female. This exploration was given deeper expression as Jones created the quintessential diva Jomama Jones. Jomama is a celebrated performer who left the oppression of the United States for Switzerland in the 1980s, then returned to continue her artistic activism through song. She spreads a message of life-giving energy that is reflected in many of her song titles— "Sunbeam," "Radiate," "Sunflower," "Endless Summertime." Through Jomama, Daniel Alexander Jones focuses female *àṣẹ* to invite audiences to remake their lives through joy—but it is not a naïve joy, for Jomama has known hardship, a hardship that contributes to her diva status.[28]

Through Jomama, Daniel Alexander Jones pushes audiences to experience gender anew. Jomama is not part of the long lineage of men performing women for misogynistic comic effect from Flip Wilson to Tyler Perry, but instead Jomama offers an opportunity to applaud gender nuance, self-naming, and the blurred gender contours of tease and seduction. Here, Jones's childhood visions of Horne and Baker move through him to the full radiance that is Jomama.

Jones's powerful female mentorship has a very specific relationship to Yoruba cosmology. In employing Yoruba cosmology as an analytical approach to theatrical jazz, it is useful to remember that the artists featured in this volume do not practice specific Yoruba-based traditions, but Yoruba spirituality becomes a way of examining their lives and their aesthetics.

Jones's debt to women is beautifully acknowledged in his eulogy for his grandmother, Bernice "Bunny" Leslie, when he writes in her funeral program, "may we meet change, may we greet life with the surety of a bird in flight—held aloft through a combination of grace and will, guided by the wisdom of experience, protected by courageous openness and confident of the Earth's eventual embrace."[29] From a Yoruba vantage point, it is telling that this homage to a revered female elder is associated with the power and beauty of birds.

Figure 28. "Leroy and Moon," by Walter Kitundu. For seven months in 2005, Kitundu tracked and photographed a red-tailed hawk as the bird moved through the urban nooks of San Francisco. Later, he found and photographed Leroy, the hawk in this photo. The command, beauty, and fierceness of Leroy is an apt image for the *Ìyàmí.* Photo by Walter Kitundu.

Women hold a very particular authority and influence in Yoruba-based traditions. They are at once feared and revered as *Àjé*[30]—women with the Divinely given authority to make things happen. *Àjé* are known by many names—*Ìyámi*, Divine Femininity, Primordial Mothers. They are charged with carrying out the mandate given by *Òrúnmìlà*[31] as the supreme knower of destiny. Whatever *Òrúnmìlà* decrees, *Ìyámi* manifests. In this way they have a distinct relationship to *àṣẹ*—the force of manifestation. These powers are represented as birds throughout *Odù* (Divine scripture), *oríkì* (praise), and proverbs. A dynamic representation of female power is found in the beaded crown of Yoruba *Ọba*s, or kings. These elaborate crowns can be as tall as three feet, and typically feature birds encircling the top of these conical royal symbols of authority. While *Ọba*s are most often men,[32] it is women as birds who encircle his *Orí* or head, his first Divinity and destiny. Women also ritually maintain the crowns and actually place the crown on the *Ọba*'s head at the time of installation. The *Ọba* cannot be invested without the sanction of female *àṣẹ*.

For Jones, birds are mysterious prophets—and occasionally avengers—who haunt and tantalize with their oracular messages. In addition to the bird references in the titles of *Earthbirths, Jazz and Raven's Wings* and *Phoenix Fabrik,* and the allusion to winged flight of *Clayangels,* Jones often includes birds in his texts. There is the "loud caw of raven" that marks the disappearance of Harper from the opening scene of *Earthbirths,* along with slides of birds, additional raven sounds, and sightings in dreams. In the play, Mabel, who refuses to be dead, tells Brother, "For now, take this dollar—Annie Mae's fixin to go to the store, have her put it on 344 for nest. With you coming and all, I seen a bird's nest in my sleep last night, big enough to hold Annie Mae's feet."[33] In this moment, birds and the conjuring energy of playing numbers are twin powers. Later in the play, a feather duster prop sheds feathers throughout the space, creating flight on stage, and the ravens come to Harper's father with messages deep in the night.

In *The Book of Daniel, Chapter 7: Immortality,* the character Malcolm X speaks of lessons learned from hummingbirds when he states, "Gentle. Gentle. Gentle. Hummingbirds go through an almost daily hibernation. Because if they used energy at the same rate they do during the day they would run out of gas and die in the night = so their rate of breathing, their heart systems slow way, way down. So that, in the morning, if you happen upon a hummingbird, you can lift it off its perch and it won't have the energy to go anywhere because they have to ramp themselves up. Gentle. Bet on gentle, what's beget."[34]

One of Jones's most dynamic use of these winged symbols of the female is found in *Phoenix Fabrik* when the conjurer/healer Mother Dixon explains how white racist killers will face justice. She declares, "Cowardly pack of dogs. But on the wing, above the trees and eye sharp as a blade, it's another hunter. She hunts alone. Circles and circles and circles. One will walk off by himself. On his way to the field, to the barn, to the outhouse. On they own they small as a mouse, as low to the ground and soft. This hunter? She fix them with her eye. She move quick, quick. So quick they don't feel the blade 'til too late. Land on they shoulders. Stuff they mouth with cotton while they squeal like a pig at the slaughter. They was on their way but . . . never come back. One at a time. Down to the river. Bleed them, gut them, render them, grind them. Down to ash. Surrendered clean unto the Lamb."[35]

These fierce avenging raptors are the very image of the *Ìyàmí,* the force of female rage and justice. The Yoruba Primordial Mothers pluck out the eyes, tongues, and intestines of those who offend them, especially those who have transgressed against women. They work specifically at the behest of *Ifá,* implementing all that he has ordained. In *Phoenix Fabrik,* Jones's voracious winged avengers demonstrate the etymological union of "raven" and "ravenous." It is also important to know the archaic meaning of raven as a collective of conspirators. Birds are rife with telling allusions in Jones's work.

While the *Ìyàmí* may destroy in order to bring cosmic balance, the female force of theatrical jazz is generative. Indeed, destruction often makes way for a new order. As Mother Dixon points out, "What is foul is made pure again by sacrifice."[36]

Sound takes on a distinctive importance in Jones's work. Specific music references, extrasensory radios, the creaking mechanics of a turntable, musicians, singing (often his own), create a soundscape of meaning, as if sound itself carries truth. In *Earthbirths,* Harper notes this power when he begins to understand his father through an aural clarity:

> My father in the black chair.
> Feet, hand, chin, eyes almost closed.
> I'm a shadow on the stairs behind
> *Don't know even if he know I'm there.*
> Just know him cause
> she's
> here.
> Her voice lifts out the record player
> in the corner,
> with the scratch and pop of needle in groove.
>
> (SINGS) ***Them that's got shall get,***
> ***them that's not shall lose,***
> ***so the Bible says and it still is news,***
> ***mama may have.***
>
> Only time I know my father . . .
> she
> haunts the room,
> makes the breathing easy,
> makes the softness on his face,
> slow and steady.
> Eyes closed almost . . .

And it still is news . . .
Then blue
and almost not at all,
the sound
comes
from him.
Bass notes catch in the wood. *Mama may have . . .*
Notes set in my eyes. *Papa may have . . .*
Sound of my father and her together.
Flood the room full night comes on
First drops
of rain
fall.
I am safe.
Something about my father and Billie
makes sense.
Something holy
for which there are no words,
only sound
sound
sound through to the hiss and scratch
and record's ending skip skip crank as the arm
moves and sets clacks off and the silence moves back in.
I'm sitting at the bottom of the stairs
Don't know even if he know I'm there.[37]

Harper closes the play with a near-verbatim repetition about Billie Holiday's transformative powers, except that by the end of Harper's experience in piecing together the fragmented photographs of his family, his mother is also more fully understood through Holiday's mesmerizing sound. The birds return to mark the importance of the moment. Harper tells the audience:

something about my parents
and Billie
makes sense
something
holy
for which there are no words
only sound.
slide rr (flock of ravens)

(A flock of ravens fly out through the stairs. Loud cries from ravens. End piece.)[38]

While the bird images of Jones's works resonate with Yoruba cosmology through the *Ìyámi,* these resonances are ones that I see, not ones that Jones con-

"ULTIMATELY WE ARE RESPONSIBLE FOR FINDING OUR OWN LANGUAGE, FOR OUR OWN SPIRITUAL JOURNEY. THE HARD WORK IS THAT YOU HAVE TO FIND YOUR OWN."*
—DANIEL ALEXANDER JONES

* Phone interview with author, May 2011.

sciously creates. His spiritual influences are many. In considering how the images develop in his work, Jones says, "It is important to me that I be clear that the symbols always came to me, or I was always attracted to them, and then, as a result I would seek out a larger context/ conversation. I have not ever, nor do I anticipate doing a particular tradition. I listen to many voices. So my interest in Egyptian cosmology, while strong, is not the defining feature of my belief system."[39]

Although theatre eventually captured Jones's artistic sensibilities in high school, he found his first artistic home in painting. He began to paint in earnest when he visited his Aunt Terry, a landscape painter, in California. She presented him with a canvas, brushes, and a small set of paints, and encouraged him to explore. Ms. Camp, one of his high school art teachers, also gave him a special gift. Classical High School planned to relocate during Jones's senior year. In preparation for the move, at the end of his junior year, Ms. Camp gave him the key to the art-supply closet and told him to take whatever he wanted because the school would be getting all new materials at its new location. Jones's stash of supplies lasted him for years.

Visual art shapes Jones's understanding of theatrical space. When he directs his own work, the performance venue is often transformed into a patchwork of porous locations with the audience enveloped in the entire world of the piece. In this way, the space approximates the seriate structure of the written text. Jones describes this resonance between the spatial/visual and the written/aural when he stated, "When I was introduced to jazz music and jazz culture it all made sense. When I was introduced to the visual work of artists like Romare Bearden or Jacob Lawrence or Lois Mailou Jones it all made sense, because it was about pastiche and collage and all of these things coming together."[40] In much of Jones's work, the pastiche is in the design and use of space as well as the written and spoken text. He describes his painting in this way: "A lot of my painting technique was self-taught, through trial and error. Intuitive and driven, like my writing. Painting was possession—I would sit in front of a canvas for hours until the picture revealed itself to me."[41] In an essay for *Parabasis,* Jones again notes the relationship between his painting and his writing: "There is a distinct metaphysical process related to each play I write. I've got to take it through to the end which is the beginning again. Sometimes I feel like the love child of Romare Bearden and Julia Child. *Finished cooking feeding started. Finished painting seeing started.*"[42] For Jones, jazz was the connective tissue joining his artistic roads.

In Jones's work, the visual and the written come together through a jazz-inspired commitment to hope. Jazz eschews despair. Scholar Robert G. O'Meally acknowledges this relationship as he notes, "Writers and visual artists who project jazz rhythms into their art express a jazz timekeeper's base-clef sense of time.

The feeling, as Ralph Ellison once put it, that as blues-beset as life may be . . . the real secret is somehow to make life *swing,* to survive by staying in the groove."[43] Jones moves his characters toward a groove, a hopefulness in spite of pain, sorrow, or fear that is visually evoked through the transformative potential of portals. In Jones's work, the visual portal acts as the jazz break, where the magic happens, where the soloist takes flight, where the character goes deeper.

Jones's *Bel Canto* tells the story of Benjamin, a Black gay teenager who struggles to make peace with estrangement from his father. This narrative is the most linear and the least jazz-inflected in Jones's corpus of writing. Although music is prominent in the work, with Marian Anderson appearing as a celestial guide for Benjamin, the narrative structure and impulses owe more to opera than to jazz. It is not surprising, then, that the set also evokes some of the formality and consistency of operatic structure.

In both the 2003 production at Actor's Express in Atlanta, designed by Kat Conley, and the 2004 production at Pillsbury House in Minneapolis, designed by Seitu Jones, the landscape for the performance is a stark thrust stage that nevertheless maintains a strong proscenium perspective and influence. Dramatically marked upstage entrances, platforms, and a simple contrasting color palette characterize both productions.

Figure 29. *Bel Canto,* set designed by Kat Conley, Actor's Express. I took this photo after a production that included Vinie Burrows and was directed by Jasson Minadakis at the Actor's Express in Atlanta, 2003. Portals between worlds that are often featured in Jones's work are found throughout the set. Photo by Omi Osun Joni L. Jones.

The two upstage entrances allow actors to get on and off stage, and the set offers no other physical opportunities for moving between realities. These entrances suggest the mystery of Benjamin's attempt to be a self he has yet to know. The picture frames, unlike the entrances, seem to encase nothingness instead of harkening possibility. In production, the performers did not interact with the frames, which further highlighted their potential as change agents.

Seitu Jones's set puts emphasis on the epic operatic features of the play with bold lines that accentuate the dominant upstage center position of the entrance. In both productions of *Bel Canto,* Benjamin's progress from confusion to greater clarity occurs against the backdrop of the liminal reality of portals, that place of transformation, otherworldliness, and possibility, though the portal as visual statement and metaphor does not solidify for Jones until his later work.

For the 2006 production of *Phoenix Fabrik* at Pillsbury House, Jones renewed his collaboration with designer Leilah Stewart. Stewart has a long acquaintance with a theatrical jazz aesthetic, having designed *Heavenly Shades of Night Are Falling* (by Erik Ehn, directed by Jones), *con flama* (by Sharon Bridgforth, directed by Laurie Carlos), and *Alaskan Heat Blue Dot* (by a team of writers, directed by Carlos). She is currently the resident designer for The Rude Mechanicals, an internationally lauded experimental theatre company based in Austin, Texas. This background makes Stewart uniquely suited for the nonlinear time-traveling work of Jones's *Phoenix Fabrik.* The play brings together transtemporal spirits who are joined by their relationship to both a defunct German-owned doll factory and a revivalist shaman. Here, the power of a portal is more thoroughly integrated into the verbal text, and likewise more layered into the visual world of the piece.

Jones introduces the idea of a portal in his opening stage directions when he writes, "The doll factory wall, and its window—a wide white mouth. The window becomes a porthole in a Trans-Atlantic steamer."[44] In spite of this direction, Stewart did not create a literal ocean liner with window between the ship and the factory; her use of the portal was more subtle and evocative. Not only do hidden boxes under the stage and rectangular niches in crumbling walls create stylized portals, but in *Phoenix Fabrik,* Jones introduces a river that functions in a similarly transformative way as do the more obvious thresholds between realities. In the stage directions, Jones writes, "At the lip of the whole, a river flows. Dark, steady, relentless."[45] Stewart transforms this idea into a textured river of doll dresses and sparkling blue ornaments that diagonally intersect the stage, marking the porous space between the decaying doll factory and the revival tent where Eleanor tries to understand her spiritual past.

The jazz of the set design is in the surprise of the materials and the rhythm of their composition, dividing the set into two overlapping/competing worlds, creating a dynamic tension. The flow of doll memories as river shimmers tantalizingly. The spiritualist Mother Dixon warns The Boy, "Sleep by the river isn't safe. Trouble come quick. Cottonmouth or cracker."[46] The river looms large in the African American consciousness, at once baptismal font and lyncher's secret. In this play, the gateway to transformation has become a fluid site that visually extends into and out of time and place, and occupies the dominant visual space of the set.

In Jones's 1996 direction of Edwin Sanchez's *Unmerciful Good Fortune,* set designer Kym Koym likewise created a visual separation between blurred worlds—one, an accused murderer's detention cell; the other, a dying woman's surreal bedroom. What is distinctive here is the literal bridge Koym builds between these worlds so that the characters' crossings are marked by their ability to balance and tiptoe and leap and trudge from one reality to the next. Importantly, this bridge extended up through the audience, implicating us in each of the characters' choices. This bridge, like Stewart's river, is an acknowledgment of the charged passage between human and the Divine that is experienced as communitas and liminality, and is the visual otherworldliness of a Thelonious Monk spirit-filled ka-plunk on the piano.

For *The Book of Daniel: 35:1,* Jones not only conceived, directed, and performed the work, he also designed it. Given his control of all artistic elements of the production, it is not surprising that this iteration of *The Book of Daniel* is a full expression of his union of a jazz verbal text with a jazz visual text. Here, his painter's eye is given full sway. *The Book of Daniel* presently exists as a series of ten installments that examine specific moments in his self-evolution. Each installment lived as performance installations visually packed with carefully careless artifacts, giving this work a kinship to a Bearden collage in which details are layered upon more details.

The audience entered a dimly lit, cavernous world of possibility when they arrived at the 2005 performance of *The Book of Daniel: 35:1.* As they made their way to their seats, composer Walter Kitundu's sounds were already filling the space. The audience seating was dispersed throughout the performance area in small groupings of four to six chairs, a painted floor design suggested a possible road, bare lights in clear bottles were suspended from the ceiling, a video screen occupied a traditional elevated stage area, a bullet-riddled lectern was mounted on a platform in one corner, Kitundu was playing one of his handcrafted turntable-stringed instruments, a mysterious alcove partially covered with chicken wire was on the house floor opposite the screen, a tiny table covered in white cloth was near Kitundu and his musical museum—all of this was a tempting playscape where Jones, Kitundu, and the audience would together build each moment. Jones did not create a fixed verbal text for this work, as he improvised each seriate segment within an established structure.

The space becomes a birthing room that mirrors the self-discoveries in the verbal text. After the audience was seated, Jones slid/danced/stretched from the alcove into the audience seating through an eerie orange light, clad in a flouncing mesh skirt embellished with delicate jangling bells. This birthing put him and the audience in the same imagined world without the sharp demarcations of stage and house, of fantasy performance and real audience. By placing himself on the same physical plane as the audience, Jones suggested that he and they were

Figure 30. Daniel Alexander Jones in *The Book of Daniel 35:1* at allgo showing performance floor, 2005. He is performing on his floor grid that created performance pathways winding through the audience/witnesses. Photo by Bret Brookshire.

joined in a common journey. In this 360-degree playscape, Jones, Kitundu, and the audience could riff off of one another. The staging required the audience to function more as co-creators than as observers. This very particular relationship to the audience heightens the vulnerability and subsequent potential for audience transformation. Jones nudges that transformation through a dense and challenging verbal text and a visual landscape that literally encompasses the audience in the world of the work.

The vitality of the production was not in merely doing away with the proscenium, nor was the power solely in the environmental vision of the space; Jones conjured a place of freedom, unfettered by the predictability of a stage and rows of audience chairs. The performance space was like a playhouse full of toys strewn about for Jones, Kitundu, and the audience to enjoy. An audience member in one area of the room would not see the same details as another audience member across the way. Some would have to crane their necks, turn around in their seats, or simply accept that they were not meant to see every moment of the performance. The effect is that of having very individual yet simultaneous audience experiences. The freedom in the space is the freedom longed-for in the verbal text. The delight, the wonder, and the force of the work is the open opportunity suggested by the environmental staging, which privileges audience idiosyncrasy and the nonlinear improvised text. As with musical jazz, one looks for—longs for—the surprises—the way Louis Armstrong could attack a note and blow the mute off his trumpet, the way Billie Holiday could drag across the rhythm, the way Betty Carter could make you hear a familiar song for the first time.

Jazz aesthetics push the present moment to a fever pitch, a jazz-induced desire living in our shared humanity as we move through portals, cross rivers and bridges, sit together with the tension and sweat of spontaneous creation. Jones's work vibrates with this potential as it evokes freedom, not stasis; unimagined promises, not answers; the unforeseeable, not certainty. In writing about his use of jazz aesthetics, Jones states, "a Jazz practice is whatever our 'literal' art practice may be (writing, painting, choreographing, etc.) *and* is simultaneously our expansive response to any limitation in life."[47] In this way, Jones invents for himself and his audience a home of possibility.

DANIEL'S LINEAGE*

Daniel . . .

sees Laurie Carlos's picture in a book of *for colored girls* and pins the picture to his wall

performs the lady in blue monologue originated by Laurie for his high school Drama Club

studies with Aishah Rahman while a grad student at Brown (Rahman brings Laurie Carlos to Brown to direct a reading of *The Mojo and the Sayso*; Carlos casts Jones as the sad and volatile Blood, classmate Nilo Cruz played Acts)

directs fellow grad student Shay Youngblood's project starring undergrad Rhonda Ross for New Play Festival at Brown

directs reading of Shay Youngblood's *Talking Bones* at Brown

attends the National Black Theatre Festival in Winston-Salem, South Carolina, where Laurie Carlos and Robbie McCauley perform *Persimmon Peel*; Ntozake Shange and Idriss Akamoor perform *The Love Space Demands*; Keith Antar Mason and Hittite Empire perform *Shango Walk Through Fire*; Rhodessa Jones performs *Big Butt Girls, Hard Headed Women*; Sekou Sundiata, Stephanie Alston, and Craig Harris perform *The Circle Unbroken Is a Hard Bop*; Omi Osun Joni L. Jones also attended the festival, and saw each of these shows except *Persimmon Peel*

performs the role of Oz in *Talking Bones* directed by Robbie McCauley with Kathryn Coram Gagnon as Ruth, Laurie Carlos as BayBay, Lou Bellamy as Mr. Fine, Amy Waddell as Eila, choreographed by Marlies Yearby, set by Seitu Jones, lights by Mike Wangen at Penumbra (Gagnon performed in Youngblood's *Shakin' the Mess Outta Misery* at Penumbra, in Jones's *Earthbirths* at the Walker Center, in Bridgforth's *lovve/rituals & rage* at the Playwright's Center, Jones's *Ambient Love Rites* at the Frank Theatre, and in Luis Alfaro's *Straight as a Line* directed by Carlos)

performs the role of Glena in Moving Spirits' production of *Feathers at the Flame*

directs Shay Youngblood's *Talking Bones* with Zell Miller III, Cynthia Taylor-Edwards (later, Cynthia Alexander), Starla Benford, and Richard Smith at Hyde Park Theatre (HPT)

collaborates with Margery Segal

performs in Erik Ehn's *Enfants Perdus*, directed by Vicky Boone with Lisa D'Amor, Ruth Margraff (as voice installation), Shana Gold, Megan Monaghan, Jason Phelps, Kristen Kosmas, choreographed by Margery Segal at Hyde Park Theatre (Ruth Margraff and Lisa D'Amor taught playwriting at UT, Vicky Boone was Artistic Director for Hyde Park Theatre)

directs *Unmerciful Good Fortune*, by Edwin Sanchez, with Amparo Garcia, Adelina Anthony, Daniel Dodd Ellis, Stacey Robinson at Hyde Park Theatre

performs in Grisha Coleman's HotMouth with Helga Davis

---

* This partial listing of events, productions, and publications gives a sense of the interconnections among theatrical jazz artists. See Jones's excerpted CV (Appendix II) for production details.

directs his *Earthbirths, Jazz and Raven's Wings* with Daniel Dodd Ellis at Hyde Park Theatre

directs Shay Youngblood's *Black Power Barbie at Hotel de Dream* at Hyde Park Theatre

becomes a Many Voices Fellow with the Playwrights' Center, Minneapolis

becomes a Jerome Fellow with Bridget Carpenter, Ruth Margraff, Naomi Iizuka, and Carlos Murillo in his cohort

writes and performs *Blood:Shock:Boogie* at Hyde Park Theatre

performs *Blood:Shock:Boogie* at Outward Spiral Theatre Company, Minneapolis, with Daniel Dodd Ellis and Jason Phelps

performs *Soul Seeds Variety Pack* for Late Nite at Penumbra Theatre

curates the Frontera@Hyde Park Guest Artist Series with Laurie Carlos performing *The Cooking Show*, Grisha Coleman performing *Modern Love*, Chris Wells performing *Liberty!*, Mauricio Cordero, Niobe, and Zell Miller III performing *Mad-Izm*

writes with Todd Jones *Clayangels*, performed by the brothers Jones, directed by Laurie Carlos, music by Grisha Coleman, set by Kim Koym, graphics by Porn Siphanoum, dramaturged by Omi Osun Joni L. Jones at New World Theatre; later Sonja Perryman as Production Assistant at Hyde Park Theatre

writes *Ambient Love Rites* performed with Jones, Carlos, Amparo Garcia, Elissa Adams, and Omi Osun Joni L. Jones, directed by Bridget Carpenter at Hyde Park Theatre

performs in Djola Branner's *Homos in the House* in Minneapolis

performs in the Ordway Music House musical *Ruthless!*, preventing him from directing Sharon Bridgforth's *blood pudding*

recommends Laurie Carlos to direct Sharon Bridgforth's *blood pudding* when he was unable to

directs Shay Youngblood's *Shakin' the Mess Outta Misery* with Cynthia Taylor-Edwards (later Cynthia Alexander), dramaturged by Omi Osun Joni L. Jones for First Stage Productions; later Omi Osun Joni L. Jones joined the company as a performer

creates and performs, with Grisha Coleman, *Cab and Lena* at Penumbra's Late Nite Series curated by Laurie Carlos; also performed at Frontera@Hyde Park; work was developed by both artists during a Yaddo residency

writes *La Chanteuse Nubienne*, produced at 3 Legged Race

directs Erik Ehn's *Heavenly Shades of Night* (written for and about Carlos) with Florinda Bryant, Zell Miller III, Sarah Richardson, Raul Castillo, and Omi Osun Joni L. Jones at Hyde Park Theatre

directs Renita Martin's *Five Bottles in a Six Pack* for Solo Stage Boston and Theatre Offensive

directs Carl Hancock Rux's *Smoke, Lilies and Jade*

writes *Bel Canto*, directed by Robbie McCauley with Oni Faida Lampley in readings at the Public Theatre (New Work Now!) and Sundance Playlab (later fully staged with Renita Martin at Theatre Offensive), directed by Omi Osun Joni L. Jones as a reading with Faye Price (Producing Director of Pillsbury

House) and C. Denby Swenson at Penumbra; directed by Jasson Minadakis
    with Vinie Burrows at Actor's Express
conducts workshops for the Austin Project (tAP)
writes and performs *The Book of Daniel: jazz rite in lecture form* for the Warfield
    Center as part of tAP
directs staged reading of Zell Miller III's *Arrhythmia* with Miller, Sonja Parks, Amy
    Bryant, TruthMaze, Tookie Wright at Penumbra, Sharon Bridgforth as dra-
    maturg, hosted by Laurie Carlos for Penumbra's Cornerstone Reading Series
directs Zell Miller III's *Evidence of Silence Unbroken* at Pillsbury House, with Wal-
    ter Kitundu as DJ
directs Laurie Carlos's *Marion's Terrible Time of Joy* with Carlos at the Playwright's
    Center, Minneapolis
writes *Phoenix Fabrik*, performed by Daniel Alexander Jones, Daniel Dodd Ellis,
    Helga Davis, Barbara Duchow at allgo; later with Vinie Burrows, Rhonda Ross,
    Namir Smallwood, Barbara Duchow at Pillsbury House with set by Leilah
    Stewart, dramaturged by Sharon Bridgforth, program note by Omi Osun Joni
    L. Jones; later still, with Robbie McCauley, Sonja Perryman, Namir Smallwood,
    Barbara Duchow at the Todd Mountain Theatre Project; all directed by Jones
writes and performs *The Book of Daniel: 35:1*, with Walter Kitundu performing
    and composing, and contributed text from Robbie McCauley, Erik Ehn, Grisha
    Coleman, Rachel Harper; Jaclyn Pryor provided program notes; Krissy Mahan
    and Camille DePrang provided technical support; at allgo with the Warfield
    Center
directs reading of Oni Faida Lampley's *Tough Titty* for BRIC, Brooklyn
performs in Sharon Bridgforth's *love conjure/blues*, conducted by Helga Davis
    with Sonja Perryman, Florinda Bryant, Marlah Fulgham, Daniel Dodd Ellis,
    Sean Tate, Gina Houston, Fred Cash Jr., Carsey Walker, Greg Rickard, and
    Omi Osun Joni L. Jones. (Gina Houston, Carsey Walker, and Kathryn Coram
    Gagnon perform in *A Raisin in the Sun* at St. Edward's University)
directs Renita Martin's *Blue Fire on the Water*
receives Alpert Award in Theatre (previous theatrical jazz ẹgbẹ́ winners include Erik
    Ehn, Carl Hancock Rux; Rux takes position as Head of Performance Writing
    at CalArts [succeeding Suzan-Lori Parks] as Ehn becomes Dean of the School
    of Theatre at CalArts; Grisha Coleman and Virginia Grise received their MFAs
    from CalArts)
becomes New Dramatists' Resident Writer (2003–10)
writes and performs *The Book of Daniel, Chapter 7: Immortality*, with Tea Alagic,
    Azure Osborne-Lee, Patrick McKelvey, set by Leilah Stewart, stage managed
    by Ana-Maurine Lara for the Warfield Center
directs E. Patrick Johnson's *Sweet Tea* with E. Patrick Johnson for About Face The-
    atre at Viaduct Theatre for the Ellen Stone Belic Institute for the Study of
    Women and Gender in the Arts & Media, then headed by Jane Saks
performs Jomama Jones at Joe's Pub, Soho Rep, Victory Garden's through the Ellen
    Stone Belic Institute for the Study of Women and Gender in the Arts & Media,
    and Pillsbury House

Sharon Bridgforth

B. MAY 15, 1958
CHICAGO, ILLINOIS

I see this work as my spiritual practice, and I must do it.
When I do it, I'm a better person.
—Sharon Bridgforth

The ancestors are here, talking, dancing, breathing on your shoulder.
      Yemọnja asesú, asesú Yemọnja
                  Listen for their wisdom.
      Yemọnja olódò, olódò Yemọnja
                       Receive their blessings.

BRIDGFORTH IDENTIFIES as an L.A. girl, though her spirit is shaped by many places. Although she was born in Cook County Hospital in Chicago, she and her mother, Sonja Annjeanette Bridgforth, moved to Los Angeles when Bridgforth was about three years old. It was her childhood years in Memphis living with relatives from her mother's side of the family that rooted her in her mother's bloodline. It was New Orleans—what she calls her psychic and spiritual space—that gives her her blood memories from her father's people. Even with this complex landscape that created her brand of jazz—the people, the spirits, the histories, the sounds of each location—Los Angeles is Bridgforth's *àdúgbò,* the place that most forged her ideas of community solidarity, of family particularities, and of Black art in the everydayness of identity formation and social interaction. Place and family are central to Bridgforth's identity. Her longing for home and her journey through family reconciliations have fueled much of her work. She ran the streets of Century, Manchester, Florence, Slauson, Western, Denker, Normandie, and Vermont, full of Tennessee, Louisiana, Georgia, Texas, Mississippi, and Alabama migrants, BBQ shacks, and soul food restaurants. Her bus rides through Hollywood, Echo Park, Venice Beach, Little Tokyo, the Miracle Mile District, and downtown L.A. made her familiar with a range of truths, and taught her something about the richness and variety of the world, including the density of Black life. The meticulous details of Black possibilities give her work a fullness and specificity, and a comfort and familiarity. During her childhood bus trips, she discovered how rich and varied the world is. This appreciation for diverse ways of life laid a foundation for an expansive and inclusive Blackness in her adult writing.

Figure 31. Sharon Bridgforth composing *River See* at Rockefeller Memorial Chapel. Bridgforth has developed a distinctive style of storytelling—of composing—in which she improvises the evolution of the performance by giving the performers and audience/witnesses specific signals indicating what is needed. This performance was produced by Links Hall in 2013. Left to right: Adriene Patrice Barber, Sonja Parks, Joshua L. Ishmon, Kathleen Purcell Turner, Sharon Bridgforth. Barber, Ishmon, and Turner are company members with Deeply Rooted Dance Theatre. Photo by Matthew Gregory Hollis.

---

bunched up bookstores with half naked ladies dance in windows beckon readers
come / boys not yet men walk the dividing line swinging tight jeans crop tops
and plenty ass / temporary
furniture stores pawn shops motels hotels liquor stores and thriftys
match box churches with stick suit preachers shout
while folks at the giant donut hole in the sky wait   more motels liquor stores
and thriftys
vacant lots tattered apartments houses insurance offices barbershops beauty shops and
shoe shine stoops / rib joints you-buy-we-fry head shops record shacks check cashing
windows and bean pies / hamburger hangouts
temporary drug stores boys is where the
girls are / at the catch
i see everything°

° Sharon Bridgforth, "con flama" (unpublished manuscript 2002), 32.

Bridgforth initially attended St. Cecilia Grammar School and Holy Cross Middle School in predominantly Black areas of L.A., then took two city buses to Echo Park in order to attend Our Lady of Loretto High School, a predominantly Latina all-girl school near the intersection of Beverly and Alvarado. Her mother wanted her to continue with the strong education she believed Catholic schools provided, and Bridgforth chose Our Lady of Loretto because she thought they offered karate classes. Bridgforth was mistaken about the karate classes, but she found an excellent sports program and a nurturing environment at Our Lady of Loretto. Her daily bus trips to and from school—two hours each way—took her through a wide range of neighborhoods: West Indian, Jewish, Japanese, Chicana/Chicano, Filipina/Filipino. These names alone do not capture the complex class, racial, and national identities of Los Angeles in the 1960s. She soaked in the dense weave of traditions as she traveled to and from school each day, and came to understand the world as rooted in culture, family, and lineage. Her *àdúgbò,* or neighborhood, was creating an understanding of *ẹgbẹ́,* or work group, that was organically diverse.

---

looking out the window i see

memories unfold / in condemned mirrors

crumpled pictures of never again places and gone times / stand in broken doors

i

see who we are and what we wanted to be.

looking out i look in

the eyes of people passing / witness

the landscape

that created

me °

° Sharon Bridgforth, "con flama" (unpublished manuscript 2002), 41–42.

Bridgforth has spent many years working to have healthy relationships with her family members. In most cases, this has meant a wrenching estrangement, followed by mutual respect and welcome visits that were once filled with an unspoken pact not to traverse explosive territory. Bridgforth's work has been the site where some of these relationships are explored and mollified. Indeed, the work seems to be the very method for making inner peace with family, a peace derived from a complex perception of living relatives, along with rigorous self-examination and deep ancestral remembering. The work is an act of self-making. The writing process exposes truths Bridgforth needs to examine for herself, and once she does so, her primary character, Gurl, must do so as well. Bridgforth's work, then, enacts the crucial vulnerability that is theatrical jazz in which one's personal inner work *is* the artistic public work.

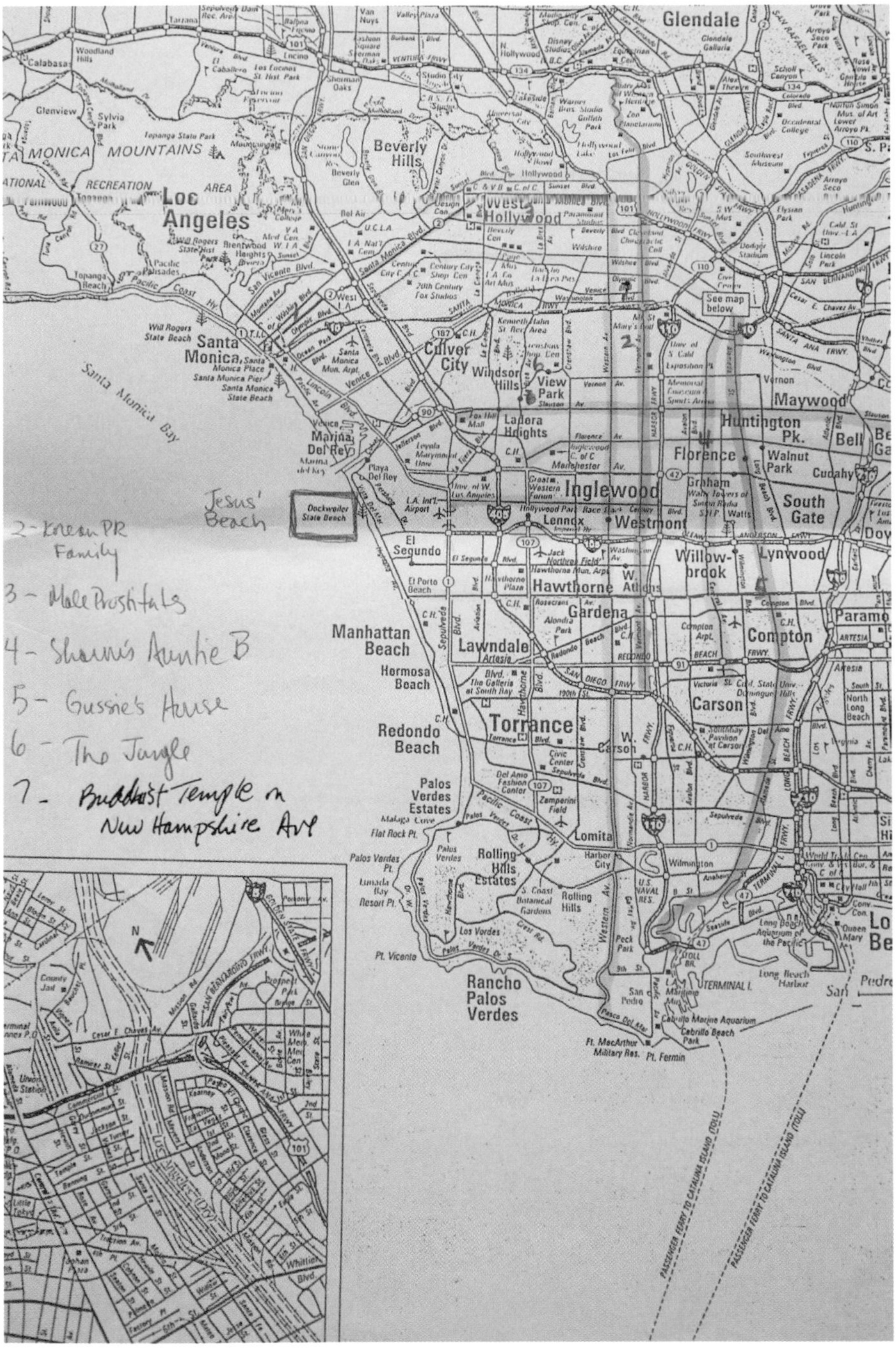
Glendale
Beverly Hills
West Hollywood
Los Angeles
Santa Monica
Santa Monica Bay
Culver City
Marina Del Rey
Jesus' Beach
Dockweiler State Beach
2 - Korean PR Family
3 - Male Prostitutes
4 - Shawn's Auntie B
5 - Gussie's House
6 - The Jungle
7 - Buddhist Temple on New Hampshire Ave
Inglewood
Westmont
Lennox
El Segundo
Hawthorne
Gardena
Huntington Pk.
Florence
South Gate
Lynwood
Willowbrook
Compton
Manhattan Beach
Lawndale
Hermosa Beach
Redondo Beach
Torrance
Carson
Palos Verdes Estates
Rolling Hills Estates
Rolling Hills
Lomita
Wilmington
Rancho Palos Verdes
San Pedro
Maywood
Bell
View Park
Windsor Hills
Ladera Heights
See map below

Figure 32. L.A. map used in *con flama*. Carlos used this map of Los Angeles as a guide to blocking Bridgforth's *con flama* produced at Frontera@Hyde Park Theatre in 2000. The highlighted streets are referenced in the text, and were important during Bridgforth's childhood. The key to the left identifies specific locations that I marked on the map for the cast to orient themselves to Bridgforth's world. Photo by Elisa Durrette.

Figure 33. Sharon Bridgforth and her family. Here, a young Bridgforth is surrounded by relatives in Los Angeles at one of many family gatherings. Behind her is Auntie Bea, who raised her mother. In the right of the photo is Bridgforth's mother, Sonja Annjeanette Bridgforth.

Bridgforth spent two years living in the Orange Mound area of Memphis with a family friend while her mother remained in L.A. to work and attend night school so that she could make a better living to support herself and Bridgforth. Ultimately, the family friend subjected Bridgforth to vicious forms of emotional and physical abuse. Bridgforth's family finally wrested her from this horrendous situation, and relocated her to the family house, where she developed strong bonds with loving great-aunts, great-uncles, great-grandparents, and cousins. Through much of her work, Bridgforth seems to be consoling the girl-self separated from her mother and abused by a friend. A character named Gurl appears again and again in Bridgforth's work. Gurl is often working through childhood trauma in order to achieve an adult peace. In *blood pudding,* Gre Gre Gurl is exploring her father's lineage to find her place as a leader in her community; in *con flama,* Gurl is resolving the mysteries in her mother's lineage and the specific tensions with her mother; in *love conjure/ blues* Isadora Africa Jr., whom the elders call Our Gurl, finds homeplace in a queer community touched by music and the Divine forces of nature; and in *delta dandi* The Gurl survives trauma to declare her self-definitions. *Con flama,* completed in 2002, presents another character named Gurl who frequently asks, "who are our ancestors?" By the time Bridgforth arrives at *delta dandi* in 2010, The Gurl stands confidently as an adult and proclaims, "i wear hat and suspenders / pants with high waist and cuffs / tie and pointed shoes shining . . . today i say / i am right to be here . . ."[1] She concludes the performance piece with: "Ask your question child." Here, the works have come full circle as the questioning child evolves into the adult who eagerly invites—almost commands—the children to ask what they need to know. The Gurl assures them that they can ask whatever they like, for she is a strong, loving adult who will answer and protect them. While Bridgforth's work is not a simple retelling of her own life events, her struggles and her growth are played out in her performance work. Forging work through the crucible of writing assists Bridgforth in understanding her own life and, importantly, in moving to a deeper place of spiritual and artistic development. These steps are marked by Gurl's progress through Bridgforth's work. Through performance, Bridgforth's potent memories are exposed, like a theatrical homage to the moments of childhood she variously relished or dreaded, like a thank you to the people who helped her make sense of the world, like a prayer for the sorrow to dissolve under the stage lights with a witnessing audience.

---

she hit me she hit me she always hit me with brush and broom with stick and fist she hit me in the night. cursing she drag me to the shed in the woods and slam and chain the door. *nobody hear you crying gal cept the devil out here in the dark.* scared to scream to tremble to moan I stop breathing don't breathe till morning. shed not big enough to stretch. i stand in pools of piss with maggots swarming. wake in a ball on the floor in wet with stink and bugs and heat and haunting. i hear her through the broken slats. always she fling the door open with the sun and pull me out by my hair. Must tend field and house before eat.

why nobody come. why they not come get me. why i here i wonder every day
every day
every day
i hate her.

must hide thoughts. can't breathe. no talk. no mumble. no scream. my kin live
down
the dirt road.
they sold me i think to the devil for a few chickens and a barrel of shine.

with bruised body and heavy eyes i sag in my spirit and spine.

i five. i think.°

° Sharon Bridgforth, *delta dandi*, 199.

summers in memphis with my best friend cynthia running along railroad tracks
    walking
for miles
in the sun-adventures.
i spent hours and hours and hours
with my great aunts   at card parties and social lady functions / and mostly at
        department stores where they bought me one chocolate turtle nut cluster
        and a troll doll   i ate
both   delighted each time by the richness of it all / their color coordinated
        splendor
i'd watch them / and eat fascinated
by the way they commanded the white cashiers take their money / respectfully
in the not legally-still-segregated separate but not equal
south.
my great uncles visited their momma's and sister's houses
pressed / with suspenders / shoes shined / hats off / soft under the breath chuckles
        and clear
twinkling eyes
            except for uncle gus who became a wino after he got out the army.
cousins by the end of each day wore sagging socks and crooked clothes / their
        bellies
hanging out like   me
droopy draws
red
slim
and pumpkin were my names.°

° Sharon Bridgforth, "con flama" (unpublished manuscript, 2002), 36–37.

Bridgforth became well known for *the bull-jean stories,* her Lambda Award–
winning anthology of linked stories that centers around the life of bull-dog-jean,
a Black Southern butch woman who loves women, dresses like a man, and fights
for the right to be exactly who she is. This early work of Bridgforth's is rooted in
the blues, and like the musical tradition that anchors them, these stories are full of
pathos, basically linear, and saturated with Southern sensibilities—rules of deco-
rum, family connectedness, and constricting racial politics. A profound achievement of the work is in the vivid, emotionally complex Black queer characters who
reflect a Black queer life rarely expressed in literature. Even as Bridgforth went on
to incorporate jazz structures, the blues remained an important pulse in the work.
It is no surprise that Bridgforth's jazz rests deep inside its blues roots given the
abundance of sexually transgressive women she creates. As Angela Davis points
out in her analysis of blues women, they "openly challenged the gender politics

Figure 34. "Boom Boom Girls," by Tonya Engel. Bridgforth felt very connected to this painting. The angularity of the central figure's body, the bright colors, the references to music suggest the lively juking environments that Bridgforth frequently includes in her work. Photo by Tonya Engel.

implicit in traditional cultural representations of marriage and heterosexual love relationships."[2] The blues locales of juke joints and river banks, the blues narratives of thwarted romance and transgressive desire, and, significantly, the female Blues singer who is the very sign post of Black female agency,[3] can still be found in Bridgforth's jazz works—*love conjure/blues, delta dandi,* and *blood pudding.* Interestingly, in spite of its name, *love conjure/blues* uses the jazz structures of nonlinearity, simultaneity of time and place, and polyphonic narratives even as it retains blues themes. Bridgforth moves away from the rather homogenous Southern lesbian world of bull-jean to the more sexually diverse and ambiguous world that her several Gurl characters occupy. Laurie Carlos notes that *con flama* was the first time bull-jean didn't speak in Bridgforth's work, giving space for the wounded Gurl to finally have her say.[4]

Bridgforth luxuriates in the details of Black life, often working to resurrect a vanished homeplace, or to construct the home that never quite existed. Her deep craving for a remembered L.A. while she lived in Austin, San Antonio, New York, and Chicago may reflect her persistently nomadic life. In *con flama*, Gurl confesses:

> so i took the biggest grant out of town
> and explored civilization
>
> till the chill of missing home consumed me / back
> down century normandie slauson western adams crenshaw venice la cienega
> wilshire westwood santa monica la brea sunset echo park figueroa century and
> back again down hollywood i went
> never finding the spaces that used to fit me
>
> and now i ache for home now / i nurse
> a yearning for
> a place that no longer exists
>
> i wonder
> where i belong
> and now
> my heart hurts
> from starting over
> again
> and again / trying to settle[5]

Although Bridgforth's mother's family mostly attended Baptist churches, and she attended Catholic schools—notwithstanding a stint as a born-again Christian and attending a Seventh-Day Adventist school for the third grade—her current adult spiritual life draws from indigenous traditions and her own evolving relationship with the Divine. She has said many times, "My work is my spiritual practice"; being a writer, then, is a spiritual calling, and spirituality is infused throughout her work. For Bridgforth, the chief ingredient in this art as spiritual practice is the act of being present. This core habit pervades her writing and her facilitation process, "Finding Voice."[6] In workshops, she requires that participants reflect on a mantra for sharpening attention—"What am I feeling, what is that about, and how does that affect my work?" It was this abiding commitment to being present, to feeling whatever she was feeling in each moment, that ultimately insinuated itself into her own life in 1995.

> I stopped drinking. I haven't drunk since 1995. And I think the process of becoming sober and getting clear also helped to shape [my spiritual practice] . . . if I can just be present, the stories are everywhere. If I am clear and I focus doing my work I don't have to worry about everything else in terms of the writing . . . you create a life that allows the work to live and thrive and be present . . . I did sweats, I fasted, I called the spirit down with the work, had rituals, all of that. [My spiritual practice] used to look much more detailed in terms of an indigenous-based form of spirituality that was in my life and in my work . . . [now] the thing that I strive for is to be present and to be as loving as I'm able . . . right now [my spiritual practice] just looks like me being present.[7]

After six years of touring, in 1999 Bridgforth disbanded The root wy'mn Theatre Company,[8] the Black female jazz aesthetic ensemble she founded as a way of mounting her work. root wy'mn toured the United States with Bridgforth's *dyke/warrior-prayers, lovve/rituals & rage,* and *no mo blues,* receiving strong reviews in each city. In spite of the national visibility touring garnered and the many contributions root wy'mn made to the development of theatrical jazz in Austin, serving as the company's producer, booking agent, and artistic director made it impossible for Bridgforth to maintain her spiritual practice of writing. Discontinuing root wy'mn allowed her to return to and maintain the present-tense-ness that writing demands.

Figure 35. The root wy'mn Theatre Company. Left to right: Anoa Monsho, Sonja Parks, Arriama Matlock-Abdullah, and Kaci Fannin. Photo by Rita DeBellis.

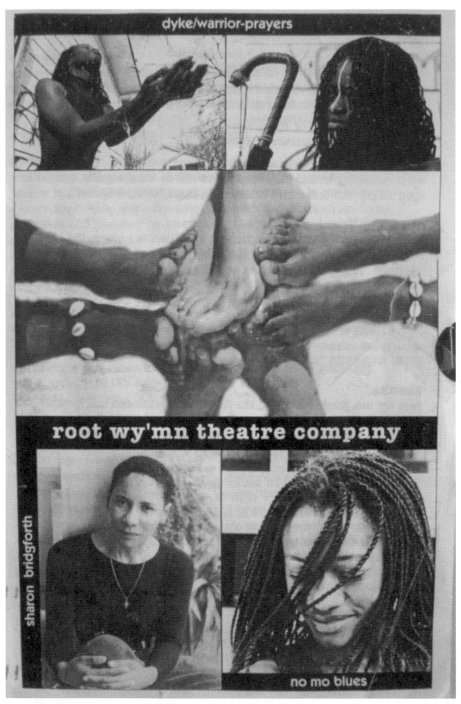

Figure 36. The root wy'mn Theatre Company flyer. In April 1996, The root wy'mn Theatre Company mailed out promotional flyers soliciting support for their work. The interior of the flyer indicates the company's connections to Austin institutions such as East Side Café, Dance Umbrella, St. James Episcopal Church, and Women and Their Work. Photos and design by Rita DeBellis.

Given the emphasis on being right here right now in Bridgforth's personal life, and its importance to her spiritual and artistic philosophies, it is understandable that coffee holds a central place in Bridgforth's world. The caffeine prods the drinker into alertness, makes one ready for the work at hand; and the international rituals and production of coffee pull together Bridgforth's respect for communal ceremonies with her profound appreciation for the history and diversity of indigenous life generally, and Black life specifically.

Her characters also use coffee knowingly, even seductively, as in the song that bull-jean sings to a prospective lover in *the bull-jean stories*. This song was performed in the 1996 production of *dyke/warrior-prayers*:

I'd like to be
The coffee in yo cup,
The first thang you put yo lips on
Each day

I'd like to be
The coffee in yo cup
What you grind
At night
To get on yo way

Let me
Be the coffee in yo cup
Hold me close / smell
Yo memories
Wake

Black / with
A little sugar
Made to fit your taste
Stir and sip me slow
Don't let none go to waste

I need to be yo coffee, baby
Long as you want yo cup filled up / I'd
Like to be the coffee / baby
Waiting for you   in yo cup[9]

In *con flama,* the importance of coffee is expressed through its careful preparation. One of the unnamed characters says:

ohninny
we better get to making some fresh coffee cause you know how your aunt bobo

despise a cuppa chololo brew
and first thing home from work too
quick / quick
we best get to getting now[10]

In an appendix to the script, Bridgforth defines chololo as "a very weak cup of coffee," a definition she credits to the *New Orleans 7th Ward Nostalgia Dictionary, 1938–1965*. The offense of weak coffee is so profound, it requires its own name, definition, and citation. Weak coffee means feeble concentration.

In *love conjure/blues,* there are three references to coffee, each connected to the importance of clarity or presentness. In one moment, the notoriously misbehaving big bill announces her love to bettye, who "just sit with she coffee stare off the porch till big bill ready to tell it."[11] The fact that bettye is drinking coffee is a sure sign that what is to follow is of major significance; it is a cue for her and the audience to pay attention. The other two references to coffee in *love conjure/blues* happen when the storyteller wants to be sure the audience knows that liquor is not allowed in "bettye's jernt," that instead she serves "strong ass coffee." One particularly lively storyteller explains the presence of coffee at bettye's this way:

see / bettye don't allow no drinking in she jernt.
not since she lost her first love lushy boudreaux to the guzzle.
naw / lushy ain't dead
thats her yonder holding up the back of the jernt.
bettye lost lushy from she bed   when she kicked that drunk ass out one last
    time.
been upset about that ever since. mostly at herself / say she got so caught up
    loving what
lushy could have been / she wouldn't see what lushy really was.

anyway

lushy don't drink no more / bettye don't like the smell of the drink / reminding
    her of the hard times / so we all forced stay in our right minds when we
    come to bettye's
    well not all of us / cause you know any fool can find a way to tilt they cup if
    they   want to. but bettye's no liquor rule do cut down on the free flow-
    ingness of it
which is a relief really
because usually with the drinking come the looking and the looking bring the
    knives / cause folk can't just look at they own peoples they gots to always cast
    a looking at somebody's somebody else / and the knives bring the cussing
    and the cussing bring the swoll chest and the swoll chest
always
interrupt the good time.[12]

When coffee appears for the final time in the performance, it is just before a mighty wrong gets righted. Two-timing lushy finally apologies to bettye for cheating with the songstress prophetically named change. Right after change sings a song so fine that the patrons' "drool get wiped," lushy tells bettye: "for all the ways that i acted a fool I know i was / wrong / and i was sho nuff wrong / for fucking change bettye . / i am sorry honey. / i am sorry."[13] In Bridgforth's work, clear and loving choices come from a lucid mind. While alcohol can tire and distort the spirit, coffee can clear and focus it.

SHARON'S PERFECT CUP OF COFFEE*
THE HISTORY

I love Coffee[†]
and a lot of writers / artists that I know love Coffee.
there is a bit of ritual that goes into making Coffee,
and offering it / and taking it in
so some of it is the ritual—
the smells / the feel / the brewing of it / the nuances of brewing it

of course the taste

it as an offering to something that can be a gateway for expression
to help people get beyond needing a treat or being tired or being unable to focus
the caffeine of it
as much as taking it in / of making the cups / and taking it in.

Coffee has the desired effect every time.
Even people who don't drink it express the comfort from smelling and watching
      others get excited about it.

I prefer very hearty very dark organic brands of Coffee that are created in fair trade.
If money or location doesn't allow me to get to this / then I do Bustelo.

I didn't grow up with Coffee drinkers
my Auntie Bea drank Coffee, but it was Folger's Instant
what I found out is that when Sonja [Bridgforth's daughter] was about five /
      sometimes Auntie Bea would babysit while I was at work / and she was giving
      Sonja Coffee / which I would have never done / and I found that out when
      Sonja told me that when she was a teenager

---

* E-mail message to author, May 15, 2011.
† Note Bridgforth's use of capitalization for Coffee. This is a sure sign of its profound importance for Bridgforth, who also capitalizes Divine, Ancestors, and Spirit. Coffee, then, has the spiritual weight of a cosmic force.

what Auntie Bea told me is that when she grew up in Memphis / she was the
    second to the oldest / and she said they would give the kids Coffee so the
    kids could work
she grew up with her grandmother because there were so many kids
her grandmother was mean / and would give Auntie Bea Coffee so she could work
so she didn't think there was anything wrong with it.

I didn't start drinking Coffee until I was in my last two years of college / Sonja was
    little / and I was just simply trying to stay awake
I drank instant / from the machine at school / I didn't care about or have any sense
    of being a Coffee connoisseur.

I became a connoisseur
it wasn't until I was in a relationship with a Puerto Rican from the Lower East Side.
I began to fall in love with the ritual of Coffee / and the richness of loving Coffee.
we drank Bustelo.
we heated the milk
it was very much a meditative ritual with making it
and huge fanfare with every cup for us
and for every guest that came to the house
it was just damn good
we made it in espresso pots on the stove
it was special / for you.
extremely strong
and just a wonderful taste.

I always had special cups
the biggest cup I can put my hands on
Some people go with pretty / but I go for big.
Helga has two very beautiful China cups and she has a big cup
and that's the one that I use.
Sonja and her dad gave me one one birthday.

The Recipe

I make Coffee many ways using many instruments.
espresso machine / Melitta filters / the good old sock drip / espresso pot.
for groups, I have a large thermos thing that I wash and fill with boiling hot water
let it sit with the water for a while
I get a large Coffee pot that gets the water really hot
and I pour in a fair trade organic deep dark rich roast or Bustelo
and I just dump it in there
then I put some more in
then I brew the Coffee

pour out the hot water from the thermos thing
and pour the Coffee into that thing
then I have available half and half / soy creamer / raw sugar / Splenda so that
    people can
make their Coffee
and large paper cups

I don't let Coffee sit all day
I'll make a new batch
it will be there fresh when the people arrive for a workshop
then before a break / I give people a writing assignment
then I'll make the Coffee / and at the break it will be there waiting for them

I used to make Coffee in ice trays but I don't do that no more

drinking Coffee is part of my meditation practice / one large cup in the morning as
    part of
my meditation
and I'll drink one cup of decaf later on in the day / and that's because as I have
    gotten
older and hormonally challenged I have to be mindful that I get a good night's sleep.

and I will take a train and four buses and jog 10 blocks uphill to get to Peet's and
    Café Mundi
at Café Mundi they have great Coffee / and the owner has created an environ-
    ment that
nurtures and supports the ritual of Coffee.
at Pete's the Coffee is just exquisite / for a big business their politics are great
they supported local artists when they were based in Austin / actively supported
    artists
through their donations / they approached me
I used to go in there all the time and they're very much about finding out what's
    going on
in the community they are in
they knew I was curating events for allgo / and they just offered / they would
    deliver it sometimes
and Café Mundi has done the same thing / provided free space for events /
    donated Coffee
and snacks for events that I have curated / myself and others

The most common mistake people make when making Coffee—

low quality beans
make it too weak
and let it sit too long

that's the ruination of Coffee
and don't get the water hot enough

the relationship between Coffee and people of African descent is complicated
    through
slavery / colonization / and capitalism
maybe that's why it's important
that we celebrate each cup
with mindful ritual and intention
and important to gift it to loved ones in that way

The act of being present is often represented in Bridgforth's work by prayers and praying. Indeed, she founded root wy'mn as "an act of learning how to pray through art."[14] When working on *con flama*, Laurie Carlos said of the piece, "The prayer was the real writing. The rest was what she thought was expected of her. The kid [in the script] wanted to say the prayer to the mother . . . She brought those photographs [from her childhood to rehearsal]. *That's* what she wanted to talk about."[15]

When I worked as a dramaturg on con flama *in 2000, I wasn't really sure of my role. I knew that I wanted to document the work—I videotaped most rehearsals and took copious notes on everything from the foods we ate on breaks to the specific movements that Laurie introduced in rehearsals. I wanted this detail because I knew there was some truth in it, a truth that I am still working to name and to live. In addition to the documentation, I also researched different references in the text— Japanese relocation camps, the Brown Beret, forced*
sterilization in Puerto Rico, the Watts riots of 1965, maps of Sharon's childhood neighborhood. I loved piecing together details of the text, it felt so concrete against the open explorations in rehearsal. It made me feel useful in a room full of very creative and pliable artists. I also knew that being a dramaturg often means closely responding to the print text. I was able to draw on my training in Oral Interpretation, work that I had not used in years, work that helped me to really love a text, and work that seemed so removed from the spontaneous
discovery of these rehearsals. Over the years I had seen dramaturg Megan Monaghan and Laurie talk through knotty issues of structure and intention, I'd heard performers describe the spaces of muddiness in the text or incomprehensible emotional shifts. I wanted to likewise provide such insights, and offered Laurie and Sharon some feedback on the text of con flama. *Early in the rehearsal process, I sent a lengthy e-mail to Sharon and Laurie in which I commented on the water/fire and transportation/movement images, the bus trips as a structuring device for the entire piece, the monologues as spiritual personal narratives, and the contrasting list of artists and works. I wrote,*

PENUMBRA THEATRE PRESENTS

CON FLAMA

BY SHARON BRIDGFORTH

ORIGINAL MUSIC BY LOURDES PÉREZ & ANNETTE D'ARMATA | DIRECTED BY LAURIE CARLOS

Celebrate the cultural landscape of American life.

Figure 37. *con flama,* Penumbra Theatre program cover. This program cover for the 2001 Penumbra Theatre production of *con flama,* directed by Carlos, features a young Bridgforth (probably six or seven years old) with the Watts Tower looming to the right of the image.

From page 31 on, the script has the potential for moving toward a kind of
sentimentality. I don't know if this is what you want, but those last pages
seem to arrive at a quick "you can do it if you try"
solution that contrasts the specific social and personal pain that is so clearly
played out in the rest of the script.

While many of my other observations seem to have withstood the test of time, I
realize now how I missed the force of the ending of the work. What I described as
"sentimentality" was actually the core of the work
for Laurie, who gently but conclusively said to me "no . . . no . . . no (shaking her head
slowly) the ending is not sentimental. What she wants is to get to that prayer."

> "RAGE IS THE COLLECTIVE GRIEF
> AND TRAUMA THAT BLACK PEOPLE
> FROM THE SOUTH WORK WITH."*
> —SHARON BRIDGFORTH
>
> * Interview by author, New York, July
> 2003.
>
> "LOVE THAT COMES FROM A
> SPACE OF OPEN SPIRITS CON-
> NECTING IS LIKE CREATING THE
> PERFECT COMBO, AND LIKE JAZZ,
> IT SHIFTS TIME."*
> —SHARON BRIDGFORTH
>
> * Phone interview with author, January
> 2007.

Cornel West makes a plea for Black love when he writes, "Like alcoholism
and drug addiction, nihilism is a disease of the soul . . . Nihilism is not over-
come by arguments or analyses; it is tamed by love and care
. . . a love ethic has nothing to do with sentimental feelings
or tribal connections. Rather it is a last attempt at generating
a sense of agency among a downtrodden people."[16] That nihilism is born of a righteous rage with few appropriate places for
expression. Bell hooks speaks to agency as a healthy by-product
of addressing rage when she tells us "renewed, organized black
liberation struggle cannot happen if we remain unable to tap
collective black rage."[17] If Bridgforth's productions merely reveal
the trauma without ameliorating it, without providing medi-
cine, without productively directing the rage, she could not save
herself or her family line. The jazz aesthetic work affirms the
human spirit, and Bridgforth's affirmations are often expressed
as prayer. Prayer is the enactment of *àṣẹ*, the faith that what one
calls for will come to be.

Creation in the jazz aesthetic is exactly the work of self-
making. In order to craft this work, the writer must pry open the most concealed self and speak from that place of verity. This is the spiritual work of the
practice. The writer prepares by developing the psychic muscles for telling
the truth and loving the self. Bridgforth describes a watershed moment of self-
revelation intimately linked with artistic clarity around the development of *con
flama*:

> . . . myself, the composers Lourdes Perez and Annette D'Armata, and Laurie
> were meeting up for coffee before going into the first rehearsal. Or at least I
> thought we were having coffee, you know a lil happy time before work. Chile,
> Laurie came in, she looked at me, she held the script up in the air, and she
> threw it down on the floor. Lourdes and Annette backed up, my mouth dropped,
> Laurie said, "this is a piece of shit. Oh it's pretty, cause you're a good writer. But
> you have not said what you need to say, and until you do, you will be writing

the same thing over and over for the rest of your life!" Laurie leaned in close, pointing at me, Lourdes and Annette were almost out the door, Laurie said, "you need to write about why that little girl was on the bus. Where was her mama? What did she want from her mama? What is that little girl's story? That's what this piece is about. Until you write THAT . . ." Well, at that I started crying. I was crying cause I knew she was right, cause deep down the little girl had already been talking to me and I didn't want to deal with her. That little girl—me—had been waiting all her life for someone to pay attention. She wanted very much to tell her story. I cried, Lourdes and Annette cried, Laurie cried. Laurie hugged me. Then we pulled ourselves together and went to rehearsal. That night I stayed up till I was done. I wrote in the voice of the little girl.[18]

In her most recent works, the primary characters are looking for a healing—with their mothers, with their ancestors, with themselves—and that healing is often achieved near the conclusion of the piece through prayer. Just before the primary character offers her closing words in *con flama,* the community chorus enfolds the audience in collective supplication to the Divine:

may remembering be our shield
may love be our weapon of choice

may we live life
like a drum driven dance
connected
may we
love ourselves
give compassion
walk in Spirit
and
may the flame
in our heart be
love.[19]

Near the end of the 1998 version of *blood pudding,* Bridgforth calls for an invocation:

my mother paints the leaves in autumn / fans
earthquakes and hurricanes beneath her skirts my
mother will clean for you / but
do not disturb her
if you are not ready for the visit / she cyclones destroys outward structures when
she sweeps
maw'mn is ready
dancing by the tombstones
till changing time come / call[20]

Bridgforth then concludes the piece with a prayer:

> *Ancient breeze*
> *softly send*
> *my Soul fly home*
> *with You / i pray*
> *Heaven be here*
> *on Earth*
> *in my Heart and actions*
> *please change me clean*
> *for Thee / THY WILL BE DONE*
> *HOLY AND SACRED ONE*
> *make me*
> *a channel of*
> *THE PEACE AND GOOD WILL OF THE CREATRESS*
> *make me*
> *a channel of*
> *THE PEACE AND GOOD WILL OF THE CREATRESS*
> *make me*
> *a channel of*
> *THE PEACE AND GOOD WILL OF THE CREATRESS* [21]

Prayer is also central to *love conjure/blues*. One of the final lines declares: "I am the answered Prayer / the manifested Light" [22] Overt references to spirit are infused throughout much of Bridgforth's work. Indeed, the evolution of her work charts a path to self-love in spite of everything, and that path is a deeply spiritual one. Like Bridgforth herself—who has stopped drinking, has reconciled her relationships with both her mother, who was uncomfortable with Bridgforth's sexuality, and her father, who was absent during the early years of her childhood, has lovingly and vigorously reclaimed her relationship with her daughter, has declared herself a working artist, and has wrestled with cervical cancer—the Gurl of Bridgforth's performances comes through her fractures with a profound sense of self-sanctity.

Giving voice to language reflects the Yoruba concept of *àfọ̀ṣẹ*, the ability of words to make things happen. Spoken prayer, then, calls forth a Divine manifestation, as sound, vibration, and will conspire toward creation. While all theatre could be imagined as potential examples of *àfọ̀ṣẹ*, the overtly spiritual nature of prayer invigorates Bridgforth's work with the added authority of conscious spiritual communication.

Bridgforth did not come to theatre as a playwright. She came as a writer. Because of this indirect route to the theatre, and because of the specific type of performance works she creates, Bridgforth has struggled with categorizing each of her performances. She has borrowed the term "biomythography" from Audre Lorde, and has also used "performance pieces" to describe some of her work. *Love conjure/blues* she calls a "performance novel," while the San Antonio production of *con flama* is called a "word opera." She identifies *blood pudding* as "a spoken word blusical," and *geechee crossing* as a "theatrical/opera that uses words-as-music in a jazz aesthetic." With *delta dandi* she originally intended to create a "word orchestra complete with gospel choir." Bridgforth was exploring this specific form with choir as early as 2000 with *geechee crossing* when she described the work in the stage directions as

> an interdisciplinary piece based in an African and African-American circular form. This work is a theatrical/opera that uses words-as-music in a jazz aesthetic. Movement/gestural language should be used however the focus of this work should be on the delivery of the vocal orchestrations and words. Number of cast members may vary but there should be at least four (three wy'mn and one man or four wy'nm), plus a choir and a quartet.[23]

The emphasis on music is made explicit in the full title of the work—*geechee crossing marsha's overture.*

SHARON'S DISCOGRAPHY OF IMPORTANT MUSIC AS OF 2014*

"DIDN'T IT RAIN," SISTER ROSETTA THARPE, *THE GOSPEL OF BLUES*

"WHAT A DIFFERENCE A DAY MAKES," DINAH WASHINGTON, *UNFORGETTABLE*

"MY FUNNY VALENTINE," SARAH VAUGHAN, *LIVE IN JAPAN*, VOL. 1

"SEE LINE WOMAN," NINA SIMONE, *THE DEFINITIVE COLLECTION: NINA SIMONE*

"UNCHAINED MELODY," JIMMY SCOTT, *THE SOURCE*

"OH HAPPY DAY," ARETHA FRANKLIN WITH MAVIS STAPLES, *ONE LORD, ONE FAITH, ONE BAPTISM*

"AT LAST," ETTA JAMES, *AT LAST*

"MY ONE AND ONLY LOVE," JOHN COLTRANE AND JOHNNY HARTMAN, *JOHN COLTRANE AND JOHNNY HARTMAN*

"IT'S YOUR THING," THE ISLEY BROTHERS, *BEST OF THE ISLEY BROTHERS*

"SAY IT LOUD—I'M BLACK AND I'M PROUD," JAMES BROWN, *SAY IT LOUD—I'M BLACK AND I'M PROUD*

"JESUS CHILDREN OF AMERICA," STEVIE WONDER, *INNERVISION*

"BUTTERFLIES," MICHAEL JACKSON, *THE ULTIMATE COLLECTION*

"THE GODS HAVE FEET OF CLAY," HELGA DAVIS

* Sharon Bridgforth, e-mail message to the author, June 6, 2014.

"ALL ON A MARDI GRAS DAY," WILD MAGNOLIAS, *LIFE IS A CARNIVAL*

"BLESSED," THE EMOTIONS, *REJOICE*

"LADY MARMALADE," LABELLE, *NIGHTBIRDS*

"SHAKE YOUR MONEY MAKER," DEACON JOHN, *LIVE AT THE 1994 NEW ORLEANS JAZZ & HERI-*
    TAGE FESTIVAL

Given Bridgforth's exploration of form and dedication to musicality, her indebtedness to Ntozake Shange's *for colored girls* is not surprising. She explains,

> . . . the only theatre I ever remember going to, was to see *for colored girls* in San Francisco. It was in the 70s, of course, and I didn't really know what I was going to do. I was kind of tripping around, had gone to college for a year or so and I didn't really find a fit there . . . I saw this advertisement and I went by myself. It was my first memory of being in theatre . . . and it just changed my whole life. Then I got the book and read the book and you know kind of, it just gave me the freedom to imagine telling the truth, to imagine using language in a way that really worked for me. It allowed me to imagine that I could do art and it was liberating and, just really important to see those black women on the stage doing what they were doing . . . most significantly I think that the way that the piece was structured, being nonlinear, using movement, barefoot, simple costumes, light, but really the power of the word and the word was poetic and the freedom to explore rhythm with language, stories from the body and realness in terms of being a black woman talking life it—it opened a door that for me as a writer . . . significantly shaped how I wrote and how I came to write and how I became clear that it was important to control how I wanted to do things, as opposed to believing the message that the way I was doing it was wrong.[24]

The musicality of Bridgforth's language and her ability to paint the page with distinctive punctuation, multiple fonts, bold, and italics, and the play of flush left / flush right / center derive in large part from the freedom she discovered through Shange's *for colored girls*. Bridgforth strives to put what she internally hears and how she hears it on the page.

Bridgforth earned her B.A. from California State University, Los Angeles, in 1985. She originally attended St. Mary's College in Moraga, California, for a year, where she majored in physical education. Although she loved the idea of teaching P.E. and kinesiology, she injured her back and was distracted from her studies by drugs and alcohol. When she enrolled in Cal State L.A., there was no single department that encompassed her interests and talents. Her experience with *for colored girls* validated a multigenre approach to her writing. To accommodate her unique curricular needs, a program was created especially for her—Creative Writing and Broadcast Media.

Bridgforth's work has become increasingly expressive of spirit. The 1999 *bull-jean stories* references spirit, but in that work spirituality comes mostly through romantic love and the rhythms of juke joints. By the time Bridgforth pens *delta dandi* in 2009, the entire work is engulfed in an otherworldly realm designed to bring Gurl, and the audience, to a state of inner transformation. It might be that "communal invocation" best names the more directly spiritual work she is now creating. Bridgforth's friends lovingly, perhaps prophetically, call her Reverend

When Bridgforth declares "My work is my spiritual practice" this not only suggests the content and structure of the work, it also reveals the spiritual inspiration that brings the work forth, and the spiritual aspirations she holds for her audiences. The ancestors and the forces of nature are venerated Divinities as well as collaborators for Bridgforth.

It is in her more recent works such as *blood pudding, con flama, love conjure/blues,* and *delta dandi* that Bridgforth turns her attention more fully to the blend of the past with the present—a hallmark of theatrical jazz—as she makes manifest the power of ancestral embodiment. Stephanie Batiste describes Bridgforth's particular response to time in *delta dandi* as an "aquanova," that "borrows the mystery and vastness of outer space in its suggestion of the multiple layers of cosmic existence—time, location, distance—as a primary element in water's movement between and across spaces."[25] Prior to these works, Bridgforth concentrated on the individual, giving less attention to the self within community. Her particular writer's voice—poetic, bluesy, full of whiskey and regret, love and personal redemption, and many tongues—expands as she moves away from her mostly southern present-dwelling Black women/dykes and into gender-variant, racially, geographically, and temporally complex characters. Even with this evolution in character, content, time, and space, the South remains her favored locale. Her writer's voice now speaks in multiple tones while retaining a specific acknowledgment of Southern ancestral authority.

Ancestors are *égún,* those who now inhabit *òrun,* or the world of spirit. In Yoruba cosmology *aiyé,* the earth, and *òrun* have a cycling spiraling relationship of mutual influence. This relationship is often depicted as the two halves of a calabash, a vessel with interdependent units. Some *égún* are elevated to the status of *Egúngún,* commonly understood as an ancestral masquerade, a whirling assemblage of a lineage's respect for a family member or a Divine concept such as the Primordial Mothers. Painter and art historian Moyo Okediji provides additional intricate understandings of *Egúngún* when he writes,

> The *Egúngún* masquerade celebrates the end of death, or the death of dying. It is a celebration of a vision in which people do not die. The Yoruba people of West Africa have this vision, which they call *Egúngún,* or something that is perfect. *Gun* means symmetrical. *E-gun-gun* means symmetrical perfection. When life is in symmetrical perfection, people do not die. The Yoruba people have therefore developed a vision in which people do not die, but transform into ancestors.[26]

In Okediji's articulation of *Egúngún,* Bridgforth's works bring the ancestors back to *aiyé* for a performance party in their honor, what Okediji calls "a festival of deathlessness."[27] They bless us with the assurance of our interconnectedness. Indeed, as Toni Morrison acknowledges, "When you kill the ancestor you kill yourself."[28]

The ancestors know things that we need. And Bridgforth's work gives us an opportunity to learn from them. The African diaspora is full of wounded phantoms who come to the living with messages. They have seen horrors, been split, chewed deceit, shat terror, and they must tell the tales so that we can fully be. They interrupt our thoughts, tell us stories we don't understand, sing us a forgotten memory—each act reminding us how the dead and the living are inextricably bound. Her work asks that we contribute to an ancestral healing in which the river joy caresses the turquoise sea, in which the birth of tortured memories brings us all to the ultimate freedom of our truest selves. Ancestral transgressions, grief, and trauma must be scraped from the spirit like grime that makes the skin grey with mourning, must be trashed like a pair of ill-fitting shoes that cause a perpetual limp. The ancestors are insistent. We are their best hope for a long-sought good night's sleep. Toni Morrison describes ancestral importance in this way: "these ancestors are not just parent, they are sort of timeless people whose relationship to the characters are benevolent, instructive, and protective, and they provide a certain kind of wisdom . . . the presence or absence of that figure determined the success or the happiness of the character . . . whether the character was in Harlem or Arkansas, the point was there, this timelessness was there, this person who represents this ancestor."[29] As the *Egúngún* swirls through the community, *Oya*'s wind cleanses us of the debris that prevents us from being our best selves. When the ancestors call, it's best to just sit and listen.

---

i saw my Ancestors in the eyes of strangers / sitting on the bus. I   collected
their   stories   on   the bus / in   the   creased
faces   the   bent   backs   the
*   blistered   hands the   pieces   of   memory*
*   flickering   neath the blackbrowntanyellowredwhitebeige flow*
of   skin
the   lilt   and   curve   of   languages
*   spoken   and   silence   the music blasting hair wavy kinky straight*
curly shaved gone doors swinging open laughter strutting broken yelling fists crumpled
smells somebody's dinner rushing in from streets we passed closed curtains weeping
silence and smiles stepping aboard / i saw myself. who do they look out the window
for / wait to return home from work   who are their Ancestors
i wondered.

i saw my Ancestors in the eyes of strangers / sitting on the bus
i collected their stories / created my story
proudly. °

° Sharon Bridgforth, "con flama" (unpublished manuscript 2002), 25.

For Bridgforth, writing is a visitation. She begins to feel the presence of the ancestors as new writing comes—cigar smoke from juke joints, the swish of sassy petticoats, the tinkle of laughter, and the slosh of whiskey in jelly jars. Her work comes to her in dreams in the night, in the early azure hours before sunrise—the ancestors send out the call and her performance works are the response. *Egúngún* are ancestors returned. They speak to Bridgforth, and her performances function like their masquerades, giving the ancestors a festive space to be present in the here and now.

As the ancestors guide her, she begins vigorous research. Bridgforth is a voracious reader, especially of musical biographies. The lives of blues singers, jazz pianists, R&B crooners feed the ancestral call to write, to tell the stories so the truths won't die. These biographies sometimes stimulate specific characters and moments in her work, as with Linda Dahl's biography of Mary Lou Williams that helped produce the no-nonsense piano player, honeypot, who originally appeared in the Long Center for the Performing Art's production of *delta dandi*. More often, the biographies keep Bridgforth connected to the multifarious world of music and the rigors of making art. Her writing process blends the physical practice of reading and writing with the psychic process of listening to the other world speak.

SHARON'S READING LIST

TO BE OR NOT . . . TO BOP: MEMOIRS, BY DIZZY GILLESPIE

MORNING GLORY: A BIOGRAPHY OF MARY LOU WILLIAMS, BY LINDA DAHL

BEYOND CATEGORY: THE LIFE AND GENIUS OF DUKE (ELLINGTON), BY JOHN EDWARD HASSE

LENA, BY LENA HORNE AND RICHARD SCHICKEL

FAITH IN TIME: THE LIFE OF JIMMY SCOTT, BY DAVID RITZ

BROTHER RAY: RAY CHARLES' OWN STORY, BY RAY CHARLES AND DAVID RITZ

RAGE TO SURVIVE: THE ETTA JAMES STORY, BY DAVID RITZ AND ETTA JAMES

DREAM BOOGIE: THE TRIUMPH OF SAM COOKE, BY PETER GURALNICK

THE BIG SEA: AN AUTOBIOGRAPHY, BY LANGSTON HUGHES AND ARNOLD RAMPERSAD

I WONDER AS I WANDER: AN AUTOBIOGRAPHICAL JOURNEY, BY LANGSTON HUGHES AND ARNOLD RAMPERSAD

THE LIFE OF LANGSTON HUGHES (VOLUME 1 & 2), BY ARNOLD RAMPERSAD

JAMES BALDWIN: A BIOGRAPHY, BY DAVID LEEMING

THE AUTOBIOGRAPHY OF MALCOLM X: AS TOLD TO ALEX HALEY

THE WARMTH OF OTHER SUNS: THE EPIC STORY OF AMERICA'S GREAT MIGRATION, BY ISABEL WILKERSON

MY SONG: A MEMOIR, BY HARRY BELAFONTE AND MICHAEL SHNAYERSON

The jazz aesthetic is just the right dwelling place for raucous wandering ancestors, because here, time and space are fluid. Ancestors and deities and nature and humans hum, holler, stomp, spit, and make worlds together, aware or unaware of each other's presence. These spirits intensify, then Bridgforth puts her fingers to the keyboard and lets them guide her. She stated: "I think for me my more mature writing or my actual writer's voice came when I started the ancestors' work, when I started hearing the whispers, hearing my grandmother talk to me, hearing stories, cause I always kinda *saw* but I started *hearing* them."

19.
feathers
colors
light.
singing
dancing
voices.
whispers
warmth
knowing.
Ancestors
Dreams
Awake.
the hairs on my neck stand up
i see them
Africans Indians Geechees kiss my face / rumble when not happy
tell me the stories
My Ancestors
save me from myself.
when i was drunk
    they kept dancing
when i was running
    they kept guiding
when i was broken
    they kept singing
when i gave up
    they didn't.
my mother's people
    from arkansas mississippi memphis chicago

my father's people from
  louisiana Geechee / Black Indians
made remembering wake.

all my Life
i've been recording it all
in my writing / It is
my Spiritual Practice
making Words shaped by Blood.°

° Sharon Bridgforth, "interlude #21: The road to Higher Power."

---

the Ancestral feel of my own tongue in my own mouth / the
birth name of the birth place of my people / the
sound of the ancient leader i could
have been named for
i wonder.
i run
in my mind / over and over
try to recall my truths / i wait
to become me
again.°

° Sharon Bridgforth, "con flama" (unpublished manuscript, 2002), 41–42.

Even the titles of Bridgforth's work reveal something of the ancestral spiritual landscape she often travels, and to which she pays homage. *love conjure/blues, blood pudding, lovve/rituals & rage, geechee crossing, amniotic/flow, no mo blues, delta dandi*—all acknowledge an earth-based spirituality that knows the power of ancestors and lineage, the power of place, the power of the Divine forces of nature, the power of love to create the ultimate authenticity.

Bridgforth opens *con flama* with Gurl's search for her identity as she says, "my earliest memory is of my grandmother's laughter when i was three and we lived in chicago / . . . who are our Ancestors grandmother? / i used to ask her / cause i was hoping i had more grandmothers somewhere." By beginning the work with these lines, Bridgforth establishes the importance of ancestors/lineage/home, not only for her characters but for herself as well. On the page, the point is underscored by capitalizing "Ancestors"; capitals are consistently Bridgforth's markers of respect and honor. Grandmother frustratingly responds to Gurl's question with a series of gibberish answers. She says the ancestors are "kassa shaka mutu," then "kuta mako mo," then "kaba zula we," and finally she tells the truth:"shit gal / i don't know." Gurl tells the audience: "that was a very unsettling moment. / why / didn't she

Figure 38. Florinda Bryant, Ana Perea, Zell Miller III, and Sonja Parks during *con flama* production at Frontera@Hyde Park Theatre. This photo of the 2000 Frontera@Hyde Park Theatre production of Bridgforth's *con flama* directed by Laurie Carlos illustrates the simultaneity and the use of abstract gestures that characterizes theatrical jazz. In the background Miller (left) and Parks mirror non-mimetic movements, while in the foreground Bryant (left) and Perea engage in their own conversation with the audience/witnesses. Photo by Bret Brookshire.

know i wondered. / why don't i know / i wonder / i wonder / why / i am crying / i am crying now / now i cry." In the Hyde Park Theatre production of *con flama,* Gurl's acknowledgment that her Grandmother's response was unsettling often elicited a bit of laughter from the audience, perhaps discomfort with the Grandmother's insensitivity. However, this was not humorous for Gurl or for Bridgforth. Not knowing ancestors makes it more difficult to know one's self.

As Gurl of *con flama* moves through neighborhood after neighborhood on her daily bus trips, she comes to understand the importance of familial roots and the need for ancestral clarity. In *love conjure/blues,* Bridgforth's characters make family from their associations with one another, but in *con flama,* Bridgforth also examines the power of the blood connection—truly a self-journey toward healing a relationship with her own mother and preparing for the healing with her daughter, Sonja Perryman, as expressed in the CD of *amniotic/flow,* which the mother–daughter artistic team collaboratively created. The stories from the ancestors help Bridgforth to make sense of her own life. While many spirits and natural forces move through her work, ancestors hold a place of primacy; one must work to get right with kin before truly being right with anyone else. The stories, family histories, use of language, omnipresence of music, and social protocols from her

Figure 39. Florinda Bryant, Ana Perea, and Sonja Parks during *con flama* production at Frontera@Hyde Park Theatre. In this photo from the 2000 Frontera@Hyde Park Theatre production of Bridgforth's *con flama* directed by Laurie Carlos, the performers are working in separate planes but are also in concert with each other. Photo by Bret Brookshire.

mother's and her father's sides of her family were the foundation for Bridgforth's writing that opened a path to ancestral artistic guidance. Family—the living and the dead—is one's first *egbẹ́*. It prepares us for the community responsibility that will follow as we make theatrical jazz.

In much of Bridgforth's work, ancestor veneration is present as *ìtanlẹ̀*, the defining of a lineage. The *ìtanlẹ̀* is a critical community performance that records the evolving history and linkages of a people. Naming names, identifying places, highlighting key events are central to the *ìtanlẹ̀*'s content. While *ìtàn* is often translated as history, the Yoruba scholar Olabiyi Yai warns against equating this vital Yoruba concept with a Western one. Yai suggests that *ìtàn* "means to illuminate, enlighten, discern, disentangle" chronology and geography. In this way, history is understood as a maze or a riddle. Enacting *ìtàn*, then, is "to 'de-riddle' history, to shed light on human existence through time and space."[30] Bridgforth's productions themselves are richly theatricalized *ìtanlẹ̀* as she works to "de-riddle" her own specific lineage and Black life generally. Near the end of *love conjure/blues*, one of the unnamed voices evokes the power of *ìtanlẹ̀* as the audience is reminded of the community they met through the performance:

bettye figurman slim figurman luiscious boudreaux cat lil tiny ruthieann soon-
yay peachy soonyay bitty fon king creole red guitar sam mannish mary kokomo
j.b. duckie smooth cora adam fathead sims change big bill henry b mama ston-
well marvis jackson sherriff townswater booker chang joshua davis reverend
honré sooky lewis sooky lewis jr. pauline ms. sunday morning sweet t lashay big
paw uncle daddy ma-dear the drummer the Houma the Fon the Ibo the Yoruba
the Wolof the Tunica the Choctaw the Chickasaw isadora Africa jr. isadora
Africa jr. isadora Africa jr. isadora Africa jr. isadora Africa jr. isadora Africa
jr. here with me here in me / are   me . . .

our gurl she
carry the conjuration her mama she mama she mama she mama
and that first African woman pass on[31]

In a similar passage from *con flama,* a voice tells us:

and when she asks who her Ancestors are
i tell her
Missouri Kirk and Calvin Mitchel Black and Joseph Hadley Black and Georgia
Ana Hicks and Georgia Lee Black and / i go on and on naming them all and
i tell her i don't know the names of the Africans but your daddy's daddy can
name all the names on that side your tree / including
the Indians and the Africans.

my daughter you see
gets to keep all her dreams
because we have made it so
and through her
my mother gets to dream again too.[32]

The *ìtanlè* clarifies history so that the present moment can be one of authority. The storyteller recounts the names and places so that the next generation can
live grounded in the certainty of their identity and power. As Okediji points out,
remembering is a kind of birthing, a deep living. For him, the opposite of remember is not forget, but dismember, a severing from lineage and therefore the self.[33]

Blood pudding, con flama, and *delta dandi,* when considered together, form a
trilogy in which Gurl simultaneously embraces through remembering, and releases
through exorcising, those ancestral bonds that either sustain her or mean her no
good. *Blood pudding* addresses Bridgforth's relationship with her father, Lanny
Ross, and his people from Algiers, Louisiana. In *blood pudding,* Gurl soaks in the
dense mysteries of Louisiana through the ways of the French, the Spanish, many
Native Americans, and many Africans. *Con flama* examines Bridgforth's relationship with her mother, and the family history from Chicago to L.A. Here, Gurl's
world has broadened beyond the Southern root. At the end of *delta dandi* just as

Figure 40. The ensemble during *blood pudding* production at Frontera@Hyde Park Theatre. *blood pudding,* by Sharon Bridgforth, directed by Laurie Carlos at Fronter@Hyde Park Theatre, 1998. Left to right: Florinda Bryant, Zell Miller III, Stacey Robinson, Renita Martin, Djola Branner. Photo by Bret Brookshire.

the adult Gurl is centered enough to say "ask your question child," and prepared to help the next generation be fully themselves, Bridgforth has satisfied the ancestral need which must be appeased before entering other Divine realms. In Yoruba-based spiritual traditions, the *égún,* or ancestors, are ceremonially propitiated before approaching the *Òrìṣà.* Bridgforth has mirrored this necessary sequence by fully exploring Gurl's relationship to and interdependence with her ancestors. As Bridgforth notes, "my Ancestors taught me about the Orisha a long time ago."[34] While Bridgforth has included references to the *Òrìṣà* in much of her work (*blood pudding* is dedicated to *Oya, delta dandi* includes many references to *Yemọnja* and *Òṣun, geechee crossing* is "a work for Elleggua, the Divine trickster-linguist / chief engineer of the da / master of the nommo / keeper of the crossroads," and *love conjure/blues* opens with an homage to the pantheon of many Yoruba *Òrìṣà*), it seems the completion of this ancestral trilogy paves the way for an even deeper dance with the *Òrìṣà.*

Bridgforth passes her ancestral appreciation on to the many writers she has mentored in the style of *ìkọ́ṣ'ẹ́,* an elder–apprentice relationship. Florinda Bryant and Virginia Grise both demonstrate their debt to Bridgforth's ancestral insights as they craft their own work. Under Sharon's dramaturgical tutelage for *Half-Breed Southern Fried (check one),* Bryant writes:

Holy Jesus, father god bless her.

                                   Holy ancestors mother earth bless her.

Stop trying to remember.

                                   Stop trying to forget.

There is only pain there.

                                   There is only pain there.

Holy Jesus, father god bless her.

                                   Holy ancestors mother earth bless her.[35]

Bryant unconsciously demonstrates her Bridgforth lineage as she invokes the ancestors she has learned to acknowledge through years of working closely with Bridgforth. Bryant began working with Bridgforth in 1995 through weekly workshops in history and politics held at Bridgforth's home. Since that time, she has performed in *blood pudding, love conjure/blues, delta dandi,* and readings of *Ring Shout* (which later became *River See*), and has participated in the Austin Project while Bridgforth served as Anchor Artist (2002–9). Bryant has also been directed by Carlos and Jones. She is steeped in theatrical jazz even as she works the Hip Hop principles that also shape her art.

Similarly, Virginia Grise began to mine her family's history as a catalyst for her creativity after working with Bridgforth at the Esperanza Peace and Justice Center in San Antonio. In working to name herself an artist, Grise examined her Chinese and Mexican histories through the poem "Rasgos Asiaticos":

wanting to step out of full moon sadness
and into the body of a red dragon woman
breathe life to memory

large cabezas de budah left in mesoamerican lands
tiny jaguar children con rasgos asiaticos

i.
memories de mi bisabuela
que nunca conocí
whose picture
i never saw
whose stories
i never heard

my great grandmother was a cantonese refugee
who traveled to the shores of tampico
port city to the world
narrow streets
lined by buildings that block the sun
ruins of houses
in the discards of the petroquímica refinería empire

she died there
unkempt grave
separated from her family by an ocean
in foreign land

when my great grandmother arrived in mexico
immigration and naturalization services renamed her concepción

concepción was her name

memorias de mi bisabuela
que nunca conocí
whose picture i never saw
whose stories
i never heard

concepción wong

what was my great grandmother's real name?[36]

The persona of Grise's poem is reminiscent of Bridgforth's insistent Gurl long-ing to know her ancestors. Bridgforth is committed to training the next legion of truth-telling artists through her Finding Voice method. Her legacy resides, in part, in those writers who model her artistic courage and her belief in the importance of plumbing an ancestral lineage for artistic and personal wealth.

Push GURRL . . . WRITE!

By Tracey Boone Swan
For Sharon
who always encouraged me to write

Push GURRL!
she says
WRITE

as i struggle with myself
with those words wrapped up inside
tangled with those things I've heard
battling with what came into my ears
from people meaning well
advice about not wasting time
and being practical with life
all those fucked up nuggets
people dropped off, left
piled up in my mind

like dirty towels after a visit
that lasted far too long

Push GURRL!
she says
WRITE

i fight with those words that I've heard
those fucked up nuggets
stacked up in my mind
like the dirty dishes
left in the kitchen overnight
with caked on dried up residue
that no one scraped off
stinking shitty words
from the writing teacher asking
hasn't this story already been told?
telling me:
the story has potential
but something is missing . . .
never revealing what that
something is

Push GURRL!
she says
WRITE

i battle with those words that I've heard
those fucked up little nuggets
dropped off and left out
and offered without regard
by the people meaning well
who do you think you are?
telling secrets that shouldn't be
written, mentioned, said out loud
you don't have time for this
writing when you should be
working not wasting life
you need to concentrate on
something concrete
like an education
like a real job, getting ahead
and not that shit you do
when you should be working
to pay the rent and the bills
for food and diapers
and the student loans

PUSH GURRRL
she says
WRITE!

as i try to drown the words already inside
shaped and formed from self doubt
who do you think you are?
have you lost your mind?
wasting wasting wasting
time money space
when you've never won a prize
never published a sentence
never sold a book and knowing
you don't have time, money or space
let alone a room of your own
there are bills and children
your boyfriend, or girlfriend, or your
partner needs . . .

PUSH GURRRL
she says WRITE!

I gather them all together
all those words I've heard
from the people meaning well
and even from myself

PUSH

those shitty fucked up little nuggets
that build a wall inside my mind

PUSH

and block every gentle beautiful
raw ephemeral word longing
to be written and released

PUSH

and I listen . . .

then
I write.°

° Tracey Boone Swan, "Push GURRL" (unpublished poem, 2003).

Although much of Bridgforth's work has demonstrated the primacy of ancestors, she has also consistently been responsive to the *Òrìṣà*, the Divine forces of
nature, most specifically *Yemọnja,* the white crest of the ocean and the authority
of motherhood. Bridgforth believes that *Yemọnja* claimed her as her child one day
when Bridgforth was scooped up by the sea. She weaves this initiatory event into
delta dandi:

> i don't know how to die so i just go along. carry all
> these things. all these things. till once in the
> black/blue of day i jump. i jump where the waters meet.
> i jump. cold cold cut me. i jump. pray/carry me to the
> ocean. please. maybe i find my mama there. i jump.
> go under. come up. go under. come up. jump. jump. jump.
> can't float down. the water won't take me. again again
> again i jumping till look see. there right there a woman
> tall tall naked and shining in the water stand smile
> smiling down at me in the water. i run out. run stand under
> giant tree with weeping arms. look through bending
> branches. still still. no breathing. can't move. can't
> turn head. can't close eyes. no look away. the woman tall
> tall naked and shining in the water stand. stop laughing.
> stare. stare. stare. stare telling me something
> i don't know what.
> ~ ~ ~ ~
> *silver pearls and turquoise. yams and seaweed. blue skirts 7 layers. peacocks and*
> > *fish*
> > *watermelons and grapes. monday. shifts.*
> > *north star half moon rivers and pound cake.*
> > *strength.*[37]

In Bridgforth's telling of this event, the ocean carried her far out to sea and
then dropped her back on shore. *Yemọnja,* also known as *Yemaya* in many parts of
the diaspora, could have taken her to the other side, but she didn't. Instead, she left
her imprint on Bridgforth, who acknowledges their union in much of her writing.
Isadora Africa Jr., the unborn spirit in *love conjure/blues,* lives in the ocean with
her ancestors; many of the people in *con flama* play by the ocean and are replen-
ished by it; and in an essay Bridgforth declares, "my mother is *Yemaya* / *Yemaya*
is Big Mama / She governs wo'mn-business / wombs belong to her / . . . / *Yemaya*
Rebirthed me. / I am cancer free."[38] It is the ocean, as well as her family relations,
that draws her so persistently to L.A.

The *Òrìṣà* give us lessons about ourselves. They vibrate in us and help us to
fulfill our Divine mission. In this way, they are experienced less as malevolent or
benevolent external forces, but rather as energies both within us and beyond us
with which we must make relationship. Our *Orí,* or destiny, allows us to make decisions at every turn. People are not merely buffeted about by nature; we are given

Figure 41. "Yemaya," by Yasmin Hernandez. Photo by Yasmin Hernandez.

opportunities to create inner balance with Ọ̀ṣun (as joy, healing, community) or Ọya (as change, spontaneity), or Ògún (as work, endurance, commitment), or any of the several Divine forces with which we consciously or unconsciously interact. With this understanding, if there is no joy in one's life, it is not because Ọ̀ṣun does not like us; rather, we should look to what choices we are making that block joy in our lives. If we are in the midst of an unjust situation, this does not mean we have offended Ọbàtálá; instead we could consider the way we mete out justice and gratitude to those around us. In understanding the Òrìṣà as energies in and around us rather than external forces waiting to punish or reward us, Yemọnja did not punish Bridgforth with cervical cancer, but the location of this cancer—Yemọnja's realm in the human body—suggested that Bridgforth had mother issues to examine. Bridgforth was given information that something was amiss with the Yemọnja vibrations in herself.

Mother–daughter issues have long been in focus for Bridgforth. In addition to the confusion of being sent away from her mother in Los Angeles to live in Memphis as a child, Bridgforth had to contend with her mother's initial discomfort with Bridgforth's sexuality. As a result, Bridgforth was estranged from her mother for many years before they silently agreed not to discuss the tensions between them. An even more difficult Yemọnja issue was embedded in her relationship with her daughter, Sonja Marie Perryman, who Bridgforth sent to live with Perryman's father when Perryman was about eight years old. In *con flama,* Bridgforth recalls this time:

> *i love no one more than my mother*
> *except my daughter   who i sent to live down south with her father*
> *and his home house people when she was little / and i was learning how to*
> *enjoy laughter without beer.*[39]

In an important way, Gurl in Bridgforth's ancestral trilogy might simultaneously stand in for Bridgforth's mother, Sonja Bridgforth; for Bridgforth's daughter, Sonja Perryman; and for Bridgforth herself. Sonja Bridgforth, Sharon Bridgforth, and Sonja Perryman were each separated from their mothers at a young age. The same tune was being played from one generation to the next, until Bridgforth broke the rhythm through a commitment to her art and to self-healing that included sobriety.

Today, Bridgforth and Perryman enjoy a hearty healthy relationship forged from courage, hard work, and love. The collaboratively generated CD *amniotic/ flow* charts the journey to strength Bridgforth and Perryman have traveled. In developing *amniotic/flow,* Perryman and Bridgforth wanted to reflect on their relationship, with Bridgforth specifically using this collaboration as an opportunity to release her daughter to the adult phase of her life. Many of the songs/poems speak of memories together or apart. Near the end of *amniotic/flow,* which was performed live as part of a CD release party, they sang a brief reference to the painful time apart:

and i am wondering how to keep you safe
remembering
over and over
i wish i wonder
if only
what kind of mother i wonder i wish
if only how could i / why
i wish i wonder
if only
over and over i grieve.
time lost words said
ignorance / i wish i hada over and over
i wish i wonder
if only
i remember

      until

      i

      bruise.

but
you
are
beautiful
and
you
are
kind
and
you
are
smiling
despite my mistakes.[40]

The healing between Bridgforth and her daughter set the stage for mending her relationships with her mother and father. It was essential that the cycle of rejection and absence be broken. The *égún* have been accommodated through *blood pudding, con flama,* and *delta dandi* by rigorous self-examination that paves the way for stability and prosperity.

Daniel Alexander Jones directed a staged reading of *amniotic/flow* at Esperanza Peace and Justice Center in San Antonio, and brought all the demands of theatrical jazz to the rehearsal process. Bridgforth and Perryman arrived at the first rehearsal with written pieces they imagined for the performance. Not unlike Laurie Carlos in responding to *con flama,* Jones made it clear that they needed to more deeply examine their relationship if the music was going to have power. Through emotionally strenuous exercises, tears, and determination, the women created lyrics that spoke to the regrets, the joy, the humor, the secrets, and the promise of their lives together. Jones helped generate the mother–daughter healing that is inextricable from the ancestral fabric. He often plays this role in the development of Bridgforth's work, providing a seasoned understanding of how theatrical jazz operates and how even practitioners can unintentionally skirt the rigors of the form. Because they talk to each other almost every day, they become unofficial collaborators on every project.

In Bridgforth's work, queer is the norm. Him/shes and bull daggers and men loving "one the other" raise families, make a living, nurture gardens, go to church, drink too much, cheat, brandish razors, and love loud and soft—and in their very everydayness explode the Black middle-class propriety that has tried to make them unspeakable dirty laundry. As Rinaldo Walcott puts it, "Black queers mess with that desired respectability [of the Black middle class] by bringing their shameful and funky sexual practices to it."[41] Bridgforth's work insists that we fashion Blackness queerly, that those gay folk who populate every corner of straight life create a Blackness that is instantly recognizable even if for its presumed disgrace—what Walcott calls "a sociality of mutual recognitions."[42] And because so many of Bridgforth's characters are pursuing, crafting, sneaking up on love, they insinuate themselves into our expansive understanding of humanity because we recognize that search, that longing.

As Sharon worked to fully imagine delta dandi, she scheduled a public improvisational "conduction" of the piece in a classroom at the University of Texas. This was not a conduction of the brand that Butch Morris has invented and mastered; instead it was Sharon's own imagining of conducting the audience as choir with key solo voices. This event was sponsored by the Warfield Center for African and African American Studies, and as such, was required for students taking AFR 301, Introduction to African American Culture—a large lecture class with a demographically varied student population. The classroom was packed with mostly people of color, many sitting on the floor and hanging in the doorway. AFR 301 often has an unusually high ratio of Black male athletes, and they were present in force along with Department of Theatre and Dance students, faculty from many departments, and a diverse gathering of Sharon's loyal Austin supporters, many of whom are queer artists. There we all sat, sweating in the overcrowded room, greeting one another from one corner to the next, already munching on the reception food in the hallway where so many who could not fit inside were standing. Sharon passed out slips of paper with text, and gave us somewhat ambiguous instructions. Much later she would perfect this technique, but on this night she told us that when she pointed at us, we were to read. When do we stop reading? Are we trying to read together, or were individual flourishes welcome? Were we to listen and feel for cues from one another?

With this delicious uncertainty, it began. Sharon read in her throaty patterned voice, pointed at one section of the room, and a blaring cacophony followed. People laughed, Sharon's brows were knit, and we went on. She read, pointed to another group as she continued reading, and this group tried to speak in unison. Sharon nodded, circled her hand as if indicating they should continue, then she pointed to another section of the room—many voices, styles, histories, worlds reverberatinq in the walls. And Sharon read the story of a man recalling through stutters how his brother, just returned from the war and still in uniform, was beaten almost to death by white men because he didn't respond when they "called him out of his name." The room was awkwardly silent as she read and pointed to one person to echo her words,

then pointed to another group to read from their paper. She then told the story of the man in the juke joint who lost his woman to another woman right before his eyes, and as the audience laughed, Sharon pointed again, and people tried to read their papers through the humor. Some of the athletes laughed—perhaps at the bawdiness, perhaps at recognition, perhaps at embarrassment—but they nonetheless joined the communal laughter—these athletes as those university emblems of all things heterosexual— sharing words, and sweat and improvisation within a room full of straight, queer, and "neithers." They were following the instructions of a woman whose self-performance reads queer and creole, a woman whose presence

often generates raised brows and second looks. All of us were under the spell of performance in which our shared humanity, our individuality, was deeply shaped by the queer Black world that Sharon offered us. Performance created the space where we all were able to participate in a queer Blackness, in which our very presence helped to validate a queer Blackness. For just a moment queer created a space of safety and community rather than terror and isolation.

Through the embodiment and full imagination that is theatre, Bridgforth is able to create worlds where queer can fully be. When Gurl comes to the end of *delta dandi* and proclaims "I wear hat and suspenders . . . ," it is easy to imagine Bridgforth having also found a place of freedom inside her realities. *Yemoṇja,* the oceanic force of motherhood, was the delta's destination, a homeplace of reconciliation. In this way, theatrical jazz created the space for multitemporal truth-telling, an inclusive Blackness, and a spontaneous generation of community.

In 2010 Bridgforth's work took a significant turn with *River See.* The work began as *Ring Shout,* the title a clear declaration of its spiritual focus. The title is also an indication of a radical shift through the use of capitalization; Bridgforth assigns holiness to all things capitalized. The psychically and structurally consistent central figure of Gurl has become SEE in *River See*—no longer the designation of an inexperienced child, but now a visionary gifted with insight, and, importantly, expressed in all caps. *River See* is the least linear of Bridgforth's texts, with the script existing as seriate units that can be ordered as each production sees fit. This structure also allows for the essential layering that Bridgforth incorporates into *River See* in production. What began as a practice similar to Lawrence "Butch" Morris's conductions with a standing-room-only audience in a classroom at the

University of Texas evolved into a precise improvisatory relationship with the audience/witnesses in which some offer gestures, some translate and speak passages of text in various languages, some sing from whatever traditions they know, and some walk the space as gossipers—all following Bridgforth's signals and working with the performers who have rehearsed particular moments of the text. In this way, in performance she composes layers of sonic and physical narratives that respond to the immediate vibrations in the room. This composing puts her directly in the production, and suggests the polyrhythms, jazz lines, and structured improvisation of jazz. With *River See,* her work is moving toward a new variant of theatrical jazz that is communal ritual guided by the immediacy of the moment, and further from linear, mimetic, proscenium-based theatre. What Bridgforth retains is a commitment to *ikọṣ'ẹ* as she brings many artists into the development of *River See* and into the demands of theatrical jazz. The continuation of an artistic *ẹgbẹ* remains essential to Bridgforth's understanding of how spirit is sustained.[43]

---

chicago.°
railroad tracks
biscuits and bacon
my grandmother's laughter and beer.
backyard parties sour pickles green olives
little stevie wonder the staple singers jerry butler cannonball adderley
bid whist neck bones greens cobbler sweet tea
great aunts great uncles cousins grandmother auntie bea remembering
cynthia smitty tart cigarettes spin the bottle tonk gin pass out.

los angeles.
cars buses honking exhaust street lights billboards wide streets liquor stores
  motels crowded sidewalks soul food restaurants
my mother's laughter.
pork chops potato salad orange crush sweet potato pie
ottis redding martha reeves and the vandellas the supremes the miracles the radio.

memphis los angeles memphis los angeles
great aunts great uncles cousins grandmother auntie bea my mother
her friends so pretty
los angeles. the Beach up up and away concrete fried chicken the hooptie junebug
  lying johnny guitar watson bb king millie jackson freda payne Dionne warwick Johnny mathis lou rawls
james brown Aretha franklin gladys knight and the pips marvin gaye the
Ocean the Waves Dancing my mother the Moon dancing her friends with
men dancing us children in the living room dancing.
Up denker in the car in the kitchen on the phone parties bar-b-que
laughter the Ocean

° E-mail from Bridgforth to author, January 1, 2010.

The song of Solomon the book of psalms I wonder as I wander nobody
knows my name nikki-rosa running on rooftops riding the bus up western
normandie Vermont alvarado Crenshaw century Manchester pico Beverly
Melrose sunset Hollywood me wild
Beer tequila parties concerts clubs underage at the park after curfew
cisco kid dance to the music say it loud nutbush city limits
RESPECT you need emotion hey sister go sister Minnie riperton rufus and chaka
    khan fried fish for colored girls who considered suicide when the rainbow
    is enuf
My mother's laughter the Beach blood memories great aunts great uncles cousins
    my grandmother my mother remembering laughing talking the old days new
    lives talking dancing laughing remembering like dizzy and Charlie parker
    intersecting time and space like etta james deacon john honey boy Edwards
    sam cooke jimmy scott like stirring gumbo
dreaming
The circle is made again the circle is continued the circle is us
Hold on . . .

my memory the topography of a good story

SHARON'S LINEAGE[*]

Sharon . . .

sees Ntozake Shange's *for colored girls who have considered suicide/when the rainbow is enuf*

hangs out at Beyond Baroque in Venice Beach, California, and becomes friends with Michelle T. Clinton; sees work of Wanda Coleman and Keith Antar Mason

is mentored by Marsha Ann Gomez, raulrsalinas, and meets Cherrie Moraga

writes *sonnata blue*, produced by Word of Mouth Women's Theatre Company, performed by Starla Benford

creates The root wy'mn Theatre Company with performers Anoa Monsho, Sonja Parks, Kaci Fannin, Arriama Matlock-Abdullah; Lori Wilson manager, Omi Osun Joni L. Jones provides actor training; Michelle Parkerson guest directs; Marsha Ann Gomez designs living altar set

writes and produces *lovve/rituals & rage*

writes, produces, and tours *no mo blues* and *dyke/warrior prayers* through root wy'mn with Sonja Parks performing and Lori Wilson as production manager

writes *the bull-jean stories*, RedBone Press

wins Lambda Literary Award for *the bull-jean stories*

writes *blood pudding*, directed by Laurie Carlos, with Florinda Bryant, Zell Miller III, Djola Branner, Renita Martin, and Stacey Robinson at Hyde Park Theatre; later, directed and choreographed by Baraka de Soleil, composed by Helga Davis with Ted Cruz, Helga Davis, Baraka de Soleil, Omi Osun Joni L. Jones, Francine Sheffield, Monica McIntyre, Pam Patrick, Negaysha Walcott for SummerStage Festival, New York

writes *geechee crossing marsha's overture*, curated by Carlos, dramaturged by Robert Baum, directed by Kamesha Jackson, with Tezra Bryant, Tonia Jackson, Mankwe Ndosi, Sonja Parks, Devin West, and Joe Wilson at Penumbra as a reading; later directed by Omi Osun Joni L. Jones with Theresa Burke, Aisha Conner, Zell Miller III, and Sonja Perryman as a workshop at UT

dramaturges Zell Miller III's *Arrhythmia*, directed by Daniel Alexander Jones, with Miller, Sonja Parks, Aimee Bryant, TruthMaze, Tookie Wright, hosted by Laurie Carlos for Penumbra's Cornerstone Reading Series

contributes writing to *Alaskan Heat Blue Dot*, directed by Laurie Carlos, with Florinda Bryant, Zell Miller III, Emily Cicchini, Richard Smith, and Omi Osun Joni L. Jones at Hyde Park Theatre

writes and performs in *amniotic/flow* with her daughter Sonja Perryman; directed by Daniel Alexander Jones for Esperanza Center, San Antonio; later directed by Lisa Byrd; composers included Amy Vanpatten, Camille Rocha, Lourdes Perez, and Annette D'Armata, installation by Omi Osun Joni L. Jones, performance and CD release party at allgo with Women and Their Work

---

[*] This partial listing of events, productions, and publications gives a sense of the interconnections among theatrical jazz artists. See Bridgforth's excerpted CV (Appendix III) for production details.

writes *con flama*, directed by Laurie Carlos with Florinda Bryant, Zell Miller III, Ana Perea, Sonja Parks, dramaturged by Omi Osun Joni L. Jones, set by Leilah Stewart at Hyde Park Theatre; later directed by Carlos with Zell Miller III, Ana Perea, Djola Branner, Aimee Bryant, Ambersunshower Smith, and Mankwe Ndosi, set by Seitu Jones at Penumbra

dramaturges Daniel Alexander Jones's *Phoenix Fabrik* with Helga Davis, Barbara Duchow, Daniel Dodd Ellis, and Daniel Alexander Jones at allgo; later with Vinie Burrows, Rhonda Ross, Barbara Duchow, and Namir Smallwood at Pillsbury House; later with Robbie McCauley, Sonja Perryman, Barbara Duchow, and Namir Smallwood at the Todd Mountain Theatre Project

dramaturges *Half-Breed Southern Fried (check one)* by Florinda Bryant, directed by Laurie Carlos, with Florinda Bryant, Jaclyn Pryor, Monique Cortez, Laura Rios, Terence Stith as DJ, videography by Krissy Mahan for the Warfield Center

writes *love conjure/blues*, directed by Helga Davis, with Florinda Bryant, Sean Tate, Carsey Walker, Marla Fulgham, and Omi Osun Joni L. Jones for the Warfield Center; later directed by Helga Davis, with Florinda Bryant, Sean Tate, Gina Houston, Daniel Alexander Jones, Daniel Dodd Ellis, Sonja Perryman, Fred Cash Jr., Greg Rickard, and Omi Osun Joni L. Jones for the Warfield Center

dramaturges Laurie Carlos's *The Pork Chop Wars (a story of mothers)*, directed by Carlos and Deborah Artman, with Florinda Bryant, Sonja Perryman, Lisa L. Moore, Virginia Grise, Courtney Morris, Bianca Flores, Renita Martin, Rene Ford, and Omi Osun Joni L. Jones for the Warfield Center

writes *delta dandi* and co-directs with Helga Davis and Baraka de Soleil, with Florinda Bryant, Monique Cortez, Leigh Gaymon-Jones, Karla Legaspy, Andrea Edgerson, Sonja Perryman, and Azure Osborne-Lee through the National Performance Network and Women and Their Work at the Long Center for the Performing Arts, Austin, Texas

writes *Skin Deep* for Baraka de Soleil, performed at Dixon Place

becomes a New Dramatists' Resident Writer

writes lyrics for Jomama Jones—"Jomamasong," with Bobby Halverson, and "Sunbeam."

receives a commission from the National Performance Network Creation Fund for *River See*, co-commissioned by Links Hall, in partnership with Living Arts of Tulsa, Diaspora Vibe Cultural Arts Incubator, Pillsbury House Theatre, The Theatre Offensive and NPN

receives support for *River See* through a Pillsbury House Theatre MAP Fund Award

PART TWO

The Break / *Awo* / Process

To call Conduction an experiment is a grave error.
Any time you synchronize the spirit and still give it liberty,
you open many doors to the primus, where the intimate necessity of possibility reigns,
where we find and realize our individual and collective freedoms.

—Lawrence "Butch" Morris[1]

Vocabulary is only the basis for a language, not the language itself.

—Tori Haring-Smith[2]

I don't want to hear what you know,
I want to hear what you don't know.

—Joao Costa Vargas[3]
(echoing his teachers)

You are not in a process of discovery if you are not
(more than a little) lost.

—Erik Ehn, "Chaos"[4]

The moment of greatest jeopardy
is your moment of greatest opportunity.

—Albert Murray[5]

THE JAZZ AESTHETIC in theatre can be as elusive to document as jazz music was to document for Jelly Roll Morton. Morton attempted to explain jazz in print so that the music he helped pioneer would be more widely understood and accepted, and so that his own style of playing would be comprehensible to the musicians with whom he worked. Here, I set forth some of the basic principles of the form, always keeping in mind what Laurie Carlos said—"You can't write this stuff down! You can't name it!" This naming that I offer is a guide to both creating and experiencing this work; it cannot replace the understanding that comes from the lived experience, or the *ikǫ́ṣę́* in the elder–apprentice relationship. That being acknowledged, here goes.

Figure 42. "Boddica," by Carl E. Karni-Bain "BAI." Photo by BAI.

The break in jazz music occurs when a soloing musician veers away from the prescribed melodies and invents new musical realities on the spot while the rest of the band pulls back the sound, or is silent. Morton says, "A break is like a musical surprise. Without breaks and without clean breaks and without beautiful ideas in breaks, you haven't got a jazz band and you can't play jazz. Even if a tune hasn't got a break in it, it's always necessary to arrange some kind of a spot to make a break."[6]

This idea of opening a "spot" in the work often happens in a theatrical jazz aesthetic when an individual performer releases into the work with courage, abandon, and mastery. In theatrical jazz, the break can also be conceived of as an entire performance when all of the company members respond to the electric demands of the moment. An inner hidden dynamic is brought forward to an outward expression, something palpable yet almost indescribable is brought into the room. There is a powerful fusion between the degree of risk-taking and honesty in the performer's personal life and the degree of idiosyncratic creativity the performer unleashes in the performance. Performance then becomes a place of freedom rather than a place of hiding—behind technique or from self-secrets. In this way, the performer has nothing to fear from the otherworldly visitation that is performance; indeed, she/he welcomes the wonder into her/his experience.

During the fall of 2004, I was able to see both Robert Wilson and Bernice Johnson Reagon's The Temptation of St. Anthony *at the Brooklyn Academy of Music and Ralph Lemon's* Come home Charley Patton *at BAM's Harvey Theatre. Helga Davis and Carl Hancock Rux were in* St. Anthony, *which made the experience all the more exciting. I had worked with both Helga and Carl through the Austin Project, and both have been collaborators with Daniel, Laurie, and Sharon. I was intrigued by what Johnson and Wilson might create given the sharp contrast in their aesthetic sensibilities. The production was beautiful. It was full of the intricate and dramatic lighting and stylized spatial relationships for which Wilson is known. The music was new and fresh, and the lyrics were densely packed, essential strands of the narrative. The colors were lush and the costumes regal. The performers were in full command of the work, with strong voices and confident presences. This was the work of seasoned professionals all around. The next evening I saw* Charley Patton. *The racially and nationally diverse cast enacted iconic moments from the Civil Rights Movement complete with Lemon being hosed down so forcefully he could barely remain standing, along with what seemed to be private personal moments—a young man at home in bed, encounters at school. The dancers careened around the stage as if tormented or in deepest ecstasy. They sprang into the air, then hurtled to a heap on the floor. During one home scene, a dancer fell from a top bunk bed, then climbed back up only to crash down again. They danced as if there was something urgent at stake. The pace was swift, terrifying even. I was enthralled by the work—the fearlessness and virtuosity of the performers, the porous compelling narrative units, the vulnerability and humility of the exploration. While both* St. Anthony *and* Charley Patton *were exceptional productions conceived by master artists,* Charley Patton *resonated with me more deeply.* St. Anthony *was an extraordinary work that was visually and sonically stunning.* Charley Patton *was this, and something else. Neither was better than the other—simply different. I spoke about this with Laurie, who had also seen both productions. She said, "Oh yeah,* Charley Patton *was the marrow in the bone." That was it. And, of course, Laurie would name the marrow. The production itself was the break, it was the inner meat, it was the very place of life. It revealed something beyond technique and skill—a humanity, an openness, a sense of exposure. The break is the marrow, the place of profound vitality.*

In Yoruba-based spiritual ceremonies much time is spent preparing for the arrival of forces from *ọrun,* or the spiritual home of ancestors and Divinities. The hours of drumming, of percussive dancing, of all-night cooking, and completion of sacrifices, of fervent singing and prayers—these necessary ingredients leave participants spent, with their senses simultaneously numb and primed, in an altered state ready to receive and transmit messages from the Divine. Jazz acting is similar to this sensation in that one invites the mystery through conscious play within the form or, even more courageously, by yielding to impulses and instincts that seem to have their own set of intentions. Jazz acting relies on technique and craft that are used to facilitate deep exploration. The ability to fully inhabit one's own body, command of vocal variety and flexibility, familiarity with narrative styles and structures, and understanding of multiple relationships with audiences are the technical strengths on which jazz acting builds. Such competency creates the safe strong parameters within which play and experimentation can flourish. In addition to these standard acting techniques, jazz acting insists on listening and spontaneity—this is where the deep exploration is housed. In theatrical jazz, standard acting techniques can easily become armor inhibiting the very listening and spontaneity the jazz acting demands. When technique becomes a way to display one's proficiency for the admiring gaze of audience, or when technique becomes a goal in itself, technique can seriously impede jazz acting.

Along with performing for approval, traditional forms of character and scene analysis can also stunt jazz acting, which puts it in unique tension with the most widely used actor training in the United States. As of this writing, Yale, Julliard, New York University, Carnegie-Mellon, Actor's Conservatory Theatre, and CalArts include some adaptation of actor training that developed from the Group Theatre of the 1940s. Lee Strasberg's brand of training relied on emotional memory, a recall strategy in which actors layer onto a character their own emotional reality from experiences similar to the character's. Other techniques often grouped under the umbrella term Method Acting include Stella Adler's use of "given circumstances" and Sanford Meisner's use of "daydream." These techniques share with theatrical jazz the desire for aliveness and spontaneity in performance; however, theatrical jazz rarely operates in psychological realism, mimesis, and "fourth wall" relationships to the audience—the mainstays of Method Acting.

In a jazz aesthetic, the actor prepares not by in-depth psychological exploration of the character but with a rigorous personal excavation that leaves the actor supple, fluid, open, and ready. Jazz acting asks the performer to confront herself— her resistance to exploration and play, her attachment to habitual aesthetic and personal choices, her insistence on an intellectual understanding of the performance experience—in order to commit to the immediacy of the process. The performer is able to bring everything she/he is actually experiencing to each onstage reality while continuing to move the production along. This might mean a story that is told full of energy one evening will be slow and contemplative the next. Rather than pretending to be energetic, the performer embraces her/his actual energy level and

Figure 43. *Alaskan Heat* rehearsal. *Alaskan Heat Blue Dot* was collaboratively developed by a group of writer-performers through a workshop process conducted by Carlos, Jones, and Ehn. Daniel Alexander Jones, not pictured, guides us through one of several writing exercises. Left to right: Erik Ehn, Jason Phelps, Margery Segal, Emily Cicchini, C. Denby Swanson, Omi Osun Joni L. Jones, Zell Miller III, Leslie Belt, and Peck Phillips. 1999. Photo by Bret Brookshire.

massages that into the work. This does not allow her to rely on her research or even what she learned in rehearsal last night; instead, her job is to be poised for whatever comes next in the moment, now.

Theatrical jazz requires acting techniques that are at once deeply personal and intimate as if something has opened inside the performer, and at the same time separate, in that the character does not necessarily extend from some part of the performer's experience; indeed, the character might not be a character per se but an idea or a sign. Jazz acting is often more presentational than representational, and can be likened to Brechtian techniques in which the actor demonstrates rather than becomes the character. Surprise and invention are key ingredients to the form. Jazz acting has a kinship to acting in other non-realist work; it is the sort of acting that Tori Haring-Smith describes as performing a "figure" rather than a character, and telling the character's story rather than becoming the character. Theatrical jazz rehearsals tend to focus on acquiring flexibility and spontaneity—the elements of play. Because theatrical jazz operates outside the parameters of realism, the palette of spontaneity includes idiosyncrasy and unpredictability. While the performer's rehearsal time is also spent in learning verbal and physical directions, the emphasis remains on playing inside a sensibility rather than repeating lines and movement.

Since its inception, Laurie has been a guest artist with the Austin Project (tAP)—a
collaboration of women of color artists/scholars/activists and their allies who learn art
as a tool for social change. In 2005 she was asked to offer a public performance as a
part of her work with tAP. She was developing Marion's Terrible Time of Joy, *and chose*
the opportunity with tAP to move the piece
forward. As usual, I didn't know Laurie's plan, but, also as usual, I trusted her to
bring her extraordinary gifts to the performance—and I didn't need to know any
more beyond that. She'd told me she was going to read from the evolving script; that
was a perfect use of this venue that had been home to the development of other
nontraditional work. As Sharon and I prepared 2.180 in the Winship Drama Building
for Laurie's performance that was to happen in less than an hour, Laurie turned to us
and said, "I'd like you to read with me! I have extra scripts—here!" Sharon let out one
of her characteristic WHOOP!s and I just jutted my head forward and widened my eyes
in panic and delight! And it was on! We read the piece
moving about the stage riffing off of each other. I had no idea what my character was
about or what word was coming next. What I did know is that I had two other people
in the space with me, and we were making something totally new together. This felt
reminiscent of Lawrence "Butch" Morris's conductions, though with his improvisational
adventures, the performers already know the text and he directs each word! I'd seen
Morris stand before a group of vocalists each prepared to offer sounds or words based
on the most subtle flick of his wrist or bold explosion of his gesticulations.[7] The only
things I could rely on as I contemplated working with Laurie and Sharon in the five
minutes before the performance would begin were my trust
in them, my training in how to listen, to share space, to feel as I read, and my deep
desire to push beyond boundaries of the known.

As I describe the road to jazz acting, I am aware that many of my descriptions share the language and intentions of the very traditions I contrast. The work of the Group Theatre sought to find a vitality and immediacy in acting that corresponded to the then new ways of making theatre that were heavily influenced by the intimacy of film, the grittiness of naturalism, and the despair of Western modern life that struggled to understand the role of humanity in the face of potential annihilation and global responsibility. Like the jazz acting being described here, Method Acting encouraged being present and taking risks, as did the so-called Stanislavski Method to which Method Acting owes a heavy debt. Like jazz acting, more traditional Western acting approaches may ask performers to "be present" and "honest" on stage, but any performance strategy, including jazz acting, loses its potency when it becomes rote and formulaic.

While performing in Alaskan Heat Blue Dot *under Laurie's direction, I struggled*
mightily to do a "good job." I tried to understand the key to theatrical jazz, but it
eluded me. I couldn't find my way in. One night during the performance, I was moving
through the lines and walking the complex diagonals of the stage that Laurie had

given all of the performers. It was like being the ball in a pinball machine, flipping from one invisible block to the next, turning instantly just as another performer was headed your way. I said the lines, turned sharply, sat on the
edge of the large bed upstage right as I had been directed to do, then abruptly rose from the bed and headed in a new direction across the stage. Only, on this night, I got to the bed, bent my knees, jutted out my butt ready to connect to the bed, but I didn't quite make it to a full sitting position.

Figure 44. The ensemble on the bed during *Alaskan Heat* production, Frontera@Hyde Park Theatre. Directed by Laurie Carlos, 1999. Left to right: Zell Miller III, Emily Cicchini, Richard Smith, Omi Osun Joni L. Jones, Florinda Bryant. Photo by Bret Brookshire.

Instead, I abruptly took my assigned diagonal downstage. It was a fraction of a second in which I moved with the energy of the moment. Laurie had precisely choreographed the work so that the angularity of the language was matched with the erratic fluidity of movement, so that the quiet spaces in the verbal text were joined with energetic gestures and walking. In that instant when my butt didn't quite touch the bed, I was moving inside of Laurie's choreography with my own developing impulses instead of following her direction by rote. After the performance Laurie noted this moment and said, "Joni, ah, when you didn't really sit down? Beautiful!" This was the first bit of praise I had received from Laurie on this work, and I clung
to it. So every night thereafter, I strained to repeat the exact same action—get to the bed, bend my knees, poke out my butt, miss the bed, take the diagonal. Laurie had said this choice was beautiful and I decided that meant the action itself was right rather than the spontaneity that spawned the action. I was determined to "get it right" so each night I repeated the same thing, only on subsequent nights the action was hollow. It no longer had the spark of invention or
presentness. It became the thing to do so that I could be deemed "a good actor." At that time I did not understand that what really worked in that moment was my imagination spinning in the instant; the act of missing the bed was secondary. I tried to make a rule out of a process and thereby emptied the action of its vigor.

The surprise in jazz acting is the break in the pattern, it is the juxtaposition of disparate experiences such as telling a horrific tale while performing abstract movements, it is leaving room for the audience/witnesses to make their own sense of the work. Nonmimetic movements are particularly important in this regard as they work to unmoor Blackness from discursively enforced limitations and predictable associations. The surprise constitutes a break itself, a break from the expected in performance, a kind of fissure in the work that the audience/witnesses are left to fuse into their own sense of reason, or to dismiss as incomprehensible and inconsequential. The audience/witnesses are not required or expected to comprehend each element. In this way, the break exists as features of the visual/aural aesthetic as well as a shift in the conventions for audience behavior.

This idea of surprise is often achieved through the layering of elements. The verbal text has layers, to which the soundscape—especially breath and music—is added as more layers, to which nonmimetic movement builds even more layers. This layering does not occur from a prescribed sequence. The experience might start with breath, then layers are added in the order in which they are discovered. While breath and music soundscapes, movement, and text are the primary layers that are manipulated in theatrical jazz, of course costume, set, and lights can also create powerful juxtapositions.

In 1996, I was cast in Alaskan Heat Blue Dot *under Laurie's direction. The script grew out of an extensive writing workshop produced by Frontera@Hyde Park Theatre. The workshop consisted of an eclectic group of artists including playwrights, directors, dramaturgs, dancers, and actors who met for about six weeks completing various writing assignments and engaging in a range of exercises Laurie gave us. Laurie took the writing that each workshop participant generated and shaped those works into a single text. The result was a jazz script—multiple overlapping*

narratives, fluid time and place, ensemble facility, choral and solo vocal work. I was not initially cast in the performance, and I was disappointed. I told Laurie I would like to work on the show in any capacity, and was then invited to be the dramaturg. At the first rehearsal, one of the actors, Jason Phelps, was absent and I was asked to read his part. He was not able to continue with the production, and the part was given to me. The company consisted of Florinda Bryant clad in a costume reminiscent of The Good Witch of the North, Zell Miller III in casual pants and shirt, Emily Cicchini variously in lounging wear or a full slip, Richard Smith in a shirt and tie, and myself in a sleek pantsuit and heels. The costumes gave some notion of who our characters were, though the characters did not represent coherent

psychological realities or single personalities. We moved in and out of scenes, text, dialogue, and movement as we followed an order that lived inside of Laurie rather than inside of the script or characters. The set pieces included a large bed that could hold all five cast members and a refrigerator. The performance

tools I brought to the experience did not fit. I was working with four other performers, two of whom had worked with Laurie before and both seemed at ease with the mapping of nonliteral movements onto the words of the text. I, on the other hand, was floundering. My body seemed alien to me,

Figure 45. The ensemble with gestures during *Alaskan Heat* production, Frontera@Hyde Park Theatre. Directed by Laurie Carlos, 1999. The company performs a series of Carlos's characteristic abstract gestures. Left to right: Emily Cicchini, Zell Miller III, Omi Osun Joni L. Jones, Richard Smith, Florinda Bryant. Photo by Bret Brookshire.

my voice arch and contrived, my focus utterly scattered. And eventually, I became angry. This work uprooted my sense of myself as a good performer, and forced me to begin relinquishing my old methods.

While I struggled to understand the aesthetics of the world I found myself in, I often asked other cast members how they were managing with what I found to be incomprehensible directorial choices. They would give me maddening suggestions like "Just relax," or "I don't know what I'm doing either," or "Don't ask questions. Just do what she says." Completely unable to see any

wisdom in these comments, I finally went directly to Laurie and asked, "What can I do? I don't know what's going on and I know I'm just not getting it!" Laurie threw up her hands, said "I can't help you with that!" and walked away. I was left bewildered and scared. I was experiencing a deeply painful yet necessary break before the jazz work could take hold. It was not until a few years later, working under Daniel's direction of Erik Ehn's Heavenly Shades of Night Are Falling, *that I began to build new possibilities for performance using the break that occurred in* Alaskan Heat.

In 1998 I was invited to take over Laurie's role in Heavenly Shades *when she contracted pneumonia. Erik wrote the piece for Laurie, and Daniel would be directing it at Frontera@Hyde Park Theatre. Here I was facing another jazz aesthetic experience after having felt so out of sync in* Alaskan Heat, *and I was being asked to step into shoes made expressly for Laurie—the mentor to us all. I would also be working with Florinda and Zell again, who had experienced my*

awkwardness and anxiety in Alaskan Heat. *This was a "Legba Moment" in which the Òrìṣà of Divine possibility presented me with an opportunity, and my own ìwà or character would determine how I would respond. I could turn down this offer and retreat to the safety and stagnation of my known experiences, or I could dare to live life without ready answers and inside mystery and wonder. I agreed to do the role, though at the time the decision didn't feel courageous or empowering. A small barely discernable part of me was eager to have another shot at doing this work, though I couldn't articulate why. I sensed, even if I couldn't name it, that doing this work was about living fully with my arms spread open to the vitality of life, and if I said no to it, I would succumb to stasis and conventionality. It was a pivotal moment in which I could be more fully alive and more fully*

myself, or turn away from life in the guise of security and reason.

Because the play was about and for Laurie, the bulk of the lines went to the main character, L'Ash, whom she would have played. Now I was L'Ash, and the memorization for the role was daunting. I was onstage for most of the performance and I seemed to be talking all the time. I struggled to memorize the often abstract nonlinear language, and I had to ask producer Vicky Boone if we could delay the opening by a week to give myself more time to get the language down. She graciously agreed, and I had seven more days to strengthen my relationship with Erik's poetic language and nonlinear narrative and Daniel's unique gestural vocabulary. Daniel sat in the cold small theatre space and fed me lines as I moved around the stage trying to link lines with movement. He was patient and generous. He never demonstrated any frustration with my slow process or any anxiety about the development of the show. He would just

Figure 46. *Heavenly Shades of Night* poster. This large poster of Laurie Carlos made clear that Carlos was to be featured in the 1999 Frontera@Hyde Park Theatre production of Erik Ehn's *Heavenly Shades of Night Are Falling,* directed by Daniel Alexander Jones. Photo of Carlos by Dani Werner. Photo of poster by Elisa Durrette.

methodically give me one line after the other. I would flop around the stage slowly integrating one phrase at a time. And finally the opening night came—Erik's fantasy of Laurie's life was going to live with the audience bearing witness to it all. I managed to get through the first act pretty well.

Figure 47. Zell Miller III, Sarah Richardson, and Omi Osun Joni L. Jones in *Heavenly Shades of Night* production, Frontera@Hyde Park Theatre. *Heavenly Shades of Night Are Falling* by Erik Ehn, directed by Daniel Alexander Jones, 1999. Set design by Leilah Stewart. Given the centrality of my character to the piece, I was glad to have a rare moment of rest. Left to right: Miller, Jones, and Richardson. Photo by Bret Brookshire.

A script carefully placed backstage was my savior during the few moments when I was off-stage. I would cram in the next scene, then fling myself into the performance space knowing that the other performers would push my body into the right place when the blocking eluded me. In the second act, I began to release anxiety about the lines I didn't know, and the fear of humiliating myself. This anxiety actually kept me from responding to the environment and the other performers because I wasn't really there—instead I was mentally and psychically backstage scanning my script even as my body moved onstage. Inside of this release, it felt like
playing! The lines were tenuously hanging somewhere in my consciousness, precariously waiting to be rescued by my mouth and tossed into the air. My body was poised to sense every nuance of the other performers—if they shifted right that was my cue to do the same, if their eyes flashed quick with fear, I knew I'd better move off the center stage trunk and head downstage.

Figure 48. Raul Castillo and Omi Osun Joni L. Jones in *Heavenly Shades of Night* production, Frontera@Hyde Park Theatre. *Heavenly Shades of Night Are Falling* by Erik Ehn, directed by Daniel Alexander Jones at Frontera@Hyde Park Theatre, 1999. Set design by Leilah Stewart. I sit with Raul Castillo (right). Daniel Alexander Jones used a similar "back-to-back" position in his direction of Shay Youngblood's *Shakin' the Mess Outta Misery*, a strategy that generates a productive physical angularity and emotional tension. Photo by Bret Brookshire.

My mind was curiously free because I couldn't possibly think of the next moment since I didn't have a clue what that next moment might be! I had no choice but to be present, to respond to the tiniest internal impulses
that might be a shadowy memory from rehearsal, and to really vibe with the other performers and let their knowledge guide me. I felt broken and free and terrified. By the time I sat on the floor at the end of the play as L'Ash nestled between the legs of

my mother played by Florinda—me staring vacantly out at the audience, she reflecting
on her life choices, the lone stage light focused
directly on us so that the shimmering gold makeup on my skin and the auburn
highlights in her hair glowed—by the time this final

Figure 49. Florinda Bryant and Omi Osun Joni L. Jones in *Heavenly Shades of Night* production, Frontera@Hyde Park Theatre. The closing image in the 1999 Frontera@Hyde Park Theatre production of Erik Ehn's *Heavenly Shades of Night Are Falling*, directed by Daniel Alexander Jones, set design by Leilah Stewart. Byrant (left) and Jones. Photo by Bret Brookshire.

scene from the play happened, I was spent and grateful and exhilarated. We had done
it. We made it through. Missed cues, improvised blocking, flubbed abstract language
that was more about pulse than it was about sense—we did it.
And my performance life would never be the same.
Several months later, I was hosting a prospective faculty member at East Side Café.
Our waiter took our drink orders, then turned to me and said: "I loved your work in
Heavenly Shades of Night! That last scene with the light on you and the other actress
was just amazing!" I resisted the impulse to respond in self-deprecating disbelief,
and instead thanked him and continued my conversation with the other UT faculty. I
wondered if that young man could know that I was so terrified in those moments that
I could hardly speak the last words. And indeed, the very palpability of my terror, of an
electrically alive moment, may have been precisely what moved him.

Jazz acting asks the performer to be herself rather than be someone else. This means that the performer is herself in the process of discovering the character who may own the lines. The performer's vocal quality, physical reality, personality all come together through the words of the script. This also means that one's insecurities, one's desires are all visible—and should be woven into the experience of the work. This is most clearly seen when Carlos choreographs voices for a piece. She is interested in the exact texture the performer brings, not the performer's ability to pretend to sound like or be someone else. In this work, the performers get to be who they *are*.

During rehearsals in 2002 for Sharon's con flama, *I watched as Ana Perea struggled in much the same way I had in* Alaskan Heat. *She is a talented performer who was making her first encounter with Laurie's use of movement and soundscapes. I saw myself as she worked to understand why Laurie had made certain physical choices. The task is not to understand, but to feel, to incorporate, to make Laurie's choice one's own. The insight is not likely to arrive like an intellectual epiphany, but instead as a physical knowing. Your muscles will get it before your mind does. The entire company was aware of Ana's frustrations. The assurances I offered her from my own experience did not appear to help. Then, on opening night, she got it. Her body was present and direct and in charge. When Laurie and I talked about this later, Laurie simply said, "Oh yeah! She just stepped up to the plate!"*

I saw this amalgamation of gesture, sound, nonmimetic movement, text, and performer once again with Daniel's direction of E. Patrick Johnson in Johnson's Sweet Tea *at About Face Theatre in Chicago.* Sweet Tea: Black Gay Men of the South *is Patrick's extraordinary volume of sixty-three interviews of Black gay men from the Southern United States. He originally adapted the book into a one-man performance in which he sat on a stool, read from the script, and gave vocal and emotional clarity to each of the men he performed. Patrick had been touring this minimalist production for about two years when he collaborated with Jane Saks, then executive director of the Ellen Stone Belic Institute for the Study of Women and Gender in the Arts and Media at Columbia College Chicago, to mount a fully staged production of* Sweet Tea. *By this time, Patrick truly owned the work—he had interviewed and befriended the men of the book, he birthed the 570-page volume, and he had been performing from the book around the country for the previous two years. Daniel is a skillful and generous director who introduced Patrick to an array of theatrical jazz methods. As with many performers who engage with this work for the first time, Patrick was stymied. He worked to apply Daniel's abstract gestural vocabulary to the many varied and emotionally dense monologues of the script. When we talked on the phone, Patrick often sounded exhausted and exasperated, yet committed. For him, Daniel's gestures didn't "make sense," but he trusted Daniel's vision and was willing to release his own ideas about "good performance" to discover something new. On one occasion, Patrick strongly disagreed with a set of physical choices Daniel recommended. Patrick tried the movements, but*

*they continued to conflict with his own ethnographic ethics that require as faithful
a performance of fieldwork as possible. When Patrick approached Daniel about his
concern, Daniel quickly agreed to change the movements, telling Patrick, "What you
really feel would have come out on stage anyway! You need to be at ease." "At ease"
did not mean Patrick would not work and stretch, but "at ease" did mean that Patrick
would not have to betray himself. On opening night, Patrick worked his way through
the movements, the language, the interplay with the audience—he was strong and full.
It was good work. As Patrick performed one of the men
who described warding off sexual advances from a family friend, he gingerly placed
tinsel on a huge tree that dominated the set stage left. Later, as an elderly man
describing the flurry of activity surrounding prostitution in his day, Patrick pointed
upstage, spoke some of the text, then pointed downstage, spoke more text, then
pointed up again, took a few steps downstage and repeated the sequence of gestures.
Later, he squatted center stage and then glided on his belly upstage right as he began
a scathing commentary on homophobia in the Black church. All of this was executed
precisely, though not organically. When I saw the production two weeks later, Patrick
strode about the stage filling
every abstract gesture with its own full and complex set of meanings—meanings that
were not made explicit for the audience, but meanings that lived inside of Patrick. The
tinsel was now handled fondly, the pointing was deep inside of the elder's storytelling
style smoothly rolling with and through the words, and the backward glide became a
venomous slither. The gestures had fully marinated into a meaning that existed inside
the work. Patrick had traveled the performer's journey of theatrical jazz.*

The work is about process. It is about the performers finding their way, bringing their distinctive gifts to the work and letting those gifts ring forward through
the character or symbol or "figure," through the breath of the company. As Carlos
is fond of saying, "Everything is already in the room." What the performers bring
is exactly what is needed—their joys, insecurities, fears, ecstasies are just what is
required for the fulfillment of the work. In Yoruba-based spiritual work, elders
often take note of who is present, which priests have come to contribute their *àṣẹ*
to the work. The focus of *Ọbàtálá*, the authority of *Ṣàngó*, the cultural perpetuation
of *Ọ̀ṣun*—the particular forces of nature that are present will be the ones to mold
the work. And in a jazz aesthetic, the distinctive histories, personalities, geogra-
phies of each performer are the exact ingredients needed. They are not asked to
leave themselves at the door; instead their full selves are invited in to play.

Rehearsals in a jazz aesthetic are a time for developing a kind of psychic flexibility, a readiness to engage in the work. A great deal of time is spent working
through exercises, some of which are suggested by the text, and others that the
director feels will push the company to greater honesty and vulnerability. Carlos
uses rehearsals to make her own discoveries rather than lay down predetermined
blocking and movement. Much of what she proposes in rehearsals is designed to
stimulate her imagination as well as the performers'.

During rehearsals for Sharon's con flama, Laurie was slowly and precisely mapping out the physical reality of the piece. There is a passage in which the main character, Gurl, performed by Sonja Parks, is talking about the elder women who she remembers as a child. As Sonja speaks, Ana Perea improvises actions of adornment—applying makeup, putting on perfume. A beautiful union between the women developed with Ana assuming the role of a seasoned teacher, and Sonja practicing some of the moves of beauty-making. Laurie watched these moments evolve into deepening intimacy as she instructed the women to repeat the scene again and again. Eventually, Laurie asked Ana to gradually lift Sonja

onto her back, and walk while Sonja spoke. It had been a long rehearsal that was energized once the work on this passage began. Both women were eager to work, and trusted Laurie's judgment. This made them willing to try whatever she asked—a critical consent granted a director by theatrical jazz performers. We all watched as Sonja began the passage for the umpteenth time. She slowly and lovingly climbed on Ana's

Figure 50. Laurie Carlos carrying Ana Perea during *con flama* rehearsal, 2000. To help Perea understand how to carry Sonja Parks, Carlos has Perea feel what it is like to be carried while Parks determines where her abdominal muscles should rest while being carried. Photo by Bret Brookshire.

Figure 51. Ana Perea carrying Sonja Parks during *con flama* rehearsal, 2000. After being carried by Carlos, Perea now carries Parks while Carlos ensures that both performers are balanced and secure. Photo by Bret Brookshire.

back—like a sleeping child being carried to bed, arms wrapping around the parent's neck in acknowledgment of trust and safety, and the head flopping to the side having found familiar comfort. Sonja's legs dangled free and peaceful as they straddled Ana's back. For the first time, it was clear how this elder in the text supported and prepared the child as Ana took wide strides across the floor, her back willingly bent under Sonja's weight. Lourdes and Annette audibly sighed at the beauty and strength of that sight. We were all moved to witness this moment—two performers finding something so potent that its rarity and vulnerability shifted us all. Surprisingly, Laurie did not stage the passage in this way for the public production. The little girl atop her elder's back became a visceral and psychic memory the performers carried with them rather than a staging technique to be shared with the audience. The point of this discovery was not to find the picture that would work in performance; instead, it was to assist performers in weaving a union between them that would be felt in the scene even when different production choices are made.

Finding oneself as a performer inside of this tradition is much like the role of an *Ìyàwó,* the title given the newly initiated in Yoruba-based practices in the United States, who is grappling with his or her new status in the spiritual community. Frequently the *Ìyàwó* will ask, "How do I learn all I need to know for my priesthood? Why doesn't the elder spend more time with me? What are the mysteries of my *Òrìṣà*?" The *Ìyàwó* may want to get to the end of the journey rather than experience the unfolding truths. Impatience and anxiety often dominate the initiation year. As with a theatrical jazz performer, the *Ìyàwó* must work from a space deep inside to find union with the tradition and not expect direct answers from the god parent, that elder who has initiated them and is primarily in charge of their spiritual training. The most abiding lessons come not from being told the way but from discovering the way through sometimes painful trial and error. The performer and the *Ìyàwó* must stretch the boundaries of their skill and knowledge by venturing a bold attempt in the world. Without such attempts, the performer and the *Ìyàwó* never quite experience the full breadth of their *iwà,* their distinctive character or essence. The newly initiated must be willing to live inside of "the break," apart from linear time and place, where their identity is full of possibility. Living inside of this space creates a new daily existence in which art and spirit are not compartmentalized; the choices made change one's life.

Ìwà rere[8]—good character, character as one's crowning jewel—requires being one's self in spite of public opinion. It is not merely doing the right thing, but doing *your* thing, and doing that thing connects us with the Divine. Do the job you are here to do, no matter what. One is virtuous by following the Divine mandate. This is Ornette Coleman blowing a solo while the other band members do their own thing. Coleman's head bobbing, the sax bleating out each note. He is soaring in some other place following the dictates of an unseen force. It is Sonja Perryman speaking Carlos's words in *The Pork Chop Wars (a story of mothers)* and finding her own story as she realizes that she is also talking about her recently hospitalized father. That moment was not for the audience/witnesses or her mother or Carlos. She was communing with the Divine and, in yielding to the fear and pain of that moment, she was exhibiting *ìwà*, virtuosity that is good character. It is Jones almost every time he performs, with a kind of wicked jig, a melodious voice, and a presence so compelling one can hardly look at anything else. *Ìwà* is about one's relationship with the Holy; it is the self in vibration with the Divine.

Rowland Abiodun notes that in Yoruba cosmology, *ìwà* is the child of patience, and patience is born of the Supreme Being.[9] So, to exercise *ìwà* is to link with the Divine. And to experience *ìwà* requires patience—as in practice, as in working with the same group of people on similar journeys, working over and over again, each person offering patience to one another.

Legba is in charge of "the break." He presents us with an opportunity, and our response is not limited to an either-or binary of either exercise *ìwà* (character and virtuosity) or back away; there are as many responses possible as there are degrees of good character. I painfully recall the times in my spiritual practice when *Legba* was at the door and I chose not to open it. And choosing *not* to builds character in its own way. The work in theatrical jazz is similar. We either draw upon our most present and powerful selves or we opt for some measure of shrinking, resting on familiarity and a false sense of safety. When one is accustomed to walking with a fierce integrity in the personal life, then one can access this muscle more readily in the aesthetic life.

In 1995 I was invited to perform in a staged reading of Daniel's Ambient Love Rites *at Frontera@Hyde Park Theatre. It was directed by Bridget Carpenter, who was flying in from California to work on this production. Elissa Adams, from Minneapolis, Amparo Garcia, from Austin, Laurie, and Daniel completed the cast. This reading marked an important moment for Daniel when he would once again share the stage with his mentor Laurie after having performed with her in* Talking Bones, *directed by Robbie McCauley. It was an important moment for me as well. I knew I was rolling with the big dogs and was excited to just be in the room. The play was a love story juxtaposed against an omnipotent radio talk-show host and a mystic who knew the destinies of the characters. Most of my scenes were with Amparo, who played the Spanish-speaking mystic; I was her translator. In rehearsal it was challenging and often humorous when we tried to get the timing of her*
Spanish with my English. I know some Spanish but not enough to riff when Amparo got creative! At this point in my experience with a jazz aesthetic, I was working closely with the lines and less so with the freedom of improvisation or being flexible in the present moment. I also had not yet had my necessary and unnerving experience with Laurie in Alaskan Heat, *so I wasn't yet fearful of or truly open to the work. I was just glad to be there. During one of the performances Amparo, a seasoned performer very accustomed to the give-and-take of improvisation and audience interaction, began to play with the text as she felt the vibe from the audience. I was on stage, stuck! This was indeed a "Legba moment," but I was not connected to Yoruba deeply enough at that time or fluent enough in a jazz aesthetic to do anything with this opportunity*

except stare at it in wonder. On stage, I remember looking with a bit of shock as Amparo smoothly found delicious nuances in the printed text. Then she turned to me and said something like "You've got to keep up!" This elicited a well-deserved rumble of laughter from the audience, and left me embarrassed and off-kilter. Amparo had it right. She played the moment and expected me to go on the ride with her, but I couldn't. Her comment beautifully acknowledged what was clearly happening on stage so that the artifice of theatre had this moment of real life as the audience saw that I was dumbfounded and they could also see that Amparo was improvising. A beautiful moment that I could not sustain. In hindsight, I thought of several retorts I could have made: "You're right! You're flying too fast for me!" Such a comment would have addressed the reality of her leaving me behind in her improvisational flourish and it would have allowed me to be a full participant in the moment. Even "Nobody can keep up with you!" would have kept the energy moving forward, though the tone of it is a bit mean, as if Amparo and I were playing the dozens, trying to outdo each other in our ability to spontaneously be clever.

Legba *tossed me the ball, and I couldn't play.*

Many years later, when I was performing in Sharon's performance novel love conjure/ blues, Legba *generously gave me another chance to be fully in the moment. The John L. Warfield Center for African and African American Studies at the University of Texas at Austin first presented* love conjure/blues *in the spring of 2004 in the Winship Drama Building, room 2.180, under the musical direction of Helga Davis. On the strength of this work, I decided to create the Performing Blackness Series through the Warfield Center that would premiere a new work related to the jazz aesthetic each year. In the fall of 2004, the series opened with the completed text of* love conjure/blues. *We performed in a moderate-sized classroom that we re-envisioned as an arena space. For the fall version we were joined by piano player Greg Rickard and bass player Fred Cash Jr. Near the end of the first half of the performance, just as the cast was exiting the space, Helga began a call-and-response*

chant that she had developed with the cast during rehearsals. Helga is a master performer who is so keenly present, she can feel the most subtle shifts in tone, intent, and energy. All the performers were on our feet as Helga called out to us in that intense magical way that she has. Helga: ga ga ga. We: GA, ga-ga-ga GA, ga-ga-ga GA. Helga: ga ga ga. We: GA, ga-ga-ga GA, ga-ga-ga GA. Then somehow I lost the rhythm and added another vocal pulse to the sounds! Rather than this being an error, Helga turned to me directly and verbally challenged/cajoled me into a guttural duet. It was as if she said, "OK Omi, let's go for it together! Let's do this toe-to-toe!" I matched the sound. She replied. I matched the sound again. We did this for a bit, back and forth. It was exhilarating but I couldn't take it higher. I could only match what I had been given, I couldn't find something

new inside the experience. Helga felt this and ended the moment by exiting the stage. Once again, Legba *showed me a door. This time, I stood on the threshold rather than back at some distance, but I still did not walk through. I was inside of the break but could not / would not let my own music come forward.*

A fundamental concept of Yoruba spiritual practice is process. One does what is right and cannot be tied to the outcome. This is the same in theatrical jazz. Take the risk, be present, do the work, and enjoy the ride. In spiritual practice, you can do everything just right and still not "win." Winning—an overt marker of success—is not the point. Serving the planet, serving humanity is the point. If one does spiritual work because you will "go to heaven" or because people will like you or because of anything other than increasing *iwà* and committing to the continuation of humanity, you have lost the very spirit that you were seeking to discover. In jazz, the point is not the applause. Working for applause means stepping out of the present moment to construct a particular value-laden future. Carlos often reminds performers, "Don't expect your friends to like this work. Don't even expect them to get it." This is how to live life—without commitment to a narrowly prescribed outcome, fully in the present.

As with all features of theatrical jazz, the break becomes a way of life in at least two ways. First, there are breaks in one's life that creak open those dank spaces of fear and terror. These personal breaks—a death, confrontation with illness, financial windfall or devastation, birth, natural disasters, relocation—require one to invent new ways of moving forward. The tried and true no longer work in a world where the foundation has shifted. Such life breaks can leave a person feeling exposed, vulnerable, and directionless, yet this is the very time when relying on one's inner resources can make a person the strongest and most fearless they have ever been. Taking away the known allows for a full exploration of the unknown.

Second, one begins to live the breaks, to feel the break as the norm, the surprise as the expected. Spiritual elders often remind us when we are doing *Òrìṣà* work, to always leave room for X. Rather than being thrown by the unexpected, one can live in such a way that the unexpected is an opportunity to use ingenuity, practice grace, and move with Divine rather than human order. It is a reminder that the plan is never solely of one's own making.

In Yoruba practice, *iwà* is the basis of priesthood. As a priest, one must know a litany of prayers and praises, must know the precise order in which sacrifices must be performed, must understand detailed protocols for everyday living; but if a priest masters each of these activities and has not learned to practice *iwà rere*—good character—in every instance, the priesthood will be bereft of its most potent force. It is the development of good character that allows for mindful improvisation of priestly responsibilities. Each ceremony moves in its own way, which requires that the participants know how to respond to the unique circumstances that have been presented to them. They know the customary structure, but their integrity helps them to make the appropriate decisions when the customary structure isn't available or doesn't quite work. In this way, *iwà* has an important relationship to virtuosity, whose root word is virtue. Virtuosity is a paradox of humility and fearlessness. The artist must submit to creation, to the force of the group's *àṣẹ*, to the demands of the spirit that move through the space, and at the same time connect so deeply with spirit that their own *iwà*/character/beauty soars.

This critical blend of competing forces is part of the mastery of a jazz aesthetic in theatre. The group relies on you to take the solo when it is tossed your way, and to hold them up during theirs. The group needs each performer to fully bring themselves to the art, to stand tall and bold—willing to take risks, to appear foolish, to be ridiculed in the pursuit of the Divine. If a performer does any less than this, the group cannot rise to its destined heights. The group then falls short of its spiritual and artistic mission—and indeed the two missions are actually one. Learning this ability to be egoless in service to the group and utterly self-/Divinely possessed in the act of creation is *ìwà* in action.

In Yoruba diasporic practice, priests must be relied on to know what is needed at any moment in ritual. While each priest may have her or his own specialty— divination, *oríkì,* beadwork, herbology—they must also know some of each priestly element so that they do not leave weak spaces in the life of an *ilé*.[10] This multifaceted priesthood may be a modification made in the diaspora as enslaved populations could not entrust a specific corpus of spiritual knowledge to single individuals; instead each priest had to be familiar with many layers of secrets and rituals so that if one priest was lost through the decimation of slavery, the tradition could continue.

Practicing the necessarily improvisational experience of *ìwà* creates what Bridgforth calls "new forms in traditional ways." She believes that jazz aesthetic work is "something that we deeply know that is old. This is not no new thing. It is getting inside of the ancient traditions and then creating something new."[11] This synthesis of new and old makes the jazz aesthetic in theatre at once familiar and strikingly novel.

The break in a jazz aesthetic can also occur just in the gathering and composition of the audience/witnesses. The work attracts people from a variety of neighborhoods, racial/gender/sexuality identifications, ages, and educational backgrounds. The break, experienced as the necessary rupture for something new to spring forth, is manifest in the demographics of the audience/witnesses as people who would not ordinarily occupy time and space share the moments of a work that is consciously about the formation of new world possibilities. In this way, to even sit in a room together is a transgression that opens the possibility for new structures and new life choices. This is the power of liminality that pushed political regimes to outlaw artists in different eras around the world. In this break created by the diverse theatrical jazz audience/witnesses, the established social order is suspended; one's sense of oneself and others is disrupted. There is more chance for acknowledgment across divisions when people share in the transgressive and transformative experience of performance. The more diverse the gathering, the more likely the shifts in self-definitions and in the understandings of others. The break in a jazz aesthetic creates a portal through which the audience/witnesses move.

The break—that opening into *awo,* mystery—also occurs in the set design and staging of the work. Often, the set seems to be a series of found objects randomly/ artfully arranged so that abstraction rather than mimesis governs the experience.

A bag of dirt, a chicken-wire fence, a bentwood chair, photographs strewn about the floor—these are set pieces that tend to evoke individual understandings among the audience/witnesses rather than common meanings. The work valorizes individual audience experiences. The abstract set pieces are positioned in such a way that the audience/witnesses sitting house right might see images that are not visible to those sitting house left. In this way, the director is less concerned with creating a world for a common audience experience, and more concerned with creating a world that stimulates each audience/witness and evokes a sense of mood and tone. And in much of this work, the mood is tinged with age so that objects have a worn patina. This situates ancestors subliminally in the work even when ancestors are not specifically referenced.

Theatrical jazz tends not to solicit audience identification which asks the audience/witnesses to see aspects of themselves in the work. Neither does it ask for empathy, a kind of feeling with the experience often predicated on some sort of sadness or pain. Instead, theatrical jazz hopes to achieve resonant frequencies with the audience. Audience/witnesses will connect with those moments, ideas, people, feelings, colors, sounds with which they sense a vibration, and they are not held accountable for those experiences in the production that do not resonate with them. The notion of resonance allows for an inarticulable vibrational over-lapping of truths between audience/witnesses and performances; unlike empathy and identification, which seem to require conscious connection, resonant frequencies can hum in the unconscious. Repeated experiences with theatrical jazz are likely to create more and more points of resonance as audience/witnesses begin to tune into jazz structures and techniques from one performance to the next.

In the staged reading of Florinda Bryant's *Half-Breed Southern Fried (check one)* presented in the Oscar G. Brockett Theatre at the University of Texas, Carlos directed some scenes in intentional visual obscurity. Carlos placed one scene far up left, next to the tiered seating in the theatre. This position meant that about a third of the audience could not see the scene at all, and those closest to the scene had to sharply crane their necks to see even a glimpse of one of the performers. In another moment in the production, one performer sat on a stool with her back to the audience while the three others faced the audience and performed the lines. Carlos did not reference the back-facing performer or attempt to clarify how this choice coordinated with the lines being spoken. Understanding became the work of the audience/witnesses, not the requirement of the director. Carlos uses space in such a way that she creates animated paintings throughout the space. If that means the best painting is staged against a mostly hidden wall, so be it.

Half-Breed also took full advantage of simultaneity. In addition to four performers often positioned upstage behind music stands, there were three video monitors running continuously. Two monitors displayed footage of Bryant's grandparents' land in Central Texas where she was "allowed to get dirty,"[12] and the third monitor showed images of the performers live as they embodied the work on stage. At any given moment, the audience/witnesses might experience the four live

Figure 52. *Half-Breed Southern Fried (check one)* poster. Painting by Tonya Engel. Directed by Laurie Carlos for the Performing Blackness Series of the John L. Warfield Center for African and African American Studies at the University of Texas at Austin, 2006. Photo by Ruth McFarlane.

performers, video of a rooster running across the road, live video of the women as they performed, and video of Bryant's relatives discussing a family quilt. No two people in the audience were likely to have the same experience, as attention and desire were internally and individually guided.

The video work in this production was particularly intriguing. There was something both disorienting and seductive about seeing a tight close-up of one woman on video while the same woman was performing live, or having a profile perspective from the video while seeing the performers frontally, or seeing one performer silently watch the others speak as displayed on the monitor while one's attention in the live embodiment is on the speaking performers. In an important way, the videographer and camerawoman, Krissy Mahan, was a co-director with Carlos as Mahan made instant artistic decisions about which live moments to display on the monitor. Carlos gave Mahan very little specific guidance on when and what and how to capture this live work on video. While this was a little disconcerting for Mahan, it was an indication of Carlos's trust in Mahan's skill and instincts. Mahan, like most of the performers in *Half-Breed*, had worked previously with Carlos on jazz aesthetics. This meant that Mahan knew, though perhaps unconsciously, the principles of random juxtaposition, of jagged contrasts, of shifting focus, and of simultaneity that characterize this work. During each performance, Mahan moved through the space turning on and off the videos of Bryant's central Texas home, and selecting which performer, which angle, which surprise she wanted to video and display to the audience in an awareness of the multiple and varied visual/aural conversations her choices might stimulate. As Mahan responded to the performers, to the audience/witnesses, and to her own impulses, each performance became its own nonlinear and evolving narrative.

The use of diagonals for stage crosses—a trademark of Carlos's direction—elongates the space and seems to radiate the experience out beyond the confines of the performance. In *Half-Breed*, Carlos staged several moments with the four performers—Florinda Bryant, Monique Cortez, Jaclyn Pryor, Laura Rios—walking quickly forward on the deepest diagonal in the space, then having them walk slowly backward down the same diagonal. The DJ, Terrence Stith, was positioned in an aisle at the downstage end of this diagonal in close proximity to the audience. His DJ table was a strong anchor in the visual space, and underscored the diagonal planes Carlos favored. Given the shape of the Brockett Theatre, walking the diagonal meant that none of the audience could experience this very forceful walk straight-on. Everyone had to see profiles and shadows.

Carlos's use of space is reminiscent of the expressionist staging techniques found for a short period in U.S. theatre at the top of the twentieth century. Deep, long cross lines, bodies in shadows, often stylized/danced angular movements were identifiable features of Eugene O'Neill's *The Hairy Ape* and Elmer Rice's *The Adding Machine*. In *Half-Breed*, Carlos also played heavily with shadow so that performers and set were often obscured or fuzzy. These lighting choices, along with blocking that did not yield to conventional notions of sight lines, were dictated primarily by Carlos's directorial vision and less so by the constraints of the space itself.

Jones likewise relied on diagonals in the 2005 installment of *The Book of Daniel: 35:1*. He created a performance grid on the floor of allgo much like a game board. The audience/witnesses were seated irregularly around the paths and performance circles of the space. Few audience/witnesses shared the same view as Jones walked his jaunty dance from one location to the next. In this instance, the diagonals created energy and added to the sense of community, as audience/witnesses could look across a diagonal to see other audience/witnesses experiencing the moment. Diagonals were also central to the production of *con flama,* as Carlos used a Los Angeles map to configure the spatial relationships of the performers. In the second incarnation of *love conjure/blues* at the University of Texas, Helga Davis also directed the work with a heavy emphasis on diagonals. The performers sat on wooden cubes divided into two groups placed at diagonals to each other, and each body was often torqueing at the torso, thereby creating more diagonals. It seemed that none of the performers were facing the same direction. Dynamic tension. A little like dissonance or surprise in music. In *blood pudding* directed by Carlos at Frontera@Hyde Park Theatre, even when the performers were in a line in front of the audience, they stood three-quarters, creating individual diagonals with

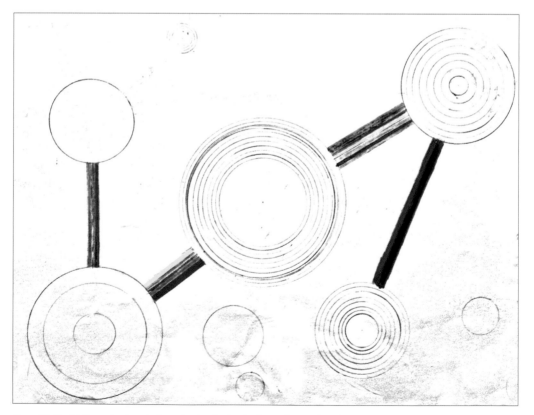

Figure 53. Daniel Alexander Jones's floor plan for *The Book of Daniel 35:1*. Photo by Daniel Alexander Jones.

the audience/witnesses. In Jones's direction of Shay Youngblood's *Shakin' the Mess Outta Misery,* also at Frontera, he staged one emotionally powerful scene by placing the two performers seated in chairs with the chair backs touching each other on the diagonal. This meant the performers had to fully know the energy of the scene while facing in opposite directions, without looking at each other. This surely created the common directing dictum "give the actor an obstacle to work through," as the performers had to struggle for intimacy, but equally important, this choice veered the work sharply away from realism, and gave the audience/witnesses an opportunity to tap their own imaginations. I was moved by how not looking at one another actually created an intense intimacy between the performers. Given the unique shape of Hyde Park Theatre—with the limited audience seating in an L-shape—it was almost impossible to achieve anything *but* a diagonal relationship with the audience/witnesses. It is critical to remember that so much of the jazz aesthetic created by this arm of the lineage was developed on this very stage. Audiences' expectations of staging at Hyde Park Theatre were broken and remapped as they experienced the work, literally, from a new vantage point. What began as an imaginative response to the constraints of Hyde Park Theatre may have evolved into a common, unstated, theatrical jazz, directorial principle.

Much theatrical jazz is set in arena or deep thrust staging, which makes the audience/witnesses a part of the performance, as one sees both the performance and the audience/witnesses at all times. Arena staging also encourages the use of the entire performance space since the demarcation between performance and audience is blurred. Both incarnations of *love conjure/blues* through the Warfield Center at the University of Texas made use of arena staging as the audience/witnesses encircled the performances. In the original spring 2004 version, the performers were also seated in a circle, occasionally rising to move around their seats or through the performance circle. Such usage can activate and enliven the *àṣẹ,* the life force of the production. Artist, activist, and scholar Susanne Wenger explains this phenomenon when she writes, "Everything has *àṣẹ,* but *àṣẹ* operates only after a motive stimulus: It has neither life nor will of its own."[13] Utilizing all parts of the performance space as the world of the performance can act as the "motive stimulus" that will spark the *àṣẹ.*

The circle is the dominant geometry for the transfer of *àṣẹ.* Power is passed from *òrun,* the realm of deities and ancestors, to *aiyé,* the material plane. The *àṣẹ* is carried back to *òrun* through those humans who become ancestors. Similarly, the *àṣẹ* among the living in *aiyé* resonates in *òrun.* These circular relationships are manifestations of the circular Yoruba cosmos in which *òrun* and *aiyé* are intimately linked. Yoruba lidded bowls and divining trays are physical representations of this intimate relationship between *òrun* and *aiyé,*[14] and the authority of the circle. *Babaláwo*s and *Ìyáláwo*s—those priests who have apprenticed as diviners and are consecrated to *Òrúnmìlà,* the Divinity of divination—often conduct their work on an *opón,* a circular divining tray that corresponds with the joined worlds of deities and humans. *Òrúnmìlà* sends a message from *òrun* onto the *opón.* Given the centrality of divination to Yoruba reality, it is significant that the *opón* is most often carved in the very shape of the Yoruba cosmos. In performance, the arena staging becomes *àyíká,* the circle as the cosmos, thereby creating *iyíká* and *yímiká,* the acts of encircling and encircling me respectively. In the Yoruba spiritual diaspora of Brazil's Candomble and the United States' *Ìṣẹ̀ṣẹ̀* practices, in which dances for deities are often done in a circle, and of Haiti's Vodoun, which acknowledges the power of the central *poteau-mitan,* there is *àyíká* containing and protecting the energy. In this way, the performance circle actually creates a dynamic place for strengthening the Divine–human connection through performance.

The set, like the intricate scoring of voices, becomes another way of layering ideas and creating individual private understandings within the group communal intimacies of performance. A buried cross mentioned in the text is visible only to those seated house left. An embroidered riding jacket cannot be seen by those seated center. Frequently, the sets in these jazz works evoke archeological digs strewn with artifacts where historical documentation speaks with today's headlines and each artists' memories. In this way, the sets often function like installations—discrete yet unbounded locations within which the performers could live.

The jazz aesthetic productions are often realized in unmasked spaces, revealing the beams, exit signs, and warehouse doors of the actual facility. The sets, then, physicalize the open space free of pretense suggested by the form itself and mirrored in the world of possibility found in the staging. This *mise en scène,* then, puts the audience/witnesses in the performance. We—everyone present—are sharing and creating as we are encompassed by the same walls, ceiling, lighting, floor. The set encourages this to be our experience jointly. Working the whole space as the world of the performance also suggests a jam session in which we are all crafting these moments together. In discussing the qualities of his conductions, Lawrence "Butch" Morris speaks of "the art of environing" in which the physical world and much more is considered. He explains, "By observing the cultural, social, and historical potential in both the individual and the collective, we arrive at a specific momentary logic."[15] It is key that Morris addresses the *potential* of the performers, not just their established skill. This deep awareness of the complete experience of performance is reminiscent of Oyin Ogunba's exploration of Yoruba festival dramas that employ "imaginative collaboration,"[16] the establishment of just the right physical and psychic space for artists, audiences, and artifacts to make mutually influencing work together.

In theatrical jazz, the space calls attention to the here and now rather than evoking another location or era. The audience/witnesses are encouraged to be here inside of the current experience so that they can feel themselves into what is actually occurring on stage. The minimally detailed stage pulls us into now, cocreating together. A spare stage space encourages a spacious inner awareness among audience/witnesses, an inner curiosity and knowing that is sparked by the potential of the sparse stage.

The staging in a jazz aesthetic is rarely mimetic. Performers often use their bodies in abstract ways while giving voice to rich dense language that may approximate everyday speech but often has more textures than the everyday generally allows. The bodies act as one rhythm, or set of rhythms, with language creating a counterpoint. The audience/witnesses, then, must work to create sense of this seemingly random union of verbal and physical languages. This work to understand and feel with the performance requires a specific commitment and engagement from the audience. Rather than the "willing suspension of disbelief," the audience/witnesses are asked to discover, through vigorous mental and intuitive participation, the truths and distinctive contours of beauty and dissonance inside the work. The bodies are often choreographed into a series of gestures, postures, walks, and exhalations of breath that reappear throughout a production. When both Carlos and Jones direct, they move about the space half-dancing, half-channeling some private and demanding muse. As they hear the performers' voices and feel the harmonies and discordant strains across those sounds, they inject an ensemble gesture or series of stylized movements here, or toss in a loud breathing pattern there. The intent and effect may be clear for the director, but this clarity is typically not provided for the performer, who must uncover her or his own truth through repetition and a willingness to yield to nonreason. Even in Jones's *Phoenix Fabrik,* a work more on the linear end of the continuum than many in this aesthetic, the actors engage in identifiable actions that do not always mirror the words being spoken. Indeed, not having body and sound in mimetic concert is precisely the point. Erik Ehn explains that these works "[create] a sense of the infinite through a layering of patterns, medial."[17]

Alaskan Heat Blue Dot *was the first time I was directed by Laurie, and I was self-conscious and rigid—physically and psychically. I had seen Daniel's work and had been a dramaturg for Laurie. I had offered workshops for Sharon's company as she developed root wy'mn, but this was the first time I attempted to fully embody what I had previously experienced at some distance. During rehearsals, I was more worried about what Laurie thought than what I was discovering. After a particularly long rehearsal, just a few days before the show opened, Laurie worked with me on a monologue I had been struggling with for some time. The lines suggested a self-absorbed person who had a propensity for*
rambling. I tried to make those characteristics into a character. I pushed the words and forced the movement. I was trying to be like the character I imagined, and each choice felt strained and artificial. I was embarrassed not to "get it" the way the other performers seemed to, and I just wanted to conclude this exposure of my inabilities as soon as possible. After some attempts to get me to respond vocally by saying the lines in different ways, Laurie gave me a series of hand tosses that she choreographed into the print text. As is customary in this aesthetic, the gestures did not have an obvious literal relationship to the words. Indeed, that was the point, though I didn't know it at the time. I also didn't realize that Laurie simply took my nervous gestures—those awkward hand motions that are supposed to look informal and conversational but read as loud displays of uncertainty—and gave them back to me in a choreographed manner. I was stymied. I couldn't even do my own gestures in the way Laurie wanted! I see now that my task was to allow my body to incorporate the gestures rather than

understand the psychology behind them.[18] *The break often comes as a mirror that illuminates the performer's resistance. At that time, I could not see my reflection, only what I thought was Laurie's distortion of me.*

The texts in a jazz aesthetic imagine time as coterminous realms—rarely linear, discrete, or fully knowable. Worlds interact across time and space, and characters often move in and out of temporal, spatial, and psychic sites. According to Ehn, in such work "time and space are omnisciently available."[19] This temporal quality is particularly clear in *Phoenix Fabrik*, in which the "now" of the play is tantalizingly ambiguous. In the opening stage directions, Jones notes: "The dramatic structure of *Phoenix Fabrik* is rooted in the ring shout. Time and space are specific, yet not linear. You will note that the play unfolds through two 'rings.' The language (its rhythm and tempo in particular) is the key to unlock the circular movement in the playing of *Phoenix Fabrik*."[20] Jones joins together transtemporal spirits. Although he has situated this play in South Carolina in 1945, the abandoned German-owned doll factory where much of the action takes place serves as home to the presumably flesh-and-blood characters of Eleanor and The Boy, as well as the more ephemeral Inga. Inga seems to live in the very brick and mortar of her father's doll factory as she appears in the building's crumbling walls and shadowy niches. This spirit girl interacts with Eleanor and communes with other forces. She is in the here and now, and in the then and was—and this puts the entire text in the realm of the possible or the "what if" or the nonmaterial future. Richard Schechner notes the fluidity of time and space that is possible as work moves between efficacy and entertainment. Those works that value efficacy veer toward "timeless time—the eternal present."[21] The timelessness of the jazz aesthetic, then, links this aesthetic to efficacy even when the creators do not have a specific efficacious aim in mind. The very challenge to established aesthetics means that there is a subliminal challenge to sociopolitical structures that undergird established aesthetics—and in this way the jazz aesthetic's nonlinear use of time predisposes it to exist as theatre for social change.

Some scholars associate future-oriented time with notions of progress that are bound up in an uninterrogated status quo.[22] In the United States the focus on the future is a drive toward an unattainable middleclass perfection complete with a college education, a house, marriage, children, health care and a solid retirement package. Eliminated from this future fantasy are those who cannot participate due to structural racism and sexism, and due to an utter erasure of queer people from the formula. The obvious preference for families, the disregard of systematic forces that disproportionately hinder families of color from gaining a firm foothold within the middle class, the elimination of queer people because they are not uniformly allowed (as of this writing) the dubious move to middle-class respectability that marriage confers—all make for a future-time orientation that excludes Black and queer possibilities. Such a future attempts to dehistoricize and depoliticize race and sexuality. The present in theatrical jazz does not dismember[23] the past facts of racialized and sexualized violence and oppressions, as the present requires body-to-body engagement with an abundantly complex Blackness, and with queer self-performances and queer love. The body holds the histories and the desires. Now holds more richness than a product-driven future contains. Living in the present allows us to be responsive to who we really are in the room.

The nonnormative pleasures that are theatrical jazz create queer time, a time committed to the present that includes the competing historical truths of the past, a time that relinquishes the progress and product orientation of the future, a time that invites a reconsideration of our personal narratives and our ways of being in the world. Most Black people inevitably occupy queer time as we are systematically eliminated from the linear constructions of respectability, and as we retain visceral memories of violent oppression that have no place in a sanitized tomorrow. The now insists on everyone being exactly who they are in the moment.

In a 1998 interview I conducted with Craig Harris and Sekou Sundiata about the development of *Elijah, the Return of the African* (later refashioned as *Udu*), Sundiata explained how time functions in that work: "The character I was doing was Elijah [an enslaved African] . . . but the thing is, he really starts out speaking from the point of view of the 20th century . . . in terms of time and space, I like the idea of breaking . . . I like the idea of time being that fluid . . . it's a poetic sense of time. And space . . . which means it's largely metaphorical and he doesn't respect real time all the time. I like that idea. Because the music is like that, too."[24] Sundiata makes the critical connection between time, space, and music— a connection that appears repeatedly in theatrical jazz texts. The jazz aesthetic writer is keenly aware of the pulse and vibration in language, and shapes that language as a composer might with attention to the layering of harmonies, the force of dissonance, the vigor of competing rhythms. This attention to sound as vibration and animating force is the principle behind *àfòṣe*, the ability of the word to manifest reality. Words—when sounded—are a very particular making, are their own distinctive kinesis as the words transform the physical plane and *are* action.

This brand of space travel defies linear plot construction, and thrives within a seriate structure that exists as often autonomous units of time and space joined by language, or theme, or image, or by the very fact of performance within determined locations. In describing the structure of Yoruba performance, Margaret Thompson Drewal uses the visual art concept of seriation, the assignment of meaning based on context and the relationship among narrative units rather than a linear and causal narrative truth. This seriate structure allows a narrative—or several—to unfold from multiple perspectives without necessarily giving primacy to any one angle of truth. In Bridgforth's *delta dandi,* simultaneity of time and space is essential to the psychological liberation of the main character. Many worlds swirl together as one fragment of story trails to a close, and another piece of memory or truth from a different time and place is taken up. Like persistent visitations, the Elder, Chorus, Blues, and Spirits assure The Gurl, "all at the same time in all directions / we are here / talking talking talking talking / singing your praises."[25] And their disparate melodies return again and again to blunt the blues The Gurl has had to bear.

The works in a jazz aesthetic are unabashedly about hope—about love as the antidote to annihilation, about joy as a birthright. These writers disdain despair and futility, and offer up worlds in which we might actually find communion with ourselves first, and with others as a welcome by-product of self-love and affirmation. For Carlos, love manifests as food. Again and again in her texts, food is talked about, prepared, eaten, and shared. The care given to selecting the ingredients, and a chef's eye for artful arrangement, shape character interaction and create a gustatory and olfactory presence in her work. In *Marion's Terrible Time of Joy*, Ananya and Monkey understand that food is both physical and spiritual sustenance. The opening stage directions prepare the reader for the primacy of cooking, which gives way to a conversation that roots food in love:

ANANYA

You are standing here with our hands stirring pots / Who are we feeding?

MONKEY

I can only smell this river / The pots are filled with regret? / When will the regrets get gone? / Move into the foam? / Become soot /

ANANYA

Who are we going to give all this food to? / Who is going to say thank you and clean the plates? / Lick their fingers? / Who will clean the nail with the tongue? / Who are we feeding? /

MONKEY

I've made salads of cresses with endive, olives, goat cheese and chervil / I don't eat them / I serve them up to whoever wants them / Who is gonna want them? / That's how it is / I don't clean the dishes or eat the left overs or even serve / Just let them spoon and pick /[26]

Monkey's generous sharing provides an example of community building for the skeptical Ananya. Food—carefully selected and richly prepared food—is the way to ward off ugliness of spirit, isolation, and destruction.

The works in a theatrical jazz aesthetic most often offer hope as a possibility and love as the strategy. Love both requires and generates hope. This is what transforms the world. This is the new way—and such a way requires the break—the realm of possibility where individual identity features blend into new realities, never fixed, always evolving. Performance Studies scholar Dwight Conquergood wrote of the discipline of Performance Studies as a caravan rather than a carnival—ever shifting and evolving.[27] Theatrical jazz moves in a similar fashion, as one does not hold fast to gender, race, class, sexuality or nationality; instead one dances inside the possibility of malleable identity—not without details and anchors—but fluid nonetheless, moving.

In the conclusion to *Phoenix Fabrik,* the worlds of the living and the dead—in perhaps the ultimate expression of human liminality—morph and slide as the evangelist Mother Dixon helps the son she aborted acknowledge his betwixt and between life.

> MOTHER DIXON. Open your eyes.
> THE BOY. What do *you* see?
> MOTHER DIXON. Sunflowers. Only sunflowers in every mouth, in every hand,
> in every ear.
> THE BOY. The seeds are tears. Happy as glass.
> END PLAY.[28]

The Boy—newly named Pluto—enters into this new phase of his death with his eyes open and full of the promise and sunshine that sunflowers evoke, "Happy as glass." Even in death Jones finds hope and happiness. This is not hope for a peace in the afterlife; Jones's hope is full of beauty that should characterize both death and life. As Jones states: "The Divine continues to assert itself. And this does not come without sacrifice, because you had to choose it."[29] Jones uses the dwarf planet Pluto as his reference point here. He explains that as the farthest planet in the solar system, Pluto suggests those terrible truths of our collective Black consciousness that get pushed into private spaces as if they never happened.[30] When The Boy is named Pluto, he is claiming a necessary self-assertion as he pulls the crusted isolated secrets into public view—a supreme act of freedom and self-making.

For these writers, love is the most radical move we can make. Love builds for a fertile ripe tomorrow, a hoped-for continuation of the love itself and for humanity. Love connects us with the deepest mysteries of the universe, and accessing that love is a spiritual path, a covenant with ancestors, the Divine, and an unknown tomorrow. Erik Ehn concludes *Heavenly Shades of Night* with an exchange between a reunited mother and daughter. They say together, "Fill our hearts / Fill our hearts with suffering / Break our hearts with suffering / And open us to joy. / Awake in the world let us suffer. Break our suffering with joy. / We concentrate on peace. / Break our hearts with suffering. / Open us to joy." L'ash, the daughter, has the final words of the play, "Love is pulse."[31] In *Heavenly Shades of Night,* love is the very heartbeat of life; and after a play filled with lethal betrayals and tragic deaths, this mother and daughter can sit together declaring the necessity of choosing life.

Such a love is indeed a transgression, because it flies in the face of the social order that asks us to diminish ourselves, to keep boundaries, to be dreamless for the sake of familiarity and predictability. Societies, nations, function best with an automated efficiency in the absence of improvisation, spontaneity, and fluidity, with few openings for individuality and magic. In these structures, the present moment is lost in the machinery of the future, in delimiting tomorrow at the expense of the full potentiality of the here and now. The way these structures respond to the unwieldiness of their size and complexity is by encouraging uniformity and an erasure of detail and specificity. The love in these theatrical jazz works holds great promise for tomorrow, though in production the love happens right in the present tense with the audience/witnesses.

In *love conjure/blues*, Bridgforth's characters move in and out of love, many of them finding the deepest meaning in unions that transgress social boundaries. A seriate unit that typifies the genuine power of love occurs with Joshua Davis and Booker Chang, who "found themselves over a poem." The narrator tells us,

> this is how booker chang and joshua davis found each other. in
> blistering sun / working days never ending / backs bent in toil / in
> the company of men they claimed each other
> declared themselves
> adorned each other with words. united
> in heart / booker chang and joshua davis married one the other
> with a poem.[32]

The transgression here is love itself, the love of two men, the declaration of hope and joy, even in a world that tries to ensure that one's very Blackness is the epitome of sorrow, in a world where combating oppression assures the prominence of pain.

Bridgforth ends *love conjure/blues* with the lyrics "the Peace we Pray / the poem we pen / the bridge we make / the song / the dance / is us / and we are // free / free / Free. / cause / We are / Love";[33] and the narrator leaves the audience/witnesses with "I am the conjurer come back to love / remember / remember / remember / remember."[34]

When I was serving as a dramaturg on con flama, *I misunderstood the very heart of the piece. Sharon's revisions, based on Laurie's suggestion that the girl's prayer was actually Sharon's focus, compounded the very elements I questioned. Laurie understood that this work gives primacy to love—real love—which is an inner freedom. I was applying a logic to the work that did not grow from theatrical jazz tenets on which the work is based.*

Working the jazz aesthetic in theatre requires being present with *awo*—mystery, possibility, the vulnerability of pursuing the unknown—that can open us to the deepest potential for love or transformation while acknowledging those places of terror that hinder our access to joy.

PART THREE

The Bridge / Àṣẹ / Transformation

I learned that how to act had to do with survival,
not only of my individual body,
but also of the integrity of my people's story.
It was years later that I got
the life changing awareness that the *art* of acting
is a powerful tool for transmitting truth
about implicit, unspoken social conditions.

—Robbie McCauley[1]

We co-exist with our future and with our past.
We carry the genes of history.
We manifest the genetic traits of our history in our present
body [un]conscious.
We cut across different temporalities.

—Grisha Coleman[2]

The tragedy of the contemporary age (the genocidal era) is not that we have gone mad,
but that at every step, conscious choices are made that deliver us up to the symptoms of
madness. Art, when it counters, does so by creating safe spaces for waiting for witness,
for union—spaces that may be approached by but not made by reason.

—Erik Ehn[3]

This project will be based in urban areas and uses water from rainfall and melting snow
to play records chosen by those who live in the surrounding community. I propose
building rain activated acoustic phonographs that will sit curbside like musical hydrants,
waiting for the rain.

—Walter Kitundu[4]

THE JAZZ BRIDGE prepares us for a return to the original melody. But
the return bears the marks of the journey. One does not arrive at the exact
point of origin, for that familiar place is now imbued with the experience
acquired through the bridge. The bridge is the shift in the music when a new
refrain or key is introduced. The music takes a sonic turn as it heads to the next
aural idea. The bridge transports, transforms, and elevates. It takes us somewhere.

Theatrical jazz is the bridge itself, carrying the audience/witnesses through the recognizable selves that entered the performance—with their understandings of Blackness and theatre—and delivering them, at the end of the performance, anew.

The works in theatrical jazz can be imagined as catalysts for animating *àṣẹ*. Like enzymes when placed with other properties, the work makes things happen, indeed makes something that did not exist before. *Àṣẹ* is the Yoruba concept for life force; it is the energy that pervades all things, and the authority to make things happen.[5] *Àṣẹ* is the force that unifies all persons and things into symbiotic relationships. When the *àṣẹ* of one is depleted, others are required to replenish it; in this way we have a deep and abiding responsibility to one another and to all living beings—animal, plant, mineral.

Àṣẹ exists in many verbal forms. The two that are most clearly connected to theatrical jazz are *ìgèdè* and *àfọ̀ṣẹ*. *Ìgèdè* is understood as incantation, the use of language to invoke and to evoke. *Àfọ̀ṣẹ* is the power of the word to manifest. It has a kinship with the Dogon word *nommo*, which theatre scholar and playwright Paul Carter Harrison describes as the ability of the word to animate the spiritual world.[6] While among the Dogon *nommo* is understood to be ancestral forces, some Afrocentric scholars (Asante, Karenga), following Janheinz Jahn's discussions of the concept in *Muntu* and *Neo-African Literature*, understand *nommo* to be the power of the word. This power is deeper than language itself in that it encompasses the will to expression, the ability of language to catalyze enactment. Harrison suggests that Black Theatre is a theatre of *nommo*, performance that makes something shift in the world.[7] In this way, *nommo* has kinship with *àṣẹ*, which artist/philosopher/priest Susanne Wenger regards as "the motive force inherent in the Word, the living pulsation of *Odù*, the heartbeat of *Ifá*'s sacred number symbolism."[8] Indeed, during prayers by practitioners of Yoruba-based spiritual traditions in the United States, the priests say *àṣẹ* to acknowledge the power of the prayer; in this way the word *àṣẹ* is used to signify "so be it," it is used to affirm the actions that the potentiality of the words unleashed.

The union of *àṣẹ* and words is crystallized in *Èṣù*, close kin to *Legba* and *Ellegua* in African diasporic spiritual traditions. *Èṣù*, the Divine force of indeterminacy, opportunity and linguistics, is the bearer of *àṣẹ*. *Èṣù* is the communicative impulse "that activates the physical-metaphysical, intellectual communicative affinities and reaches."[9] Several scholars, including Sandra Richards, Joyce A. Joyce, Nathaniel Mackey, Graham Lock, and Henry Louis Gates, Jr., have noted *Èṣù*'s animating power in their analysis of Black performance and literary texts.[10] The weave of words and action make theatre the ideal spark for *àṣẹ*. Words, life force, and manifestation are interlocked.

JOHN MASON: "*Èṣù* is not just the guardian of vital life force but is synonymous with it."°

° *Orin Òrìṣà: Songs for Selected Heads*, 54.

Àṣẹ is also a physical substance that empowers its owner with miraculous abilities. Only specialists deeply responsive to *Ìṣẹ̀ṣẹ̀* traditions can be entrusted with this form of *àṣẹ* because the substance has the tremendous ability to bring things to action. Hence, the physical *àṣẹ* and the metaphysical *àṣẹ* share the vitality of action

Figure 54. "Untitled," by Wura-Natasha Ogunji. In Ogunji's drawing, waves of *àṣẹ* flow through the woman's fingertips, filling the image with her blue-green energy. Photo by Wura-Natasha Ogunji.

and potentiality. Margaret Thompson Drewal's straightforward definition of meta-physical *àṣẹ* makes the relationship between both properties clear when she defines *àṣẹ* as "performative power; the power of accomplishment; the power to get things done; the power to make things happen."[11]

The goal for these artists—in varying degrees and ways—is the act of transformation, of invigorating *àṣẹ*, a kind of "making holy," in Bridgforth's words. The artists seek to create work that writes their own identities into the world and, in so doing, generates a distinctive set of possibilities for others. Rather than each of the performers, writers, or designers individually serving as change agents, the elements of production collectively carry the power to transform.

Those who write in this form first encounter this power to make things happen as they examine themselves for truths to put on the page, to release into the studio, and/or to live their lives with greater generosity and humility. The truth might be a forgotten memory, word, idea, or image that triggers clarity, or a move-

Figure 55. "Self Portrait," by Minnie Mari-anne Miles. In the painting, Miles seems to be introspective while still directing her gaze outward. She is almost one with her surroundings as her skin and the wall share a range of ochre hues and a transparent yet layered density. This inward pull happens even as her eyes look outward beyond her here and now. Photo by Ricky Yanas. Courtesy of the John L. War-field Center for African and African American Studies, University of Texas at Austin.

ment and breath that open the body to new territory. In this way, the writers are shifting their self-foundations by sharing their personal discoveries or exposing the difficult questions they need to pursue. Performers of this work redefine what it means to create a character or to sustain a scene or moment. For performers encountering the work for the first time, there is a shedding that often happens as previous training is sloughed off so that the emergent methods can be embraced. The self as performer uncovers humility, vulnerability, and release of expectations for approval. Audience/witnesses can experience the theatrical jazz bridge or shift through an engagement with a potentially disconcertingly expansive Blackness, with nonlinear transtemporal narratives that encourage new strategies of comprehension, and with varied physically collaborative methods. Indeed, each of these features acts as emotional, psychic, or physical forms of participation. The more present these forms of participation, the more likely the internal shifts within the audience/witnesses will occur.

The animating force of *àṣẹ* has a kinship to Kim Benston's notion of methexis, "a communal 'helping-out' of the action by all assembled."[12] In his discussion of methexis, Benston describes a road to a proposed transformation when he writes,

> [Methexis] is a process that could be alternatively described as a shift from display, the spectacle observed, to rite, the event which dissolves traditional divisions between actor and spectator, self and other, enacted text and material context. And through this process, the black beholder has been theoretically transformed from a detached individual whose private consciousness the playwright sought to reform, to a participatory member of communal ceremony which affirms a shared vision.[13]

Like methexis, the *àṣẹ* activated by theatrical jazz is set in motion by transforming audience/witnesses into participants, co-creators. Unlike methexis, the *àṣẹ* of theatrical jazz does not rely on "a shared vision" with the audience/witnesses.[14]

BRANDI CATANESE: "Black performers taking the stage play a crucial role in helping audiences understand what blackness is. Their work challenges old ways of seeing blackness and makes new ways of being black possible."[*]

[*] "Politics of Representation in African American Theatre and Drama," 20.

Indeed, the tension and unsettledness that occurs from an engagement with an *un*shared vision of Blackness is precisely a primary way in which theatrical jazz generates transformation. In theatrical jazz, the primary shared ground between the performance and audience/witnesses may be Blackness itself, though the work stretches what Blackness might be. For some, Blackness may function as a fundamental resonant frequency.

Because theatrical jazz frequently introduces characters, themes, plots, and artifacts that may not be commonly associated with Black Theatre, theatrical jazz has the potential to stretch audiences to deeper possibilities for Blackness and, consequently, deeper possibilities for everyday realities. Expanding on Brandi Catanese's claim, if theatre creates new possibilities for Blackness, it inevitably creates new social and political possibilities generally.

The active engagement with audience/witnesses that is stimulated by theatrical jazz reflects the present tenseness that is fundamental to the form. Curiosity, disease, epiphany, synthesis, frustration, recognition, even alienation and disconnection keep the audience/witnesses right here right now, keep the audience/witnesses alert and aware of what they are feeling. Being keen to what one is feeling is necessary for individual personal transformation as well as for broader social change. Theatrical jazz shines a spotlight on an audience's *now* as the work challenges theatrical conventions, narrative structure, and concepts of Blackness.

Figure 56. Program for *The Book of Daniel, Chapter 7: Immortality,* designed by Daniel Alexander Jones. It invites the audience/witnesses to reflect on their own life choices just as he reflects on his own during the performance. Jones (upper left) with family members (middle and lower left); Malcolm X (upper middle); Josephine Baker (upper right); collaborators Tea Alagic and Walter Kitundu (lower left). The program is also another example of the care Jones takes in shaping the visual experience with his work. The reverse side of the program included the complete text of the performance. Photo by Elisa Durrette.

When Daniel brought his The Book of Daniel, Chapter 7: Immortality *to the Warfield Center's Performing Blackness Series, I was thrilled. Daniel's way of stimulating audiences with complex narratives, exceptional artistry, and nonrealistic* mise en scène *would surely prompt vigorous discussion during the talk backs.*

Sitting in the audience, I was less sure about the impact Daniel's work might have. I wanted the Black folk to really go at the controversial ideas he presented—"allowing" a Croatian woman to speak of her oppressions alongside the oppressions of Black people, mocking the performance styles of some brands of Black Theatre in which vocal and facial histrionics are the norm, applauding the activism of Josephine Baker, who some Black folk imagine to be solely an exploited misguided nude dancer—surely some of this would spark

dialogue! To my right were a group of Black graduate students who appeared to be uninterested (though in private conversations with them later, it was clear that that was not the case), to my left were a handful of Black faculty members who did not appear to be engaged in the performance, and around me were a few Black non-UT folk who also seemed rather passively involved in the experience. The majority of the audience members were white UT students, some of whom were required to attend as part of the participation grades in their theatre courses. When there was laughter, much of it came from the white people. In general the Black folk did not appear to connect.

During the talk back the white theatre people dominated the discussion, which centered on the use of space, the process for creating the work, the style of acting. In my memory, no one—not even the few Black folks who made comments—engaged with the ideas that were present in the piece—immortality, Black life in light of mortality, human interconnectedness. What I had hoped would be an opportunity for community, for a conversation about Blackness, became a rather static discussion of theatrical aesthetics. Talk backs are often awkward moments when audiences are asked to publically discuss something that has just landed in their psyche. Some may need to process silently and over time rather than immediately with a group of strangers. Could the very structure I thought would stimulate discussion actually silence Black audience members?

Is such silence part of active engagement?

Was there some feature of theatrical jazz in the work that might have encouraged wider discussion if framed for the talkback?

What is a Black Theatre that leaves Black people speechless?

And was it the performance or the talk back itself that left many people silent?

Bridgforth refers to audiences in this aesthetic as "witness participants." In so doing, she calls forth a host of political and social associations with the role of witnessing—the deep and abiding responsibility to the act being collectively experienced. Dwight Conquergood understands the audience in similar ways, as demonstrated by his term "co-performative witness," whom he describes as "the ideal spectator" because he or she is "deeply engaged" through the act of empathy.

JILL DOLAN: "Stories, embodied with such grace, such care, such imaginative detail, offer the audience a utopian performative, a glimpse of what it might feel like to regard friends and lovers, strangers and those most different from ourselves with respectful, intersubjective consideration and care."°

° "'Finding Our Feet in the Shoes of (One An) Other': Multiple Character Solo Performers and Utopian Performatives," 502.

Jones also references empathy in considering audiences' engagement when he suggests that theatrical jazz fosters a "radical empathy"[15]—a rigorous commitment to feeling inside the complexity and fullness of someone else's world. In this way empathy in theatrical jazz has a place, but by itself is limited. While audience empathy has a long-held position within theatre as an ideal to be achieved, its insistence on one person understanding another diminishes the breadth of transformation that might be possible, for in this schema, if an audience member does not understand the character or experience in the performance, the transformation is narrow or even nonexistent. Understanding in the sense of knowing or believing is not the primary goal for a theatrical jazz audience. A broader and less nameable shift may occur as audience members experience resonant frequencies, an internal vibration with a moment, a word, a person, or an idea in the performance. In discussing the utopian performative, Jill Dolan notes that the stories unfolding on theatrical stages are rarely images of a utopia, but instead the act of sharing a live experience creates the soil where a more responsive humanity can grow. This aptly describes the bridge that is possible, and desired, in theatrical jazz—a bridge all the more sturdy for the resonant frequencies the work can create.

In theatrical jazz, even if the audience does not empathize with the experience of the performance, their very encounter with the form pulls them into the work in profound ways. The work is in their consciousness. Jones calls this "active witnessing" a way of implicating the audience. They build the work with the performers; their hands are also covered with sweat and spirit. To participate in Yoruba is *kópa.* The root word, *ipa,* means role, making *kópa* "to take or gather a role." From a Yoruba worldview, the audience's presence places them *in* the performance. The audience cannot escape, physically, psychically, or morally, what they have co-created through witnessing.

The shift the audience/witnesses experience as a result of attending such work positions theatrical jazz as a method for social change. For a brief moment in Austin's history, audience/witnesses rubbed elbows regularly across class, and more often across race. This was especially true for Frontera@Hyde Park Theatre, but was also experienced at other Austin venues—Women and Their Work in the 1990s when Black performance was a regular part of its National Performance Network roster; any place where root wy'mn performed; ProArts Collective; Las Manitas with its regular poetry performances; and Capital City Playhouse. People from many backgrounds came to have these experiences. Those performance events were so ripe with social possibilities; the very act of sitting next to someone across a social divide in a site of democratizing communitas creates shifts and unions that are the foundation of a reimaged society. One could be transformed by sitting among the audience/witnesses through the act of witnessing/co-creating the performance. The jazz aesthetic imagines and generates an audience that genuinely reflects the worlds we want to live in—a dense world of organic racial/social/ sexual/gendered/spiritual/national diversity, where people understand how race and privilege work, how material excess contributes to social blinders, how adherence to rigid identity boundaries stunts the potential for humanity's evolution. We cannot create a world of genuine justice and respect and active participation when we practice such isolation in life's rehearsal halls called theatres.

Yoruba theatre scholar Oyin Ogunba describes the "imaginative collaboration"[16] of Yoruba spiritual performance as the specific ways the community participants interact with and shape the direction of the performing masquerades. These spontaneous participants sometimes improvise their responses by dancing with the masquerades, shouting out directions, or verbally and physically competing, and other times they carry out predetermined actions as they pour water over a masquerade, or "dash" a masquerade by placing money near its head, or offer an *oríkì* or praise song for *Òrìṣà* who arrive at a ceremony. Although theatrical jazz does not move through a town like a masquerade, audience/witnesses contribute to the performance even from the relatively stationary location of their theatre seats.

During the summer of 2006, my daughter Leigh and I attended the annual Black Arts Festival in Atlanta. We were both eager to see Ron K. Brown / Evidence, a company we'd heard a great deal about. I had experienced Brown's "Grace" performed by the Alvin Ailey American Dance Theatre some years before in Austin and looked forward to reawakening the energy I felt then. On this night, there seemed a union between the audience and the performers that began even with the house lights still up.

The audience was predominantly Black, and they appeared willing and eager to see some mirrors. The woman in denim capri pants and the child with her who sat in front of me and Leigh, the band of crew-cut, tank-topped, heavy-shoe-wearing women who swaggered

to the front rows just as the house lights were dimming, the many middle-aged couples in their elegant, sharply pressed Afrocentric wear—it felt as though the almost full house brought their best hopes to the performance, a chance to see themselves, to be uplifted, to get the spirit. This was surely my feeling as I sat immersed in all the energy around me. It was like the anticipation of something spiritual about to happen. It's like being in the outer circle of the bèmbé as the priests press the energy from the drums outward. It felt as though the audience wanted to go there, they seemed ready to party and shout hallelujah.

Even before the stage lights come up, the performance has begun. The entire room is the performance space, and Brown choreographs this knowingly. As the curtain rises and the dancers stand in silhouettes—dark figures in blue light radiating spirit—the audience starts to whoop and whistle, just like at a Sweet Honey In the Rock concert or an Urban Bush Women performance. It is so enticing, the expectation of such ecstasy that the audience inserts themselves fully into the moment, signaling their support, their offering, granting the dancers permission to transport them—anticipation based on perceived connection, embracing their responsibility to co-create.

Brown took everyday movements and made them shine. That slow walk upstage,

one foot peels off the floor while the hips rotate forward and the arms casually, purposefully swing behind, grazing the buttocks. Just like Ọ̀ṣun *helps us to see the beauty in our everyday selves.*
Ìkópa. *Though not theatrical jazz per se, the performance expertly employed its audience collaborators, and in so doing, used one of theatrical jazz's most potent tenets.*

While the resonant frequencies between audience/witnesses and performance accounts for some of the electricity in theatrical jazz, the transportation in the moment relies on the willingness of the audience/witnesses to be transformed—their willingness not merely to believe, but to be changed, to experience the alterity of opening to the unknown, a willingness to be so fully in the now that you can let go of it, a willingness that may not be consciously perceptible. Without resonant frequencies—some of which may be stimulated by identification and/or empathy—the work can't lift up.

During the SummerStages production of blood pudding *in 2010, I had to stand as Chief. After a wrenching self-examination around my father, approval, and independence that occurred during rehearsal, I felt the inner and outer spirals in the moment of performance—loving Harlem from afar since high school as I imagined a renaissance of art and power, and now I was performing in Marcus Garvey Park in the heart of Harlem; having just released myself from leadership in a specific Yoruba-based community, and now I was embodying a Mardi Gras Indian Chief leading my people. The Harlemites gathered for* blood pudding, *including the unexpected* bèmbé *or drum circle that was in full force when we arrived. Many in that circle were dressed in white, a specific symbol of identification for Yoruba-based practitioners in the West, and soon the* blood pudding *performers would likewise be clad in our white costumes. Their drumming opened the door for* blood pudding *as the spiritual, the everyday, the theatrical melded together. Respectfully, the drum circle stopped when* blood pudding *began, and the drummers became an invigorated part of our audience. Harlem was our witness, applauding Helga's otherworldly sounds, talking back when we tricked the settlers into giving us their guns, laughing as Baraka de Soleil offered Legba-inspired movements, stomping with me as I strode across the stage as chief. Many lingered after the performance to share their appreciation, to ask questions about the* Òrìṣà *in our lives, to give us suggestions for the next performance. In those moments,* blood pudding *reflected the people back to themselves. We were all working together through the spontaneous communitas generated by performance.*

Theatrical jazz thrives on a willingness to be communal, to share among the performers *and* the audience/witnesses. Jill Dolan describes the transformative potential of live performance when she writes, "the presence of the actor in front of breathing spectators implies an expectation that sharpens our watchfulness, our awareness of ourselves as a group, and the potential for our hope to translate into action."[17] This is what theatre can do—make us feel each other, not merely feel with the performance but to feel with the other audience/witnesses present—and the more eclectic that group, the more profound the transformation because we then get to see ourselves mirrored in disparate others. Mirrors tell us who we are and are not, who we want to be and when we are being our best. The mirrors of a jazz aesthetic are not narcissistic, but are communal, revealing a complex "we." This collective mirroring is the need to feel; it is the antidote to the nihilism, denigration, and erasure Black people endure in the larger society. This ability to feel is an active resistive choice. In this way, theatrical jazz with its focus on a participating audience creates a space for Black survival and Black freedom.

While the eclectic audience composition, the physical involvement and aliveness, the multiple racial casting, and jazz acting and directing prod audience/witnesses to a deep internal participation with this work, it is probably the nonlinear narrative structure and the transtemporal experience with time that most encourage audience/witnesses to attend in a vigorous way. For the writer, the ordering and juxtaposition of moments may be precisely planned, but the narrative logic of this ordering and the fusion of now/then/will be may not be intellectually understood by audience/witnesses; this makes way for a tacit knowing.

While seriation can aptly describe how the moments in a theatrical jazz narrative are organized, it does not fully account for the narrative's distinct relationship to time and place. Instead, the ethnographic concepts coterminous and coeval get at the temporal and spatial realities in these artists' works more precisely. Time and events in theatrical jazz are often coterminous, having coincident boundaries. Perhaps multiterminous more accurately expresses the many worlds that share space and time in theatrical jazz. The simultaneity implied by coeval also seems to get at a response to time in which seemingly anachronistic items coexist as realities from the other times and live as if contemporary with realities from the present. These spatial and temporal concepts describe the ways that theatrical jazz narratives make meaning.

Theatrical jazz suggests something other than character psychology as the narrative drive. Memory, mood, sound, movement may each constitute their own narrative material and ordering. In this work, there is the frank acknowledgment of something other than what is materially known. Spirit is. Encountering such worlds, audience/witnesses have to work, have to reach, have to allow for points of understanding as well as points of confusion and inarticulable clarity.

The jazz aesthetic performance, then, is efficacious; it creates an intense relationship with the audience/witnesses that is designed to move things, to break some things open, to make way for something new, to cross the bridge—indeed, the performance *itself* is either the bridge to change, or a bounded platform maintaining the status quo, or some rickety structure between the poles of stasis and transformation.

During the fall of 2007, Porgy and Bess *was produced in Austin. This history-making opera created by George and Ira Gershwin and DuBose Heywood provided rare performance opportunities for Black classically trained singers of the 1930s while also reinforcing racist stereotypes. I had never seen* Porgy and Bess, *and as a teacher of African American Theatre History, it seemed I should "see for myself" what the controversy was about. It was also important to me that I support the Black performers who were participating in the production. For these reasons I found myself in the midst of racist narratives on stage and in the theatre building.*

The audience was predominantly white. There were some Black audience members and a handful of other people of color. Porgy and Bess *was being presented in a newly renovated space that was not yet complete. The house seating was awkwardly arranged with loose chairs inconveniently located in aisles. Bodies squished past each other as people struggled to find their seats in poorly marked chairs and a poorly lit auditorium. I pressed my way to the women's room, where a very polite young white woman said: "Your scarf is beautiful! Do you mind my asking*

what you call it?" I was happy to tell her that in Yorubaland, the "scarf" is known as a gèlè. *At that time, I had waist-length dreadlocks and tied my head daily in a* gèlè—*a large swath of cloth that is usually of the same fabric as one's clothing and is tied on the head in many simple to elaborate patterns. The young woman seemed interested in my "difference," and respectful of it. I then made my way to the bar to buy some snacks. I had been at the university all day and did not have time to eat before coming to the theatre. While standing at the bar, a middle-aged white woman said to me, "Do you know the story behind*

Porgy and Bess?" *And she proceeded to tell me about how authentic the music was and how hard the Gershwins worked to ensure this authenticity. And then, before I could stop her, she reached out and touched my locks and said, "Your hair is beautiful!" I turned away mortified! I couldn't say a word to her. I stammered to the waiter behind the bar, "She touched my hair!" The young white man looked at me confused as I repeated over and over "She touched my*

hair!" In Yoruba cosmology, the Orí—the head—is one's first Divinity. It is your destiny and holds your essence. It should be protected and regularly cleaned of psychic debris. And this stranger—full of her power and privilege—had defiled it. I paid my $5.00 for a vending-machine-sized packet of peanuts and walked away, angry that I had come to this production, but still feeling that I should finally see this work. I squeezed through the crowds toward my seat as another white woman reached out and patted my gèlè *saying "How pretty!" I waved my hand at her and said "NO!"*

Now, this was ridiculous! What was really going on here? I think what was really going on was the preshow enactment of the convenient, disempowering stereotypes that were soon to be depicted on the stage. Some of the white audience members extended a well-worn, theatrically substantiated understanding of Negroes to the real-life Black people in the audience. I was a fiction in their imagination with virtually no distinction from Bess, Sportin' Life, and all the rest of the sorrowful inhabitants on Catfish Row. And just as some had paid their money to see the packaged Negroes on stage, they treated me as if I, too, had been bought.

In spite of all of this, I stayed for the production. No surprises there. The largest darkest Black man was the villain. The light-skinned long-haired slim Black woman was the vixen love interest. The full-bodied Black woman mothered everyone and was the only person in town brave enough to confront the violent men. There were no mirrors for me here, just the bent glass in the house of horrors.

These audience encounters might have happened at a theatrical jazz production, but I believe the possibility of such is slim. If a production creates new symbol systems for the audience, indeed, if the audience has never encountered the specific production nor any work in a jazz aesthetic, they are less likely to confidently assert their narrow expectations of Blackness on those around them when they do encounter theatrical jazz. Surely, if more people of color had been in the audience, the white audience members would have had less sense of entitlement and less certainty in the unconscious enactment of their privilege.

In the liminal moment, in "the break," anything can happen; the bridge can occur or a stultifying status quo can be concretized through perpetuation.

If performance does not offer something new, is not a conscious bridge, it can dangerously affirm the rusted social systems that already exist. Because performance is always co-creating with an audience, it can co-create expansive social possibilities as fully as it co-creates dehumanizing social constraints.

The potential for transformation that audience/witnesses experience, first happens for the creators of the work. Indeed, the performance is often an exploration of how they have moved from various forms of self-denial and self-destruction to positions of self-affirmation. This is in sharp contrast to a host of jazz luminaries who lived hard tragic lives. Through drunken, misogynistic, violent bouts, Charley Patton created a singular Delta blues sound. During years of heroin addiction, Billie Holiday found a way to drag a note across a beat that has become legendary. Although Charlie Parker's official causes of death were listed by the coroner as pneumonia and a bleeding ulcer, his heroin addiction and alcoholism surely sped his death along. Even when the theatrical jazz artists are not successful at achieving the personal health they desire, it is this goal that fuels many of their conversations and provides the content for much of their art. Because theatrical jazz insists on being present and telling the deepest truths, the artist is striving to choose life, to choose the present. This is the very antithesis to the self-destruction associated with many blues and jazz musicians and singers. *Àṣẹ* is about creating, is about life. And the artists featured in this book strive to live as healthy human beings, not tragic artists.

The propensity for transformation connects theatrical jazz to social change and social justice. Theatrical jazz transformation is built on truth telling, present-tense-ness, and a dedication to joy, hope, and life. To tell the truth in the present moment means an acknowledgment of a host of social devastations; such acknowledgment positions even the most autobiographical theatrical jazz as an act of social consciousness. As Jones points out, his autobiographical work is seeking the "we in me."[18] In considering the social justice threads of the three artists featured here, it is useful to remember that Carlos worked with the artistic unit of the empowerment organization Mobilization for Youth, Jones created theatre for social change performances with Rebecca Rice, and Bridgforth worked for Planned Parenthood, offered art and social justice workshops from her home, and from 2004 to 2006 was the artistic director of allgo, Texas's queer people of color organization that had a specific social-health component from 1996 to 2002. Each artist had a commitment to social change outside of their art, a commitment that consciously or unconsciously informs their artistic work.

Among the theatrical jazz *egbé*, Robbie McCauley and Erik Ehn are best known for iconoclastic artistic work that foregrounds activist desires. Both have worked closely with Carlos, Jones, and Bridgforth, and both have earned a national reputation for their insurgent artistic productions. Robbie McCauley[19] co-created the Sedition Ensemble in 1979 with Ed Montgomery. The company performed live and also recorded poetry with a jazz ensemble while offering an explicit critique of racism, capitalism, and patriarchy. McCauley, like her close friend Carlos, was a major figure in the East Village avant-garde theatre scene of

ROBBIE MCCAULEY: "My life as a black woman is the lens through which I gaze. Theater is the process through which I focus. This intelligence about what I do is my jazz, gives me permission to play for people."°

° "Dear Omi," 253.

the 1970s, having appeared with Carlos on Broadway in *for colored girls,* and having created Thought Music with Carlos and Jessica Hagedorn. She performed in Joseph Chaikin's *Tourists and Refugees II* at LaMama ETC[20] and in Adrienne Kennedy's *A Movie Star Has to Star in Black and White,* directed by Chaikin at the Public Theatre.[21] McCauley acknowledges the work with Chaikin and his philosophy on art and social transformation as criti-

cal in the development of her own strategies for art and justice. Her community collaborations—The Buffalo Project, examining the Buffalo riots of 1967; The Mississippi Project, dealing with voter registration; the Boston Project, centering around busing issues of 1993—used an interviewing technique and devising method that she created expressly for this work. McCauley began a series of family explorations that included *San Juan Hill, My Father and the Wars,* and *Sally's Rape,* for which she is probably best known. The Obie Award–winning *Sally's Rape* has received more scholarly attention than any of her other work, and excerpts were recorded in the documentary *Conjure Women,* making the performance more accessible for study and reflection. McCauley assumes a Black feminist stance when she acknowledges how the particulars of her life story can speak for and to others. In her most recent solo work—*Sugar*—she examines the interconnectedness of diabetes, the slave trade, and the exploitation of Black bodies. For McCauley, art and activism are deeply intertwined.

ERIK EHN: "We exchange with Rwanda because it is a global center for cultural innovation and because the damage there results from a failure to witness—to be with."°

° "A Space for Truth," 34.

Erik Ehn[22] has worked in elements of theatrical jazz for many years even before naming the work as such, and has recently turned his attention squarely to the politics of humanity in his plays. His annual sojourns to Rwanda, begun around 2001, have generated conferences on genocide and art at California Institute for the

Figure 57. Robbie McCauley in *Sugar*. McCauley is testing her blood-sugar level in performance excerpts from her *Sugar* in the Performing Blackness Series of the John L. Warfield Center for African and African American Studies at the University of Texas at Austin, 2008. Photo by Sharon Bridgforth.

Arts, as well as a trilogy of intimate plays that probe into the inner lives of those who commit genocidal acts and/or hold genocide in their psyches. The Rwandan trilogy along with Ehn's *Heavenly Shades of Night Are Falling*—which includes historical details of a racist massacre in Oklahoma—were written with Carlos in mind.

While social commitment surely characterizes Ehn's work, his notion of activist theatre is larger than the creation of specific productions that address pressing social concerns. He is interested in reimagining the entire enterprise of U.S. theatre, a radical reinvention based on "personalized economy" rather than institutions and grants. In an interview he explained, "I think the future for artists is going to be person to person . . . We're going to have to rely on ourselves much more than in the past . . . I think we're what's going to be left after it all burns down . . . I was just working with this big foundation with lots of money—that just went away. So, what's left after it goes away are the people you had lunch with. The lunches are bigger than the institutions."[23] Theatrical jazz—while rooted in Black political and artistic sensibilities—is not racially exclusive. Ehn's work demonstrates how white artists can be committed to elements of theatrical jazz, can acknowledge the racial conversation inevitably imbedded in aesthetics while

Figure 58. Erik Ehn's *Maria Kizito,* the Soulographie Series. *Maria Kizito* was directed by Emily Mendelsohn, with set by Jeff Becker and costumes by Cybele Moon for Ehn's Soulographie Series: Our Genocides, a commemorative performance cycle. The play examines the real story of Rwandan nuns who were complicit in the 1994 genocide. Standing: Esther Tebandeke; Sitting left: Lynette Freeman; Sitting right: Sharon Wang. Photo by John Eckert.

navigating the tricky terrain of appropriation, distortion, condescension, and erasure. Like McCauley, Ehn fashions a theatre that capitalizes on "the bridge" of transformation afforded by performance, a theatre that grows from a deeply politicized understanding of community responsibility.

The theatrical jazz impulse toward hope, love, joy, personal health, and life are intimately linked not only with social justice but with environmental awareness as well. Being present and fully responding to the demands of self-love and the deepest love for others necessitates attention to and respect for the Earth. *Abínibí*, understood as natural or something in its natural state, implies an awareness of nature itself. *Àṣẹ* is the life force that animates all things. Together these fundamental Yoruba concepts establish the interconnectedness of life. Theatrical jazz creates a thriving in the present moment. In a pre-performance talk entitled "Chaos, Anarchy, Ecology," Ehn described the ecological drive of Theatre Yugen's work as "a way of being with chaos on a practical level. If Eden is a garden, we remain in a garden but have fired the gardener and must do our own weeding. Relatedness is not extensive past the horizon of our perception— it is available to our love and responsibility."[24]

"Ẹní da ilẹ̀ á bá ilẹ̀ lọ."

"To break the oath, is to die."

also

"Violating our covenants with one another is betraying our responsibility to the earth."

also

"If you betray the earth, you will be consumed by it."

Theatrical jazz cannot make a commitment to hope and life without making a similar commitment to that which sustains life.

Although the face of the environmental movement in the United States is typically white, Black people have a powerful relationship with the land and with environmental justice. From George Washington Carver[25] and his revolutionary understanding of the power in the versatile legume misclassified as a nut in the late 1800s to Majora Carter and her renovation of a South Bronx waste site into the Hunts Point Riverside Park in 1997, there have been Black people who understood that green values are Black values.

VAN JONES: "Caring about the Earth and future generations is very consistent with African indigenous values. . . . Our great-grand-mother's values are coming into vogue."°

° "Black and Green: The New Eco-Warriors," 98.

Black spiritual practices that performed baptisms in rivers, held worship services under the trees, and poured libations to ancestors in the ground attest to a Black and green relationship. Among the *ẹgbẹ́* members who are greening theatrical jazz are Grisha Coleman with her series of environmental explorations known collectively as *echo::system* that explore the reverberations between people and nature, and Walter Kitundu with several works, especially his *Ocean Edge Device*, a large wooden musical instrument that relies on the waves of the ocean to produce sound.

Coleman creates what Stephanie Batiste calls "alternate worlds that reproduce, critique, and re-imagine our environment and our place in it . . . Like an ecosystem, the performances are collaborative, patterned, and improvisational."[26] In Coleman's *echo::system/ActionStation #2 The Desert,* at On the Boards in 2005, the program beckons, "Welcome to a temporal home, our house of mixed meanings, where we rest the soul by troubling it."[27] Through a short, narrow, dimly lit corridor, the audience/witnesses arrive in a small space—the size of a modest living room—that can only accommodate approximately fifteen audience/witnesses, mostly seated on floor pillows. From the disorientation upon entering the space, the audience/witnesses know they are encountering something new. Sitting so close to the performance created a humbling intimacy, and it required a distinct experience with simultaneity. In the small room with such close proximity to the performance, my eye could not take in the entire picture; I had to choose one area to watch while my ears took in the sonorous information from another part of the space. I was always aware that so much more was happening that I couldn't take in. So, audience/witnesses should come again and again as they attend to different elements at each performance. The repetition can become a ritual or ceremony that generates its own community. This happened with Bridgforth's *love conjure/blues* when it was presented at the University of Texas. People came again, sat in new places, and could hear a fresh rhythm, or feel a different body near them. Through proximity, the tactility of the audience is as much a part of the experience as the work being done by the performers.

To one side in *The Desert,* Coleman is suspended upside down, harnessed on each side by sturdy ropes. The wall behind her is covered with rough white paper that is repeated on the three-step platform extending from the wall. In front of this image, there are treadmills with Gatorade bottles dangling overhead in an undulating pattern of heights. The clear bottles are variously filled with sand or sea salt, and topped with orange caps. There are 272 hanging bottles, each with a tiny unlit Christmas light inside; the night before they opened, the fire marshal forbade the company from actually switching on the lights. In another area are the technicians, the scientists with whom Coleman collaborates—an ecologist, an architect, an electroacoustic designer—men who manipulate their onstage equipment, thereby adjusting the performance, complete with population graphs shifting behind them and televisions broadcasting fluctuating desert images in front of them. They watch, they move through the space, they prod and record. Land, technology, and imagination are woven throughout the experience, prompting questions about the relationship between the environment and humanity. The audience/witnesses in this work must choose to build identification, must elect to open to empathy—these responses are not assured because the prompts for such identification are not already established in the cultural lexicon. A diverse range of works adheres to the basic tenets of theatrical jazz, leaving ample room for innovation within the form. Audience/witnesses that connect with Bridgforth's *love conjure/blues* may not know the appropriate audience cues or semiotic rules for *echo::system*. The audience/witnesses must work to uncover coherence or anchors as they release narrative expectations, common visual metaphors, and previously held notions of what theatre might be. This very release may open them to resonant frequencies.

GRISHA COLEMAN: "Environmental issues relate directly to issues of our own survival, and artwork offers another way of navigating these relationships."[*]

[*] *echo::system/ActionStation #2 The Desert* (Program Note, On the Boards, 2005).

In *echo::system/ActionStation #2 The Desert,* the performers sit on the floor in a circle with their backs to one another facing the audience, the technician/scientists, and the walls of the space. In this imagined seven-day journey across the desert—what the program describes as "a migration to a new habitat"—the performers begin by sifting piles of sand through their hands, perhaps tuning in to the environment in which they find themselves. An intricate chant begins as the sounds pass among them. There is an initial tentativeness as the chant progresses—not nervousness or confusion, but an evolution of connectedness, a working

Figure 59. Program cover from Grisha Coleman's *The Desert.* Coleman is in the foreground in a beige suit. Production took place in 2007 at the New Hazlett Theater in Pittsburgh. Coleman's look at the future is imbued with her interest in community, the land, art, and design. Photo by Tim Friez.

it out right there and then, in front of and with the audience/witnesses. They sync up sonically, get miked for performance, then begin the next phase of their trek. The costumes are gender neutral. The performers, four women and one man, are phenotypically diverse, with no easy designations of race or nation. The scientists appear to be white except for one Black man. In this work, Black is not foregrounded though race surely is as one considers who populates this present-day landscape of the future.

In addition to being a musician, instrument maker, and photographer, Walter Kitundu is an ecological innovator. His concern with time and place have yielded environmentally animated performance events in specific geographic locations. From his website, he writes:

My recent work inevitably reveals time as an element in its aesthetic consideration. Our relationship with time is culturally specific and it evolves as we do. The rising and setting of the sun, the waxing and waning of the moon, changes in the air that signal the turning of seasons. These rhythmic reference points once delineated our generations and life spans. Now these natural cycles have been catalogued and subdivided down to the millisecond. The geologic and environmental pulses that once formed the basis for our measures have been systematically observed, ordered and refined until our standards no longer rely on or reference their source. Nature now fits our system. We can readily explain and deduce the causes of natural phenomena and our visceral and immediate relationship with the natural world has transformed into one of distance and control. That which we cannot control we strive to predict in the hopes of insuring [*sic*] the insulated dominion we hold over our lives and landscape.[28]

A response to Kitundu's ideas of an "insulated dominion" over nature is his *Ocean Edge Device,* at once performance and object. In 2002 Kitundu crafted this musical device with water wheels, pulleys, wind chambers, a melodica, an accordion, wind chimes, a turntable, and stool on which he could lean while playing

Figure 60. Walter Kitundu's "Ocean Edge Device." Here, Kitundu plays his Ocean Edge Device in 2005 with the help of several friends at the Headlands Center for the Arts. Photo by Laurie Lazer.

the clarinet. With generous community support from the Headlands Center for the Arts, on an early morning in June 2005 Kitundu stood astride this Ocean Edge Device and was pulled into the Pacific. This handcrafted instrument took flight as an exploration into the union of time, sound, space, humanity, and nature. Men hoisted the instrument into the air and walked it into the ocean. Kitundu's website shows detailed photos of him diligently playing the clarinet as the Ocean Edge Device was buffeted by the waves while his friends worked to keep the fantastical object steady. The waves spun the wheel, which generated sound. Kitundu, clad in a suit and tie befitting the ceremonial and respectful dance between human and sea, would jump down to help keep the device upright, then climb aboard again to play his clarinet and to occasionally blow into a red tube linked to the pump housing that assisted with the positive pressure needed by the pump. In his website he writes, "After surviving fifteen minutes in a rising tide, the main wheel is ripped off by the waves and the recovery begins."[29] The performance was ephemeral and lasting, leaving pieces in the sea and memories for all gathered. Kitundu's artmaking has taken him, like Coleman, directly to nature, joining art and environment in perhaps the most radical, even if inevitable, move that an expansive love can take us.

Kitundu and Coleman's work highlights the danger of prescription. All the work in the jazz aesthetic will not look this way or that, but the works share similar impulses—the impulse to invite the audience/witnesses to take on a new role, the impulse to feel the complete space of the performance, the impulse to cast with a race self-consciousness harkening a new world order, the impulse to bring to bear all that one is onto the work, the insistence upon creation in the moment, the implementation of narrative innovation—these principles join the works of theatrical jazz. The jazz aesthetic is also dedicated to hope and love and freedom. That's the world the artists and most of their characters want to live in and try to find/make. Within these broad parameters, theatrical jazz can branch in many directions. Coleman and Kitundu put the earth at the center of the theatrical experience, linking ecology and race, love and possibility, the fullness of the present moment. There can be no environmental sustainability with racism, sexism, homophobia, classism, or any other oppressions. *Abínibí.* Such forces are antithetical to the life force that propels theatrical jazz, for theatrical jazz is regenerative. Regeneration is transformation. To engage in such performance is, then, intertwined with sustainability—personal, social, ecological. Both theatrical jazz and ecology require what Coleman calls "listening when the land talks back."

It is not only a belief in the possible, a commitment to social and environmental truths, that connects McCauley, Ehn, Coleman, and Kitundu with Carlos, Jones, and Bridgforth. These artists have worked closely together over many years. Although their art practices are uniquely their own, they have informed each other through the saturating process of collaboration.

WALTER KITUNDU: "I learned a great deal about myself and ocean, the nature of waves, and the generosity of the art and science communities . . . The materials will be recycled into the next versions. There won't be an old version lying around . . . it will just keep evolving based on the lessons learned from the sea."°

° Walter Kitundu's website, accessed 2006, kitundu.com.

Figure 61. "The Three Graces," by Carl E. Karni-Bain "BAI." Photo by BAI.

It was amazing! Robbie McCauley, Laurie Carlos, Vinie Burrows, Daniel Alexander Jones, Sharon Bridgforth, Ana Perea, Erik Ehn, and me—all at Double Edge Theatre in Ashfield, Massachusetts, for a weekend retreat around Erik's work! We read Erik's Drunk Still Drinking, Every Man Jack of You, Cordelia, Heavenly Shades of Night Are Falling, Maria Kizito. It was magical to hear Vinie crackling like the fire in the text and allowing the French to dance
on her tongue, to sit next to Daniel as he playfully developed each character with such a distinctive vocal and physical personality, to learn from Ana's directness and

Figure 62. The Soulographie Series reading at Daniel Alexander Jones's apartment. Several artists came together in 2007 for a reading of the first collection of Erik Ehn's Soulographie plays. The complete collection of seventeen plays was later presented as a durational performance event at La Mama ETC in 2012 under the title "Soulographie: our genocides, a commemorative performance cycle." Left to right, top row: Erik Ehn, Helga Davis, Sonja Perryman, Barbara Duchow, Morgan Jenness; bottom row: Sharon Bridgforth, Shaka McGlotten, Ana Perea, Lucy Thurber, Vinie Burrows, and Rhonda Ross. Photo by Daniel Alexander Jones.

seeming simplicity. All of us had worked on Erik's productions before, and the web of connections among us was incredible. Vinie has been directed by Daniel, Robbie has directed Daniel, Daniel has directed Robbie, Laurie has directed Ana in one of Sharon's productions, Ana has performed in Erik's work, Robbie and Laurie go way back, Daniel has performed in Sharon's work, and they talk with each other about their work every day, and I have been a producer, performer, or dramaturg for each of them! This is the theatrical jazz version
of "A Great Day in Harlem" except we were here to jam, not pose!
Ana had driven up from New York, so Sharon, Daniel, and I jumped in her car when we finished the work at Double Edge and headed for NYC. On the way, we stopped by Daniel's home in Springfield. I got to see the street where he grew up and to greet his mother in the kitchen where he first cooked his vegetarian greens. I had somehow forgotten that his mother was a painter, and her work was throughout the house. It was a full day, a reminder of the centrality of family and neighborhood, of the importance and stability of ẹgbẹ̀s of all types, the variety of ways that theatrical jazz can manifest and bind us to the art as our common concern.

Living healthy and well requires that we pay the utmost attention to the present moment. Yoruba cosmology and jazz focus so intently on the now that the moment explodes, that the corners of this instant morph into doorways to transcendence, to new form, to a vibrant shimmering now.

When I'm standing in the grove praying I have to let go of everything else; it is just me and the space that is opening in the ọ̀run to receive my message. Every hair on me has to be tuned in the same direction. When I am working in theatrical jazz, I have to release what I did last night, the tension
in my lower back, the expectations of the audience and the director. All the energies of ọ̀run are waiting for me to step up, to step up, to be me, abínibí, me—the best hope my égún have going at this time, the best hope my ẹgbẹ̀ has going at this time. Imitation only stagnates the planet. It is time to live the life we know to live in our Orí.

Jazz, like queer, can be redeployed as a strategy of resistance. Jazz need no longer be tainted by dubious origins, no longer attached to artists outside of its own making, no longer reputed to be dying but instead vibrantly alive in theatre and beyond. Theatrical jazz *claims* jazz as its name. In this way, jazz, like queer, gets to name itself, is allowed to burst in order to find itself—as historically rooted, resistive, and insurgent. If Black embraces joy and jazz, it snatches back itself, it becomes an affront to hegemonic forces that seek to inhibit self-naming. In challenging normative notions of Blackness, Black undermines the State's ability to control through naming. Theatrical jazz turns Blackness on its head through the joyous blue note of surprise and mystery. Roderick Ferguson's "queer of color critique" reminds us that queers, by self-definitions and practices, subvert the political narratives of progress that are linked to the interwoven experiences of naming, heteronormativity, and social stasis.

What if joy *is* Black? This becomes a fundamental social transgression as Black then lives outside of hegemonic ideas of joy that position Black as a tool, as an object to create joy. When Black becomes agent, Black cracks utilitarian understandings of what joy might be in which Black and joy only come together as commodities serving others. The multiplicities of Blackness and the necessity of improvisation/innovation disrupt the ability to name, and therefore control, who and what Black is.

The expression of joy under oppression might be understood as an irreconcilable contradiction. Expressions of joy within this context could feed a voracious white supremacist appetite for fabricated racist justifications, offering the infantilizing "Happy Darkie" trope as evidence of a benign enslavement and the need for subsequent dehumanizations.[30] Because Black people have been positioned by the larger society as nonhuman and therefore abject—indeed the larger society needs this construction in order for it to exist—Black joy, which is contrary to all that society needs Blackness to be, is the very image of joy itself, the enactment of light and promise, enthusiasm and faith, delight and hope. Is *abínibí*.

Under racist realities, Black joy may appear to be the excess, the overflowing, that thwarts respectability, a respectability that is actually the yearning for an impossible acceptability. Joy as excess makes Blackness boldly visible, audible, olfactory, gustatory, tactile, kinetic; joy is the evidence of the uncontainability of Blackness. And as excess, Black joy could create shame for those Black people who may unconsciously align Black worth with social and institutional approval. Theatrical jazz encourages an embrace of Black joy as a space of agency with the potential for mitigating the constrictions of racism.

In "Black Atlantic, Queer Atlantic," Omise'eke Tinsley offers Black love as the enactment of our humanity—transgressive because nonhumans can't love, transgressive because such love through the degradation of the Middle Passage sought tenderness and union and was not concerned with the limitations of a supposed "legitimate" sexuality; legitimate sexuality as another State requirement buttressing both patriarchy and white supremacy.[31] Tinsley speculates that Black Love is an integral fact of Blackness, an ability to make a way out of no way, evidence of the pulsing life principle that—even momentarily—unshackles Black people from social death in spite of physical shackles and imprisonment. Our joy does not erase oppression, fear, rage—it lives alongside these feelings, which makes it all the more powerful. To know joy within oppression—to seek love as Tinsley suggests even in the bowels of slaving ships—is an acknowledgment that Black is more than a social construction, that we live outside of that construction even as we live within it.

In theatrical jazz, the belief in and pursuit of love and joy become the ultimate Black blue notes, the unexpected drive that keeps Blackness outside of well-worn mainstream definitions and expectations. As such, the drive toward joy is an act of resistance—consciously or unconsciously—a declaration of Blackness that eludes the stranglehold of socially established defining hands.

As the remaining pages of this book begin to dwindle, I am keenly aware of the aliveness of theatre, jazz, and Yoruba-based spiritual practices, and the corporeal nature of queer and Black. These concepts don't end, as this book inevitably will. You will stop reading, close the cover, and put the book down. The book doesn't do what jazz and theatre and Yoruba do—revise, repeat, sample, come back next week and do it again with a signal difference. This book, my offering, gives the appearance of being definitive, whereas Jones has created ten iterations of *The Book of Daniel,* Carlos has returned many times to reimagine *The Cooking Show,* and Bridgforth's *love conjure/blues* has lived as ensemble work, film, solo performance, and conducted audience orchestra. Theatrical jazz is a living practice. The aliveness is the form. Although I am mindful of how "the reader became the book"[32] through my artistic and intellectual roots in oral interpretation, which notes how print texts "live," this understanding recognizes the changes in the *reader* as she or he revisits the book while the *book itself* remains the same. So, for this text to truly live as a jazz document, you, the reader, are invited to come back to it again and again perhaps discovering something you missed that was there all along. In this way you might take the bridge, seize the break, and in community pitch the moment higher.

What a journey this has been. The river winds and I learn the ways of fish. Bringing down the spirit—that is this work. Nothing short of spiritual invigoration.

At Northwestern, waiting to give my offering, a solo performance of love conjure/ blues—I sat backstage, side stage really, a short wing curtain separating me from the stage and the audience, my eager and courageous collaborators. Their swelling voices soothe me as I sit with my head bowed, finding connection. Their anticipation is also mine. I was in all white, feeling cool and ready, a surprise to myself. I am here, allowing the spirit to be.

My ẹgbẹ̀ is with me, Laurie saying: "I can't help you with that," and my knowing that she already has. Daniel's fierce improvisations do their jig in my heart and I remember his patience as I struggled to learn lines years ago. Sharon's words resting in my lap, the years of shared rehearsals and casts and scripts and promises.

In this performance, my skin is alive. I hear all the words for the first time and am moved, so startlingly moved.

The bounty is here. And must be shared. Loving gardeners share their fruits.

"I never left you / I been right here,"
"Lift now / Fly now / Free now / Be now / it's okay, not alone, not alone, not alone, not alone / always / We,"
"Praise memory,"
"our gurl don't yet understand that the pressure of not feeling / explodes / poisons the Spirit . . . which liable to make the lesser way seem right at the crossroads,"
"I am the conjure, come back to love."

And then I know. I am not an actor, I am a priest, I am a conjurer, helping the people to their own prayer, sentient first then passing it on. This is a holy place, this theatre. It is where we can dream and build our worlds together. This is sacred business. No purely commercial ventures here. It is me in the river once each month in my own rituals with omi, it is Daniel saying goodbye so he could say hello, it is Sharon stepping out of herself to be herself, it is Laurie finding her way down the hallway through the darkness. A display of talent is not what is required, it is my virtuosic commitment that must be summoned. It is knowing that everyone here is willing, that my tears cleanse us all, that the spirit I sought was right here all along, in the place that I feared for its power, for its potential to expose my failures and my hunger. It was here waiting for me to arrive, for me to step one toe in at a time, to let my lip curl in that ugly way, for me to spin with my arms spread, to splash through the words saying thank you to Mama and Daddy at each whirl.

So this is it. My Legba moment. The marrow in the bone. And I laugh from my knees. It was here all along, strumming its fingers on the pulse, patient. Splashing water on

those around me in baptism, the swish of the Egúngún panel, the sound of my own
voice. Never again to fear the freedom in truth. So funny. I'm giggling.

"I am the conjure / sacrificial blood made flesh."
Oh yes.

Theatre is the Divine public space, the theatron and orchestra of public discourse, the
sacred grove where anything is possible.

"I am the answered prayer."
It is true.
Each of us is sufficient and required for this manifestation.

"remember / remember / remember / remember / LOVE"

Indeed.

Robbie said "the end of the work is often the beginning."

And so it is.

Ẹbọ dá

Figure 63. "Devotee," by Arleen Polite. It seems fitting at this
moment of pause in the work to greet Ọ̀ṣun in gratitude.
Photo by Wura-Natasha Ogunji.

APPENDIX I

Laurie Carlos

AN ABBREVIATED CHRONOLOGY OF WORK
(DATES ARE APPROXIMATIONS)

A Raisin in the Sun *by Lorraine Hansberry* *director*	**Production** Vortex Theatre Austin	**2013**
Moreechika *by Ananya Dance Theatre* *performer*	**Production** Southern Theatre Minneapolis	**2012**
Kshoy!/Decay! *by Ananya Dance Theatre* *performer*	**Production** Southern Theatre Minneapolis	**2010**
Washed *writer & performer*	**Production** Warfield Center, UT Austin	**2008**
Marion's Terrible Time of Joy *writer & performer*	**Staged Reading** Warfield Center, UT Austin	**2007**
	Production Playwright's Center Minneapolis	**2003**
Half-Breed Southern Fried (check one) *by Florinda Bryant* *director*	**Production** Warfield Center, UT Austin	**2006**
The Pork Chop Wars (a story of mothers) *writer & director*	**Staged Reading** Warfield Center, UT Austin	**2005**
con flama *by Sharon Bridgforth* *director*	**Production** Frontera@Hyde Park Theatre Austin	**2000**

Feathers at the Flame, Next Dance *writer & performer* *with Movin' Spirits Dance Company*	**Production** Guthrie Lab Theatre Minneapolis	**1998**
	Aaron Douglas Hall NYC	
blood pudding *by Sharon Bridgforth* *director*	**Production** Frontera@Hyde Park Theatre Austin	**1998**
Ambient Love Rites *by Daniel Alexander Jones* *performer*	**Workshop** Frontera@Hyde Park Theatre Austin	**1997**
The Cooking Show & How the Monkey Dances *writer & performer*	**Production** Frontera@ Hyde Park Theatre Austin	**1997**
Clayangels *by Daniel Alexander Jones & Todd Jones* *director*	**Production** Frontera@Hyde Park Theatre Austin	**1997**
	New World Theatre Amherst	
Everlasting Arms *by Rebecca Rice* *director*	**Production** Penumbra Theatre Minneapolis	**1996**
Big White Fog *by Theodore Ward* *performer*	**Production** Guthrie Theatre Minneapolis	**1995**
Talking Bones *by Shay Youngblood* *performer*	**Production** Penumbra Theatre Minneapolis	**1994**
The Food Show *writer & performer* *with Robbie McCauley & Jessica Hagedorn as Thought Music*	**Production** Nuyorican Poet's Café NYC	**1992**
Persimmon Peel *writer & performer with* *Robbie McCauley*	**Production** The Working Theatre NYC	**1992**
	Sushi Performance Gallery San Diego	
	La Mama ETC NYC	**1990**
	Brooklyn Bridge Anchorage NYC	
White Chocolate for My Father *writer & performer* Bessie Award	**Production** BACA Downtown NYC	**1990**

Teenytown *writer & performer* *with Thought Music*	**Production** Franklin Furnace NYC	**1988**
	Danspace Project/St. Mark's Church NYC	
	The Whitney Museum NYC	
	The Schomburg Center for Research in Black Culture NYC	
Heat *writer & performer* *with Urban Bush Women and Thought Music* Bessie Award	**Production** The Kitchen NYC	**1988**

Nonsectarian Conversations with the Dead
(an evening of performance in four movements)

    1. Nonsectarian Conversations with the Dead
    2. Phosphorescent
    3. Claypainters
    4. An Organdy Falsetto

writer & performer

Written	**1985–86**

for colored girls who have considered suicide/ **when the rainbow is enuf** *by Ntozake Shange* *performer* Obie Award	**Production** The Booth Theatre NYC	**1976**

Daniel Alexander Jones

AN ABBREVIATED CHRONOLOGY OF WORK

Plays and Performance Texts

Phantasmatron

2011	Workshop	Ruth Easton Series The Playwrights' Center	Minneapolis
2010	Reading	New Dramatists	NYC
2009	Workshop	The Playwrights' Center	Minneapolis
	Workshop	New Dramatists	NYC

Hera Bright

2009	Reading	New Dramatists	NYC
2008	Workshop	The Playwrights' Center	Minneapolis

Phoenix Fabrik

2007	Production	Todd Mountain Theatre	Project Roxbury, NY
2006	Workshop	Playtime / New Dramatists	NYC
	Production	Pillsbury House Theatre	Minneapolis
2005	Workshop	Pillsbury House Theatre	Minneapolis
2004	Reading	New Dramatists	NYC
	Workshop	allgo	Austin

Bel Canto

2004	Production	Pillsbury House Theater	Minneapolis
2003	Production	Actor's Express	Atlanta
	Production	The Theater Offensive	Boston
2002	Workshop	Sundance Theatre Lab	Utah
	Reading	NY Theatre Workshop	NYC
	Reading	Penumbra Theatre Co.	St. Paul
2001	Reading	The Public Theater	NYC

La Chanteuse Nubienne

| 2001 | Production | 3 Legged Race | Minneapolis |

Cab and Lena

2000	Production	The Green Room	Manchester, UK
	Production	W. Yorkshire Playhouse	Leeds, UK
	Production	The Theater Offensive	Boston
	Production	FronteraFest	Austin
	Workshop	Penumbra Theatre Co.	St. Paul

Earthbirths

1999	Reading	The Jungle Theatre	Minneapolis
1998	Reading	Center Stage	Baltimore
1995	Production	Frontera@Hyde Park Theatre	Austin

Blood:Shock:Boogie

1997	Production	Outward Spiral Theatre	Minneapolis
	Production	Indigo Productions	Austin
1996	Production	The Theater Offensive	Boston
	Production	Frontera@Hyde Park Theatre	Austin
	Workshop	Portland Stage Company	Portland, ME
	Workshop	The Playwrights' Center	Minneapolis

Ambient Love Rites

1998	Production	Cara Mia Theatre	Dallas
	Production	Frank Theatre	Minneapolis
1997	Workshop	Frontera@Hyde Park Theatre	Austin
1995	Reading	The Playwrights' Center	Minneapolis

Clayangels

| 1997 | Production | Frontera@Hyde Park Theatre | Austin |
| | Workshop | New World Theatre | Amherst |

Performance Art and New Music Theatre

Bright Now Beyond (collaboration with composer Bobby Halvorson)

| 2013 | Workshop | Salvage Vanguard Theater | Austin |
| 2012 | Workshop | Center For New Performance/CalArts | Valencia |

Radiate

JOMAMA JONES (collaboration with composer Bobby Halvorson)

2013	Concert	The Theater Offensive @ Hibernian Hall	Boston
	Concert	Salvage Vanguard Theater	Austin
2012	Concert	Kirk Douglas Theatre	Los Angeles
	Concert	Pillsbury House Theatre	Minneapolis
	Concert	Victory Gardens Theatre	Chicago
2011	Concert	Soho Rep	NYC

In Concert

JOMAMA JONES *(collaboration with composer Bobby Halvorson)*

2013	Concert	Joe's Pub	NYC
2012	Concert	Los Globos	Los Angeles
2011	Concert	Symphony Space	NYC
2010	Concert	Joe's Pub	NYC
2009	Concert	Fire & Ink Cotillion	Austin
		Dixon Place (BlackOUT)	NYC

Qualities of Light

2009	Invited Sharing	Speicherstadt	Hamburg, Germany

The Book of Daniel

2011		Late Nite Series Pillsbury House Theatre	Minneapolis
2010		Genderfusions Columbia College	Chicago
		Jazz Aesthetic Series Links Hall	Chicago
2009		Rites and Reason Brown University	Providence
2008		Flipfest Angel Orensanz Center	NYC
		Texas A&M University	College Station
2007		Alpert Residency CalArts	Valencia
		Warfield Center, UT	Austin
2006		Summer Theatre Lab University of California	Santa Barbara
2005		allgo	Austin
2003		Goddard College	Plainfield
2001		University of Texas	Austin

Selected Acting, Singing, Dancing, Voice Work

love conjure/blues *by Sharon Bridgforth*   *principal actor*

2004	Staged Reading	Warfield Center, UT	Austin

HotMouth *conceived and composed by Grisha Coleman*   *principal singer*

1999		Dublin Theatre Festival Civic Theatre	Dublin
		Peacock Theatre	London
		U.S. Tour	various cities over 3 months
1998		Brooklyn Bridge Anchorage	NYC
		Manhattan Theatre Club	NYC

Feathers at the Flame by Marlies Yearby's Movin' Spirits Dance Theatre   *principal actor*

1998	Guthrie Lab Theatre	Minneapolis
	Manhattanville College	Rye, NY
	Aaron Davis Hall	NYC

Ruthless!   *principal actor (Sylvia St. Croix)*

| 1998 | Ordway Music Theatre | St. Paul |

Selected Shorts   *reader*

| 1999–present | Symphony Space/WNYC | NYC |
| | Tour | Ithaca, NY; Philadelphia |

Bloomsday on Broadway   *reader*

| 2001–present | Symphony Space | NYC |

Homos in the House by Djola Branner   *actor*

| 1998 | Intermedia Arts | Minneapolis |

Enfants Perdus by Erik Ehn   *principal actor*

| 1996 | Frontera@Hyde Park Theatre | Austin |

The Underground Project by Robbie McCauley   *principal performer*

| 1995 | Penumbra Theatre Co | St. Paul |

Coming of the Hurricane by Keith Glover   *actor*

| 1995 | Penumbra Theatre Co. | St. Paul |

Talking Bones by Shay Youngblood   *principal actor (originated role of Oz)*

| 1994 | Penumbra Theatre Co. | St. Paul |

Commissions

2010	Full Stage Commissioning Program	for *Jomama Jones*Radiate*
2007	McKnight Residency and Commission	for *Hera Bright*
2001	Tenderloin Opera Company	for *Love:Supreme*
2000	Three Legged Race	for *Whale*

Recordings

2014	Jomama Jones	*Flowering*	Aries Records
2012	Jomama Jones	*Six Ways Home*	Aries Records
2011	Jomama Jones	*Radiate*	Aries Records
2010	Jomama Jones	*Lone Star*	Aries Records
2007	Selected Shorts CD	"Solomon's Big Day"	Symphony Space Recordings
1995–99	Educational CDs	Various Short Stories	Holt, Reinhardt & Winston

Music Videos

2012	Jomama Jones	*Bones*	dir. Vicky Boone
2012	Jomama Jones	*Supernova*	dir. Ezekiel Sun
2012	Jomama Jones	*Unknown*	dir. Kevin Doyle
2011	Jomama Jones	*Out of Time*	dir. Owen Cook

Films

| 2005 | Actor (Gary) | *Attack of the Bride Monster* | dir. Vicky Boone |
| 1998 | Actor (Paprika LaMay) | *Homo Heights* | dir. Sara Moore |

Directing
(full productions, unless marked with asterisk to indicate workshop)

Wedding Band *by Alice Childress*

| 2010 | | Fordham Theatre Co. | NYC |

Sweet Tea *by E. Patrick Johnson*

| 2010 | | Viaduct Theatre | Chicago |

Slavey* *by Sigrid Gilmer*

| 2007 | | Clubbed Thumb | NYC |

Blue Fire on the Water* *by Renita Martin*

| 2007 | | Dixon Place | NYC |

Marion's Terrible Time of Joy *by Laurie Carlos*

| 2003 | | Playwrights' Center | Minneapolis |

Evidence of Silence Broken *by Zell Miller III*

| 2003 | | Pillsbury House Theatre | Minneapolis |

Tough Titty* *by Oni Faida Lampley*

| 2003 | | BRIC | Brooklyn, NY |

Dirty Blonde *by Claudia Shear*

| 2002 | | Perseverance Theatre | Douglas, Alaska |

A Slight Headache* *by Alyson Pou*

| 2002 | | The Crain Theatre | NYC |

Smoke, Lilies and Jade* *by Carl Hancock Rux*

| 2001 | | The Public Theater | NYC |
| | | Penumbra Theatre Co. | St. Paul |

Five Bottles in a Six Pack *by Renita Martin*

| 2000 | | The Theater Offensive | Boston |
| 1999 | | Solo Stage Boston | Boston |

Heavenly Shades of Night Are Falling by Erik Ehn

| 1999 | Hyde Park Theatre | Austin |
| | The Playwrights' Center | Minneapolis* |

Shakin' The Mess Outta Misery by Shay Youngblood

| 1997 | First Stage Productions | Austin |

Cracking Amber/Breathing Red by Margery Segal

| 1997 | MSNerve Dance Company | Austin |

A Roomful of Men by Amparo Garcia-Crow

| 1997 | Frontera@Hyde Park Theatre | Austin |

Unmerciful Good Fortune by Edwin Sanchez

| 1996 | Frontera@Hyde Park Theatre | Austin |

*Mister XMas** by Bridget Carpenter

| 1996 | The Playwrights' Center | Minneapolis |

Gat Him to His Place by Ruth Margraff

| 1995 | Red Eye Collective | Minneapolis |

Black Power Barbie in Hotel de Dream by Shay Youngblood

| 1995 | Frontera@Hyde Park Theatre | Austin |

Talking Bones by Shay Youngblood

| 1994 | Frontera@Hyde Park Theatre | Austin |

Sharon Bridgforth

AN ABBREVIATED CHRONOLOGY OF WORK

Publications

Books

Experiments in a Jazz Aesthetic: Art, Activism, Academia and the Austin Project, University of Texas Press, Summer 2010
Eds. Omi Osun Joni L. Jones, Lisa L. Moore, Sharon Bridgforth

love conjure/blues, RedBone Press, 2004
Urban Spectrum Black Book Award / National Best Book of Prose by Black Lesbian Writer

voices for racial justice: eliminating racism, empowering women, YWCA of Greater Austin, 2004
Eds. Sharon Bridgforth and Jennifer Margulies

the bull-jean stories, RedBone Press, 1998
Lambda Literary Award / Best Small Press Book

Anthologized Work

delta dandi in *solo/black/woman* anthology, Northwestern University Press, 2013
Eds. E. Patrick Johnson and Ramon Rivera-Servera

The love conjure/blues Text Installation in *Blacktino* anthology, Duke University Press, forthcoming
Eds. E. Patrick Johnson and Ramon Rivera-Servera

blood pudding in *Geechee to Gumbo* anthology, RedBone Press, forthcoming
Eds. Marlon Moore and L. H. Stallings.

con flama excerpt in *Windy City Queer: GLBTQ Dispatches from the Third Coast,* University of Wisconsin Press, 2011
Ed. Kathie Bergquist

Finding Voice writing exercises included in *Wingbeats: Exercises and Practice in Poetry,* Dos Gatos Press, 2011
Eds. Scott Wiggerman and David Meischen

Compact Discs

amniotic/flow, writer and performer with Sonja Perryman, allgo, 2003

the bull-jean stories audio book, writer and performer with Sonja Perryman and Deacon John, RedBone Press, 1998

Lyrics

Wrote *Love,* which is featured on World Traveler CD by Jimmy Lopez, 2011

Wrote *Sunbeam,* which is featured on Jomama Jones—Radiate CD by Daniel Alexander Jones and Bobby Halvorson, 2010

Co-wrote *Jomamasong* with Bobby Halvorson, which is on Jomama Jones—Lone Star CD by Daniel Alexander Jones and Bobby Halvorson, 2009

Films

Leading "Ladies": The Life and Times of It's All Right to Be Woman Theater
Featured speaker
Documentary by Sue Perlgut, co-directed by A. C. Warden, forthcoming

The love conjure/blues Text Installation
Writer, Performer, Director, Executive Producer
Jen Simmons, Director of Photography, Editor, Producer, 2007

Suite 4, pilot for a new GLBT entertainment show
Interviewee with Gretchen Phillips, Rob Nash, Melissa Ferrick, Malcolm Ingram, Amy Cook, Pick Up The Mic, and Ola Salo
Jenn Garrison, host; Jenn Garrison, filmmaker, 2007

Just Between Us: Documenting the Lives of Black Queer People
Interviewee with Bobby Blake, Faith Trimel, Maurice Jamal, Christopher David, Rudolph Carn, Zandra Conway, Brandon Bragg, and Layli Phillips, Ph.D.
Ken Jackson, filmmaker, 2005

Production History

Dat Black Mermaid Man Lady
Staged Reading: New Dramatists, New York, 2014

River See
Production: The Theater Offensive, Boston, November 2014
Premiere: Links Hall, Chicago, June 2014
Workshop Production: Pillsbury House Theatre, Minneapolis, 2013
Workshop: Links Hall @ University of Chicago Rockefeller Memorial Chapel, 2013
Workshop: The Theater Offensive, Boston, 2013
Workshop: Links Hall @ South Side Community Art Center, Chicago, 2012
Workshop: Pillsbury House Theatre, Minneapolis, 2012
Staged Reading: New Dramatists, New York, 2012

blood pudding
Production: Grace Exhibition Space, New York, 2012
Production: Summer Stage Festival, New York, 2010

Staged Reading: New Dramatists, New York, 2010
Workshop Production: Links Hall, Chicago, 2009
Staged Reading: Jungle Theatre, Minneapolis, 1998
Production: Frontera@Hyde Park Theatre, Austin, 1998

delta dandi
Staged Reading: New Dramatists, New York, 2010
Staged Reading: Fire & Ink Black Queer Writers Festival, Austin, 2009
Workshop Production: The Long Center for the Performing Arts, Austin, 2009; produced by Women & Their Work and The National Performance Network
Staged Reading: Fire! New Play Festival, Freedom Train Productions, Brooklyn, 2008

The love conjure/blues Text Installation
Production: The South Dallas Cultural Center, Dallas, 2008
Production: The Off Center, produced by Conjure Productions, Austin, 2007

love conjure/blues
Staged Reading: Part of the non-English Speaking Spoken Here: The Late Nite Series, Curated by Laurie Carlos and E. G. Bailey. The Pillsbury House Theatre, Minneapolis, 2005
Staged Reading: Part of Dyke Nite. Walker Art Center, Minneapolis, 2005
Staged Reading: Produced by The John L. Warfield Center for African and African American Studies, University of Texas at Austin, 2004

con flama
Production: Penumbra Theatre, St. Paul, 2001
Production: Frontera@Hyde Park Theatre, Austin, 2000

geechee crossing   marsha's overture
Staged Reading: Penumbra Theatre, St. Paul, 2000

the bull-jean stories
Staged Reading: Michigan Womyn's Music Festival, Acoustic Stage, Walhalla, MI, 1999

Founder, Writer, Artistic Director—The root wy'mn Theatre Company, 1993–98
The root wy'mn Theatre Company touring roster includes the following:

dyke/warrior-prayers
Production: Randolph Street Gallery, Chicago, 1997
Production: Outcharlotte Festival, Charlotte, 1997
Production. Frontera@Hyde Park Theatre, Austin, 1996
Production: Michigan Womyn's Music Festival, Walhalla, 1996

no mo blues
Production: King Arts Complex, Columbus, 1998
Production: Randolph Street Gallery, Chicago, 1998
Production: Outcharlotte Festival, Charlotte,1997
Production: Dyke Nite, Walker Art Center, Minneapolis, 1997
Production: The Theatre Offensive, Boston, 1996
Production: Michigan Womyn's Music Festival, Walhalla, 1995
Production: Frontera@ Hyde Park Theatre, Austin, 1995
Production: La Pena Cultural Center, Berkeley, 1995
Production: Diverseworks Artspace, Houston, 1994

lovve/rituals & rage
Production: Jump-Start Performance Company, San Antonio, 1994
Production: Randolph Street Gallery, Chicago, 1994
Production: The Vortex Theatre Company, Austin, 1993

Dramaturgy

It's the Seeing by Renita Martin
Late Night Series, The Cherry Lane Theatre, New York, 2007

Phoenix Fabrik by Daniel Alexander Jones
Playtime Developmental Studio, New Dramatists, New York, 2006

Half-Breed Southern Fried (check one) by Florinda Bryant
Performing Blackness Series, The John L. Warfield Center for African And African American Studies, University of Texas at Austin, 2006

The Pork Chop Wars (a story of mothers) by Laurie Carlos
Performing Blackness Series, The John L. Warfield Center for African and African American Studies at the University of Texas at Austin, 2005

Phoenix Fabrik by Daniel Alexander Jones
allgo (Texas statewide queer people of color organization), Austin, 2004

Arrhythmia by Zell Miller III
Penumbra Theater Company, Cornerstone Reading Series, Minneapolis, 2002

NOTES

Introduction

1. Omi Osun Joni L. Jones, "Conversations with History: Sekou Sundiata, Craig Harris, and *Elijah.*" 417.

2. Throughout this conversation, I use aesthetics to mean the structure, order, method associated with a particular artform. In this usage, aesthetics refers to beauty only in that those creating such works deem their choices to be beautiful or right or good, and those analyzing such works should do so using these criteria. In this way, I do not view aesthetics as ahistorical, apolitical, or hierarchical—a critique that has been leveled indirectly against aesthetics by Jacques Derrida and Jurgen Habermas, among others. For a thorough review of these positions, see Hal Foster, *The Anti-Aesthetic: Essays on Postmodern Culture.*

3. In this discussion of theatrical jazz, I use "performance" to mean those aestheticized, rehearsed, embodied works created specifically to be shared. In this way, my usage reflects Richard Schechner's definition of performance as "showing doing" in *Performance Studies: An Introduction* (6), even as some of the artists in this book push against a readily identifiable "doing" by abstracting the everyday-life referent, or omitting such referents altogether, and limiting static repetition through improvisation. This use of performance is in contrast to the everyday life performances, or "doings," studied by a host of conversation analysts such as Robert Hopper, Nathan Stucky, and Leslie Jarman, and in contrast to the performative features of everything from words to gender. While I embrace the everyday as performance and the performativity of language and social constructions, in this work, performance will reference a more traditionally theatrical set of conventions unless otherwise noted.

4. Robert G. O'Meally, *Seeing Jazz: Artists and Writers on Jazz,* 85.

5. E. Patrick Johnson, *Sweet Tea: Black Gay Men of the South.*

6. Throughout this work, I employ the term "Yoruba" as common shorthand for the specific Ìṣẹ̀ṣẹ̀ practices of égún, Egúngún, Òrìṣà, and Ifá. K. Noel Amherd identifies Ìṣẹ̀ṣẹ̀ practices as those spiritual methods of a wide range of Yoruba people prior to colonization (*Reciting Ifá: Difference, Heterogeneity, and Identity*). Yoruba, on the other hand, specifically refers to a *Kwa* subgroup language and has come to name a group of people living primarily throughout Southwestern Nigeria, Togo, Benin, and parts of Ghana. Outside of Nigeria, many practitioners refer to Ìṣẹ̀ṣẹ̀ spiritual work simply as Yoruba spirituality.

7. Kimberly W. Benston, *Performing Blackness: Enactments of African-American Modernism,* 8.

8. Omi Osun Joni L. Jones, "Conversations with History: Sekou Sundiata, Craig Harris, and *Elijah.*" 417.

9. Theatre of Cruelty, Dada, and the earliest Performance Art of Allan Kaprow all sought to challenge narrative structure, the performance–audience relationship, and the location of truth in art. The conscious radical manipulation of theatrical conventions positions these European traditions as antecedents to the theatrical jazz of Carlos, Jones, and Bridgforth.

10. Harry J. Elam Jr., "The *TDR* Black Theatre Issue: Refiguring the Avant-Garde."

11. Fred Moten, *In the Break: The Aesthetics of the Black Radical Tradition,* 12–16.

12. Ibid., 32–33.

13. See Henry Louis Gates Jr., "Chitlin Circuit", and Werner Sollors, *Amiri Baraka / LeRoi Jones.*

14. In the 1920s and 1930s jazz dance had a decidedly Black association. Anthea Kraut situates Josephine Baker in the Jazz Age as an "entertainer who epitomized black primitivism" ("Between Primitivism and Diaspora," 434). Brenda Dixon-Gottschild similarly notes how jazz stands in for Blackness in describing what she calls "the Africanist principles of Jazz Dance." Dixon-Gottschild enumerates these principles as "an attitude (in the sense that African Americans use that word) that combines composure with vitality. Its prime components are aesthetic visibility and lucidity . . . and luminosity, or brilliance. The picture is completed by facial composure, the actualized 'mask of the cool'" (*Digging the Africanist Presence in American Performance,* 16). For Dixon-Gottschild jazz *is* Black and the term is used then to "Blacken" dance in specific ways. In examining poetry, L. L. Dickson discusses the much-studied relationship between jazz music and poetry, and identifies the "jazz elements" in poetry as "the use of syncopated rhythms which hope to approximate the sounds and cadences of jazz . . . , and the focus on specifically named jazz musicians to enhance imagery or theme" ("Keep It in the Head," 29) Here, jazz *is* Black through a West African understanding of rhythm and through the acknowledgment of a Black artistic lineage.

15. Fred Wei-han Ho has discussed his rejection of the term jazz in many writings. An early print version of this discussion appears in "What Makes 'Jazz' the Revolutionary Music of the 20th Century, and Will It Be Revolutionary for the 21st Century?" Later, Ho famously stated, "I don't use the word 'jazz' because in my understanding of its etymology, it is a racial slur" ("Interview with Chris Mitchell," 83).

16. George Lewis, "Improvised Music after 1950: Afrological and Eurological Perspectives."

17. Wynton Marsalis, *Making The Music: A Teacher's Guide To Jazz,* 15.

18. Fred Wei-han Ho discusses the deep authority of the blue note as a *way* of playing a note rather than the fingering of the note itself. In discussing the Blues he says, "Musically, the blues is first and foremost a unique system of temperament: African American temperament! It is not as Eurocentric musicology may attempt to codify, flatted or lowered thirds, sevenths, and fifths (noted in Western musical theory as sharp or raised seconds, dominant sevenths, or sharp or raised 11ths). Blue notes can be played on Western instruments without fingering minor thirds, dominant (flatted) sevenths and flatted fifths if the player has the African American temperament. The African American system of blues temperament is the product of synthesizing the Western European fixed, diatonic temperament system with an amalgam of West and Central African pitch and modal systems. With this new temperament system, the distinction between major and minor is irrelevant" ("Revolutionary Music," 285). In this way, the blue note is less a physical technique and more an emotional and political stance.

19. Annamarie Jagose, *Queer Theory: An Introduction,* 99.

20. Moten, *In the Break.*

21. Thomas DeFrantz, "Performing the Breaks: African American Aesthetic Structures," 31.

22. Christopher Calloway Brooks, "Cab Calloway: Sketches."

23. Quoted in Daniel Belgrad, *The Culture of Spontaneity: Improvisation and the Arts in Postwar America,* 192.

24. In responding to my question "How do you name yourself," Jones wrote in an e-mail, "I am unnameable—as I ultimately believe all people are—we assume names in incarnation, but they are the lenses through which we focus our light. I hate biracial, used it a few times out of necessity. So I really do think I would self-describe out of all those names right now. The Navajo word for the two-spirit person is 'one who constantly transforms'[;] that feels closest to the way I experience myself. I am happy to say that my experience includes or is rooted in various aspects of those

identities—but I hope that my discussions about my life reflect, ultimately, that indefinable light" (Daniel Alexander Jones, e-mail to author, June 13, 2010).

25. David Kessler, *Queer Ideas: The David R. Kessler Lectures in Lesbian and Gay Studies,* 11.

26. E. Patrick Johnson and Mae Henderson, "Introduction: Queering Black Studies / 'Quaring' Queer Studies," 5.

27. From the first printing of *This Bridge Called My Back* (Moraga and Anzaldúa, 1981) through the first printing of *Black Feminist Thought* (Collins, 1991) to the appearance of *Shadowboxing* (James, 1999), many radical Black women have continued to practice liberatory politics through the use of the term feminism. This has been persistent in spite of Alice Walker's important inclusion of the term womanism into U.S. feminist philosophy. The politics of feminist naming is also seen in the work of Oyeronke Oyewumi, who notes that Walker did not coin the term womanism; she argues that the term came into being from West African feminists seeking to differentiate their work from the allegedly antimale Western feminists. Ironically, West African feminist and literary scholar Mary Kolawole embraces womanism as a way to avoid the ethnocentrism of Western feminists, and cites Walker as the theorist/artist who imagined the term. There is even deeper irony in the use of Walker's brand of womanism by some African feminists seeking to avoid the lesbian associations with feminisms, given that Walker's definition allows for "a woman who loves other women, sexually and/or nonsexually" (*In Search of Our Mothers' Gardens,* xi–xii). This tussle over naming reveals the fraught nature of African diasporic feminisms, and suggests that nomenclature for Black people remains a vital expression of self-determination.

28. Moten, *In the Break,* 269.

29. E. Patrick Johnson, "'Quare' Studies, or (Almost) Everything I Know about Queer Studies I Learned from My Grandmother."

30. This exploration of Yoruba diasporic dramatic texts can be found in Omi Osun Joni L. Jones, 2005. For additional work using Yoruba cosmology as an analytical tool, see Sandra Richards's "Yoruba Gods on the American Stage: August Wilson's *Joe Turner's Come and Gone*" (1999).

31. A *bèmbé* is a celebration for the Divine forces of nature in which drumming, dancing, and the *àṣẹ* of all those gathered are needed to make those forces manifest on the spot. *Bèmbé*s are particularly associated with the *Lukumi* traditions of Cuba and the United States.

32. It could be more legend than fact, but some scholars and artists have discussed the "voodoo" influences on Louis Armstrong. Vodoun is intimately linked with *Ìṣẹ̀ṣẹ̀* practices and continues to serve many adherents in West Africa, the Caribbean, and the United States. Some discussion of Armstrong's relationship to Vodoun can be found in Laurence Bergreen, *Louis Armstrong: An Extravagant Life.*

33. The Yoruba were among several African peoples who found themselves in New Orleans and contributed to the evolving cultural life of the region. For a discussion of Congo Square and the enslaved populations that gathered there, see Ned Sublette, *The World That Made New Orleans.*

34. Joyce Jackson and Fehintola Mosadomi, "Cultural Continuity: Masking Traditions of the Black Mardi Gras Indians and Yoruba *Egúngún.*"

35. Originally produced as a short film in 1976, Martinez's documentary, "The Black Indians of New Orleans," is an examination of the spiritual underpinnings of and community commitment to Mardi Gras.

36. Some writers have leveled famous critiques against either the term "free jazz" or the musical form itself. In an interview with Lynn Novick, co-producer of the PBS documentary "Jazz," critic/essayist Albert Murray stated, "Ornette Coleman comes up and says, 'This is free jazz.' But what is freer than jazz? As soon as you *say* jazz, you are talking about freedom of improvisation. The whole thing is about freedom, about American freedom. So why would anybody want to free it from its forms?" (quoted in Geoffrey Ward, *Jazz: A History of America's Music,* 343). Controversial cultural critic Stanley Crouch has questioned the usefulness of what he calls avant-garde in a 2007 interview with critic/pianist Ethan Iverson: "To me, the question is: What is jazz music? What I really don't like is how the avant-garde, which is more like contemporary European music, is treated as the solution to jazz to the exclusion of real jazz. I realized the problem years ago when Roland Kirk complained to Cecil Taylor in Downbeat that Cecil wouldn't let him sit in with his

band. Cecil said they had arrangements, and that's why he didn't let Kirk sit in, but that's not a good reason. That's what holds the music back. It is a real problem that there is no agreed-upon place for avant-garde musicians and the musicians who play real jazz to play together. Because if the avant-garde musicians stay away from the jazz musicians, their music gets to the point where it has less and less to do with jazz. I don't like that. Some people do; I really don't!" Note that in the same interview Crouch goes on to speak of his appreciation of Free Jazz through Ornette Coleman's ability to respond so intently to each musician in the ensemble (Ethan Iverson, "Interview with Stanley Crouch").

37. Harry Garuba, "Explorations in Animist Materialism: Notes on Reading/Writing African Literature, Culture, and Society," 265.

38. Here, and throughout, I use the term "tribe" mindfully as I seek to evoke notions of kinship that are outside of nation-state formations and sanctions. In spite of the way the word has been traditionally deployed to privilege specific government, family, and religious structures, the independence suggested by the word makes it useful in my discussion of transgressive aesthetic and political constructions.

39. The Austin regulars included Florinda Bryant, Zell Miller III, Daniel Dodd Ellis, Megan Monaghan, Sonja Parks, C. Denby Swanson, Amparo Garcia, Sonja Perryman, Jason Phelps, Leilah Stewart, Bret Brookshire, Kim Koym, Cynthia Alexander (then Taylor-Edwards), Jeffrey "Dashade" Johnson, and myself. The less frequent, though equally important, Austin participants were Starla Benford, Emily Cicchini, Gina Houston, Marlah Fulgham, and Ana Perea. Many of these artists continue to work with Carlos, Jones, and Bridgforth whenever they are given the opportunity to create the vibrant jam sessions of theatrical jazz. Because Carlos, Jones, and Bridgforth often lived and worked outside of Austin, they attracted to Austin their more distant yet consistent collaborators—including Erik Ehn, Helga Davis, Jen Simmons, Shay Youngblood, Djola Branner, Walter Kitundu, Grisha Coleman, Carl Hancock Rux, Robbie McCauley, Baraka de Soleil, Renita Martin, Adelina Anthony, Virginia Grise, Djola Branner, and Stacey Robinson.

40. Part One provides a selective chronology of work for Carlos, Jones, and Bridgforth that reveals their many repeated collaborations with a wide range of artists.

41. Robert Faires, "Wandering Preachers, Holy Fools."

42. Ibid.

43. I served as Associate Director of the John L. Warfield Center for African and African American Studies from 2001 through 2007. I assumed the position of Director of the Warfield Center in 2008. In these roles, I began the Performing Blackness Series with the mission to premiere new work by African diasporic artists, and founded the Austin Project (tAP), which was an annual eleven-week artistic collaboration and personal excavation among women of color artists, scholars, activists, and our allies. For additional information on tAP, see Omi Osun Joni L. Jones, Lisa Moore, and Sharon Bridgforth, *Experiments in a Jazz Aesthetic: Art, Activism, Academia and the Austin Project.*

44. *Ìyíká* translates as "to encircle" and is closely related to the verb *yímiká,* or encircle me, and the noun *àyíká,* or circle.

Part One: The Ensemble

1. Paul Berliner, *Thinking in Jazz: The Infinite Art of Improvisation,* 17.

2. Robert G. O'Meally, Brent Hayes Edwards and Farah Jasmine Griffin, *Uptown Conversation: The New Jazz Studies 1,* 1.

3. Wynton Marsalis, *Making The Music: A Teacher's Guide To Jazz,* 5.

4. Daniel Alexander Jones, phone interview by author, January 11, 2007.

5. Bukola Kpotie, e-mail message to author, September 16, 2009; Oladotun Ayobade, e-mail message to author, February 22, 2014.

6. *blu* was also a 2007 finalist in the Kennedy Center Playwrights' Competition. Grise subsequently was invited to become a Playwriting Fellow at the Eugene O'Neill Center for Playwrights

in 2008. The Yale Drama Series Award for *blu* included a $10,000 prize and publication of the play by Yale University Press.

7. Richard Sennett, "The Spaces of Democracy," 19.

8. Catherine Coquery-Vidrovitch, *The History of African Cities South of the Sahara,* 165.

9. The more recent texts include Afolabi A. Epega and Philip John Neimark, *The Sacred Ifá Oracle* (New York: HarperCollins Publishers, 1995); S. Solagbade Popoola's *Ifá Dídá: An Invitation to Ifá Divination, Volume 1*; Ayo Salami's *Ifá: A Complete Divination*; Fasina Falade's *Ifá: The Keys to Its Understanding*; Fa'Lokun Fatunmbi's *Awo: Ifá and the Theology of Orisha Divination*; and Chief Fama Aina Adewale Somadhi's *Reflections on the Wisdom of Ifá.* Among the earlier *Ifá* texts are William Bascom's *Ifá Divination: Communication Between Gods and Men in West Africa* and Maulana Kalenga's *Odù Ifá: The Ethical Teachings.*

10. Many historians give an account of the split between Armstrong and Oliver, with most attributing the final split to Lillian Hardin's insistence that Armstrong develop his own style and take charge of his own money. See Scott Allen Nollen's *Louis Armstrong: The Life, Music and Screen Career,* 20–23; Eileen Southern's *The Music of Black Americans,* 381.

11. I directed *Sister Overpass* when it was presented at the Blue Theatre in Austin, 2002. The piece stimulated community conversations hosted by Florinda Bryant and Piper Anderson.

12. Florinda Bryant, "How Do You Break Down the Science of the Cipher?," 325.

13. Quoted in Brian Lanker, *I Dream a World: Portraits of Black Women Who Changed America,* 56.

14. It was this impulse that led her to produce *Medea* in 1972 for Black actress Betty Howard, directed by Andrei Serban. When Howard was called to Broadway, Priscilla Smith took the lead role. This production was performed in Greek at Palace of Dionysus in Baalbeck, Lebanon, and later toured France. The U.S. and Lebanese reviews lauded the production. Although she may not have been recognized by some as an important contributor to Black Theatre, it seems she, like Adrienne Kennedy, fell into a Black blind spot, outside the popularly held ideas about how best to make Black art.

15. Lanker, *I Dream a World,* 56.

16. Rahman uses the term in her 1993 essay in *Moon Marked and Touched by Sun,* though she had been ruminating on theatrical jazz for many years prior. She references a new theatrical form in "Tradition and a New Aesthetic," 23–26; and in her introductory comments to *Mojo and the Sayso* (first published in 1986). In her *Obsidian III* interview with Afaa Michael Weaver she discusses her earliest interests in jazz and theatre. Given Rahman's early work in this form—*Lady Day* (1972), *Unfinished Women Cry in No Man's Land While a Bird Dies in a Gilded Gage*—and her continued exploration with *Mojo and the Sayso,* she is one of the earliest playwrights to stake out artistic territory specifically identified as theatrical jazz. Although Ntozake Shange's *for colored girls who have considered suicide/when the rainbow is enuf* and Adrienne Kennedy's *Funnyhouse of the Negro* have theatrical jazz elements, and Shange's vital "Unrecovered Losses" speaks of structures similar to those named by Rahman, it is Rahman who specifically situates herself within a jazz aesthetic for theatre. For greater detail on Rahman and her pioneering work on the development of theatrical jazz, see Aishah Rahman, "To Be Black, Female and a Playwright," and Alicia Kae Koger, "Jazz Form and Jazz Function: An Analysis of *Unfinished Women Cry in No Man's Land While a Bird Dies in a Gilded Cage.*" See also Brandi Wilkins Catanese's "'We must keep on writing': The Plays of Aishah Rahman."

17. Catanese, "We must keep on writing," 130.

18. McIntyre, phone interview with author, June 15, 2010.

19. Along with McIntyre, "Fly: Five First Ladies of Dance" included Jawole Will Jo Zollar, Bebe Miller, Carmen de Lavallade, and Germaine Acogny. See Claudia La Rocco, "Autumnal Choreographers in Full Bloom," for a review of this event.

20. The three primary artists being examined in this book who developed work at Frontera@ Hyde Park Theatre have moved from Austin and only occasionally return to make work. Carlos directs around the United States while maintaining directorship of Late Nite at Pillsbury House. Jones is an Associate Professor of Theatre at Fordham University, and writes, directs, and promotes

Jomama Jones in song-driven productions that have generated strong reviews, CDs, and performances in New York, Austin, and Minneapolis. In 2014 Bridgforth completed an appointment as Artist-in-Residence at the University of Iowa's MFA playwriting program while she continues to be a self-employed touring artist. Grisha Coleman is an assistant professor at Arizona State University in the Department of Integrated Media Arts and continues to create installments to *echo::system* whenever funding and venues are available. As of this writing Erik Ehn is the director of playwriting at Brown University, and continues his artistic/political sojourns to Rwanda. Since receiving the MacArthur Foundation Fellowship in 2008, Walter Kitundu has become increasingly busy in San Francisco, though he has pledged to collaborate with Coleman on a new work. Robbie McCauley retired from Emerson College in Boston as a full professor, having directed both college and local productions, and performing *Sugar* at universities around the United States. Theatrical jazz continues to grow, though it is even less centralized than during the prolific 1990s in Austin. By dint of the artists working more deeply in universities, aspects of the work have the potential to become more institutionalized, surely yielding complex results on the understanding and practice of theatrical jazz.

21. Toyin Falola, e-mail to the author, July 14, 2005.

22. These ideas are discussed in greater detail in Omi Osun Joni L. Jones's "The Self as Other: Creating the Role of Joni the Ethnographer for *Broken Circles*."

23. Joseph E. Holloway, *Africanisms in American Culture*, 16–17.

24. See Edmund T. Gordon's "The Austin School Manifesto: An Approach to the Black or African Diaspora."

The Marrow (Part One)

1. Laurie Carlos, interview by author, New York, July 2003.

2. Laurie Carlos, *White Chocolate for My Father*, 31.

3. Laurie Carlos, "Feathers at the Flame, Next Dance" (unpublished manuscript), 20.

4. Laurie Carlos, *White Chocolate*, 26; *The Cooking Show and How the Monkey Dances*, 88.

5. Carlos, *White Chocolate*, 13.

6. Ibid., 3.

7. Ibid., 10.

8. A performance novel, as used by both Carlos and Bridgforth, is a written prose/poetry text typically epic in scope that is intended for performance. The layout of the text (punctuation, blank spaces, varied fonts) offers cues for embodiment, while speaker designation and stage directions are seldom assigned on the page.

9. Valerie Preston-Dunlop discusses the feeling states of dance that bring about transformations in dancers in *Looking at Dances: A Choreological Perspective on Choreography*. See also Ann Daly's study of Isadora Duncan that describes the necessity of specific breathing methods in order to achieve the proper release of the body. As dancer Julia Levien described in her own Duncan work, "Your knee must be turned out. Your hips must be thrust forward. Your breathing must be in a certain cadence. Nothing was left to chance" (quoted in *Done into Dance: Isadora Duncan in America*, 78).

10. For a detailed study of Dianne McIntyre and her work, see Veta Goler's "'Moves on Top of Blues': Dianne McIntyre's Blues Aesthetic." 205–32; and Daly, *Done into Dance*.

11. Laurie Carlos, *Marion's Terrible Time of Joy*, 163.

12. Carlos, *White Chocolate*, 9.

13. Ibid., 14.

14. Laurie Carlos, with Robbie McCauley and Jessica Hagedorn, *Teenytown*, 117.

15. Carlos, *White Chocolate*, 12.

16. Carlos, *Teenytown*, 103–5.

17. Carlos, *White Chocolate*, 14.

18. Ibid., 9.

19. Ironically, The Bobettes originally created their hit song to describe their dislike for their teacher. Atlantic Records insisted on changing the lyrics, which transformed the song into the romantic ruminations of a schoolgirl over the object of her longing. Their 1959 "I Shot Mr. Lee" gave them an opportunity to share their true feelings about their teacher.

20. Carlos, *Cooking Show,* 83.

21. Frontera@Hyde Park Theatre regularly rented rehearsal space from the Texas State Mental Hospital. It was relatively close to the theatre, offered good rates, had large open rooms where blocking could be mapped and grounds with picnic benches that allowed for a respite from the un-air-conditioned rooms that intensified the Austin summer temperatures.

22. Carlos, *White Chocolate,* 26.

23. Carlos, *Teenytown,* 100.

24. C. Denby Swanson, interview by author, Austin, TX, July 8, 2009.

25. Carlos, *White Chocolate,* 20.

26. Ibid., 14.

27. Ibid., 27.

28. Sharon Bridgforth, phone interview with author, 2007.

29. Carlos, *White Chocolate,* 27.

30. Ibid., 4.

31. Sharon Bridgforth, phone interview with author, June 16, 2008.

32. For additional details on Carlos's early life see E. Angelica Whitmal's "So Many Possibilities before You Crack the Egg: A Conversation with Laurie Carlos."

33. Among the artists Carlos hosted during the Late Nite Series—"Non-English Speaking Spoken Here"—were Sharon Bridgforth, Daniel Alexander Jones, Florinda Bryant, Zell Miller III, Robbie McCauley, Grisha Coleman, Ed Bok Lee, Jessica Hagedorn, Mankwe Ndosi, Carl Hancock Rux, Jose James, Djola Branner, and Kati KaVang.

34. Carlos, *Teenytown,* 117.

35. Carlos, *White Chocolate,* 21.

36. Carlos, "Feathers at the Flame," 17.

37. Carlos, *Teenytown,* 96.

38. Ibid., 105.

39. Ibid., 103.

40. Carlos, *White Chocolate,* 31.

41. Laurie Carlos, phone interview by author, January 2012.

42. Carlos, *Cooking Show,* 88.

43. Carlos, "Pork Chop Wars," (unpublished manuscript, 2006).

44. Ibid.

45. Carlos, *Cooking Show,* 83.

46. Ibid.

47. Laurie Carlos, phone interview by author, January 2008.

48. Here Carlos is referencing her stepmother, Lillian Louise Smith, who she always called "mom." Her stepmother died in 2006 after a long illness. Laurie shuffled between Minneapolis and New York many times as she kept vigil over her beloved "mom."

49. Here Carlos is referring to her birth mother, Milagros Smith Randall, who preferred to be called Mildred or Millie.

50. Carlos, interview, January 2008.

51. Carlos, "An Organdy Falsetto" (unpublished manuscript), 3.

52. Ibid., 6.

53. Carlos, *White Chocolate,* 27.

54. Ibid., 23–24.

55. Carlos, *Marion's Terrible Time of Joy,* 166.

56. For information on the benefits of flooding, see the PBS special broadcast website: http://www.pbs.org/wgbh/nova/flood/.

57. Carlos, *Marion's Terrible Time of Joy,* 167.

The Blue Note (Part One)

1. Daniel Alexander Jones, *CalArts Presents the Alpert Award in the Arts 2006.*
2. Daniel Alexander Jones, e-mail message to author, March 12, 2008.
3. Robert Faires, "Wandering Preachers, Holy Fools."
4. Daniel Alexander Jones, Program notes for "Service for Bernice Lucille Gould Leslie."
5. Jones, e-mail, March 12, 2008.
6. Daniel Alexander Jones, interview by author, New York, July 2003.
7. Jones was a student at Classical until it was closed at the end of his junior year. He graduated from Central High School, what Jones describes as "a big prison-like building."
8. Jones created production posters for Adrienne Kennedy's *The Owl Answers,* directed by Rhonda Ross; production posters and program covers for Robbie McCauley's *Sally's Rape*; the book cover and program cover for Bridgforth's *love conjure/blues*; the program cover for Bridgforth's *blood pudding*; and the production program cover for Shay Youngblood's *Square Blue.*
9. Jones crafted twenty-five handmade sewn and stamped copies of *Phoenix Fabrik,* set in a unique font. Jones is meticulous about his programs and flyers. For each of his productions with the Warfield Center, he created the program himself, choosing just the right image, laid out according to his keen eye, folded just so.
10. Jones, interview, New York, July 2003.
11. See *When Race Breaks Out,* by Helen Fox, and *Reproducing Racism: White Space, Elite Law Schools and Racial Inequality* by Wendy Leo Moore, for more information on racism within U.S. academic institutions of higher learning.
12. Ross directed a production of Adrienne Kennedy's *The Owl Answers* for which Jones served as dramaturg. Of that work, Jones says, "I learned more doing that project than in class. We took the script word by word and talked for days before ever walking into a rehearsal room. Kennedy came to see the production and was quite impressed" (message to author, June 19, 2008).
13. Jones, interview, New York, July 2003.
14. Ibid.
15. Aishah Rahman, "Interview with Sydne Mahone," 283.
16. Aishah Rahman, *The Mojo and the Sayso,* 317.
17. Ibid., 286.
18. Jones, interview, New York, July 2003.
19. Daniel Alexander Jones, e-mail message to author, June 11, 2008.
20. For more information on Rebecca Rice's work in D.C. and with At the Foot of the Mountain, see Charlotte Canning, *Feminist Theaters in the U.S.A.,* and Sandra M. Bemis's "The Difficulties Facing Feminist Theater: The Survival of At the Foot of the Mountain."
21. Daniel Alexander Jones, e-mail message to author, June 12, 2008.
22. Jones offers some detail about his work at the Smithsonian in *The Book of Daniel, Chapter 7: Immortality* when he states:

> We write and stage short, little, brief performances in the BLACK exhibit—FIELD TO FACTORY. For example, let's say you might come upon a Negro farmhouse in the wayback south and there we'd be inside it. SHO' IS HARD WORKIN' DOWN HERE IN THE SOUTH LAND. I KNOW THAT'S RIGHT, ELIAS! I SHO' WISH WE COULD GO UP NORTH. NORTH? DON'T BE CRAZY!!! NORTH IS THE LAND OF OPPORTUNITY. OPPORTUNITIES FOR NEGRO PEOPLE AND A WHOLE LOT LESS LYNCHIN. I GOTS MY EYE FIX ON A CITY I HEARD ABOUT CALLED PHILADELPHIA. Then we'd run out the back of the little farmhouse and run on over to the other side of the exhibit to the Negro rowhouse up North. ELIAS! WHY YOU SITTIN' UP HERE IN PHILADELPHIA WITH YO HEAD HANGING LOW? WELL, I SHO' THOT THE NORTH WAS GONNA BE A WHOLE HEAP BETTER THAN THE SOUTH. SEEM TO ME THAT THE NEGRO MAN CAN'T HARDLY GET AHEAD NOHOW. ELIAS, I HEARD OF A MAN CALLED MARCUS GARVEY—HE GOT A BOAT GOIN' TO AFRICA. AFRICA—WOMAN IS YOU CRAZY? By

the end of the summer, my enthusiasm has waned significantly. This is not the kind
of theatre that I want to be doing. (192–93)

23. Daniel Alexander Jones, *The Book of Daniel, Chapter 7: Immortality,* 193.

24. Daniel Alexander Jones, phone interview with author, January 11, 2007.

25. Jones, e-mail, June 11, 2008.

26. Ibid.

27. Jones, phone interview with author, January 11, 2011.

28. In "Traveling through Time with Ms. Jomama Jones," Deborah Paredez offers a poetic analysis of Jomama Jones as diva with the liner notes in *Jomama Jones Radiate.*

29. Jones, *Service for Bernice Lucille Gould Leslie.*

30. For a detailed discussion of *Àjẹ́* and *Ìyámi,* see Teresa Washington, *Our Mothers, Our Powers, Our Texts: Manifestations of Àjẹ́ in Africana Literature.*

31. *Ifá* is the divination system that governs much Yoruba-based spiritual practice. Given this,
some practitioners refer to the Divinity of wisdom interchangeably as *Ọ̀rúnmìlà* or *Ifá.*

32. The city of Ondo has a history of female *Ọba*s. One origin story names Pupupu, a wife of
the progenitor *Odùduwà,* as the first leader of the Ondo Kingdom in the fifteenth century. Current
rulers of Ondo are descendants of this female *Ọba.*

33. Daniel Alexander Jones, "Earthbirths, Jazz and Raven's Wings" (unpublished manuscript,
1994).

34. Jones, *Book of Daniel, Chapter 7,* 180.

35. Daniel Alexander Jones, "Phoenix Fabrik" (unpublished manuscript, 2006).

36. Ibid., 51.

37. Jones, "Earthbirths," 6.

38. Ibid., 63.

39. Jones, e-mail, June 19, 2008.

40. Jones, interview, July 2003.

41. Daniel Alexander Jones, e-mail to author, September 12, 2006.

42. Jones, "Putting Your Foot Up in It," 4.

43. O'Meally, *Seeing Jazz: Artists and Writers on Jazz,* 9.

44. Jones, "Phoenix Fabrik," 2.

45. Ibid., 2.

46. Ibid., 8.

47. Jones, "Because I Haven't Nailed Me Down" (unpublished essay, 2005).

The Roots (Part One)

1. Sharon Bridgforth, "delta dandi" (unpublished manuscript, 2010), 36.

2. Angela Davis, *Blues Legacies and Black Feminism: Gertrude Ma Rainey, Bessie Smith, and
Billie Holiday,* 41.

3. In "It Jus Be's Dat Way Sometime," Hazel Carby notes, "The figure of the woman blues
singer has become a cultural embodiment of social and sexual conflict, from Gayl Jones's novel
Corregidora to Alice Walker's *The Color Purple.* The women blues singers occupied a privileged
space; they had broken out of the boundaries of the home and taken their sensuality and sexuality
out of the private into the public sphere" (479). Angela Davis also acknowledges the way women
blues singers created agency through their lyrics, through their self-presentation, and through the
money they were able to acquire. Their transgressive behavior signaled a world of possibility for
other women. As Carby writes, ". . . we hear the 'we' when they say 'I'" (481).

4. Laurie Carlos, interview by author, New York, July 2003.

5. Sharon Bridgforth, "con flama" (unpublished manuscript, 2002), 31–32.

6. Bridgforth's "Finding Voice" is a trademarked facilitation process that has been the primary

pedagogy of the Austin Project. Bridgforth describes this process in detail in *Experiments in a Jazz Aesthetic: Art, Activism, Academia and the Austin Project.*

7. Sharon Bridgforth, interview by author, New York, July 2003.

8. Bridgforth founded The root wy'mn Theatre Company in 1993. Their tours included work at Theatre Offensive, Boston; The Walker Art Center, Minneapolis; Diverseworks Artspace, Houston; King Arts Complex, Columbus, Ohio; La Peña Cultural Center, Berkeley; and The Michigan Womyn's Music Festival, Walhalla. The members were Starla Benford, Sonja Parks, Arriama Matlock Abdullah, and Kaci Fannin, with directorial support from Michelle Parkerson, workshop intensives with Omi Jones, set designs by Marsha Ann Gomez, and choreography by Anoa Monsho. Monique Mayo worked as house manager collecting money at the door, and Lori Wilson was the production manager.

9. Sharon Bridgforth, *dyke/warrior-prayers,* 1996.

10. Bridgforth, *con flama,* 13.

11. Bridgforth, *love conjure/blues,* 16.

12. Ibid., 11.

13. Ibid., 67.

14. Bridgforth, interview, July 2003.

15. Carlos, *con flama* interview, July 2003.

16. Cornel West, *Race Matters,* 29.

17. bell hooks, *Killing Rage: Ending Racism,* 20.

18. Sharon Bridgforth, e-mail message to author, October 23, 2006.

19. Bridgforth, *con flama,* 43.

20. Sharon Bridgforth, "blood pudding" (unpublished manuscript, 2010), 27.

21. Ibid., 29–30.

22. Bridgforth, *love conjure/blues,* 88.

23. Sharon Bridgforth, "geechee crossing marsha's overture" (unpublished manuscript, 2002), 2.

24. Bridgforth, interview, July 2003.

25. Stephanie Batiste, "Aquanova: Collapsing Time in the Lives of Sharon Bridforth's *delta dandi,*" 239.

26. Moyo Okediji, "*Egúngún:* Diaspora Recycling" (unpublished essay, 2008), 2.

27. Ibid., 2.

28. Toni Morrison, "Rootedness: The Ancestor as Foundation," 344.

29. Ibid., 343.

30. Olabiyi Yai, "In Praise of Metonymy: The Concepts of 'Tradition' and 'Creativity' in the Transmission of Yoruba Artistry over Time and Space," 108–9.

31. Bridgforth, *love conjure/blues,* 83.

32. Bridgforth, *con flama,* 44.

33. Okediji, "*Egúngún.*"

34. Sharon Bridgforth, "interlude #21: the road to Higher Power," 4.

35. Florinda Bryant, "Half-Breed Southern Fried (check one)" (unpublished manuscript, 2006).

36. "Rasgos Asiaticos" was published in *Frontiers: A Journal of Women Studies* 24 2–3 (2003): 132–39, but the version printed here reflects changes Grise made to the poem she sent to me via e-mail on April 7, 2014.

37. Bridgforth, *delta dandi.* 30.

38. Bridgforth, "interlude #21: the road to Higher Power," 9.

39. Bridgforth, *con flama,* 44.

40. Sharon Bridgforth, *amniotic/flow* (Austin, Tx: allgo, 2003), 19.

41. Rinaldo Walcott, "Outside in Black Studies: Reading from a Queer Place in the Diaspora," 93.

42. Ibid., 93.

43. As of this writing, Bridgforth has conducted eighteen *River See* experiments across the United States, including in Minneapolis, Miami, Boston, Austin, and Chicago. Bridgforth is also

editing a volume on *River See* that includes essays, liner notes, and text by Bridgforth, Virginia Grise, Roell Schmidt, Robbie McCauley, Sonja Parks, Nia Witherspoon, Mike Wangen, and Omi Osun Joni L. Jones.

Part Two: The Break

1. Lawrence "Butch" Morris, "Artist's Statement."
2. Tori Haring-Smith, "Dramaturging Non-realism: Creating a New Vocabulary."
3. Joao Costa Vargas, interview by author, fall 2008.
4. Erik Ehn, "Chaos, Anarchy, Ecology."
5. Albert Murray, "Improvisation and the Creative Process," 112.
6. Quoted in Ward, 28–29.
7. Morris explains his work by saying, "What I'm trying to bring about is ensemble spontaneity; there are still a lot of people resisting any kind of total improvisation" (interview with Alessandro Cassin). In a conduction I experienced in August 2007 with Helga Davis among the vocalists, it was exhilarating to watch as the performers worked to be tuned to Morris and to one another. It was also surprising to see how visibly frustrated Morris was when his subtlest instructions were misunderstood. This was not a casual exploration but serious, painstaking artmaking.
8. The presence of *ìwà rere* implies the presence of *ìwà burúkú*—"bad character." *Ìwà* may bend in either of these directions.
9. Rowland Abiodun, "Identity and the Artistic Process in Yoruba Aesthetic Concept of *Ìwà*," 15.
10. *Ilé* literally translates as house, although in Yoruba-based traditions in the United States it refers to the specific spiritual community to which practitioners belong, that is to say, one's spiritual home.
11. Sharon Bridgforth, interview by author, New York, July 2003.
12. Florinda Bryant, e-mail message to author, June 9, 2014.
13. Susanne Wenger, *A Life with the Gods,* 198.
14. Henry John Drewal discusses the significance of lidded bowls in Yoruba life in *Nine Centuries of Yoruba Art and Life.*
15. Morris, "Artist's Statement."
16. Oyin Ogunba, "Traditional African Festival Drama," 22.
17. Ehn, "Chaos."
18. Richard Schechner describes Anna Deavere Smith's brand of acting as incorporation—"deep mirrors, proves opposite to that of 'pretend.' To incorporate means to be possessed by, to open oneself up thoroughly and deeply to another being" ("Anna Deavere Smith: Acting as Incorporation," 140). Schechner also notes that Smith does not parody the person, nor does she lose herself—what he calls a "wondrous doubling." This ability to be oneself and be in another realm has been likened to the work of mediums, diviners, and shamans, who must commune with the other world but keep clear connection with the material world so that they can actually serve the material world fully.
19. Ehn, "Chaos."
20. Daniel Alexander Jones, "Phoenix Fabrik" (unpublished manuscript, 2006).
21. Schechner, *Performance Studies: An Introduction,* 80.
22. See M. Jacqui Alexander's *Pedagogies of Crossing* for a discussion of the union of heteronormativity and linear time. Jaclyn Pryor takes up a similar theme when she writes, "Straight time produces impossibly limited frameworks for queer citizenship. Those whose life experiences neatly fit into an unspoken, pre-conceived, socially constructed notion of time get recognized, counted, validated, and extolled, while those that cannot be made to fit, because they require a different understanding of time or history or values to make sense, are left unrecognized, unseen, invalidated, and dismissed" ("Time Slips," 18).
23. Here, I am echoing Moyo Okediji's use of this phrase as he discusses the ongoing and ever-present relationship between ancestors and the living as the continuity of life itself ("*Egúngún:* Diaspora Recycling," 2).

24. Sekou Sundiata and Craig Harris, interview with author, Amherst, MA, October 9, 1998.

25. Sharon Bridgforth, "delta dandi," unpublished manuscript, 2010.

26. Laurie Carlos, *Marion's Terrible Time of Joy,* 157.

27. Dwight Conquergood, "Of Caravans and Carnivals: Performance Studies in Motion," 138.

28. Jones, *Phoenix Fabrik.*

29. Daniel Alexander Jones, phone interview with author, July 31, 2007.

30. Ibid.

31. Erik Ehn, "Heavenly Shades of Night" (unpublished manuscript, 1999)

32. Sharon Bridgforth, *love conjure/blues,* 70–71.

33. Ibid., 87–88.

34. Ibid., 89.

Part Three: The Bridge

1. Robbie McCauley, "Looking at the Study of Jazz Theater (A Work in Progress Essay)" (unpublished essay, 2010).

2. Grisha Coleman, *ECHO SYSTEM::ActionStation # 2, The Desert* (Program notes, Dance Conservatory of Pasadena, 2011).

3. Eric Ehn, "A Space for Truth," 72.

4. Walter Kitundu, "Statement."

5. John Mason, *Orin Òrìsà: Songs for Selected Heads,* 54.

6. Paul Carter Harrison, *The Drama of Nommo; Totem Voices.*

7. These ideas of *nommo* are complementary in that the ancestral energies may be the forces that carry the words to manifestation. See Paul Carter Harrison, "Mother/Word." For a discussion of *nommo* in Black Theatre, see also Kimberly Benston, *Performing Blackness,* 47–48.

8. Susanne Wenger, *A Life with the Gods,* 198.

9. Ibid., 77.

10. Gates's *The Signifying Monkey* did much to bring Yoruba cosmology into an analysis of Western forms. This work has had its critics, most notably Joyce A. Joyce, who offers an important critique of Gates's understanding of Èṣù. It is significant to note that these scholars engage seriously with Yoruba cosmology as an appropriate methodology for the study of African diasporic art forms.

11. Margaret Thompson Drewal, *Yoruba Ritual: Performers, Play, Agency,* 201.

12. Kim Benston, *Performing Blackness,* 28.

13. Ibid., 29.

14. Harry Elam offers a detailed examination of Benston's earlier formulation of methexis in "The *TDR* Black Theatre Issue." In looking at the work of the Black Arts Movement, Elam, like Benston, acknowledges the unity between the audience/witnesses and the production as critical to the animating that is methexis. See Elam, "The *TDR* Black Theatre Issue: Refiguring the Avant-Garde." In this book, I offer resonant frequencies rather than empathy or identification as an animating feature of theatrical jazz. A more densely rooted engagement than empathy or identification occurs at the level of resonant frequencies, the conscious or unconscious attunement between people.

15. In addition to Jones's usage in relationship to theatre, radical empathy is also associated with spiritual and psychological studies that seek primarily to generate understanding among contentious groups, or to identify the union between healers and suffers. See Joan D. Koss-Chiono, "Spiritual Transformation, Relation and Radical Empathy: Core Components of the Ritual Healing Process."

16. Oyin Ogunba, "Traditional African Festival Drama," 22.

17. Jill Dolan, Rude Mechanicals production program.

18. Daniel Alexander Jones, phone interview with author, July 31, 2007.

19. For critical commentaries and interviews with McCauley, see Harvey Young, "Touching History: Suzan-Lori Parks, Robbie McCauley, and the Black Body"; Sydne Mahone, *Moon Marked*

and Touched by Sun; and Robbie McCauley, "Obsessing in Public: An Interview with Vivian Patraka."

20. *Tourists and Refugees II,* by Joseph Chaikin, dir. Winter Project (collaboration), LaMama ETC (performance, New York, April 28, 1981).

21. *A Movie Star Has to Star in Black and White,* by Adrienne Kennedy, dir. Joseph Chaikin. Public Theatre (performance, New York Shakespeare Festival, New York, November 5, 1976).

22. For critical commentary on Ehn, see Celia Wren, "Saints, Sin and Erik Ehn: Mysticism Ignites the Plays—and Theories—of a Theatrical Visionary."

23. Erik Ehn, interview by author, New York, June 2003.

24. Erik Ehn, "Chaos, Anarchy, Ecology."

25. Although George Washington Carver may be best known for the multiple uses he found for the peanut, it should also be noted that he was interested in advancing the freedom of Black farmers. By providing an alternative to cotton farming, Carver created independence for Black farmers while also replenishing the soil from the depletion of single-crop farming.

26. Stephanie L. Batiste, "Grisha Coleman's /Echo::System/: Technology, Body, Environment, Myth."

27. Grisha Coleman, *echo::system/ActionStation #2 The Desert* (Program Notes, On the Boards, 2005).

28. Kitundu, "Statement."

29. Ibid.

30. In an interview with the *Life* magazine journalist Richard Meryman, Louis Armstrong acknowledged the challenges posed by his ebullient performance style when he said, "That's me and I don't want to be nobody else. They know I'm there in the cause of happiness" (*Louis Armstrong: A Self Portrait,* 42). His display of happiness was often read as "Tomming" by other musicians and some patrons, though Dizzy Gillespie famously recanted his earlier criticism of Armstrong when he said "I began to recognize what I had considered Pops' grinning in the face of racism as his absolute refusal to let anything, even anger about racism, steal the joy from his life and erase his fantastic smile. Coming from a younger generation, I misjudged him" (*To Be or Not to Bop: Memoirs,* 295–96). I offer this well-known historical moment not to defend or excuse Armstrong, whose grin and behavior deeply embarrassed me as a middle-class teenager, but to suggest that under oppression joy may inevitably be read through the lens of racism. I am considering how Black joy might exceed such boundaries.

31. Omise'eke Natasha Tinsley, "Black Atlantic, Queer Atlantic: Queer Imaginings of the Middle Passage."

32. Wallace Stevens, "The House Was Quiet and the World Was Calm."

GLOSSARY OF YORUBA TERMS

abínibí natural; organic; as it should be

àdúgbò environment; neighborhood

àfòṣe the power of the word to manifest

aiyé the cosmic realm of the material world; the earth plane

Àjé the Divine power and authority of the primordial mothers

asesú the gush of a spring

àṣe life force; the ability to make things happen; also a substance that gives the owner the ability to make things manifest

awo Divine mystery

àyíká circle

Babaláwo male diviners trained in the mysteries of *Ìṣèṣè* traditions

bèmbé a drumming circle (as it is used in the United States) as well as a ritual celebration for the forces of nature with drumming, dancing, singing, foods, and altars

bíríbírí circularity, fluidity, flow

égún ancestors

Egúngún deified ancestors; sacred masquerade

Èṣù the Divine force of choice and opportunity; the keeper of physical *àṣe*

ebo dá an invocation at the end of a ritual that acknowledges receipt of the sacrifice by the divine forces

egbé work group; community; group spiritually joined

gb'ékó receiving knowledge

ìdè beaded or metal bracelets worn by practitioners of *Ìṣèṣè* spiritual traditions

Ifá a philosophical and divination system practiced by *Ìyáláwo*s and *Babaláwo*s, women and men trained in the mysteries of destiny and the Divine; overseen by *Òrúnmìlà*, the Divine force of destiny

ìgèdè transformative power of words; invocation; incantation

ìkópa Participation

ìkó'ṣé transmission of knowledge and wisdom

ilé home

ilẹ̀ the land

Ilé-Ifẹ̀ southwestern Nigerian city; spiritual home to the Yoruba

ilẹ̀kẹ̀ beaded necklaces worn by practitioners of *Ìṣẹ̀ṣẹ̀* spiritual traditions

Iragbagba a drum rhythm of *Òṣogbo,* Nigeria, associated with *Òṣun*

Ìṣẹ̀ṣẹ̀ Yoruba spiritual practices prior to colonization; the essence of culture

ìtàn demystifying time and place

itànlẹ̀ community history

ìwà personal character

ìwà rere good character

Ìyáláwo female diviners trained in the mysteries of *Ìṣẹ̀ṣẹ̀* traditions

Ìyámi the primordial mothers

Ìyàwó in Yoruba diasporic spiritual practices, a person newly consecrated to one or more *Òrìṣà*; the literal Yoruba translation is "wife," which resonates with the diasporic usage

ìyíká to encircle

kópa to participate

Legba the Divine force of indeterminacy

Lukumi the Yoruba-based spiritual tradition originating in Cuba, sometimes referred to as Santeria, though many practitioners prefer *Lukumi* as their identification

Odù sacred *Ifá* scripture; understood to be a female force

Odùduwà the Yoruba progenitor

Ògún the Divine force of metal, physical labor, and combat

olódò owner of the river

omi water

Orí personal destiny; "head"; one's first *Òrìṣà*

oríkì praises sung typically for *Òrìṣà*

Òrìṣà forces of nature; Divinities

Òṣogbo patron city of the Divinity *Òṣun* in Southwestern Nigeria; the capitol of *Òṣun* State

Ọba ruler, commonly understood as king

Ọbàtálá the Divine force of justice

ọpọ́n the generally circular divining tray used by *Ìyáláwo*s and *Babaláwo*s

ọpẹ̀lẹ̀ divining chain used by *Ìyáláwo*s and *Babaláwo*s in *Ifá* divination

Òrànmíyàn the son of the Yoruba progenitor *Odùduwà*

Òrányàn another name for the son of the Yoruba progenitor *Odùduwà*

òrun the Divine cosmic realm of ancestors and Divinities

Òrúnmìlà the Divine force of destiny

Òṣun the Divine force of healing and fresh waters, abundant joy and luxury

Ọya the Divine force of wind, breath, change

Ṣàngó the Divine force of intellect and strategy, lightening, the drum and sound generally

Yemọnja the Divine force of motherhood and the white crest of the sea; also spelled as *Yemaya* outside of Yorubaland

yímiká encircle me

BIBLIOGRAPHY

Abiodun, Rowland. "Identity and the Artistic Process in Yoruba Aesthetic Concept of *Ìwà*." *Journal of Cultural Inquiry* 1, no. 1 (December 1983): 13–30.

——. "Verbal and Visual Metaphors: Mythical Allusions in Yoruba Ritualistic Art of *Orí*." *Word and Image: A Journal of Verbal/Visual Inquiry* 3, no. 2 (1987): 252–70.

Adewale-Somadhi, Chief Fama Aina. *Reflections on the Wisdom of Ifá*. San Bernardino, CA: *Ilẹ̀ Ọ̀rúnmìlà* Communications, 2009.

Adler, Stella. *The Technique of Acting*. 1988. New York: Bantam, 1990.

Alexander, Bryant. "Embracing the Teachable Moment: The Black Gay Body in the Classroom as Embodied Text." In Johnson and Henderson 249–65.

Alexander, M. Jacqui. *Pedagogies of Crossing: Meditations on Feminism, Sexual Politics, Memory, and the Sacred*. Durham, NC: Duke University Press, 2005.

Amherd, K. Noel. *Reciting Ifá: Difference, Heterogeneity, and Identity*. Trenton, NJ: Africa World, 2010.

Armstrong, Louis, and Richard Meryman. *Louis Armstrong: A Self Portrait*. New York: Eakins, 1971.

Ayobade, Oladotun. E-mail message to author. February 22, 2014.

Bascom, William. *Ifá Divination: Communication Between Gods and Men in West Africa*. Bloomington: Indiana University Press, 1969.

Batiste, Stephanie L. "Aquanova: Collapsing Time in the Lives of Sharon Bridgforth's *delta dandi*." In *solo/black/woman: scripts, interviews, and essays*, eds. E. Patrick Johnson and Ramon H. Rivera-Servera, 238–54. Evanston, IL: Northwestern University Press, 2014.

——. "Grisha Coleman's */Echo::System/*: Technology, Body, Environment, Myth." Unpublished essay, 2010.

Belgrad, Dennis. *The Culture of Spontaneity: Improvisation and the Arts in Postwar America*. Chicago: University of Chicago Press, 1998.

Bemis, Sandra M. "The Difficulties Facing Feminist Theater: The Survival of At the Foot of the Mountain." Vol. 1. 1987. http://www2.edutech.nodak.edu/ndsta/bemis.htm.

Benston, Kimberly W. *Performing Blackness: Enactments of African-American Modernism*. New York: Routledge, 2000.

Bergreen, Laurence. *Louis Armstrong: An Extravagant Life*. New York: Broadway Books, 1997.

Berliner, Paul. *Thinking in Jazz: The Infinite Art of Improvisation*. Chicago: University of Chicago Press, 1994.

The Black Indians of New Orleans. VHS. Written by. Maurice M. Martinez. Directed by James Hinton. USA: Chalmalma Media Institute, 1976.

Bridgforth, Sharon. "blood pudding." Unpublished manuscript, 2010.

———. *the bull-jean stories.* Austin, TX: RedBone, 1998.

———. "con flama." Unpublished manuscript, 2002.

———. "delta dandi." Unpublished manuscript, 2010.

———. *delta dandi.* In *solo/black/woman: scripts, interviews, and essays,* eds. E. Patrick Johnson and Ramon H. Rivera-Servera, 185–226. Evanston, IL: Northwestern University Press, 2014.

———. "dyke/warrior-prayers." Unpublished manuscript, 1996.

———. "geechee crossing marsha's overture." Unpublished manuscript, 2002.

———. "interlude #21: the road to Higher Power." In *Spirited: Affirming the Soul and Black Gay Lesbian Identity,* eds. Lisa C. Moore and G. Winston James, 27–38. Washington, DC: RedBone, 2006.

———. *love conjure/blues.* Washington, DC: RedBone, 2004.

———. *love conjure/blues: The Text Installation.* 2007.

———. "no mo blues." Unpublished manuscript, 1995.

Bridgforth, Sharon, and Sonja Perryman. *amniotic/flow.* CD. Austin, TX: allgo, 2003.

———. "amniotic/flow." Unpublished manuscript, 2003.

Brooks, Christopher Calloway. "Cab Calloway: Sketches." *American Masters.* PBS, April 17, 2012.

Bryant, Florinda. "Half-Breed Southern Fried (check one)." Unpublished manuscript, 2006.

———. *Half-Breed Southern Fried (check one).* In Jones, Moore, and Bridgforth 323–25.

———. "How Do You Break Down the Science of the Cipher?" In Jones, Moore, and Bridgforth 323–25.

Canning, Charlotte. *Feminist Theaters in the U.S.A.* New York: Routledge, 1996.

Carby, Hazel. "It Jus Be's Dat Way Sometime: The Sexual Politics of Women's Blues" In *The Jazz Cadence of American Culture,* 470–83. New York: Columbia University Press, 1998.

Carlos, Laurie. *The Cooking Show and How the Monkey Dances.* In *Out of Character: Rants, Raves, and Monologues from Today's Top Performance Artists,* ed. Mark Russell, 80–91. New York: Bantam, 1997.

———. "Feathers at the Flame, Next Dance." Unpublished manuscript. 5th draft. May 25, 1998.

———. "Interview with Sydne Mahone." In Mahone, *Moon Marked and Touched by Sun,* 3–7.

———. *Marion's Terrible Time of Joy,* In Jones, Moore, and Bridgforth, *Experiments in a Jazz Aesthetic,* 156–68.

———. "Marion's Terrible Time of Joy." Unpublished manuscript, 2003.

———. "Nonsectarian Conversations with the Dead, an evening of performance art in four movements." Unpublished manuscript, 1985–86.

———. "An Organdy Falsetto." In "Nonsectarian Conversations with the Dead." Unpublished manuscript, 1985.

———. "The Pork Chop Wars (a story of mothers)." Unpublished manuscript. 1st draft. 2006.

———. *White Chocolate for My Father.* In Mahone, *Moon Marked and Touched by Sun,* 6–31.

Carlos, Laurie, Robbie McCauley, and Jessica Hagedorn. *Teenytown.* In *Out From Under: Texts by Women Performance Artists,* ed. Lenora Champagne, 89–117. New York: Theatre Communications Group, 1990.

Cassin, Alessandro. "Butch Morris." *Lacan.com.* http://www.lacan.com/frameXII7.htm.

Catanese, Brandi. "Politics of Representation in African American Theatre and Drama." In *African*

Americans and Popular Culture: Theater, Film, and Television, ed. Todd Boyd, 1–22. Westport, CT: Praeger, 2008.

———. "'We must keep on writing': The Plays of Aishah Rahman." In *Contemporary African American Women Playwrights: A Casebook,* ed. Philip C. Kolin, 115–31. New York: Taylor & Francis, 2007.

Cohen, J. Cathy. "Punks, Bulldaggers, and Welfare Queens: The Radical Potential of Queer Politics." In Johnson and Henderson 115–31.

Coleman, Grisha. *echo::system/ActionStation #2 The Desert.* 2005, On the Boards. Program note.

———. *ECHO SYSTEM::ActionStation # 2, The Desert.* October 2011, Dance Conservatory of Pasadena. Program notes.

Collins, Patricia Hill. *Black Feminist Thought: Knowledge, Consciousness and the Politics of Empowerment.* New York: Routledge. 1991.

Conquergood, Dwight. "Lethal Theatre: Performance, Punishment and the Death Penalty." In *The Sage Handbook of Performance Studies,* eds. D. Soyini Madison and Judith Hamera. Thousand Oaks, CA: Sage, 2005.

———. "Of Caravans and Carnivals: Performing Studies in Motion." *The Drama Review* 39, no. 4 (Autumn 1995): 137–41.

Coquery-Vidrovitch, Catherine. *The History of African Cities South of the Sahara: From the Origins to Colonization.* 1993. New York: Markus Wiener, 2005.

Crouch, Stanley. "Interview with Stanley Crouch." *Do the Math.* Interview of Stanley Crouch by Ethan Iverson. Blog. February 27, 2007.

Daly, Ann. *Done into Dance: Isadora Duncan in America.* Middletown, CT: Wesleyan University Press, 1995.

———. "New World A-Comin': A Century of Jazz and Modern Dance." In *Modern Dance, Jazz Music and American Culture,* 31–39. Durham, NC, and Washington, DC: American Dance Festival and Kennedy Center, 2000.

Davis, Angela. *Blues Legacies and Black Feminism: Gertrude Ma Rainey, Bessie Smith, and Billie Holiday.* New York: Pantheon Books, 1998.

DeFrantz, Thomas. "Performing the Breaks: African American Aesthetic Structures." *Theater* 40, no. 1 (2010): 31–37.

Dickson, L. L. "Keep It in the Head: Jazz Elements in Modern Black American Poetry." *MELUS* 10, no.1, Ethnic Literature and Music (Spring 1983): 29–37.

Dixon-Gottschild, Brenda. *Digging the Africanist Presence in American Performance.* Westport, CT: Praeger, 1996.

Dolan, Jill. "'Finding Our Feet in the Shoes of (One An) Other': Multiple Character Solo Performers and Utopian Performatives." *Modern Drama* 45, no. 4 (Winter 2002): 495–518.

———. Rude Mechanicals. Production program for *Decameron Day 7: Revenge,* 2006.

Drewal, Henry John, John Pemberton, Rowland Abiọdun, and Allen Wardwell, eds. *Nine Centuries of Yoruba Art and Life.* Center for African Art in Association with H. N. Abrams, 1989.

Drewal, Margaret Thompson. *Yoruba Ritual: Performers, Play, Agency.* Bloomington: Indiana University Press, 1992.

Ehn, Erik. "Chaos, Anarchy, Ecology," Keynote Speech, University of Texas New Works Festival, unpublished manuscript, April 7, 2007.

———. "Heavenly Shades of Night Are Falling." Unpublished manuscript, 1999.

———. "A Space for Truth: Meditations on Theatre and the Rwandan Genocide." *American Theatre* 24, no. 3 (March 2007): 34–73.

Elam, J. Harry Jr. "The *TDR* Black Theatre Issue: Refiguring the Avant-Garde." In *Not the Other Avant-Garde: The Transnational Foundations of Avant-Garde Performance,* eds. James M. Harding and John Rouse, 41–66. Ann Arbor: University of Michigan Press, 2006.

Epega, Afolabi, and Phillip John Neimark. *The Sacred Ifá Oracle*. 2nd ed. New York: Athelia Henrietta, 1995.

Faires, Robert. "Wandering Preachers, Holy Fools." Interview with Daniel Alexander Jones. *Austin Chronicle,* November 19, 1999.

Falade, Fasina. *Ifá: The Key to Its Understanding*. 1st ed. Lynwood, CA: Ara Ifa, 1998.

Fatunmbi, Fa'Lokun. *Awo: Ifá and the Theology of Orisha Divination*. Bronx, NY: Original, 1992.

Ferguson, Roderick. *Aberrations in Black: Toward a Queer of Color Critique*. Minneapolis: University of Minnesota Press, 2004.

Foster, Hal. *The Anti-Aesthetic: Essay on Postmodern Culture*. Port Townsend, WA: Bay, 1993.

Fox, Helen. *When Race Breaks Out*. New York: Peter Lang, 2001.

Garuba, Harry. "Explorations in Animist Materialism: Notes on Reading/Writing African Literature, Culture, and Society." *Public Culture* 15, no. 2 (2003): 261–85.

Gates, Henry Louis Jr. "Chitlin Circuit." *New Yorker,* February 3, 1997, 44–55.

———. *The Signifying Monkey: A Theory of African-American Literary Criticism*. Oxford: Oxford University Press, 1989.

Gennari, John. "Baraka's Bohemian Blues." *African American Review* 37, nos. 2–3, Amiri Baraka Issue (Summer–Autumn 2003): 253–60.

Gillespie, Dizzy, with Al Fraser. *To Be or Not to Bop: Memoirs*. Garden City, NY: Doubleday, 1979.

Goler, Veta. "Dancing Herself: Choreography, Autobiography, and the Expression of the Black Woman Self in the Work of Dianne McIntyre, Blondell Cummings, Jawole Willa Jo Zollar." PhD diss., Emory University, 1994.

———. "'Moves on Top of Blues': Dianne McIntyre's Blues Aesthetic." In *Dancing Many Drums: Excavations in African American Dance,* ed. Thomas DeFrantz, 205–29. Madison: University of Wisconsin Press, 2002.

Gordon, Edmund T. "The Austin School Manifesto: An Approach to the Black or African Diaspora." *Cultural Dynamics* 19, no. 1 (2007): 93–97.

Grise, Virginia. *blu*. New Haven, CT: Yale University Press, 2011.

———. "Rasgos Asiaticos." *Frontiers: A Journal of Women Studies* 24, nos. 2–3 (2003): 132–39.

Haring-Smith, Tori. "Dramaturging Non-realism: Creating a New Vocabulary." *Theatre Topics* 13, no. 1 (2003): 45–54.

Harrison, Paul Carter. *The Drama of Nommo: Black Theatre in the African Continuum*. New York: Ultramarine, 1972.

———. "Mother/Word." In *Totem Voices: Plays from the Black World Repertory,* xi–lxii. New York: Grove, 1989.

Ho, Fred Wei-han. "Interview with Chris Mitchell." In *Wicked Theory, Naked Practice,* 64–90. Minneapolis: University of Minnesota Press, 2009.

———. "'Jazz,' Kreolization and Revolutionary Music for the 21st Century." In *Sounding Off! Music as Subversion Resistance / Revolution,* eds. Ron Sakolsky and Fred Wei-han Ho, 133–43. Brooklyn, NY: Autonomedia and Contributors, 1995.

———. "What Makes 'Jazz' the Revolutionary Music of the 20th Century, and Will It Be Revolutionary for the 21st Century?" *African American Review* 29, no. 2 (1995): 283–90.

Holloway, Joseph E. *Africanisms in American Culture*. Bloomington: Indiana University Press, 1990.

hooks, bell. *Killing Rage: Ending Racism*. New York: Macmillan, 1996.

Hurston, Zora Neale. *Their Eyes Were Watching God*. 1937. New York: HarperCollins, 1990.

Iverson, Ethan. "Interview with Stanley Crouch." *Do The Math* (blog). Accessed February 27, 2007. http://dothemath.typepad.com/dtm/interview-with-stanley-crouch.html.

Jackson, Joyce, and Fehintola Mosadomi. "Cultural Continuity: Masking Traditions of the Black Mardi Gras Indians and Yoruba *Egungun.*" In *Òrìṣà: Yoruba Gods and Spiritual Identity in Africa and the Diaspora,* eds. Toyin Falola and Ann Genova, 143–60. Trenton, NJ: Africa World, 2005.

Jagose, Annamarie. *Queer Theory: An Introduction.* New York: NYU Press, 1996.

Jahn, Janheinz. *Muntu: African Culture and the Western World.* Trans. Marjorie Grene. New York: Grove, 1994.

———. *Neo-African Literature: A History of Black Writing.* Trans. Oliver Coburn and Ursula Lehrburger. New York: Grove, 1969.

James, Joy. *Shadowboxing: Representations of Black Feminist Politics.* New York: St. Martin's, 1999.

Jefferson, Margo. "The Avant-Garde, Rarely Love at First Sight" *New York Times,* July 8, 2005.

Johnson, E. Patrick. "'Quare' Studies, or (Almost) Everything I Know about Queer Studies I Learned from My Grandmother." *Text and Performance Quarterly* 21 (2001): 1–25.

———. *Sweet Tea: Black Gay Men of the South.* Chapel Hill: University of North Carolina, 2008.

Johnson, E. Patrick, and Mae Henderson. "Introduction: Queering Black Studies / 'Quaring' Queer Studies." In Johnson and Henderson 1–20.

———, eds. *Black Queer Studies: A Critical Anthology.* Durham, NC: Duke University Press, 2005.

Jones, Daniel Alexander. "Because I Haven't Nailed Me Down." Unpublished essay, 2005.

———. "The Book of Daniel: jazz rite in lecture format." Unpublished manuscript, 2007.

———. "The Book of Daniel: 33:66." Unpublished manuscript, 2007.

———. "The Book of Daniel 34:1 dis/integration." Unpublished manuscript, 2005.

———. "The Book of Daniel: 35:1." Unpublished manuscript, 2005.

———. *The Book of Daniel, Chapter 7: Immortality.* In Jones, Moore, and Bridgforth 177–200.

———. "Clayangels." Unpublished manuscript, 1997.

———. "Earthbirths, Jazz and Raven's Wings." Unpublished manuscript, 1994.

———. "Phoenix Fabrik." Unpublished manuscript, 2006.

———. Program notes for *Bel Canto.* In *Voices Rising,* 434–81. Washington, DC: RedBone, 2006.

———. Program notes for *CalArts Presents the Alpert Award in the Arts 2006.* Santa Monica, CA: Cal Arts and the Herb Alpert Foundation, 2006.

———. Program notes for "Service for Bernice Lucille Gould Leslie." Springfield, MA, 2003.

———. "Putting Your Foot Up in It." In *Parabasis, ASK Theatreworks,* 2000.

Jones, Daniel Alexander, and Todd Jones. "Clayangels." Unpublished manuscript. 4th draft, 1997.

Jones, Omi Osun Joni L. "Conversations with History: Sekou Sundiata, Craig Harris, and *Elijah.*" In *The Color of Theatre: Race, Culture and Performance,* eds. Roberta Uno and Lucy Mae San Pablo Burns, 409–20. New York: Continuum, 2002.

———. "'Making Holy': Love and the Novel as Ritual Transformation." In Bridgforth, *love conjure/blues* (2004), xiii–xix.

———. "Performance and Ethnography, Performing Ethnography, Performance Ethnography." In *Sage Handbook of Performance Studies,* eds. D. Soyini Madison and Judith Hamera, 339–45. Thousand Oaks, CA: Sage, 2006.

———. "Performing *Ọ̀ṣun* without Bodies: Documenting the *Ọ̀ṣun* Festival in Print." *Text and Performance Quarterly* 17 (1997): 69–93.

———. "The Self as Other: Creating the Role of Joni the Ethnographer for *Broken Circles.*" *Text and Performance Quarterly* 16 (1996): 131–45.

———. "Transatlantic Transformations." In *Nigeria in the Twentieth Century,* ed. Toyin Falola, 633–38. Durham, NC: Carolina Academic, 2002.

———. "Yoruba Diasporic Performance: The Case for a Spiritually- and Aesthetically-Based Diaspora." In *Òrìṣà: Yoruba Gods and Spiritual Identity,* ed. Toyin Falola, 321–31. Durham, NC: Carolina Academic, 2005.

Jones, Omi Osun Joni L., Lisa L. Moore, and Sharon Bridgforth, eds. *Experiments in a Jazz Aesthetic: Art, Activism, Academia and the Austin Project.* Austin, TX: University of Texas Press, 2010.

Jones, Van. "Black and Green: The New Eco-Warriors." *Ebony,* July 2008, 98.

Joyce, Joyce A. "A Tinker's Damn: Henry Louis Gates, Jr., and *The Signifying Monkey* Twenty Years Later." *Callaloo* 31, no. 2 (spring 2008): 370–80.

Kalenga, Maulana. *Odù Ifá: The Ethical Teachings,* Los Angeles: University of Sankore Press, 1999.

Kessler, David. *Queer Ideas: The David R. Kessler Lectures in Lesbian and Gay Studies.* New York: Feminist, 2003.

Kitundu, Walter. "Statement." Last modified January 5, 2012. http://www.kitundu.com/statement. html (link discontinued).

Koger, Alicia Kae. "Jazz Form and Jazz Function: An Analysis of *Unfinished Women Cry in No Man's Land While a Bird Dies in a Gilded Cage.*" *MELUS* 16, no. 3, Ethnic Theater (1989–1990): 99–111.

Kolawole, Mary. *Womanism and African Consciousness.* Trenton, NJ: Africa World, 1997.

Koss-Chiono, Joan D. "Spiritual Transformation, Relation and Radical Empathy: Core Components of the Ritual Healing Process." *Transcultural Psychiatry* 43, no. 4 (2006): 652–70.

Kraut, Anthea. "Between Primitivism and Diaspora: The Dance Performances of Josephine Baker, Zora Neale Hurston, and Katherine Dunham." *Theatre Journal* 55 (2003): 433–50.

Lanker, Brian. *I Dream a World: Portraits of Black Women Who Changed America.* New York: Stewart, Tabori & Chang, 1989.

La Rocco, Claudia. "Autumnal Choreographers in Full Bloom." Review of "Fly: Five First Ladies of Dance." *New York Times,* May 22, 2009.

Lewis, George. "Improvised Music after 1950: Afrological and Eurological Perspectives." *Black Music Research Journal* 16, no. 1 (1996): 91–122.

Lorde, Audre. *Zami: A New Spelling of My Name: A Biomythography.* 1982. Freedom, CA: Crossing, 2001.

Lubiano, Wahneema, ed. *The House That Race Built: Black Americans, U.S. Terrain.* New York: Pantheon, 1997.

Mahone, Sydne, ed. *Moon Marked and Touched by Sun: Plays by African American Women.* New York: Theatre Communications Group, 1994.

Marsalis, Wynton. *Making the Music: A Teacher's Guide to Jazz* (2 Audio Cassettes and 1 Booklet Kit and 1 Poster). National Public Radio, 1996.

Mason, John. *Orin Òrìṣà: Songs for Selected Heads.* New York: Yorùbá Theological Archministry, 1997.

McCauley, Robbie. "Interview." In *Conjure Women* (film), dir. Demetria Royals. Women Make Movies, 1995.

———. "Looking at the Study of Jazz Theater (A Work in Progress Essay)." Unpublished Essay, 2010.

———. "Obsessing in Public: An Interview with Vivian Patraka." In *A Sourcebook on Feminist Theatre and Performance: On and Beyond the Stage,* ed. Carol Martin, 205–38. New York: Routledge, 1996.

———. *Sally's Rape.* In *A Sourcebook of African-American Performance: Plays, People, Movements,* ed. Annemarie Bean, 246–64. New York: Routledge, 1999.

———. *Sugar* (excerpt). In Jones, Moore, and Bridgforth 255–58.

Mississippi Chicken. DVD. Directed by John Fiege. USA: Reversal Films, 2007.

Moore, Wendy Leo. *Reproducing Racism: White Space, Elite Law Schools and Racial Inequality.* New York: Rowman and Littlefield, 2008.

Moraga, Cherrie, and Gloria Anzaldúa. *This Bridge Called My Back: Writings by Radical Women of Color.* Watertown, MA: Persephone, 1981.

Morris, Lawrence "Butch." "Artist's Statement." *Conduction.* http://www.conduction.us/main.html (link discontinued).

———. Interview by Alessandro Cassin. *Lacan.com.* n.d. http://www.lacan.com/frameXII7.htm.

Morrison, Toni. "Rootedness: The Ancestor as Foundation." In *Black Women Writers, 1950–1980,* ed. Mari Evans, 339–45. New York: Anchor Doubleday, 1984.

———. "The Site of Memory." In *Inventing the Truth: The Art and Craft of Memoir,* 2nd ed., ed. William Zinsser, 83–102. Boston: Houghton Mifflin, 1995.

Moten, Fred. *In the Break: The Aesthetics of the Black Radical Tradition.* Minneapolis: University of Minnesota, 2003.

Murray, Albert. "Improvisation and the Creative Process." In *Jazz Cadence of American Culture,* ed. Robert O'Meally, 111–13. New York: Columbia University Press, 1998.

Nicholson, David. "Painting It Black: African American Artists in Search of a New Aesthetic." *Washington Post,* December 10, 1989.

Nollen, Scott A. *Louis Armstrong: The Life, Music and Screen Career.* Jefferson, NC: McFarland, 2004.

Ogunba, Oyin. "Traditional African Festival Drama." In *Theatre in Africa,* eds. Oyin Ogunba and Abiola Irele, 3–26. Ibadan, Nigeria: Ibadan University Press, 1978.

Okediji, Moyo. "*Egúngún:* Diaspora Recycling." Unpublished essay, 2008.

O'Meally, Robert G. *Seeing Jazz: Artists and Writers on Jazz.* San Francisco, CA: Chronicle Books, 1997.

O'Meally, Robert G., Brent Hayes Edwards, and Farah Jasmine Griffin, eds. *Uptown Conversation: The New Jazz Studies.* New York: Columbia University Press, 2004.

O'Neill, Eugene. *The Hairy Ape.* New York: Boni and Liveright, 1922.

Oyewumi, Oyeronke. *The Invention of Women: Making an African Sense of Western Gender Discourses.* Minneapolis: University of Minnesota Press, 1997.

Paredez, Deborah. "Traveling through Time with Ms. Jomama Jones." *Jomama Jones Radiate.* Liner notes. New York: On Stage, 2010.

Preston-Dunlop, Valerie. *Looking at Dances: A Choreological Perspective on Choreography.* Los Angeles, CA: Verve, 2009.

Pryor, Jaclyn. "Time Slips: Queer Temporalities in Performance After 2001." PhD diss., University of Texas at Austin, 2011.

Rahman, Aishah. "Interview with Aafa Michael Weaver." *Obsidian III: Literature in the African Diaspora* 1, no. 1 (Spring–Summer 1999): 133–40.

———. "Interview with Sydne Mahone." In Mahone, *Moon Marked and Touched by Sun,* 281–85.

———. "Living in the Black Arts Movement." Unpublished essay.

———. *The Mojo and the Sayso.* In Mahone, *Moon Marked and Touched by Sun,* 286–320.

———. "To Be Black, Female and a Playwright." *Freedomways* 19 (1979): 256–60.

———. "Tradition and a New Aesthetic." *MELUS* 16, no. 3, Ethnic Theater (Autumn 1989–Autumn 1990): 23–26.

———. *Unfinished Women Cry in No Man's Land While a Bird Dies in a Gilded Gage.* New York: Broadway Play Publishing, 2011.

Rice, Elmer. *The Adding Machine: A Play in Seven Scenes.* 1922. New York: Doubleday, 1923.

Richards, Sandra. "Yoruba Gods on the American Stage: August Wilson's *Joe Turner's Come and Gone.*" *Research in African Literatures* 30, no. 4 (1999): 92–105.

Salami, Ayo. *Ifá: A Complete Divination.* Lagos, Nigeria: NIDD, 2003.

Schechner, Richard. "Anna Deavere Smith: Acting as Incorporation." *The Drama Review* 37, no. 4 (1993): 63–64.

———. *Performance Studies: An Introduction.* 2nd ed. New York: Routledge, 2006.

Sennett, Richard. "The Spaces of Democracy." *The Raoul Wallenberg Lecture.* Ann Arbor: University of Michigan, 1998.

Shange, Ntozake. *for colored girls who have considered suicide/when the rainbow is enuf.* New York: Collier Books, 1989.

———. "Unrecovered Losses." *Three Pieces,* ix–xvi. New York: St. Martin's Press, 1981.

Smith, Darrlyn A. *New Orleans 7th Ward Nostalgia Dictionary, 1938–1965.* Honolulu, HI: JADA, 1996.

Solagbade Popoola Library and Awoyinfa Kori Ifaloju. *Ifá Dídá: An Invitation to Ifá Divination.* Vol. 1. Nigeria: AsefinMedia, 2008.

Sollors, Werner. *Amiri Baraka / LeRoi Jones: The Quest for a Populist Modernism.* New York: Columbia University Press, 1978.

Southern, Eileen. *The Music of Black Americans: A History.* 3rd ed. New York: Norton, 1997.

Soyinka, Wole. "From a Common Back Cloth: A Reassessment of the African Literary Image." In *Art, Dialogue and Outrage: Essays in Literature and Culture,* 7–14. Ibadan, Nigeria: New Horn, 1988.

Stevens, Wallace. "The House Was Quiet and the World Was Calm." In *Collected Poetry and Prose.* 1954. New York: Library of America, 1997.

Sublette, Ned. *The World That Made New Orleans.* Chicago: Lawrence Hill, 2008.

Swan, Tracey Boone. "Push GURRL." Unpublished poem. 2003.

Tinsley, Omise'eke Natasha. "Black Atlantic, Queer Atlantic: Queer Imaginings of the Middle Passage." *GLQ: A Journal of Lesbian and Gay Studies* 14, nos. 2–3 (2008): 191–215.

Turner, Victor. *The Ritual Process: Structure and Anti-structure.* 1969. Piscataway, NJ: Transaction, 1997.

Walcott, Rinaldo. "Outside in Black Studies: Reading from a Queer Place in the Diaspora." In Johnson and Henderson 90–105.

Walker, Alice. *In Search of Our Mothers' Gardens.* New York: Harcourt Brace Jovanovich, 1983.

Ward, Geoffrey C., and Ken Burns. *Jazz: A History of America's Music.* New York: Knopf, 2000.

Washington, Teresa. *Our Mothers, Our Powers, Our Texts: Manifestations of Àjẹ́ in Africana Literature.* Bloomington: Indiana University Press, 2005.

Wenger, Susanne. *A Life with the Gods.* Worgl, Austria: Perlinger, 1983.

West, Cornel. *Race Matters.* Boston: Beacon, 1993.

When the Spirits Dance Mambo. DVD. Directed by Marta Moreno Vega and Robert Shepard. USA: Caribbean Cultural Center African Diaspora Institute, 2002.

Whitmal, E. Angelica. "So Many Possibilities Before You Crack the Egg: A Conversation with Laurie Carlos." *Liminalities: A Journal of Performance Studies* 8, no. 2 (June 2012) 1–17.

Wilson, August. *Jitney: A Play in Two Acts.* New York: Samuel French, 2002.

Wren, Celia. "Saints, Sin and Erik Ehn: Mysticism Ignites the Plays—and Theories—of a Theatrical Visionary." *American Theatre* 21, no. 5 (2004): 18–65.

Yai, Olabiyi Babalola. "In Praise of Metonymy: The Concepts of 'Tradition' and 'Creativity' in the Transmission of Yoruba Artistry over Time and Space." In *The Yoruba Artist: New Theoretical Perspectives on African Arts,* eds. Rowland Abiodun, Henry J. Drewal, and John Pemberton III, 107–15. Washington, DC: Smithsonian Institution, 1994.

Young, Harvey. "Touching History: Suzan-Lori Parks, Robbie McCauley, and the Black Body." *Text and Performance Quarterly* 23, no. 2 (April 2003): 134–53.

INDEX

abínibí, 3, 215, 219, 222

Abiodun, Rowland, 183

àdúgbò, 21, 28, 34, 59, 118, 120

aesthetics, 240n2, 10; Black, 5, 7, 9, 11; African, 33; and politics, 9. *See also* jazz

àfòṣẹ, 195, 200

African Traditional Religions (ATR), 18, 97

aiyé, 19, 141, 142, 191

Àjẹ́, 106

Alaskan Heat Blue Dot (Carlos), 76, 111, 162, 168 fig. 43, 170–74, 171 fig. 44, 171 fig. 45, 179–80, 183, 193–94

Alexander, Bryant, 13, 255

Alexander, M. Jacqui, 250n22

Alley Theatre, 32

allgo, a Texas statewide queer people of color organization, 79, 98, 113, 117, 133, 162, 163, 190, 212, 230, 232, 237, 239

Ambient Love Rites (Jones), 115, 116, 183, 228, 231

amniotic/flow (Bridgforth), 145, 146, 156–58, 162, 237

ancestors, 10, 21, 32, 118; as characters in work, 40, 62, 122–23, 137, 141–51, 154, 187; rituals for, 215; in Yoruba worldview, 24, 141, 168, 191, 197. See also *égún*

Anderson, Piper, 29, 57, 244n11

apprentice–elder, 2, 19, 21, 28–29, 31–32, 56, 57, 58, 58 fig. 18

apprenticeship, 19, 24, 27

Armstrong, Louis, 16, 28–29, 114, 242n32, 244n10, 252n30

asesú, 118

àṣẹ, 2, 4–5, 19,104, 106, 180, 185, 191, 200, 202–3, 211, 215, 242n31

ATR. *See* African Traditional Religions

audience, 31, 60; witness, 3, 7–8, 9, 21, 29, 38; in theatre, 30, 41, 44, 49; role in theatrical jazz, 4, 66, 78, 79 fig. 20, 91, 92, 104–5, 109

Aunt Jemima, 13

Austin Project, the (tAP), 21, 27, 29–30, 77, 117, 170, 243n43

autocritography, 5

avant-garde: 5, 6, 7, 9, 56, 212; Black, 7–8, 59, 103; companies, 32; and theatrical jazz, 7, 30, 33, 243n36

awo, 21

àyíká. See circle

Babaláwo, 191

Baker, Josephine, 80 fig. 20, 90, 104, 105, 204 fig. 56, 205, 241n14

Baraka, Amiri, 11, 30

Batiste, Stephanie L., 141, 215

Bel Canto (Jones), 103, 110, 110 fig. 29, 116, 230

Bellamy, Lou, 64 fig. 19, 102, 115

bèmbé, 16, 242n31

Benston, Kimberly, 5, 203, 251n14. *See also* methexis; autocritography

Berliner, Paul, 23

bird imagery, 43 fig. 11, 99 fig. 26, 105, 105 fig. 28, 108–9

bíríbírí, 18, 19, 253

Black Arts Movement, 6, 30–31, 43, 100, 251n14

blood pudding (Bridgforth), 35 fig. 9, 76, 116, 122, 126, 137–38, 139, 141, 145, 148–49, 149

Blood:Shock:Boogie (Jones), 78, 80 fig. 21, 81 fig. 22, 104, 116, 231 fig. 40, 150, 162, 190–91, 208, 228, 236, 237, 247n8

Bloodletting (Jones), 100

Book of Daniel series, *The* (Jones), 12, 79 fig. 20, 81–82, 90, 99 fig. 26, 102–3, 104, 106, 112, 113 fig. 30, 117, 190, 190 fig. 53, 204 fig. 56, 205, 223, 232, 247n22

Boone, Vicky, 19, 21, 115, 174, 234

Branner, Djola, 58 fig. 18, 76, 102, 116, 149 fig. 40, 162, 163, 233, 243n39, 246n33

breath work, 245n9; in Carlos's work, 9, 42–43, 49–52, 56, 70, 73, 193; for Dianne McIntyre, 31, 43; in theatrical jazz, 6, 19, 28, 38, 172, 180, 193, 202–3; and Yoruba cosmology, 19, 43–44

Bridgforth, Sharon: apprentice–elder relationship, 27, 57, 149–50; artistic lineage, 162–63; blues, 124–26, 141, 143, 195; childhood, 27, 118–24, 138; discography, 139–40; Finding Voice, 127, 151, 236, 248n6; role of ancestors, 122–23, 137, 142–51, 154; reading list, 143–44; recipe, 131–34; role of prayer, 123, 134, 136–38, 198

Bridgforth, Sharon, works of: *amniotic/flow,* 145, 146, 156–58, 162, 237; *blood pudding,* 35 fig. 9, 76, 116, 122, 126, 137–38, 139, 141, 145, 148–49, 149 fig. 40, 150, 162, 190–91, 208, 228, 236, 237, 247n8; *the bull-jean stories,* 124, 126, 129, 162, 236, 237, 238; *con flama,* 50, 53, 54, 119, 120, 122–24, 129–30, 136–39, 142, 145; *delta dandi,* 122–23, 126, 139, 141, 143, 145, 148–150, 154, 157, 158, 159, 163, 195, 236, 238; *dyke/ warrior-prayers,* 127, 129, 162, 238; *geechee crossing marsha's overture,* 139, 145, 149, 162, 238; *interlude #21: The*

road to Higher Power, 144–45; *love conjure/blues,* 24, 25, 117, 122, 126, 130, 138, 141, 145, 146, 147, 150, 154, 163, 184, 190, 191, 198, 216, 223, 224; *lovve/rituals & rage,* 115, 127, 145, 162, 238; *no mo blues,* 127, 145, 162, 238; *River See,* 119 fig. 31, 150, 159–60, 163, 237, 249n43

Bryant, Florida, 25, 27, 29, 48, 49–50, 50 fig. 12, 52, 52 fig. 14, 53 fig. 15, 54 fig. 16, 76, 77, 116, 117, 146 fig. 38, 147 fig. 39, 149 fig. 40, 149, 162, 163, 171 fig. 44, 173, 173 fig. 45, 174, 178, 178 fig. 49, 187, 189, 227, 239, 243n39, 244n11, 246n33

bull-jean stories, the (Bridgforth), 124, 126, 129, 162, 236, 237, 238

Burrows, Vinie, 110 fig. 29, 117, 163, 220, 221, 221 fig. 62

Byron, Don, 18

Cab and Lena (Jones), 104, 116, 231

Calloway, Cab, 11, 18

Calypso, 16

Carby, Hazel, 248n3

Carlos, Laurie: apprentice–elder relationship, 57–59; artistic lineage, 76–77; childhood, 41, 59–60; discography, 48; recipe, 68–70; role of food, 66–70

Carlos, Laurie, works of: *Alaskan Heat Blue Dot* (Carlos), 76, 111, 162, 168 fig. 43, 170–74, 171 fig. 44, 171 fig. 45, 179–80, 183, 193–94; *The Cooking Show and How the Monkey Dances,* 39–40, 41, 48, 65, 66, 76, 116, 223, 228; *Feathers at the Flame, Next Dance,* 38–39, 71, 115, 228, 233; *Marion's Terrible Time of Joy,* 41, 45, 65, 73–75, 77, 117, 170, 196, 227, 234; *Non-English Speaking Spoken Here,* 61, 72–73, 238; *Nonsectarian Conversations with the Dead,* 39, 61, 73, 76, 229; *An Organdy Falsetto* (Carlos), 71–72, 73, 76, 229; *Persimmon Peel,* 65, 76, 102, 115, 228; *The Pork Chop Wars (a story of mothers),* 39, 40, 42, 43, 49, 61, 62–63, 65–66, 69, 71, 73, 76, 163, 182–83, 227, 239; *Teenytown,* 39, 41, 46–47, 61, 62, 76, 229; *White Chocolate for My Father,* 38–41, 46–50, 57–58, 61–62, 65, 72, 76, 228, 245; *Washed,* 44, 77, 227

Carrill, Pepe, 14

Carter, Betty, 5, 89, 90–91, 114

Catanese, Brandi, 31, 203

Chaikin, Joseph, 212

circle: *àyíká,* 192; *ìyíká,* 21, 192, 243n44; in performance, 1, 190–92, 207, 208, 217; in rehearsal, 44, 49; in staging, 190–92, 217; *yímiká,*192; in work, 161; in Yoruba cosmology, 16, 106, 191–92, 207

Clayangels (Jones), 76, 82, 84–88, 106, 116, 220, 231

Cohen, Cathy, 13

Coleman, Grisha, 48, 76, 104, 115, 116, 117, 199, 215–17, 217 fig. 59, 232, 243n39, 245n20, 246n33

Coltrane, John, 1, 16, 59, 60, 89, 139

con flama (Bridgforth), 50, 53, 54, 119, 120, 122–24, 129–30, 136–39, 142, 145

Conley, Kat, 110, 110 fig. 29

Conquergood, Dwight, 196, 205

Cooking Show and How the Monkey Dances, The (Carlos), 39–40, 41, 48, 65, 66, 76, 116, 223, 228

cosmology, Yoruba, 4–5, 14, 27–28, 43–44, 105, 109, 141, 183, 210, 222, 242n30, 251n10

Dara, Olu, 31, 43

Davis, Angela, 124, 126

Davis, Helga, 24, 25, 35 fig. 9, 115, 117, 139, 162, 163, 167, 184, 190, 208, 221 fig. 62, 243n39, 250n7

Davis, Thulani, 43

DeFrantz, Thomas, 11

delta dandi (Bridgforth), 122–23, 126, 139, 141, 143, 145, 148–50, 154, 157, 158, 159, 163, 195, 236, 238

diaspora: African, 17, 142; theatrical jazz, 33; studies, 33

Dixon-Gottschild, Brenda, 241n14

Dolan, Jill, 206, 208–9

Drewal, Henry John, 250n14

Drewal, Margaret Thompson, 18, 195, 202

dyke/warrior-prayers (Bridgforth), 127, 129, 162, 238

Earthbirths, Jazz, and Raven's Wings (Jones), 78, 82–84, 102, 106, 107–8, 115, 116, 231

Edwards, Brent Hayes, 23

égún, 24, 141, 149, 157, 222, 240n6

Egúngún, 16, 142, 143, 240n6

Ehn, Erik, 20, 33, 76, 77, 111, 115, 116, 117, 212–13, 215

Elam Jr., Harry J., 7, 251n14

elder, 30, 31–32, 40, 57, 64, 105, 122, 100, 101, 182, 185, 195. *See also* apprentice–elder

Ellis, Daniel Dodd, 25, 80 fig. 21, 115, 116, 117, 163, 243n39

Engel, Tanya, 43 fig. 11, 125 fig. 34, 188 fig. 52

erotics, 12, 17

Èṣù, 200, 251n10. *See also Òrìṣà*

ethnographic, 2, 5, 180, 209

Experiments in a Jazz Aesthetic: Art, Activism, Academia and the Austin Project (Jones, Moore & Bridgforth, eds.), 236, 243n43, 249n6

ẹbọ dá, 22, 53

ẹgbẹ́, 21, 23–24, 26–34, 65, 97, 102, 120, 147, 160, 212, 215, 253

Faires, Robert, 20

Feathers at the Flame, Next Dance (Carlos), 38–39, 71, 115, 228, 233

Ferguson, Roderick, 222

Finding Voice, 127, 151, 236, 248n6. *See also* Bridgforth, Sharon

for colored girls who have considered suicide/ when the rainbow is enuf (Shange), 6, 31, 56, 60, 64, 76, 97, 115, 140, 161, 162, 212, 229, 244n16

freedom: art as, 2, 5, 6; artistic, 5, 26, 78; and Blackness 9, 47; in Bridgforth's work, 140, 142; in Carlos' work, 46, 47, 61, 62, 66; "drive," 7; and jazz, 8, 10, 114; in Jones's work, 114; and liminality, 11

Frontera@Hyde Park Theatre, 7, 19, 19 fig. 7, 20 fig. 8, 21, 56, 78, 116, 172, 174, 183, 190, 191, 206, 227, 228, 231, 233, 235, 238, 244n20, 246n21

Gagnon, Kathryn Coram, 64, 65, 77, 102, 115, 117

Gates Jr., Henry Louis, 200

geechee crossing marsha's overture (Bridgforth), 139, 145, 149, 162, 238

Gennari, John, 59

Gillespie, Dizzy, 143, 161, 252n30

Griffin, Farah Jasmine, 23

Grise, Virginia, 26–27, 76, 77, 117, 149, 150–51, 163, 243n39, 250n43

gb'èkó, 28

Hansbury, Lorraine, 5, 7, 227

Haring-Smith, Tori, 165, 169

Harris, Craig, 43, 103, 115, 195

Harrison, Paul Carter, 200, 251n7

Henderson, Mae, 13

Hernandez, Yasmin, 17 fig. 6, 155 fig. 41

Ho, Fred Wei-han, 8, 241n15, 241n18

hooks, bell, 136

Horne, Lena, 85, 104, 105, 143

Hurston, Zora Neale, 39, 90

ìdè, 18

Ifá, 12, 28, 107, 200, 240n6, 248n31

ìgèdè, 200

ikópa, 21, 208. See also *kópa*

ikó'sé, 19, 21, 28, 32, 56, 57, 58, 61, 149, 160, 165, 253

ilé, 33, 186, 250n10

Ilé-Ifè, 32

ilèkè, 18

improvisation, 3, 11, 18, 29, 41, 43, 90, 91, 103, 158, 159, 170, 183, 186, 197, 222, 224, 240n3

interlude #21: The road to Higher Power (Bridgforth), 144–45

Iragbagba, 16

Ìsèsè, 4, 17–18, 23, 192, 200, 240n6, 242n32

ìtàn, 147

ìtànlè, 28, 147, 148

ìwà, 21, 28, 32, 174, 182, 183, 185–86, 250n8; *rere,* 182–83, 185, 250n8

Ìyáláwo, 191

Ìyámi, 16, 78, 105 fig. 28, 106–7, 109

Ìyàwó, 182

ìyíká. See circle

Jackson, Joyce, 16

Jagose, Annamarie, 10

jazz: acting, 168–72, 179, 209; aesthetics, 2, 3, 5, 7, 10, 11, 33, 114, 174, 189, 194–95; musicians, 1, 8, 11, 16, 28–29, 31, 33, 43, 59, 89–91, 211, 241n14, 243n36; principles, 5, 29, 241n14; and queer, 11–12, 14, 124, 222; structure, 5, 11–12, 30–31, 47, 109–10, 124, 126, 160, 187, 194; styles of 8, 11, 17–18, 114, 165; theories of, 11–12, 90–91; time, 11–12, 18, 109–10, 141; and Yoruba cosmology, 3–4, 11, 14, 16, 17–19, 27, 28, 105, 185–86, 222

Jefferson, Margo, 8

Jezebel, 13

John L. Warfield Center for African and African Studies. *See* Warfield Center

Johnson, E. Patrick, 2, 13–14, 117, 179–80, 234, 236

Jones, Daniel Alexander: apprentice–elder relationship, 31, 100–102; artistic lineage, 101 fig. 27, 104, 115–17; childhood, 80–89, 93, 104, 105; discography, 89–90; Jomama Jones, 20 fig.8, 104–5, 117, 163, 231, 233, 237, 245n20; recipe, 93–96; role of visual art, 109–10, 114

Jones, Daniel Alexander, works of: *Ambient Love Rites,* 115, 116, 183, 228, 231; *Bel Canto,* 103, 110 fig. 29, 110, 116, 230; *Blood:Shock:Boogie,* 78, 80 fig. 21, 81 fig. 22, 104, 116, 231; *Bloodletting,* 100; *The Book of Daniel* series, 12, 79 fig. 20, 81–82, 90, 99 fig. 26, 102–3,104, 106, 112, 113 fig. 30, 117, 190, 190 fig. 53, 204 fig. 56, 205, 223, 232, 247n22; *Cab and Lena,* 104, 116, 231; *Clayangels,* 76, 82, 84–88, 106, 116, 228, 231; *Earthbirths, Jazz, and Raven's Wings,* 78, 82–84, 102, 106, 107–8, 115, 116, 231; *Phoenix Fabrik,* 97, 98 fig. 24, 99 fig. 25, 103, 106–7, 111–12, 117, 163, 194, 197, 230, 239, 247n9

Jones, Margo, 32

Jones, Omi Osun Joni L., 35 fig. 9, 76, 115, 116, 117, 162, 163, 169 fig. 43, 171 fig. 44, 173 fig. 54, 176 fig. 47, 177 fig. 48, 178 fig. 49, 249n8, 250n43

Jones, Seitu, 64 fig. 19, 76, 102, 110–11, 115, 163

Jones, Van, 215

Joyce, Joyce A., 200, 251n10

Kaprow, Allan, 241

Karni-Bain, Carl E. (BAI), 166 fig. 42, 220 fig. 61

Kennedy, Adrienne, 212, 244n14, 244n16, 247n12

Kessler, David, 13

kinesis, 11, 195

Kitundu, Walter, 29, 105 fig. 28, 112, 117, 199, 204 fig. 56, 215, 217–19

Klezmer, 18, 61

kópa, 206. See also *ikópa*

Koss-Chiono, Joan D., 251n15

Kraut, Anthea, 241n14

La MaMa ETC, 30, 32, 59, 212, 221 fig. 62, 228. *See also* avant-garde

Lake, Marion, 64–65

Laveau, Marie, 16

Legba, 3, 11, 174, 183, 184, 200, 208, 224. See also *Òrìṣà*

Lewis, George, 8

liminality, 11, 112, 186, 197

lineage: artistic, 6, 21, 22, 23, 30, 151, 191, 241n14; Bridgforth, Sharon, 120, 162–63; Carlos, Laurie, 76–77; Jones, Daniel Alexander, 101 fig. 27, 104, 115–17; in work, 66, 105, 122, 145–47, 150; in Yoruba cosmology, 141–42, 148. *See also* apprentice–elder

linear. *See* nonlinear

Links Hall, 119 fig. 31, 163, 232, 237, 238

Lock, Graham, 200

love conjure/blues (Bridgforth), 24, 25, 117, 122, 126, 130, 138, 141, 145, 146, 147, 150, 154, 163, 184, 190, 191, 198, 216, 223, 224

lovve/rituals & rage (Bridgforth), 115, 127, 145, 162, 238

Lubiano, Waheema, 13

Lukumi, 16, 242n31

Mackey, Nathaniel, 200

Mahone, Sydne, 58

Marion's Terrible Time of Joy (Carlos), 41, 45, 65, 73–75, 77, 117, 170, 190, 227, 234

Margraff, Ruth, 20, 31, 115, 116, 235

Marsalis, Wynton, 8, 24

Martinez, Maurice, 16

Mason, John, 200

McCauley, Robbie, 6, 7, 27, 41, 56, 62, 64, 64 fig. 19, 65, 76, 102–4, 115, 116, 117, 163, 183, 199, 212, 213 fig. 57, 215, 219, 220, 228, 233, 243n39, 246n33

McDonald, Senalka, 13 fig. 4

McIntyre, Dianne, 30, 31, 42–43, 55, 76

methexis, 203, 251n14. *See also* Benston, Kimberly

Method Acting, 168, 170

Miles, Minnie Marianne, 202 fig. 55

Miller III, Zell, 25, 29, 57, 76, 77, 115, 116, 117, 146 fig. 38, 149 fig. 40, 162, 163, 169 fig. 43, 171 fig. 44, 173, 173 fig. 45, 176 fig. 47, 234, 239, 243n39, 246n33

mimesis, 11, 168, 186

mimetic, 160, 192, 193. *See also* nonmimetic

minstrel, 41

Monk, Thelonius, 1, 23, 112

Moore, Lisa L., 29–30, 76, 163, 236

Morris, Lawrence "Butch," 159, 165, 170, 192, 250n7

Morrison, Toni, 39, 142

Morton, Jelly Roll, 165

Moten, Fred, 7, 11, 13

Murray, Albert, 165, 242n36

Nascimiento, Abdias do, 14

no mo blues (Bridgforth), 127, 145, 162, 238

Non-English Speaking Spoken Here (Carlos), 61, 72–73, 238

nonlinear: in jazz aesthetics 3, 11, 18, 36, 100, 111, 160, 182, 193, 194, 195; narrative, 36,

110, 114, 174, 189, 194, 195, 203, 209; plot construction, 140, 159, 160, 194, 195

nonmimetic, 4, 11, 31, 38, 146 fig. 38, 172, 179. *See also* mimetic

Nonsectarian Conversations with the Dead (Carlos), 39, 61, 73, 76, 229

Nicholson, David, 33

Nunes, Werllayne, xvii fig. 1

Odù, 106, 200

Odùduwà, 57, 248n32

Ògún, 3, 156. See also *Òrìṣà*

Ogunba, Oyin, 192, 207

Ogunji, Wura-Natasha, 12 fig. 3, 17 fig. 5, 27, 201 fig. 54, 225 fig. 63

Okediji, Moyo, 4 fig. 2, 141–42, 148, 250n23

olódò, 118

O'Meally, Robert G., 2, 23, 109–10

Organdy Falsetto, An (Carlos), 71–72, 73, 76, 229

Orí, 16, 24, 28, 106, 154, 210, 222

oríkì, 16, 106, 186, 207

Òrìṣà, 18, 19, 21, 23, 24, 28, 149, 154–56, 182, 207, 240n6

Ọba, 27–28, 31, 106, 248n32

Ọbàtálá, 156, 180. See also *Òrìṣà*

ọpọ́n, 191–92

ọpèlè, 12

Ọ̀rànmíyàn, 57

Ọ̀rányàn, 57

ọ̀run, 141, 168, 191

Ọ̀rúnmìlà, 106, 191, 248n31. See also *Òrìṣà*

Ọ̀ṣun, 4, 13, 149, 156, 180. See also *Òrìṣà*

Ọya, 36, 43–44, 46–47, 142, 149, 156. See also *Òrìṣà*

Parks, Sonja, 52 fig. 14, 53 fig. 15, 54 fig. 16, 76, 117, 119 fig. 31, 127 fig. 35, 146 fig. 38, 147 fig. 39, 162, 163, 181, 181 fig. 50, 181 fig. 51, 243n39, 249n8, 250n43

Penumbra Theatre, 29, 61, 64, 102–4, 115, 116, 117, 135 fig. 37, 162, 163

Perea, Ana, 50, 50 fig. 12, 52 fig. 14, 53, 53 fig.

15, 54, 54 fig. 16, 55 fig. 17, 76, 146 fig. 38, 147 fig. 39, 163, 179, 181, 181 fig. 50, 181 fig. 51, 220, 221, 221 fig. 62, 243n39

Performing Blackness Series (pBs), 21, 184, 188 fig. 52, 205, 213 fig. 57, 239, 243n43

Persimmon Peel (Carlos), 65, 76, 102, 115, 228

Phelps, Jason, 19, 115, 116, 169 fig. 43, 173, 243n39

Phoenix Fabrik (Jones), 97, 98 fig. 24, 99 fig. 25, 103, 106–7, 111–12, 117, 163, 194, 197, 230, 239, 247n9

Pillsbury House Theatre, 7, 61, 76, 99 fig. 25, 110, 111, 116–17, 163, 230, 231, 232, 234, 237, 238, 244n20

poeisis, 11

Polite, Arleen, 225 fig. 63

polyrhythms, 4, 160

Pork Chop Wars (a story of mothers), The (Carlos), 39, 40, 42, 43, 49, 61, 62–63, 65–66, 69, 71, 73, 76, 163, 182–83, 227, 239

Pozo, Luciano (Chano), 16

P. S. 122, 7, 60

queer: and artists, 158; and Black, 13–14, 124, 158–59, 223; characters, 124; as community, 122, 158–59, 212; defining, 10–14; gender, 71; jazz, 11–12, 14, 222; as possibilities, 4 fig. 2, 10, 12 fig. 3, 194; realities, 5; sexuality, 10–14; theory, 13–14, 222, 241n19; time, 11–12, 194–95. *See also* allgo, a Texas statewide queer people of color organization

Rahman, Aishah, 6, 30–31, 76, 100–101, 115, 244n16

resonant frequencies, 187, 203, 206, 208, 216, 251n14

Rice, Rebecca, 77, 102, 212, 228

Richards, Sandra, 200

Richardson, Sarah, 116, 176 fig. 47

River See (Bridgforth), 119 fig. 31, 150, 159–60, 163, 237, 249n43

root wy'mn Theatre Company, 127, 127 fig. 35, 128 fig. 36, 162, 206, 238, 249n8

Ross, Rhonda, 98 fig. 23, 100, 115, 117, 163, 221 fig. 62, 247n8, 247n12

Rude Mechanicals, 32, 111. *See also* avant-garde

Sanchez, Edwin, 112, 115, 235

Ṣàngó, 13. See also Òrìṣà

Schechner, Richard, 194, 250n18

Sedgwick, Eve, 13

Sedition Ensemble, 212

Sennett, Richard, 27

seriate, 38, 109, 112, 159, 195, 198

seriation, 195, 209

set design, 76, 109–12, 162, 186–87, 202, 249n8. *See also* Jones, Seitu; Stewart, Leilah

Shange, Ntozake, 6–7, 31, 43, 55, 56, 76, 97, 103, 115, 140, 162, 229, 244n16. See also *for colored girls who have considered suicide/when the rainbow is enuf*

simultaneity, 11, 29, 41, 43 fig. 11, 49–50, 91

Soca, 16

Soho Rep, 7, 117, 231

Soyinka, Wole, 18

staging, 92, 103, 114, 182, 186–87, 189–93

Steppenwolf, 32. *See also* avant-garde

Stewart, Ellen, 30

Stewart, Leilah, 54 fig. 16, 76, 111, 117, 163, 176 fig. 47, 177 fig. 48, 178 fig. 49, 243n39

Suite, Annie, 19

Sundiata, Sekou, 1, 7, 43, 103, 115, 195

Swan, Tracey Boone, 151–53

Swanson, C. Denby, 56, 169 fig. 43, 243n39

tAP. *See* Austin Project, the

Taylor, Cecil, 43, 59, 242n36

Teenytown (Carlos), 39, 41, 46–47, 61, 62, 76, 229

Theatre '47, 32

Tinsley, Omise'eke Natasha, 223

transtemporal work, 4, 100, 111, 203, 209

Turner, Victor, 11

Urban Bush Women, 56, 76, 207, 229

Vargas, João, 165

Vega, Marta, 16,

virtuosity, 4, 21, 167, 183, 185, 224. See also ìwà

Walcott, Rinaldo, 158

Warfield Center, 21, 24, 77, 97, 99 fig. 26, 117, 158, 163, 184, 188 fig. 52, 191, 205, 213 fig. 57, 227, 232, 238, 239, 243n43, 247n9

Washed (Carlos), 44, 77, 227

Wenger, Susanne, 191, 200

West, Cheryl, 102

West, Cornel, 136

White Chocolate for My Father (Carlos), 38–41, 46–50, 57–58, 61–62, 65, 72, 76, 228, 245

Wilson, August, 5, 7

witnessing, 123, 205–6

Woolly Mammoth, 32. *See also* avant-garde

Yai, Olabiyi, 32, 147

Yearby, Marlies, 31, 43, 56, 102, 115, 233

Yemọnja, 13, 118, 149, 154–56, 159. See also Òrìṣà

yímiká. *See* circle

Youngblood, Shay, 14, 31, 64, 78, 91

Zollar, Jawole Willa Jo, 31, 43, 56, 100, 102, 103, 115, 116, 177 fig. 48, 191, 228, 233, 235, 243n39, 244n19

BLACK PERFORMANCE AND CULTURAL CRITICISM SERIES

Valerie Lee and E. Patrick Johnson, Series Editors

The Black Performance and Cultural Criticism series includes monographs that draw on interdisciplinary methods to analyze, critique, and theorize black cultural production. Books in the series take as their object of intellectual inquiry the performances produced on the stage and on the page, stretching the boundaries of both black performance and literary criticism.

Theatrical Jazz: Performance, Àṣẹ, and the Power of the Present Moment
 OMI OSUN JONI L. JONES

When the Devil Knocks: The Congo Tradition and the Politics of Blackness in Twentieth-Century Panama
 RENÉE ALEXANDER CRAFT

The Queer Limit of Black Memory: Black Lesbian Literature and Irresolution
 MATT RICHARDSON

Fathers, Preachers, Rebels, Men: Black Masculinity in U.S. History and Literature, 1820–1945
 EDITED BY TIMOTHY R. BUCKNER AND PETER CASTER

Secrecy, Magic, and the One-Act Plays of Harlem Renaissance Women Writers
 TAYLOR HAGOOD

Beyond Lift Every Voice and Sing: The Culture of Uplift, Identity, and Politics in Black Musical Theater
 PAULA MARIE SENIORS

Prisons, Race, and Masculinity in Twentieth-Century U.S. Literature and Film
 PETER CASTER

Mutha' Is Half a Word: Intersections of Folklore, Vernacular, Myth, and Queerness in Black Female Culture
 L. H. STALLINGS